CONDITIONS OF CHILDREN'S TALENT DEVELOPMENT IN SPORT

Jean Côté · Ronnie Lidor

Fitness Information Technology

A Division of the International Center for Performance Excellence
262 Coliseum, WVU-CPASS · P O Box 6116
Morgantown, WV 26506-6116

Library of Congress Card Catalog Number: 2012948477

ISBN: 978-1-935412-46-5

Production Editors: Jennifer Bowman, Rachel Tibbs

Cover Design: 40 West Studios

Typesetter: 40 West Studios

Copyeditor: Jennifer Bowman

Proofreader: Geoffrey Fuller

Indexer: Geoffrey Fuller

Printed by Data Reproductions Corp.

Front cover photos: soccer girl and boy: © V.e.r.i.k | Dreamstime.com. Baseball boy, family biking, and hands courtesy of iStockphoto.com. Back cover photos: basketball coach, tennis lesson, martial arts, boy with basketball, and soccer girls courtesy of iStockphoto.com

10 9 8 7 6 5 4 3 2 1

Fitness Information Technology
A Division of the International Center for Performance Excellence
West Virginia University
262 Coliseum, WVU-CPASS
PO Box 6116
Morgantown, WV 26506-6116
800.477.4348 (toll free)
304.293.6888 (phone)
304.293.6658 (fax)
Email: fitcustomerservice@mail.wvu.edu
Website: www.fitinfotech.com

Table of Contents

Dedication

À ma mère et mon père, pour leur amour, soutien, et encouragement. They never failed to support me even if, at times, my goals were unclear. Their ability to nurture talent in all their children was exemplary.

Jean

CHAPTER 1

EARLY TALENT DEVELOPMENT IN SPORT: A MULTIFACETED APPROACH

Jean Côté and Ronnie Lidor

The profile of activities in which youth engage is an important determinant of their over-all development. Youth who spend long periods of time watching television or playing video games will develop different habits and skills than individuals who spend their time in more productive endeavors, such as learning a musical instrument or playing sports. The significance of sport as an integral avenue for children's development has been formally recognized by different organizations around the world as an important global issue. Sport is an activity in which youth have reported experiencing the unusual combination of high in-trinsic motivation and determined engagement over extended periods of time (Larson, 2000). Despite the positive value that sport can have in children's lives, adults often alter the experi-ence of youth in sport to achieve short-term outcomes that are not in line with children's needs and long-term development. This book focuses on how we can keep children's experiences in sport positive while still developing elite-level athletes.

The documentary *Lost Adventures in Childhood* (Harper, 2009) takes a critical look at the state of growing up in the world today. Interviews with leaders in the fields of developmental psychology and youth sport depict a grim picture of overstressed children who are severely lacking in opportunities to play without adult supervision. We are introduced to a father who keeps track of his two daughters by receiving their exact GPS coordinates, updated every two minutes, via the girls' cell phones. We are taken to a summer camp where a photographer takes 700–800 pictures of the campers each day to post on the camp's website for parents to see; the camp director then spends three to four hours each day fielding phone calls from parents concerned that their child looks upset or disengaged in one of the photos. We follow a family as they drive their two young daughters from one sport commitment to another; one of the daughters remarks about the difficulty of doing her homework in the car because of car sickness. These scenarios are in sharp contrast to images conjured up when considering the childhoods of previous generations: children of all ages playing in the neighborhood without adult supervision.

Achieving elite performance in sport is a feat that is highly acclaimed and can be financially rewarding in today's society. As worldwide youth sport becomes increasingly professionalized and institutionalized, play and child-led activities are being replaced by a professional model of sport for children driven by adults. However, this model is limited because of the implicit and unsupported assumption that high volumes of intense and adult-directed training during childhood will increase a child's chance to climb to the top as adults in elite sports.

Adult-driven sport programs for children are most often based on a *talent-identification* model, in which adults use a rigid skill-based approach to evaluate talent and weed out the less skilled children. This approach implies an early selection of talented children, an increase in resources for a special group of athletes, and training that is not always consistent with the children's motivation to participate in sports. There are a number of problems with traditional methods of talent identification when applied to children (see Pearson, Naughton, & Torode, 2006; Vaeyens, Lenoir, Williams, & Philippaerts, 2008). For example, characteristics that distinguish success in an adult athlete (i.e., size or speed) may not become apparent until later adolescence. At the same time, there is no guarantee that a young athlete who possesses a desired attribute will still possess that attribute as an adult athlete. Pearson et al. (2006) also noted that talent is dynamic and multifaceted: The characteristics of talent may be different across age groups and attempting to measure these characteristics often means that more important factors are overlooked. Additionally, there is the major concern that youths begin maturing at different times and rates; late maturing athletes could be summarily dismissed through traditional talent-identification methods (Pearson et al., 2006). Finally, there are a number of negative consequences that result from intense sport training during childhood that are associated with a strictly adult-led and rigid skill-based model of children's sport, such as an increased level of injuries, burnout, and dropout (Côté, 2009). In a review of *talent detection* and *talent-development* in sport literature, Régnier, Salmela, and Russell (1993) concluded that the long-term prediction of talented athletes based on an evaluation of children in specific youth sport programs is unreliable and inefficient.

Despite the evidence against early talent identification, the quality of effective youth sport programs continues to be measured by the performance of young athletes who reach elite performance in adulthood—with little attention being provided to those other youths who could also have eventually developed into elite-level athletes had they been given the appropriate training and environment. While talent detection can be seen as a performance process that focuses on a select number of children, a talent-development approach involves a long-term commitment to an inclusive process that focuses on children's needs and their continued participation in sport. A talent-development approach to children's sport provides the most appropriate and adapted environment for long-term development of skills for a larger number of participants. This approach to youth sport appears to be a more efficient way of designing sport programs for children (Côté, Coakley, & Bruner, 2011).

This book uses a talent-development approach to present and discuss research evidence that highlights how different activities, as well as personal and social variables, affect children's involvement in sport and the long-term acquisition of skills. Different aspects of talent-development in youth sport will be presented, including the effect of play and practice, the effect of the environment, and the influence of involved people such as coaches, parents, and peers.

The remainder of this chapter is dedicated to providing a short overview of the origins of contemporary talent-development research in sport, followed by an outline of the different chapters covered in this book.

ORIGINS OF CONTEMPORARY TALENT-DEVELOPMENT RESEARCH IN SPORT

Bruner, Erickson, McFadden, and Côté (2009) conducted a review of 229 articles, books, and book chapters that focused on models of talent development. The goal of this review article was to trace the genealogy of talent development research in sport. In general, the results were divided into four stages of research that led to our present understanding of talent-development in sport. The first two stages focused on the work of Bloom (1985) and Ericsson, Krampe, and Tesch-Römer (1993), while the remaining two stages were directed more specifically toward sport research.

The first stage of talent-development research in sport can be found in the foundation texts published between 1973 and 1991. Five texts (Bloom, 1985; Gustin, 1985; Kalinowski, 1985; Monsaas, 1985; Sosniak, 1985) at the foundation of talent-development research in sport were contained in Bloom's book on talented young people. In their pioneering research, contributors to Bloom's volume (1985) traced the development of talent through interviews with scientists, musicians, artists, and athletes who achieved a high level of performance in their specific domain. The athletes interviewed were tennis players and swimmers who had exhibited elite performance by winning international competitions, such as Wimbledon or the Olympic games. Bloom (1985) inferred a general pattern of development and psychosocial conditions that appeared necessary for reaching an ultimate level of elite performance in any domain of expertise. The other four texts at the foundation of this genealogy presented a more experimental approach to high-level talent-development that included, for example, the seminal work of Simon and Chase (1973) on expertise in chess.

The core of the second stage of talent-development research was based on the work of Ericsson and his colleagues (1993) on deliberate practice. Building on the work of Simon and Chase (1973) and Bloom (1985), Ericsson et al. (1993) analyzed the current level of training and the developmental histories of several groups of highly accomplished musicians to account for individual differences in their current level of achievement. Examples of other texts that emerged as being central to this second stage include publications by Ericsson and Lehmann (1996) and Howe, Davidson, and Sloboda (1998). These authors adopted methods and principles of cognitive psychology to develop and apply the *expertise approach,* and proposed different conditions of practice (i.e., deliberate practice) as the essential elements of expertise development. Although this second stage of talent-development research in sport referred to the work of Bloom, the literature in this stage was limited to the perceptual and cognitive aspects of skill acquisition. Aspects of motivation, social influences, and psychological variables were acknowledged by the authors of this second stage, but not seriously discussed and integrated in their approach to talent-development.

The year 1998 marked the beginning of the third stage, featuring important sport studies that focused on the longitudinal aspect of talent-development in sport (e.g., Helsen, Starkes, & Hodges, 1998). This stage included four texts (Helsen et al., 1998; Starkes, 2000; Starkes, Helsen, & Jack, 2001; Young & Salmela, 2002) that were heavily influenced by Ericsson and colleagues' original publication (1993) on deliberate practice. These sport studies focused mostly on practice activities throughout development by eliciting information from athletes through retrospective questionnaires. The main observation from these studies was that a monotonic relationship existed between the number of hours spent in relevant practice activities and the level of performance attained by athletes. When answering a retrospective questionnaire, athletes rated practice activities (i.e., deliberate practice) that were high in effort as also being high in enjoyment. This stage of sport expertise research began to revive the work of Bloom by highlighting such important aspects of talent-development as enjoyment, motivation, and psychosocial influences that were signalled as being critical. However, these aspects were not yet fully integrated in this stage.

The fourth stage of talent-development research includes texts that focus on aspects of athlete development in sport that move beyond the sole examination of practice activities. Baker, Côté, and Abernethy (2003) were the first to provide a retrospective study of athlete development that focused on practice but also integrated psychosocial aspects of talent-development, such as the role of play and other sporting activities during childhood. The design of this study was based on Ericsson and colleagues' (1993) original study of deliberate practice and the Developmental Model of Sport Participation (DMSP; Côté, 1999), which was heavily influenced by the work of Bloom (1985). The texts in this last stage continue to advocate the importance of practice, but also highlight the importance of play and sampling different sports during childhood. This fourth stage of research presents a view of athlete development that includes both psychosocial influences and training aspects of expertise (Abbott & Collins, 2004; Côté, 1999; Martindale, Collins, & Daubney, 2005).

Bruner et al. (2009) noted that this fourth stage of talent-development research in sport has largely been influenced by the work of Côté and colleagues (see, for review, Côté, Baker, & Abernethy, 2003, 2007), who conducted several studies examining the psychosocial environment and training conditions of elite-level athletes. Emerging from these studies was the DMSP, which integrates the developing person into his or her environment and pays particular attention to the childhood years of involvement in sport as the foundation of talent-development. Seven postulates associated with the DMSP and its various outcomes have been proposed (see Côté, Lidor, & Hackfort, 2009). Generally, these postulates focus on the concept of play as opposed to practice, and of early sampling as opposed to early specialization during childhood sport. The DMSP has been developed and refined over the last 12 years and presents a set of concepts about athlete development that is quantifiable and testable. In line with the DMSP, this book focuses on the developmental activities as well as the personal and social influences that impact talent-development during childhood.

STRUCTURE OF THE BOOK

This book—*Conditions of Children's Talent-development in Sport*—is centered on the fourth stage of talent-development research; it focuses on the intersecting of developmental activities (e.g., practice and play) of young athletes and the personal and social conditions that affect these activities. Although there are a number of existing useful articles, books, and book chapters that focus on the process of talent-development in sport, none of these have yet condensed the actual state of knowledge regarding the structure of the developmental activities in childhood that are most likely to lead to talent-development. Following four decades of research on the physical, psychological, and social aspects of early development in sport, the prominent research findings on these aspects will be summarized, elaborated upon, and critiqued in an academic volume that can be used by researchers and students who are interested in the multifaceted process of early talent-development in sport.

Conditions of Children's Talent-development in Sport focuses on the conditions that underpin children's investment in sport and their talent-development. Each chapter examines a different aspect of the early years of involvement in sport, from early introduction to sport through adolescence. A primary aim of the book is to outline and discuss the evidence-based conditions of the optimal learning environments required to minimize dropout and burnout, and to optimize skill development. The objective of the entire volume is to provide the most up-to-date, authoritative, and accessible presentation of core knowledge associated with children in sport and early talent-development. The content of the book has been developed to ensure full coverage of the learning process of young athletes, as well as the personal and social aspects of talent-development in children. The book is composed of 13 chapters, each written by acknowledged authorities in the field of sport psychology or motor development and learning.

As indicated above, the structure of the book is framed around the fourth stage of talent-development research in sport (Bruner et al., 2009), which includes two levels of variables: developmental activities, and personal and social conditions. Figure 1.1 is an illustration of the variables that impact talent-development during childhood. Central to Figure 1.1 are the developmental activities in children's sport. The developmental activities constitute the process by which learning occurs and motivation is developed during childhood. Four general

Figure 1.1. The influence of personal and social variables on the developmental activities of children in sport.

types of variables affect the types and structure of developmental activities in which children engage for learning—the physical attributes of the child, the mental attributes of the child, the psychosocial influences, and the environment.

The first three chapters of the book focus on the developmental activities of children in sport and the type of learning that emerges from being involved in different types of play and practice activities. More specifically, in Chapter 2, Côté, Erickson, and Abernethy provide a taxonomy of learning activities and discuss the importance of including both child-led and adult-led activities in children's sports. In Chapter 3, Masters, van der Kamp, and Capio discuss the evidence supporting the importance of structuring activities that involve implicit learning in children's sport. To conclude this section, in Chapter 4, Chow, Davids, Renshaw, and Button present principles of nonlinear pedagogy as a way of organizing learning activities that favor creativity, implicit learning, and play in children's sport. These three chapters are the core of the developmental activities for children's sport that are expanded upon in the remaining chapters of the book.

Chapters 5 and 6 focus on the physical attributes that affect talent-development in children. In Chapter 5, Malina presents an important view of motor development that would be important to consider when structuring talent-development programs for children in sport. Lidor and Ziv complete this section in Chapter 6 by presenting the pros and cons of testing physical attributes and sport skills for identifying talent in children. Together, Chapters 5 and 6 highlight how maturation and development are determinants of performance in children's sport, but also that the physical attributes of children are variable and sometimes difficult to assess for identifying talented children in sport.

Chapters 7 and 8 focus on two mental attributes associated with talent-development in sport—self-efficacy and perfectionism. In Chapter 7, Chase and Pierce review the literature on self-efficacy in children's sport and propose some concrete guidelines for enhancing self-efficacy and confidence in children involved in sport. In Chapter 8, Hall, Hill, and Appleton discuss different approaches to the study of perfectionism and examine how the sporting environment and the climate created by coaches may act to reinforce distorted views about achievement and perpetuate the dysfunction cognitive style with which perfectionism seems to be associated. In sum, Chapters 7 and 8 focus on important psychological determinants of children's participation and performance in sport.

Chapters 9, 10, and 11 consider the social influences of coaches, groups/peers, and family members as catalysts that facilitate talent-development in children. Erickson and Gilbert (Chapter 9) present an overview of the role of the coach in children's talent-development, with a specific focus on coaches' behaviors. Bruner, Eys, and Turnnidge (Chapter 10) address how groups and peers influence children's involvement in sport through variables such as friendship, cohesion, and interdependence. Finally, in Chapter 11, Fraser-Thomas, Strachan, and Jeffery-Tosoni provide an in-depth analysis of how parents and siblings impact children's participation and performance in sport. This section of the book on social influences highlights the important role other people have on children's commitment to remain in sport and develop their talent.

The last section of the book is devoted to the social environment of children's sport. In Chapter 12, MacDonald and Baker summarize the findings of two social phenomena—relative age and birthplace—which significantly bias the nurturing of talent in children's sport. Finally, in Chapter 13, Harvey, Jung, and Kirk review social variables such as gender and social class that can distort the equality of opportunities offered to children in sport for developing their talent. The social environment in which children's sport is embedded is often overlooked in talent-development research, and the last section of this book reviews variables that need to be considered as hindering or facilitating talent-development in children.

In this volume, we seek to present a comprehensive understanding of the variables involved in the development of talent in sport during childhood. Central to the book are the developmental activities of play and practice that contribute to the development of talent in sport, with a specific focus on the physical characteristics of children, their mental attributes, the psychosocial influences, and the social environment, all of which impact children's sport. We see this book as a much needed compilation of knowledge about a unique, and often not well-understood, phase of talent development in sport. We look forward to further dialogue about the theory and practice of children's talent-development in sport.

REFERENCES

Abbott, A., & Collins, D. (2004). Eliminating the dichotomy between theory and practice in talent identification and development: Considering the role of psychology. *Journal of Sport Sciences, 22*(5), 395–408.

Baker, J., Côté, J., & Abernethy, B. (2003). Sport-specific practice and the development of expert decision-making in team ball sports. *Journal of Applied Sport Psychology, 15*(1), 12–25.

Bloom, B. S. (Ed.). (1985). *Developing talent in young people.* New York, NY: Ballantine.

Bruner, M. W., Erickson, K., McFadden, K. K., & Côté, J. (2009). Tracing the origins of athlete development models in sport: A citation path network analysis. *International Review of Sport and Exercise Psychology, 2*(1), 23–37.

Côté, J. (1999). The influence of the family in the development of talent in sport. *The Sport Psychologist, 13*(4), 395–417.

Côté, J. (2009). The road to continued sport participation and excellence. In E. Tsung-Min Hung, R. Lidor, & D. Hackfort (Eds.), *Psychology of sport excellence* (pp. 97–104). Morgantown, WV: Fitness Information Technology.

Côté, J., Baker, J., & Abernethy, B. (2003). From play to practice: A developmental framework for the acquisition of expertise in team sports. In J. Starkes & K. A. Ericsson (Eds.), *Expert performance in sports: Advances in research on sport expertise* (pp. 89–110). Champaign, IL: Human Kinetics.

Côté, J., Baker, J., & Abernethy, B. (2007). Practice and play in the development of sport expertise. In R. Eklund & G. Tenenbaum (Eds.), *Handbook of sport psychology* (3rd ed.) (pp. 184–202). Hoboken, NJ: Wiley.

Côté, J., Coakley, C., & Bruner, M. W. (2011). Children's talent-development in sport: Effectiveness or efficiency? In S. W. Dagkas & K. Armour (Eds.), *Inclusion and exclusion through youth sport* (pp. 172–185). London, UK: Routledge.

Côté, J., Lidor, R., & Hackfort, D. (2009). ISSP position stand: To sample or to specialize? Seven postulates about youth sport activities that lead to continued participation and elite performance. *International Journal of Sport and Exercise Psychology, 9*, 7–17.

Ericsson, K. A., Krampe, R. T., & Tesch-Römer, C. (1993). The role of deliberate practice in the acquisition of expert performance. *Psychological Review, 100*(3), 363–406.

Ericsson, K. A., & Lehmann, A. C. (1996). Expert and exceptional performance: Evidence of maximal adaptation to task constraints. *Annual Review of Psychology, 47*(1), 273–305.

Gustin, W. C. (1985). The development of exceptional research mathematicians. In B. S. Bloom (Ed.), *Developing talent in young people* (pp. 270–331). New York, NY: Ballantine.

Harper, S. (Producer and Director). (2009). Lost adventures in childhood. *Sunday Night Entertainment,* in association with CTV Television, Inc.

Helsen, W. F., Starkes, J. L., & Hodges, N. J. (1998). Team sports and the theory of deliberate practice. *Journal of Sport and Exercise Psychology, 20*(1), 12–34.

Howe, M. J. A., Davidson, J. W., & Sloboda, J. A. (1998). Innate talents: Reality or myth? *Behavioral and Brain Sciences, 21*(3), 399–442.

Kalinowski, A. G. (1985). The development of Olympic swimmers. In B. S. Bloom (Ed.), *Developing talent in young people* (pp. 139–192). New York, NY: Ballantine.

Larson, R. W. (2000). Toward a psychology of positive youth development. *American Psychologist, 55*(1), 170–183.

Martindale, R. J. J., Collins, D., & Daubney, J. (2005). Talent-development: A guide for practice and research within sport. *Quest, 57*(4), 353–375.

Monsaas, J. A. (1985). Learning to be a world-class tennis player. In B. S. Bloom (Ed.), *Developing talent in young people* (pp. 211–269). New York, NY: Ballantine.

Pearson, D., Naughton, G., & Torode, M. (2006). Predictability of physiological testing and the role of maturation in talent identification for adolescent team sports. *Journal of Science and Medicine in Sport, 9*(4), 277–287.

Régnier, G., Salmela., J., & Russell, S. (1993). Talent detection and development in sport. In R. Singer, M. Murphy, & L. Tennant (Eds.), *Handbook of research in sport psychology* (pp. 290–313). New York, NY: Macmillan.

Simon, H. A., & Chase, W. G. (1973). Skill in chess. *American Scientist, 61*(4), 394–403.

Sosniak, L. A. (1985). Learning to be a concert pianist. In B. S. Bloom (Ed.), *Developing talent in young people* (pp. 19–67). New York, NY: Ballantine.

Starkes, J. L. (2000). The road to expertise: Is practice the only determinant? *International Journal of Sport Psychology, 31*(4), 431–451.

Starkes, J. L., Helsen, W. F., & Jack, R. (2001). Expert performance in sport and dance. In R. N. Singer, H. A. Hausenblas, & C. M. Janelle (Eds.), *Handbook of sport psychology* (pp. 174–201). New York, NY: Wiley.

Vaeyens, R., Lenoir, M., Williams, A. M., & Philippaerts, R. M. (2008). Talent identification and development programmes in sport: Current models and future directions. *Sports Medicine, 38*(9), 703–714.

Young, B. W., & Salmela, J. H. (2002). Perceptions of training and deliberate practice of middle distance runners. *International Journal of Sport Psychology, 33*(2), 167–181.

CHAPTER 2

PLAY AND PRACTICE DURING CHILDHOOD

Jean Côté, Karl Erickson, and Bruce Abernethy

INTRODUCTION

Youth sport has the potential to promote a number of important outcomes in young people's development, including performance, participation, and personal development (Côté & Fraser-Thomas, 2007). Performance, participation, and personal development interact; therefore, they cannot be seen as separate entities when designing programs for children in sport. Accordingly, performance and personal variables have to be considered as integrated components when developing learning activities for children in sport.

Bronfenbrenner's ecological theory (1977, 1999) provides an integrated approach to studying performance and personal development through sport participation (see Carlson, 1988; Côté, Strachan, & Fraser-Thomas, 2008; Garcia Bengoechea, 2002). Bronfenbrenner (1977) originally refers to the notion that human development and human behavior are the materialization of person-context interactions, and that a network of nested systems are in constant interaction with each other to result in specific developmental outcomes. When a child's overall development and health is considered, many personal and environmental factors interact to affect an individual's talent-development trajectory. Garcia Bengoechea and Johnson (2001) state that "Understanding the forces that facilitate sports participation may contribute to the development and implementation of effective programs that increase involvement in sport activities, thereby enhancing physical, social, and psychological wellness in children" (p. 20). The activities of children in specific learning environments—their person-context interactions—therefore become an important and interesting component to explore when examining early talent-development programs in sport. Côté and colleagues (2008) suggested that playing and practice activities, with and without adults, are critical catalysts for human development and talent-development in sport, acting as mechanisms of individual-environment interaction.

This chapter is divided into four main sections. The objective of the first section is to review the different types of developmental activities in children's sport. In the second section we propose a taxonomy of different motivational and learning environments. The third section discusses of how the promotion of various playing and practice activities in youth sport exposes children to a variety of learning environments, and goes beyond the acquisition of motor skills and addresses the psychosocial dimensions of talent-development. Finally, section four of the chapter focuses on the importance of child-led activities in children sport.

DEVELOPMENTAL ACTIVITIES IN CHILDREN'S SPORT

Over the years, there have been a number of different lines of research examining the type of activities that are important at different stages of development for maintaining participation and developing talent in sport. In a comprehensive review of studies on learning and skill acquisition, Ericsson, Krampe, and Tesch-Römer (1993) concluded that the most effective learning occurs through involvement in highly structured activities, defined as *deliberate practice*. According to Ericsson and colleagues (1993), engagement in deliberate practice requires effort, generates no immediate rewards, and is motivated by the goal of improving performance rather than its inherent enjoyment. Ericsson et al. (1993) demonstrated that expert performance in music was the product of extensive deliberate practice, rather than the result of innate abilities. They suggested that to achieve expert performance, deliberate practice must be sustained over a period of at least 10 years.

Recognizing that athletes tend to first experience sport through fun and playful games, Côté (1999) used the term "deliberate play" to characterize a form of sporting activity that directly contrasts with the notion of deliberate practice put forward by Ericsson and colleagues (1993). Deliberate play involves early developmental physical activities that are intrinsically motivating, provide immediate gratification, and are specifically designed to maximize enjoyment. Deliberate play activities, such as street hockey or backyard soccer, are regulated by rules adapted from standardized sport rules and are set up and monitored by the children or by an adult involved in the activity. Furthermore, it is a form of physical activity that differs from the physical play activities of infancy and early childhood (Denzin, 1975; Pellegrini & Smith, 1998; Piaget, 1962). Deliberate play shares the contextual characteristics of more primitive forms of physical activity play, such as running, climbing, jumping, and rough-and-tumble play (Denzin, 1975; Pellegrini & Smith, 1998; Piaget, 1962), yet displays more organized and unique behavioral patterns. Pellegrini and Smith (1998) suggest that physical activity play such as rough-and-tumble play in young children (1) improves control of specific motor patterns; (2) contributes to children's endurance, strength training, and economy of movement; and (3) contributes to children's regulation of emotions and cognitive performance. In the same way, the learning of motor skills through deliberate play can be illustrated with older children who have more complex sport skills. Because free play activities such as rough-and-tumble play occur at a young age on a nonregular basis, we will consider deliberate play as the first type of activity that children engage in on a regular basis for the development of talent in sport.

Deliberate play differs from the specific pedagogical games/play designed to improve performance, such as teaching games for understanding or play practice (Griffin & Butler, 2005; Launder, 2001); it is also different from the *structured practice* activities typical of organized sport. Finally, it contrasts greatly with the concept of deliberate practice activities (Ericsson, 2001; Ericsson et al., 1993) that have an objective of improving performance. In sum, deliberate practice and deliberate play are two contrasting activities that vary along several characteristics and constitute two ends of a continuum (Côté, Baker, & Abernethy, 2007). We suggest three additional types of activities that can be included on the continuum between deliberate play and practice, and are relevant to athletes' performance and motivation in sport.

The first set of activities that cannot be defined as either deliberate practice or deliberate play are the specific pedagogical games/play designed to improve performance. Although different labels exist to describe the diverse type of activities within this general category, such as teaching games for understanding (Griffin & Butler, 2005) and game sense (Light, 2006), we use the term *play practice* proposed by Launder (2001) to describe this generic type of activity. Play practice activities are led or prescribed by adults and have the overall goal of improving performance by emphasizing fun and games. An important aspect of the play practice activities is to keep young people motivated by designing learning activities that are enjoyable and typically represent the games that are played by this age group.

We use the term *spontaneous practice* to describe a second set of activities that cannot be categorized as deliberate practice or deliberate play. Spontaneous practice constitutes a form of *informal learning*. In the education literature, Livingstone (2002) defines informal learning as learning that occurs outside of the curriculum of formal institutions or programs. Spontaneous practice differs from deliberate play activities in the extrinsic-intrinsic dimension of both activities. Spontaneous practice in sport is structured by children in their free time with the goal of improving aspects of their sport skills (e.g., extrinsic value). However, in spontaneous practice children do not follow an adult-specified curriculum or necessarily work on the most important skills to improve their performance. Spontaneous practice is not systematically and pedagogically planned; rather, it originates sporadically within certain occasions that are coordinated and led by the children themselves.

Finally, participation in organized competition is another activity led by adults. This requires concentration and effort yet is generally highly enjoyable and not specifically structured to improve performance. The structure and inherent dimensions of organized competition give it a unique place among the panoply of activities in youth sport. In a retrospective study of elite athletes (Baker, Côté, & Abernethy, 2003a), organized competition was rated as the most helpful form of training for the development of perceptual and decision-making skills, and was also rated highly for developing skill execution and physical fitness. Organized competition is supervised by adults and has properties of both deliberate play and deliberate practice.

Deliberate practice, play practice, spontaneous practice, deliberate play, and organized competition do not constitute a complete and exhaustive list of all the activities of youth sport. However, these five activities are a representation of the typical characteristics of different types of involvement of children in sport. In this sense, each of these activities can be described as a *prototype* activity that exemplifies unique characteristics, ultimately representing a larger number of experiences that children might possibly encounter in their sport involvement.

Deliberate practice, play practice, spontaneous practice, deliberate play, and organized competition vary on a number of dimensions. Each of these types of activities plays an important role in children's learning of new sport skills and in the motivation to stay involved in sport. Retrospective studies of elite-level athletes suggest that the early development of experts includes involvement in a number of different types of activities that could generally be described by the prototype activities of deliberate practice, play practice, spontaneous practice, and deliberate play (e.g., Baker et al., 2003a; Berry, Abernethy, & Côté, 2008; Ford, Ward, Hodges, & Williams, 2009). These studies suggest that the different social contexts of the various play and practice activities fulfill different needs in children's current and future involvement in sport. The intrinsically motivating and self-directed nature of more play-oriented activities contrasts with the outcome-oriented and often adult-driven nature of more practice-oriented activities.

The distinguishing characteristics of different types of activities in children's sport can be summarized by the social structure of the activity and the personal value the activity provides to the participants (Hakkarainen, 1999). Accordingly, the prototype activities of deliberate practice, play practice, spontaneous practice, and deliberate play—and their corresponding dimensions—can be conceptualized along two general axes adapted from Hakkarainen's analysis of play learning and instruction in children. A first axis, representing the social structure of the activity, shows how much instruction and input are vested by supervising adult(s) (i.e., the coach) versus by the participating youth. At one end of this axis are sport activities where adults have a minimal role in providing instructions, as in play activities. At the other end of the axis are sport activities in which adults set the direction and provide instruction in a structured environment, such as the structured practices of organized sport. A second axis relates to the personal values associated with an activity, varying from extrinsic to intrinsic values. *Extrinsic values* describes activities that are performed with the goal of improving skills or performance, while *intrinsic values* refers to activities that are done for their inherent enjoyment. When combined, these two axes form a matrix in which the prototype activities of youth sport can be located and distinct learning contexts emerge (see Figure 2.1).

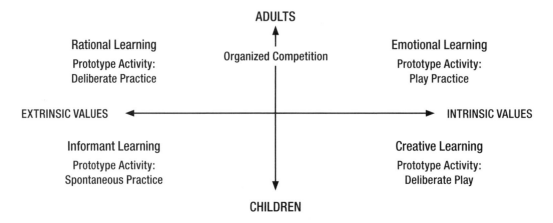

Figure 2.1. Different Settings of Practice and Play for Children

SPORT ACTIVITIES AND LEARNING ENVIRONMENTS

When a specific prototype activity is promoted in children's sport, it creates a learning context that is unique and distinct. An activity such as deliberate practice, prescribed or led by an adult to improve children's specific skills, creates a learning environment that we have labeled *rational* because of the systematic and logical nature of this activity (top left quadrant of the matrix in Figure 2.1). Adults can also create a more emotional learning environment by trying to integrate fun into skill development practice through activities such as play practice or teaching games for understanding (top right quadrant of the matrix in Figure 2.1). The bottom half of Figure 2.1 includes two general learning environments that are led by the children involved in the activity. Deliberate play activities (bottom right quadrant) produce a creative learning context by removing most of the external constraints imposed by adults and by establishing a context that minimizes the outcome of performance. On the other hand, when children engage in spontaneous practice (bottom left quadrant), they create an informal learning environment that maintains the low external pressure atmosphere of deliberate play but is directed towards specific skill development.

The social contexts created by the learning environments in which deliberate play, spontaneous practice, play practice, and deliberate practice take place are qualitatively different, as are the resultant learning and motivational outcomes. Each facilitates unique interactions between the developing child and his or her physical and social environment, thus differentiating

Table 2.1. Types of Learning and Examples of Developmental Activities in Children's Sport

Types of Learning	Prototype Activity	Illustration
Rational Learning	Deliberate Practice	Children practicing drills that are prescribed or monitored by an adult. The goal of these activities is to improve performance (e.g., a tennis player works on her backhand in training while receiving technical feedback from her coach).
Emotional Learning	Play Practice	Enjoyable learning situations are set up by an adult. The goal of these activities is to create fun learning situations in training (e.g., a coach-designed game in training where a tennis player can only score points when hitting with his backhand).
Informal Learning	Spontaneous Practice	A child deciding to practice a skill without being prescribed or monitored by an adult (e.g., a basketball player practicing shooting on her own).
Creative Learning	Deliberate Play	Children playing sport purely for enjoyment in an informal environment. Games are adapted by the children themselves to fit the environment and the players involved while keeping the game fun (e.g. getting together in a backyard to play soccer for fun.)

the nature of the proximal processes driving development within each learning context. In line with Bronfenbrenner's ecological theory (1977, 1999), it is important to promote all of these activities and provide an integrated and inclusive learning environment for children in sport. The different dimensions of the activities described in Figure 2.1 can be integrated to create sport development environments in which various types of learning can occur and, equally as important, that consider the motivational aspects of sport participation and performance. The approach proposed in this chapter suggests that having a variety of socially meaningful activities in youth sport is important for the development of children in sport. However, when adults take control of children's sport, they often promote a certain type of activity at the expense of others because of the perceived long-term benefit. A summary of the activities associated with the four different types of learning in children's sport is provided in Table 2.1. The seemingly contradictory nature of the different types of activities in children's sport may be perceived as an impediment to the creation of truly effective development environments; however, the prototype activities described in Table 2.1 complement one another to provide a comprehensive social, motivational, and learning environment for talent-development in children.

COMPLEMENTARITY OF ACTIVITIES IN CHILDREN'S SPORT

Children's sport takes place in distinctive learning contexts using different activities that can sometimes be perceived as contradictory. For example, the teaching of sport skills at a young age through deliberate practice may conflict in many ways with children's engagement in deliberate play. Although there are basic contradictions between activities such as deliberate practice and deliberate play in children's sport, participation in a range of different developmental activities exposes children to a variety of learning environments, the combination of which is most beneficial for children's motivation (Hakkarainen, 1999).

The promotion of a specific activity over another transmits distinct messages to the children involved in sport. Activities that are led by the children themselves, such as deliberate play and spontaneous practice, require an adaptable frame of mind and involve a focused but unstressed approach to sport. Child-led activities encourage children to be creative, giving them the opportunity to experiment with new skills that they might be afraid to attempt under the critical eyes of coaches or parents (Sagar & Lavallee, 2010). Further, deliberate play and spontaneous practice often take place in a mixed-age context, in which younger children are exposed to more advanced model skills toward which they can strive, while older children provide scaffolding for younger children's learning efforts and expand their own knowledge through teaching (Gray & Feldman, 2004).

In contrast, organized sport occurs within a structured environment led by a coach. Adults and coaches in organized sport typically segregate groups by age or skill level to facilitate discipline and instruction efficiency, keeping the learning focused on the specific demands of the particular sport. Deliberate practice and practice play focus on promoting performance during childhood by having adults set up the learning environment with the ultimate goal of improving children's sport performance. There are obvious advantages to having a knowledgeable coach who provides athletes with feedback about their performance, monitors success, and provides immediate instruction. However, it is unclear whether the benefits of this structured environment are superior to the benefits one gains from engagement in children-led activities during the early stages of development. Furthermore, the overly structured, competitive, and adult-driven aspects of organized sport, and more specifically, deliberate practice during childhood, can lead to negative outcomes such as early exclusion of late-maturing athletes and the increased prevalence of overuse injuries, burnout, and dropout (see Fraser-Thomas, Côté, & Deakin, 2008; Law, Côté, & Ericsson, 2007; Strachan, Côté, & Deakin, 2009; Wall & Côté, 2007), all of which can potentially limit the talent-development pool. Highly structured, adult-driven approaches to skill learning may also result in an overdependence on explicit forms of skill learning, and subsequently can limit the extent to which skill performance will remain robust under various psychological and physiological stressors (Masters & Maxwell, 2004).

There is complementarity between the different contexts of learning presented in Figure 2.1. For example, there may be advantages related to skill acquisition in setting up a rational learning context; however, these advantages need to be evaluated against the motivational strengths of an emotional learning context. Similarly, the advantages of promoting deliberate play as a creative learning process need to be assessed against the possible development of incorrect technical habits. In a review of retrospective studies focusing on the early development of elite athletes, Côté et al. (2007) showed that the integration of various types of activities defined as deliberate play and deliberate practice were characteristic of the early years of elite-level athletes. Generally, when considered with regard to the proposed matrix (Figure 2.1), activities associated with the best learning and motivational environment in the early years of an athlete's development varied across the four quadrants. Consequently, it is important to promote a balance of different types of activities (i.e., adult-led and child-led) performed for different reasons (i.e., for enjoyment or to improve performance) during childhood sport. Reducing the acquisition of expert performance in sport to involvement in a single form of activity (i.e., deliberate practice) fails to acknowledge important developmental and motivational assets acquired from involvement in play and other sporting activities. A mix of instrumental and intrinsically motivated youth-led and adult-led activities appears to be important for the development of talent during childhood (for a review, see Côté et al., 2007).

THE IMPORTANCE OF CHILD-LED ACTIVITIES FOR MOTIVATION AND LEARNING

While much has been written about adult-led activities in youth sport, comparatively little attention has been given to the child-led activities that appear to be equally critical to the development of children's talent in sport. These activities (e.g., deliberate play and spontaneous practice) share a number of characteristics that directly influence the types of motivation and learning experienced by children during participation. The motivational and learning qualities of child-led activities offer unique contributions to children's talent-development that are distinct from those in adult-led sport.

Based on findings that emerge from the general developmental psychology literature on play (see reviews by Lester & Russell, 2008; Smith, 2010), it appears that children's participation in child-led sport activities is characterized by two primary criteria, namely that the activity is (1) chosen freely, and (2) personally directed (the children themselves, rather than adults, control the structure and form of the activity). Central to this description is the agency of the child to decide what to do and how to do it, purely for his or her own values.

The specific activities constituting child-led sport participation are characterized by two further criteria: (1) a high degree of novelty and unpredictability, and (2) flexibility in their structure and form (Lester & Russell, 2008). In this context, novelty and unpredictability refer to the notion that even within familiar games with established rules, for example, children expose themselves to new physical, social, and emotional situations (e.g., adapting to new team members and opponents as teams are shuffled to keep the game competitive and fair). These physical, social, and emotional experiences are not regulated or predetermined by adults, but rather arise from the unstructured interaction of children with their environment and peers. These interactions may not always be immediately positive, but they are unmediated by adult intervention and thus are fully experienced and dealt with by the children themselves. As well, the course of a child-led sport session and the interactions occurring within it are not fixed as in more adult-led activities. Flexibility in structure and form is related to the child-directed nature of these activities. With control over structure and form, the children have the opportunity to invent, adapt, and negotiate activities and rules to suit their own wants and needs. This ownership of control means children (both as individuals and as groups) have responsibility and agency to decide what they want from their time and to structure their sport activities accordingly.

The inclusion of spontaneous practice and deliberate play within our definition of child-led sport is in disagreement with the views of some traditional play theorists. These theorists argue that the rule-oriented structure and competitive nature of these activities violate the assumptions of flexibility and lack of outcome goals inherent in true play (e.g., Pellegrini, Dupuis, & Smith, 2007; Smith, 2010). In contrast, we suggest that these arguments are more relevant to adult-led sport participation. Pellegrini and colleagues (2007) state that children follow rules in true play, but "the rules are flexible and are typically negotiated by children.... Plans [or rules] are often changed to accommodate different views so that play can be sustained" (p. 264). Spontaneous practice and deliberate play are characterized by this same child-directed negotiability of rules, necessary for providing an equitable game between players of differing abilities and physical competencies (Côté et al., 2007; Jarvis, 2007). For example, the composition of teams is often rearranged if one team is winning too easily. Younger, less-skilled players are also often accommodated or allowed to play by different rules to minimize size and skill advantages, thus exhibiting the key flexibility of child-led activities. This flexibility also reveals the nature of competition within these activities. The focus of participation is on the act or process of competing (intrinsically motivated) and on keeping the game going in a fair and fun manner (Jarvis, 2007), rather than on the outcome of winning as in adult-driven structured sport. The flexibility and negotiability of rules is thus enacted by the participants themselves, in order to maintain fun competition between players of differing abilities and often different ages (Côté et al., 2007).

Resulting from these unique characteristics, child-led sport activities have several outcomes distinct from those impacted by adult-led sport activities. It is these distinct outcomes that reveal the true potential of child-led activities to contribute to children's overall talent-development. It has been suggested that the very nature of child-led activities, and their inherent characteristics (child-directed, unpredictable, and flexibly governed), lead to their distinct outcomes (Lester & Russell, 2008; Pellegrini et al., 2007). By providing freedom to generate and experiment with new behaviors in safe but stimulating environments, child-led sport activities result less in direct learning of specific prescribed skills and more in general *learning how to learn* and how to adapt to novel or uncertain situations (both pleasant and unpleasant). It is this learning how to learn and how to adapt that marks the greatest benefit of child-led activities. Direct learning of specific prescribed skills, as in the adult-directed instruction often characteristic of adult-led sport, can only result in the transmission of existing practices (i.e., currently accepted modes of "correct" performance; Pellegrini et al., 2007). Child-led activities are unique in their ability to foster innovation—physically, socially, emotionally, and technically/tactically. This promotion and development of innovation, creativity, adaptability, and flexibility (physical, social, emotional, and technical/tactical) through child-led activities has been highlighted in both the general developmental psychology and sport psychology literature (e.g., Côté et al., 2007; Lester & Russell, 2008; Memmert, Baker, & Bertsch, 2010; Pellegrini et al., 2007).

The development of adaptability and creativity promoted by free experimentation in a safe, low-risk environment has been posited as the mechanism accounting for the empirically recorded benefits of child-led sport activities on skill acquisition and sport expertise (Côté et al., 2007). A number of retrospective studies of expert and elite athlete development (e.g., Berry et al., 2008; Côté, 1999; Ford et al., 2009; Memmert et al., 2010) have highlighted the critical role of unstructured, child-led activities during childhood. A unique contribution to this discussion is the analysis of motor learning contexts, which might be used to explain the critical role of child-led activities and the resulting creativity in skill acquisition. The characteristics of child-led activities are consistent with conditions for implicit learning (Masters & Maxwell, 2004). Implicit learning describes the learners' ability to increase performance through practice without conscious effort or processing. That is, it is possible to learn and improve at new skills without consciously trying to improve or understand performance. The opposite context, explicit learning, involves focused attention on the quality and process of practice movements during learning, often accompanied and directed by verbal instruction from a teacher or coach. Such explicit learning is often characteristic of deliberate practice activities (although it should be noted that adult-led activities can also be structured to promote implicit learning). Despite the intuitive benefits of more explicit learning provision, substantial research (see review by Masters & Maxwell, 2004; Masters, van der Kamp, & Capio, Chapter 3 in this text) has demonstrated a significant advantage for implicitly learned motor performance, particularly under conditions of stress or pressure. While initial learning may be slower under implicit conditions, the provision of instructions and focused concentration on learning in explicit learning may in some cases actually be detrimental to overall performance. Thus, in the early stages of sport expertise development (i.e., childhood), the qualities inherent to child-led sport activities may in some instances provide equally conducive learning conditions as adult-led structured practice. This is in concert with more effective promotion of the behavioral creativity and innovation purported to underlie expert sport performance (Côté et al., 2007). In sum, even from a purely skill acquisition perspective, the literature suggests that a mix or balance of child-led and adult-led sport activities—rather than a dominant focus on adult-led sport—may be most beneficial for children's talent-development.

Finally, regardless of other qualities of child-led sport activities, the self-regulation inherently guiding participation is itself associated with a number of positive outcomes, including both psychological aspects (such as enhanced self-esteem and overall well-being) and continued participation (Markland & Ingledew, 2007). Even spontaneous practice, which is situated closer to the extrinsic value end of the horizontal axis in Figure 2.1, is a self-regulated rather than adult-regulated activity. This early self-regulation has important implications for future development. Fry (2001) notes that an individual's motivational orientation appears to be set by age 12 or 13. In order to promote lifelong, intrinsically motivated sport participation and continued talent-development into adolescence and adulthood, the foundation must be set during childhood. Inclusion of high amounts of child-led sport activities early in development may provide that self-regulated foundation.

CONCLUSION

The interaction of personal and social variables is an important component to consider when describing the learning activities of children in sport. Bronfenbrenner (1999) suggests that the environment in which the processes of development occur dictates the outcome that will result from involvement in specific activities. The basic argument of this chapter is that the development of talent in sport needs a foundation during childhood that includes various learning activities, as opposed to sole involvement in one type of activity, such as deliberate practice. Support for this argument has emerged from qualitative studies of athletes' careers (e.g., Bloom, 1985; Carlson, 1988; Côté, 1999) and from quantitative studies of expert and non-expert athletes' training and experiences (e.g., Baker, Côté, & Abernethy, 2003a, 2003b; Baker, Côté, & Deakin, 2005; Berry et al., 2008; Soberlak & Côté, 2003). Furthermore, studies of dropout athletes provide additional evidence that play and involvement in various types of sporting contexts during childhood, in addition to deliberate practice, are important determinants of continued participation and commitment to sport (Fraser-Thomas & Côté, 2009; Fraser-Thomas et al., 2008; Wall & Côté, 2007).

The development of talent during childhood can only be assessed by analyzing the whole spectrum of interaction between personal, social, and learning variables that occur during various forms of play and practice. Accordingly, it is necessary to put in place different activities in children's sport that activate what may be perceived as contrasting learning contexts, but in fact are complementary activities that contribute to different dimensions of talent-development. Based on the sport expertise literature, we propose that children's sport should promote at least four different learning contexts: (1) rational learning, (2) emotional learning, (3) informal learning, and (4) creative learning. These four learning contexts are associated with prototype activities (i.e., deliberate practice, play practice, spontaneous practice, and deliberate play) that interact to optimize learning and motivation in children's sport. The interdependent nature of different types of play and practice activities in childhood sport results in a complex learning environment that ultimately promotes long-term development and commitment to sport.

REFERENCES

Baker, J., Côté, J., & Abernethy, B. (2003a). Learning from the experts: Practice activities of expert decision makers in sport. *Research Quarterly for Exercise and Sport, 74*(3), 342–347.

Baker, J., Côté, J., & Abernethy, B. (2003b). Sport-specific practice and the development of expert decision-making in team ball sports. *Journal of Applied Sport Psychology, 15,* 12–25.

Baker, J., Côté, J., & Deakin, J. (2005). Expertise in ultra-endurance triathletes early sport involvement, training structures, and the theory of deliberate practice. *Journal of Applied Sport Psychology, 17*(1), 64–78.

Berry, J., Abernethy, B., & Côté, J. (2008). The contribution of structured activity and deliberate play to the development of expert perceptual and decision-making skill. *Journal of Sport and Exercise Psychology, 30,* 685–708.

Bloom, B. S. (Ed.). (1985). *Developing talent in young people.* New York, NY: Ballantine.

Bronfenbrenner, U. (1977). Toward an experimental ecology of human development. *American Psychologist, 32*(7), 513–531.

Bronfenbrenner, U. (1999). Environments in developmental perspective: Theoretical and operational models. In S. L. Friedman & T. D. Wachs (Eds.), *Measuring environment across the life span* (pp. 3–28). Washington, DC: American Psychological Association.

Carlson, R. (1988). The socialization of elite tennis players in Sweden: An analysis of the players' backgrounds and development. *Sociology of Sport Journal, 5*(3), 241–256.

Côté, J. (1999). The influence of the family in the development of talent in sport. *The Sport Psychologist, 13,* 395–417.

Côté, J., Baker, J., & Abernethy, B. (2007). Practice and play in the development of sport expertise. In R. Eklund & G. Tenenbaum (Eds.), *Handbook of sport psychology* (3rd ed.) (pp. 184–202). Hoboken, NJ: Wiley.

Côté, J., & Fraser-Thomas, J. (2007). Youth involvement in sport. In P. Crocker (Ed.), *Sport psychology: A Canadian perspective* (pp. 270–298). Toronto, Canada: Pearson.

Côté, J., Strachan, L., & Fraser-Thomas, J. L. (2008). Participation, personal development, and performance through youth sport. In N. L. Holt (Ed.), *Positive youth development through sport* (pp. 34–45). London, UK: Routledge.

Denzin, M. K. (1975). Play, games and interaction: The contexts of childhood interaction. *The Sociological Quarterly, 16*(4), 458–476.

Ericsson, K. A. (2001). The path to expert golf performance: Insights from the masters on how to improve performance by deliberate practice. In P. R. Thomas (Ed.), *Optimizing performance in golf* (pp. 1–57). Brisbane, Australia: Australian Academic Press.

Ericsson, K. A., Krampe, R. T., & Tesch-Römer, C. (1993). The role of deliberate practice in the acquisition of expert performance. *Psychological Review, 100*(3), 363–406.

Ford, P. R., Ward, P., Hodges, N., & Williams, A. M. (2009). The role of deliberate practice and play in career progression in sport: The early engagement hypothesis. *High Ability Studies, 20*(1), 65–75.

Fraser-Thomas, J., & Côté, J. (2009). Understanding adolescents' positive and negative developmental experiences in sport. *The Sport Psychologist, 23*(1), 3–23.

Fraser-Thomas, J., Côté, J., & Deakin, J. (2008). Examining adolescent sport dropout and prolonged engagement from a developmental perspective. *Journal of Applied Sport Psychology, 20,* 318–333.

Fry, M. D. (2001). The development of motivation in children. In G. C. Roberts (Ed.), *Advances in motivation in sport and exercise* (pp. 51–78). Champaign, IL: Human Kinetics.

Garcia Bengoechea, E. (2002). Integrating knowledge and expanding horizons in developmental sport psychology: A bioecological perspective. *Quest, 54*(1), 1–20.

Garcia Bengoechea, E., & Johnson, G. M. (2001). Ecological systems theory and children's development in sport: Toward a process-person-context-time research paradigm. *Avante, 7*(1), 20–31.

Gray, P., & Feldman, J. (2004). Playing in the zone of proximal development: Qualities of self-directed age mixing between adolescents and young children at a democratic school. *American Journal of Education, 110,* 108–145.

Griffin, L. L., & Butler, J. I. (Eds.). (2005). *Teaching games for understanding: Theory, research, and practice.* Champaign, IL: Human Kinetics.

Hakkarainen, P. (1999). Play and motivation. In Y. Engström, R. Miettinen, & R. L. Punamäki (Eds.), *Aspects of activity theory* (pp. 231–249). Cambridge, UK: Cambridge University Press.

Jarvis, P. (2007). Dangerous activities within an invisible playground: A study of emergent male football play and teachers' perspectives of outdoor free play in the early years of primary school. *International Journal of Early Years Education, 15*(3), 245–259.

Launder, A. G. (2001). *Play practice: The games approach to teaching and coaching sports.* Champaign, IL: Human Kinetics.

Law, M. P., Côté, J., & Ericsson, K. A. (2007). Characteristics of expert development in rhythmic gymnastics: A retrospective study. *International Journal of Sport and Exercise Psychology, 5*(1), 82–103.

Lester, S., & Russell, W. (2008). *Play for a change: Play, policy and practice: A review of contemporary perspectives—Summary report.* Retrieved from http://www.playengland.org.uk/resources/play-for-a-change-symmary.pdf

Light, R. (2006). Game sense: Innovation or just good coaching? *Journal of Physical Education New Zealand, 39*(1), 8–19.

Livingstone, D. W. (2002). *Mapping the iceberg.* Retrieved from http://www.nall.ca/res/54DavidLivingstone.pdf

Markland, D., & Ingledew, D. K. (2007). Exercise participation motives: A self-determination theory perspective. In M. S. Hagger & N. L. D. Chatzisarantis (Eds.), *Intrinsic motivation and self-determination in exercise and sport* (pp. 23–34). Champaign, IL: Human Kinetics.

Masters, R. S. W., & Maxwell, J. P. (2004). Implicit motor learning, reinvestment and movement disruption: What you don't know won't hurt you? In A. M. Williams & N. J. Hodges (Eds.), *Skill acquisition in sport: Research, theory and practice* (pp. 207–228). London, UK: Routledge.

Memmert, D., Baker, J., & Bertsch, C. (2010). Play and practice in the development of sport-specific creativity in team ball sports. *High Ability Studies, 21*(1), 3–18.

Pellegrini, A. D., Dupuis, D., & Smith, P. K. (2007). Play in evolution and development. *Developmental Review, 27,* 261–276.

Pellegrini, A. D., & Smith, P. K. (1998). Physical activity play: The nature and function of a neglected aspect of play. *Child Development, 69*(3), 577–598.

Piaget, J. (1962). *Play, dreams, and imitation in childhood.* New York, NY: W. W. Norton.

Sagar, S. S., & Lavallee, D. (2010). The developmental origins of fear of failure in adolescent athletes: Examining parental practices. *Psychology of Sport and Exercise, 11*(3), 177–187.

Soberlak, P., & Côté, J. (2003). The developmental activities of elite ice hockey players. *Journal of Applied Sport Psychology, 15,* 41–49.

Smith, P. K. (2010). *Children and play.* Chichester, UK: Wiley-Blackwell.

Strachan, L., Côté, J., & Deakin, J. (2009). "Specializers" versus "samplers" in youth sport: comparing experiences and outcomes. *The Sport Psychologist, 23*(1), 77–92.

Wall, M., & Côté, J. (2007). Developmental activities that lead to dropout and investment in sport. *Physical Education and Sport Pedagogy, 12*(1), 77–87.

CHAPTER 3

IMPLICIT MOTOR LEARNING BY CHILDREN

Rich Masters, John van der Kamp, and Catherine Capio

INTRODUCTION

Preschoolers and even infants often act appropriately or display understanding of the world around them using complex underlying causal information that they clearly cannot explicate (see Greenbaum & Graf, 1989; Saffran, Aslin, & Newport, 1996). For example, Xu and Garcia (2008; see also Xu & Denison, 2009) showed infants as young as eight months of age a container filled with 70 red balls and 5 white balls (or vice versa). An experimenter then withdrew five of the balls from the container and placed them in a tray in front of the infant. When four white balls and one red ball were produced (an improbable outcome), the infants looked reliably longer at the tray than when four red balls and one white ball were produced (a probable outcome). If the experimenter produced the balls from a trouser pocket rather than the container, the infants displayed no differences in look times. Xu and Garcia (2008) concluded that infants "possess a powerful mechanism for inductive learning, either using heuristics or basic principles of probability," but that these abilities develop without explicit teaching (p. 5012).

Children, in other words, know more than they can tell. Motor learning by children is not different; a child learns to bounce a ball, skip a rope, or evade another child without consciously knowing how it is that such a playground feat became possible or why it can be accomplished over and over with such ease. Indeed, it seems that a child's awareness of thinking (e.g., metacognition) develops only very gradually. Flavell, Green, and Flavell (2000), for example, asked adults and 5- and 8-year-old children to "think of nothing" for 30 seconds. Adults were unable to ignore their "stream of consciousness," but children maintained that they were *thinking* of nothing. It is unclear what William James would have made of this!

Important cognitive operations, such as information processing, differ in childhood compared to adulthood. Information processing tends to be slower (Ferguson & Bowey, 2005) in children, and verbal working memory capacity only improves as a child's language abilities develop (e.g., Hulme, Thompson, Muir, & Lawrence, 1984). Verbal processes associated with early motor learning are probably absent in children, at least at a very early age, because language ability develops later than goal-directed movement skills like walking and grasping (van der Kamp, Oudejans, & Savelsbergh, 2003). Stages-of-learning models of skill acquisition (e.g., Fitts & Posner, 1976), which propose an initial cognitive stage of learning in which there is substantial verbal engagement in performing the new skill, therefore seem inappropriate if applied to children. The cognitive stage is thought to be reliant on hypothesis testing, as a learner formulates methods by which to carry out the necessary movements successfully and judges their validity using naturally occurring feedback. With extensive practice, a stage of learning is eventually reached in which the movements are highly proficient and occur automatically with little verbal engagement, but given the limited verbal processes of young children, it seems unlikely that they first pass through such an explicit stage of learning. Indeed, Piaget (1937; 1954) proposed that an ability to appropriately use logic develops during the "concrete operational" stage of childhood (about 7 to 11 years of age), but an ability to formulate and test hypotheses in order to solve problems is unlikely to develop until the "formal operational" stage of childhood, which doesn't begin until about 11 years of age.

Some developmental approaches (e.g., Karmiloff-Smith, 1992; Sun, Merrill, & Peterson, 2001) propose that the first stage of learning is typically implicit or nonconscious, only later becoming explicit through an "endogenous process of representational redescription" (Vinter, Pacton, Witt, & Perruchet, 2010, p. 113). Karmiloff-Smith (1992) argued that most of a child's knowledge is implicit; certainly, implicit learning processes are evident in many elements of development, including reading, writing, and first-language learning (Chandler, 1993; Pacton, Perruchet, Fayol, & Cleeremans, 2001), acquiring social skills (Reber, 1993), and even understanding laws of physics (Krist, Fieberg, & Wilkening, 1993). Motor learning approaches for children need to accommodate this characteristic of their evolving cognitive abilities. Implicit motor learning, therefore, may provide an appropriate framework by which to guide intervention approaches to motor learning by children.

This chapter asks, What is implicit learning? Can motor skills be acquired implicitly? What features emerge when implicit motor learning occurs? Developmental changes in cognitive processing ability are discussed with respect to motor learning by children, and the role of working memory in this context is described. The chapter then moves on to describe interventions that have been devised to bring about implicit motor learning, including errorless and reduced-feedback approaches as well as analogy learning. The potential applicability of these adult-tested approaches to children is examined, and an attempt is made to situate the framework for implicit motor learning by children within more than a cognitive carapace.

THE CONCEPT OF IMPLICIT MOTOR LEARNING

Implicit, nonconscious processes of learning are integral to the constant adaptations that are necessary for effective interaction with an ever-changing environment (Gomez & Gherkin, 1999; Reber, 1993). Implicit learning is often an unintentional process (Berry & Dienes, 1993) that is distinguished from explicit learning by a lack of declarative knowledge about the underlying rules or processes that form the basis for successful performance of the task. Many definitions of implicit learning have been proposed (Frensch, 1998), some of which remain silent with respect to the kind of knowledge that implicit learning generates. Vinter et al. (2010), for example, defined implicit learning as a form of

> unintentional learning in which, as a consequence of repeated experience, an individual's behavior becomes sensitive to the structural features of an experienced situation, without, at any time, being told to learn anything about that situation and without the adaptation being due to an intentional exploitation of some pieces of explicit knowledge about these features. (p. 111)

Crucially, all definitions of implicit learning agree that little explicit knowledge is consciously deployed to control performance when a task has been learned implicitly.

Masters (1992) extended the concept of implicit learning to the intentional acquisition of motor skills that are functionally nontrivial. Masters argued that the importance of such tasks, be they ontogenetic or phylogenetic (see Gessell, 1954), can lead to overinvolvement of conscious processes in their learning and performance, which, in Vinter et al.'s (2010) vocabulary, results in overexploitation of explicit knowledge about structural features of the task. Therefore, implicit motor learning can be thought of as the acquisition of a motor skill without awareness of, or at least without the potential for overexploitation of, explicit knowledge that underlies the movement solution (Masters, 1992).

Subsequently, an implicit motor learning approach has been investigated in tasks such as golf putting (e.g., Hardy, Mullen, & Jones, 1996; Masters, 1992), ball passing (e.g., Poolton, Masters, & Maxwell, 2007a), table tennis (e.g., Liao & Masters, 2001), basketball shooting (e.g., Lam, Maxwell, & Masters, 2009a, 2009b), hammering (Masters, MacMahon, & Pall, 2004), balancing (e.g., Orrell, Eves, & Masters, 2006a), and laparoscopy skills (Zhu, et al., 2011). A small amount of recent work has applied the implicit motor learning approach to children (e.g., Capio, Poolton, Sit, Holmstrom, & Masters, 2011), drawing upon claims that implicit learning is characteristically invariant to age (Reber, 1992).

INVARIANCE OF IMPLICIT LEARNING

Generally, a consistent conclusion emerges from research into developmental aspects of learning; age differences are evident when explicit learning (or memory) is assessed, whereas age differences are absent when implicit learning (or memory) is assessed (e.g., Hayes & Hennessy, 1996; Vinter & Perruchet, 2000). Reber (1992) argued that implicit, nonconscious processes predate explicit, conscious processes and should therefore display characteristics that differentiate them from explicit processes. Invoking basic heuristics of evolutionary biology, he proposed that implicit learning should be robust to disorders that disrupt explicit learning (or memory), unrelated to tests of intelligence that are biased towards explicit processes, low in variability between individuals, and independent of age and developmental level. For example, Reber, Walkenfeld, and Hernstadt (1991) showed that large individual differences existed between undergraduates performing an explicit problem-solving task but not when they performed an implicit artificial grammar-learning task. Moreover, performance of the explicit problem-solving task, but not the implicit artificial grammar-learning task, correlated with IQ (see also Gebauer & MacIntosh, 2007; Maybery, Taylor, & O'Brien-Malone, 1995). In the artificial grammar-learning task (see Reber, 1967), participants memorized lists of letter strings (e.g., TPPXS) generated by the artificial grammar. When unseen letter strings from the same grammar were presented after learning, in a "well-formedness" test, participants could classify them as grammatically correct or incorrect, but typically could not describe the grammatical rules that informed their decisions.

Patterns of implicit learning by adult performers are generally replicated in children. Gomez and Gerken (1999), for example, presented sequences of sounds to 12-month-old infants, which were ordered according to an artificial grammar. After the infants had become accustomed to them, new sequences of sounds were presented that either adhered to the rules of the grammar or did not. The infants oriented to the former for longer than the latter, suggesting that somehow they had implicitly learned some of the rules underlying the grammar. Meulemans, van der Linden, and Perruchet (1998) showed that children aged between 6 and 10 years displayed unconscious learning of sequences in the serial reaction time task (SRTT) equivalent to that of adults aged between 18 and 27 years. The SRTT is a paradigm often used to examine implicit motor learning. A stimulus appears at one of four locations on a screen, and participants have to respond as quickly as possible by pushing the key that corresponds to the position of the stimulus (Nissen & Bullemer, 1987). For repeating sequences of which people are unaware, repetition has been shown to eventually result in reaction times so quick that they represent anticipation of the next location in the sequence. In other words, people appear to learn the underlying order of the repeating sequences unconsciously, or implicitly. More recently, the paradigm was used in children with autism, who displayed implicit learning of repeating sequences that was comparable to age- and IQ-matched control groups of children (Nemeth et al., 2010). However, one of the criticisms of the SRTT paradigm is that participants can intentionally exploit explicit knowledge of the sequence to support performance, making it impossible to disambiguate the influences of explicit and implicit processes on behavior (Didier & Bigand, 2010).

To overcome this problem, Vinter and Perruchet introduced the Neutral Parameter Procedure (NPP), first among adults (Vinter & Perruchet, 1999) and then in children (Vinter & Perruchet, 2000). The NPP tests for implicit learning by using an outcome measure that is neutral with respect to the parameters of the task that the participants are required to learn. Using the little-known start-rotation principle, which states that the direction of movement in the drawing of closed geometrical figures is dependent on whether the starting position is at the top or the bottom of the figure (van Sommers, 1984), Vinter and Perruchet (1999) showed clear evidence of implicit learning by adult participants. The participants were asked to trace over geometrical figures as quickly and as accurately as possible, initiating their drawing from the top or the bottom and moving in a specified direction (clockwise or counterclockwise). When trials often specified a direction that defied the start-rotation principle, participants' natural drawing behavior changed without their conscious awareness. The approach was deemed neutral because attention was drawn to the speed and accuracy parameters, and away from the outcome measure (direction of rotation).

Subsequently, in a series of three experiments conducted with a large sample of children aged between 4 and 10 years, Vinter and Perruchet (2000) used the same paradigm to show that children also unconsciously (implicitly) learned to defy the start-rotation principle. Age-related differences were not evident in any of the experiments. In follow-up work, Vinter and Perruchet (2002) replicated their findings using the same paradigm, but instead of drawing over images of the geometrical figure themselves, adults or children aged between 6 and 10 years observed the figures being drawn on a screen in a direction that was in agreement with the start-rotation principle or in defiance of the start-rotation principle. Their attention was drawn away from the start-rotation direction by instructions to evaluate whether the figure was drawn with a constant speed. When later asked to trace over figures themselves, beginning either at the top or the bottom of the shape, both children and adults had learned, implicitly, to defy the start-rotation principle, a finding that further strengthened the assertion that implicit learning is unaffected by age. These elegant studies support earlier claims that implicit learning is invariant with age (e.g., Meulemans et al., 1998), but no comparisons were made with practice sessions that used explicit knowledge of the direction of rotation. This was addressed in a later study in which children with Down Syndrome were engaged in similar drawing practice sessions (Vinter & Detable, 2008). Besides the implicit learning condition, an explicit learning condition was included in which participants were given instructions about the rules governing the start-rotation direction when drawing geometrical figures. In the implicit learning condition, children with Down Syndrome, who had mild to moderate intellectual disability, performed similarly to age-matched (mental age and chronological age) controls; however, in the explicit learning condition, they displayed inferior learning compared to the controls. This finding is one that implicates working memory in explicit learning, but suggests that working memory is less involved in implicit processes.

WHAT IS WORKING MEMORY?

Working memory is described as a highly flexible, short-term mental storage system that allows information to be held and manipulated during ongoing cognitive activities (Baddeley, 2003; Baddeley & Hitch, 1974). It is thought to operate with a *central executive system* that controls the flow of information and directs attention, supported by *secretarial systems* that hold verbal or visual information temporarily (the *phonological loop* and the *visuospatial sketchpad*, respectively), and an *episodic buffer*, which integrates visual and verbal information in a temporal order and coordinates it with long-term memory.

Studies that have investigated working memory in children have shown that the proposed roles of the phonological loop, the visuospatial sketchpad, and the central executive appear to generally hold true for children. Early studies (e.g., Nicolson, 1981) suggested that memory improves with age, but not as a consequence of changes in storage capacity. Instead, the improvement has been credited to an increase in processing efficiency. The phonological loop, which is used to hold or maintain information that can be represented phonologically, is thought to be active very early in childhood. Increases in memory span that accompany development are generally attributed to increased rates of subvocal rehearsal within the phonological loop (Hulme et al., 1984; Nicolson, 1981). Hulme et al. (1984) examined the serial recall ability of children aged 4, 7, and 10, and adults, on sequences of short words, such as *egg, pig,* and *bus,* or long words, such as *banana, kangaroo,* and *umbrella.* All age groups were better at recalling sequences of short words than long words (the word-length effect), suggesting that subvocal rehearsal was occurring in the phonological loop even in 4-year-olds (more short words can be maintained by subvocal rehearsal within the phonological loop than long words). Recall was better in older children, however, suggesting that rehearsal becomes more efficient with age. Hulme et al. (1984) also found that articulation rate—the number of words spoken per second—increased with age, potentially allowing more words to be rehearsed. Additionally, the word-length effect was evident for 10-year-olds but not 6-year-olds when items to be recalled were presented visually as pictures. That is, older children use the phonological loop to remember names of items presented verbally or visually, whereas younger children do not use the loop to remember the names of items that are presented visually. These developmental changes in the use of the phonological loop were confirmed by the work of Halliday, Hitch, Lennon, and Pettipher (1990), which showed that repetition of an irrelevant word designed to cause articulatory suppression (i.e., prevent subvocal rehearsal) suppressed the word length effect for pictures in 11-year-old children, but had no effect on 5-year-old children.

It appears, then, that young children use the visuospatial sketchpad to store recently presented visual information, but they do not encode the information verbally until they are older. Good evidence for this claim was presented by Hitch, Halliday, Schaafstal, and Schraagen (1988), who showed that 5-year-old children were poor at recalling lists of pictures that had similar visual features (which presumably are difficult to discriminate in the visuospatial sketchpad), but were unaffected by the length of the names of the pictures, whereas 11-year-old children, who presumably used the phonological loop for recalling the pictures, were unaffected by similar visual features but displayed the word-length effect.

Later studies provide evidence consistent with these findings. Alloway, Gathercole, and Pickering (2006), for example, used confirmatory factor analysis to confirm that the theoretical structure of working memory is applicable to children, and showed that younger children rely on visual codes initially, but tend to recode visual material using verbal labels as they get older.

Developmental aspects of working memory play an important role in learning. Gathercole (2004) claimed that "the ease of acquiring new knowledge and skills during childhood is directly constrained by the capacity to store and manage information in working memory" (p. 367). Impaired working memory can cause learning difficulties. Children with poor working memory capacity may have good social skills but display poor attention or even motivation and can lose the thread of complicated tasks that place heavy demands on working memory, especially if information pertinent to the task needs to be stored concurrently. They may also forget instructions easily or have difficulty following verbal instructions or rules, especially if they are overly long (see Garthercole & Alloway, 2006; Gathercole, Lamont, & Alloway, 2006).

FOLLOWING THE RULES!

Age-related variability of working memory capacity and verbal development in children is associated with the use of rules to initiate an action response. Luria (1959), for example, showed that even very young children (approximately 2 years of age) can understand verbal rules, but they may not be able to reflect upon the rules in order to execute appropriate actions. When instructed "if a red light appears, squeeze," the children were able to use the rule to initiate squeezing, but generally failed to inhibit squeezing if a light other than red appeared. It seems that young children persevere with a course of action that may not be appropriate because they lack the ability to consciously reflect on the rules (Zelazo, Reznick, & Pinon, 1995); in the same way, when they are younger (8-12 months) they may gaze at the place where they saw a toy hidden, yet reach to the previous place in which it was hidden (Piaget, 1937; 1954). Older children (over 3 years of age), however, are far better at following rules because they have acquired a higher level of *reflective* consciousness (Zelazo et al., 1995).

Executive functions govern processes associated with initiating appropriate actions on the basis of verbal rules or instructions (Miyake, Friedman, Emerson, Witzki, & Howerter, 2000), so poor or impaired working memory capacity is likely to impede rule use even by children who have developed reflective consciousness. This may occur as a consequence of forgetting the relevant rules or instructions, or because of capacity limitations associated with processing the rules or instructions alongside competing working memory demands. It is unlikely that this problem is restricted to children. For example, Green and Flowers (1991) asked older participants to track and catch a blip on a screen by controlling a joystick. When participants were explicitly instructed about probability rules that predicted the direction that the blip would take, they performed worse than when instructions were not provided. Green and Flowers attributed this to the cognitive demands associated with recalling and applying the probability rules.

Given the limitations associated with verbal development and rule use by children, skill acquisition approaches that avoid loading working memory are likely to have greater efficacy for motor performance.

THE ROLE OF WORKING MEMORY IN LEARNING

Hayes and Broadbent (1988; see also Berry & Broadbent, 1988) proposed that implicit learning is an unselective mode of learning in which information underlying all actions and outcomes is entered into a data bank of knowledge that informs performance in a cognitively unconscious manner. They proposed a contrasting form of explicit learning in which a performer selectively generates hypotheses about how to perform and uses outcomes to assess the veracity of the hypotheses, retaining verifiable hypotheses and disregarding refutable hypotheses. Hayes and Broadbent claimed that implicit modes of learning do not engage working memory but explicit modes do, and demonstrated that a concurrent cognitive task designed to encumber working memory (random letter generation; Baddeley, 1966) caused the decision response times of explicit learners to become slower when performing, whereas the decision response times of implicit learners became faster. Studies of sequence-learning (e.g., Cohen, Ivry, & Keele, 1990), conceptual priming (e.g., Mulligan, 1997), and word-stem completion (e.g., Wolters & Prinsen, 1997) support this position, showing that implicit processes make fewer demands on attention, and thus working memory, than explicit processes. Berry and Dienes (1993) therefore proposed that stable performance of a concurrent cognitive task can be considered a dissociating characteristic of implicit learning.

Studies have shown that the involvement of working memory in *motor* learning and performance is also dependent on the type of learning that takes place. Motor learners normally use trial-and-error to improve their performance (Ohlsson, 1996), deploying working memory to store and manipulate information that accrues when testing hypotheses about how to avoid errors. Hypothesis testing is predominant during, but not limited to, the early stages of skill acquisition, and initially much of the information that is accrued can be accessed consciously as explicit, declarative knowledge. With repetition, the knowledge gradually becomes less accessible to consciousness as movement procedures develop. These run automatically, outside working memory, unless interrupted by controlled processing (see Masters & Maxwell, 2008, for a review of the Theory of Reinvestment).

EVIDENCE FOR IMPLICIT MOTOR LEARNING FROM ADULT STUDIES

Pew (1974) showed that participants who physically tracked a blip that oscillated across a screen improved with practice, regardless of whether segments of the oscillating pattern were random or repeated. However, superior tracking performance was evident for segments that were continuously repeated. Participants inevitably claimed to be unaware of the repetition and were powerless to describe the shape of the oscillations within segments, suggesting that they had learned about them implicitly (see also Wulf & Schmidt, 1997, and later work by Chambaron, Ginhac, Ferrel-Chapus, & Perruchet, 2006).

Although the work of Pew (1974) provided insight into implicit learning associated with decision-making when moving, the work of Masters (1992) was the first to provide insight into implicit learning of the movement control processes. The initial implicit motor learning work by Masters (1992) utilized a concurrent cognitive task (random letter generation) to reduce working memory involvement in performance of the primary task (golf putting). Motor performance improved despite the additional processing demands created by the dual-task paradigm, showing that motor learning was possible without the use of working memory for trial-and-error processes (e.g., hypothesis testing). Not only did participants display limited exploitation of explicit knowledge during performance (and limited ability to report explicit knowledge about their movements), but performance appeared to be more resilient to state anxiety caused by performance evaluation. Advantageous outcomes of the dual-task implicit motor learning paradigm have been confirmed by subsequent studies (e.g., Hardy et al., 1996; Mullen, Hardy, & Oldham, 2007), but a consistent finding is that the paradigm results in a protracted pace of learning compared to discovery learning or explicit learning (see also Mac-

Mahon & Masters, 2002; Maxwell, Masters, & Eves, 2000). Consequently, alternative implicit motor learning paradigms have been designed to discourage working memory involvement during practice, without hampering the pace of learning.

ERRORLESS LEARNING

Errorless learning probably originated from work by Terrace (1963), who used a fading procedure to shape pecking behaviors by pigeons. A consequence of gradually shaping the natural pecking behavior of the pigeons was that they learned with few errors. Sidman and Stoddard (1967) deployed the same shaping principles to train children with intellectual disabilities to discriminate circles from ellipses. The children learned more effectively and with fewer errors than children in control conditions, who made substantially more errors. Subsequently, errorless learning has been utilized widely to help people who have memory impairments (e.g., amnesia) that lower their ability to correct or avoid making errors (e.g., Baddeley & Wilson, 1994; Clare et al., 2000; Squires, Hunkin, & Parkin, 1997). "Learn from your mistakes" is not an adage that necessarily holds true if a learner has poor memory for those mistakes!

Maxwell, Masters, Kerr, and Weedon (2001) proposed that constraining the environment to prevent errors during practice would limit the need for hypothesis testing about movement solutions, which would reduce the involvement of working memory in motor performance and invoke implicit motor learning. The errorless approach was initially applied to learning golf-putting tasks (Chauvel et al., 2012; Lam, Masters, & Maxwell, 2010; Lam, Maxwell, & Masters, 2010; Maxwell et al., 2001; Poolton, Masters, & Maxwell, 2005; Zhu, Poolton, Wilson, Maxwell, & Masters, 2011), but has been replicated in a number of other tasks, including rugby ball-passing (Masters, Poolton, & Maxwell, 2008; Poolton et al., 2007a), balancing (Orrell et al., 2006a, 2006b), netball-shooting (Rendell, Farrow, Masters, & Plummer, 2011), and surgery simulations (Masters, Lo, Maxwell, & Patil, 2008). The studies have consistently shown that constraining the learning environment so that errors are reduced, particularly in the early stages of learning, results in better performance in retention tests, and as Reber's (1992) evolutionary argument suggests, performance of these implicitly learned skills has been demonstrated to remain stable in the face of physiological fatigue, performance pressure, or multitasking demands (see Masters & Poolton, 2012, for a recent review).

THE REDUCED FEEDBACK PARADIGM

Learners utilize all forms of feedback (visual, auditory, proprioceptive, tactile) to improve movement performance, with the visual sense superseding the rest (Kelso, 1982). Masters (2000), and subsequently Maxwell, Masters, and Eves (2003), therefore suggested that implicit motor learning may be facilitated by prohibiting novice performers from evaluating their performance efficacy with visual feedback. Masters (2000) and Maxwell and colleagues (2003) argued that preventing access to salient visual feedback about movement outcomes would make hypothesis testing unfeasible and reduce the need for involvement of working memory in performance. Consequently, minimal verbal knowledge about the task would accrue.

Experiments designed to test these assertions (see Maxwell et al., 2003) revealed that working memory was not completely bypassed by preventing access to visual feedback; in the absence of visual feedback, information from the other senses became more salient (e.g., proprioceptive, tactile), and performers merely switched to testing hypotheses based upon this other feedback. Followup experiments showed that besides prohibiting access to visual feedback, a visual search task unrelated to motor performance was necessary to preclude hypothesis testing, and thus bypass working memory involvement. The visual search task presumably deployed working memory in a manner that corresponded with hypothesis testing about movement outcomes.

Generally, it is argued that learning emerges from consciously directing attention to relevant stimuli (Cohen et al., 1990; Nissen & Bullemer, 1987), but learning is also possible when attention does not consciously orient towards relevant stimuli (Cock, Berry, & Buchner, 2002; Deroost, Zeischka, & Soetens, 2008) or when attention simply does not register salient information consciously (Masters, Maxwell, & Eves, 2009). Masters et al. (2009) presented visual outcome feedback to participants at a marginally perceptible threshold of awareness at which they professed to have no conscious awareness of the feedback. Putting performance became more accurate, but participants displayed little or no exploitation of explicit knowledge about the putting task when performing. Masters et al. (2009) concluded that when outcome feedback is presented below a person's conscious threshold of awareness, learning is probable but hypothesis testing improbable. Consequently, working memory involvement in performance is limited, and implicit motor learning emerges.

ANALOGY LEARNING

Studies in implicit motor learning have also applied the analogy-learning paradigm. Analogies allow a learner to utilize a familiar representation of a concept in one domain in order to understand a concept in another domain (Gentner, 1988). Liao and Masters (2001) applied an analogy based on Pythagoras' theorem to train novice table tennis players to hit a topspin forehand shot. Learners were instructed to swing their table tennis paddle up the hypotenuse of an imaginary triangle each time they hit a forehand. Evidence from this study indicated that analogy learners not only improved equally to explicit learners, but also displayed performance characteristics of implicit motor learning. That is, performance remained stable under concurrent cognitive demands, performance pressure, and even a thought suppression condition designed to deflect attention unintentionally towards exploitation of explicit knowledge about the task. More stable performance by analogy learners compared to explicit learners was also shown when they were required to hit balls to targets that could only be selected correctly by using a complex algorithm based on the color of the approaching ball (Masters, Poolton, Maxwell, & Raab, 2008; Poolton, Masters, & Maxwell, 2006).

Other examples of analogies that have been utilized successfully for implicit motor learning include "shoot as if you are trying to put cookies into a cookie jar on a high shelf" for basketball (Lam et al., 2009a, 2009b) or "move the bat as if it is traveling up the side of a mountain" for Chinese table tennis players hitting topspin (Koedijker et al., 2011; Poolton, Masters, & Maxwell, 2007b). With clinical contexts in mind, other successful analogies have included "stand like a soldier on guard" for balance training in rehabilitation (Orrell et al., 2006a) or "speak like a flat calm sea" for modulating intonation during speech production (Tse, Masters, Whitehill, & Ma, 2012).

IMPLICIT MOTOR LEARNING BY CHILDREN

The variable and evolving nature of information-processing abilities during development limits generalization of the rich adult implicit motor learning literature to children. Nevertheless, it seems clear that an implicit approach to motor learning may be expedient, given the immature cognitive resources available to developing children.

For example, although to our knowledge no studies have used analogies to bring about implicit motor learning in children, much research has attested to the importance of analogy-making by children as a cognitive mechanism for understanding the world around them (e.g., Hofstadter, 2001; French, 2007). Donnelly and McDaniel (1993; see also McDaniel & Donnelly, 1996) taught children the astronomic concept of a collapsing star, which spins faster as its size reduces. When the concept was presented to some children as an analogy of an ice skater spinning faster and faster as her hands are raised to clasp above her head, these children were far better than explicitly instructed children at inferring what would happen "if a star expanded instead of collapsing." A skater spins more slowly when her hands are outstretched, so the speed of an expanding star must decrease. In these circumstances, children display very little explicit knowledge of the rules that underlie their decisions, yet they show clear understanding of the concept presented to them, which is reminiscent of implicit learning (e.g., Hayes & Broadbent, 1988). Given the weight of evidence that analogy learning evokes advantageous characteristics of implicit *motor* learning, it is to be hoped that analogy learning generalizes to children.

One implicit motor-learning paradigm that can be claimed to demonstrate evidence of generalization to children is errorless learning (e.g., Maxwell et al., 2001). Not only does errorless learning suppress hypothesis testing, which potentially reduces the demands on immature working memory abilities of children, but it may well have a significant influence on psychological attributes that shape the motor development of children.

ERRORLESS LEARNING AND PERCEIVED COMPETENCE

Social-cognitive theories of motivation, such as achievement goal theory (e.g., Dweck & Leggett, 1988), propose that children's experiences influence their interest in and their persistence at an activity. Positive outcomes related to concerns about gaining mastery (i.e., task or learning goals) or about personal ability relative to others (i.e., performance or ability goals) play a significant role in a child's sense of perceived competence and increase intrinsic motivation to engage in the activity (Deci & Ryan, 1985; Ulrich, 1987; White, 1959).

Consequently, the importance of early experiences of success during motor learning cannot be underestimated for children. By constraining the environment to prevent errors, errorless learning achieves such an outcome, potentially encouraging not only a sense of mastery (by promoting near-perfect performance), but also reducing concerns about performance standards relative to other children (by default, errorless learning results in performance that is of a very high caliber).

Capio et al. (2011) used the errorless paradigm to teach children an object-control skill in a primary school. As a field-based study of implicit motor learning, the work addressed concerns related to both the feasibility and the application of laboratory-tested motor learning techniques in the real world (see also Renshaw, Chow, Davids, & Hammond, 2010). Two-hundred and sixteen children aged between 8 and 12 practiced a fundamental movement skill, overhand throwing, in either an error-reduced or error-strewn environment during their physical education (PE) lessons. Children completed 120 throws from 5 meters to a target on a wall, during three PE lessons. Children in the error-reduced condition (a large 2.4m^2 target that gradually reduced in size to 0.45m^2) made fewer practice errors and demonstrated superior movement patterns (Test of Gross Motor Development-2, Ulrich, 2000) and throwing accuracy (absolute error) relative to children who practiced in an error-strewn environment (a small 0.45m^2 target that gradually increased in size to 2.4m^2). Consistent with adult implicit motor learning studies (e.g., Chauvel et al., 2012; Masters et al., 2008; Maxwell et al., 2001), throwing performance of the children in the error-reduced condition was not disrupted by a concurrent cognitive task (counting backwards in two's), suggesting that they learned to throw with little need for working memory involvement. Throwing performance in the error-strewn condition was disrupted by the counting task, suggesting that the demands on their processing resources were higher. Low-ability children benefited in particular from error-reduced learning, and Capio et al. (2011) speculated that making relatively few errors during practice may be particularly beneficial for children with developmental conditions.

Motor delay is found in a wide variety of pediatric conditions, including developmental coordination disorder (Fox & Lent, 1996), cerebral palsy (Rosenbaum et al., 2007), Down Syndrome (Spanò et al., 1999), and intellectual disability (Schalock et al., 2010). The biological causes of such syndromes are distinct from each other, so the root causes of motor delay may vary, but for conditions that involve impaired cognitive processing abilities, approaches that avoid loading working memory are logical motor-learning options.

Capio, Poolton, Sit, Eguia, and Masters (2012) thus replicated the field-based study by Capio et al. (2011), but in children with intellectual disability. Movement skills of children with intellectual disability tend to be less proficient than in children without such impairments. Capio et al. (2012) found that children with intellectual disability who practiced overhand throwing in an error-reduced learning environment during adapted PE lessons displayed greater improvements in their movement patterns and their throwing accuracy than children with intellectual disability who practiced in an error-strewn environment. Despite displaying characteristic cognitive impairments, the children who experienced fewer practice errors were capable of sustained throwing performance when performing a concurrent cognitive task (singing a familiar nursery rhyme). Capio et al. (2012) also observed overhand throwing activity during free play periods before and after learning. Children in the error-reduced condition engaged in more overhand throwing activity after learning than children in the error-strewn condition. Although perceived competence was not assessed, this finding converges with theories that associate successful experiences with motivation to persist at an activity.

SUMMARY AND DISCUSSION

In summary, the developmental literature indicates that age-related differences are much in evidence for explicit, verbal aspects of learning and performance, but children generally perform as well as adults on implicit, nonverbal aspects of learning and performance. Across the age spectrum, from young infants to older adults, there is an invariant ability to learn and use implicit knowledge, and this knowledge is less susceptible to brain impairments such as amnesia or to psychological pressure or possibly even physical fatigue. Fewer attention resources are needed by implicit learning because it occurs independently of conscious awareness, and the knowledge is durable, too, lasting longer than explicit knowledge. Ask an adult to use a swing in the park 40 years after childhood and she will know immediately how to swing to and fro without a push! Ask the adult to recall Mom's 40-year-old *explicit* instructions for when to be home from the park, and likely the time will be forgotten. It also appears not to matter how high or low children score on intelligence tests—they learn implicitly just the same.

It is probably fair to recommend that when designing motor learning for younger children, primary modes of instruction should be visual rather than verbal, given that children seem to rely more on visuospatial aspects of working memory and that verbal phonological aspects only become more efficient as language develops. Developing executive functions contribute to age-related increases in the complexity of rules and instructions that children can formulate and follow (Zelazo, Muller, Frye, & Marcovitch, 2003), so learning strategies that avoid instructions and reduce cognitive processing requirements should be used to avoid taxing the limited capacity of the immature working memory system of the child. An implicit motor-learning framework appears well suited to these recommendations, but beyond the errorless-learning approach used by Capio et al. (2011; 2012), no studies of which we are aware have applied an implicit motor-learning framework to children learning functionally nontrivial motor skills.

Further work is thus needed to determine which implicit motor-learning techniques are best suited to children, both practically and theoretically. Studies of analogy learning in the implicit motor-learning literature suggest that adults are guided quickly towards a general motor solution, and that analogy learning results in motor performance that places few demands on attention. This may indicate that working memory involvement in performance is bypassed by analogy learning, but it is also possible that the analogy leans towards children's strengths by calling upon visuospatial functions of working memory (i.e., the visuospatial sketchpad) rather than verbal functions (i.e., the phonological loop). Analogy learning may, therefore, have strong potential for implicit motor learning by children, but there are complications. The ability to map relations among tasks, objects, and situations develops slowly in children and is dependent on familiarity with the relevant domains (Gentner, 1988). Additionally, Richland, Morrison, and Holyoak (2006) argued that analogy learning places an additional load on working memory by requiring a child to retrieve from memory, and then hold and manipulate, information about a concept from a secondary domain, while simultaneously processing information about the task in a primary domain.

The framework for implicit motor learning by children that we have tried to set out here is, by default, laid upon cognitive groundwork, but it nevertheless should take into account a constraints-based approach to how movement control and coordination comes about (Davids, 2010). Based upon a variety of interlinked theories (e.g., Gibson, 1979; Newell, 1986; Thelen & Smith, 1994), a constraints-based approach suggests that motor learning is a corollary of adaptations to interacting constraints that are imposed upon the motor system during the search for solutions to movement problems. The constraints are unique and can be cognitive or environmental, or perceptual or intellectual, and can even take the form of movement disorders or difficulties. Chow et al. (2007) argued that pedagogical approaches to motor learning by children should take into consideration the dynamic interaction of constraints and should identify the key constraints in order to manipulate their exploration by the child, thus facilitating the emergence of functional movement patterns.

The environment is a constraint that plays a crucial role in development (Barker, 1968; Gibson, 1979) and constantly interacts physically and perceptually with the human movement system (Davids, Araujo, Shuttleworth, & Button, 2003). Consequently, implicit motor-learning techniques that subtly influence interactions between the movement system and the environment (e.g., errorless learning) may have particular efficacy for children. So too may techniques that alter constraints in the environment cause movement adaptations without conscious awareness or involvement (Masters et al., 2009). It seems appropriate in a chapter about children to illustrate this point with an example from a story for children: The Twits (Dahl, 1980). As payback for putting worms in his spaghetti, Mr. Twit glues a sliver of wood to the bottom of Mrs. Twit's walking stick each night when she is asleep. The stick gradually becomes longer and longer and Mrs. Twit adapts to it without noticing. Eventually, Mrs. Twit realizes that something has changed. She concludes that she has the "dreaded shrinks" and feels "so trembly that she has to sit down" (p. 22). Future studies are needed to establish whether presenting information to children at a threshold of which they are only marginally conscious results in effective performance without awareness of the motor adaptations that bring about the movement solutions.

Other modes of learning warrant investigation with respect to whether they fit within an implicit motor learning framework for children. For example, observational learning or modeling (e.g., Bandura, 1962) proposes that observation elicits experiences that become integrated and structured into perceptual responses. In the course of observation, learners are thought to acquire verbal labels for the modeled behaviors. For example, Bandura, Grusec, and Menlove (1966) found that children who verbalized the actions of an observed model were better at imitating the modeled behavior than children who performed an unrelated concurrent verbal task while observing. Such evidence suggests that explicit motor learning by children may be a product of observational experiences, but Masters et al. (2008) presented evidence that adults learned a surgical suture and knot-tie procedure implicitly by observation (i.e., they showed no disruption of surgical performance when required to multitask), so it is unclear what influence observation has on implicit and explicit processes of motor learning by children.

Developmental aspects of nontrivial skill acquisition by children have previously not been considered within an implicit motor-learning framework, as is clear from the limited number of studies of implicit motor learning in children. Many imponderables exist. How well do children retain information related to outcome feedback? What is the maximum complexity of rules or instructions that children can follow to solve a movement problem? What is the consequence of conflict between instructions from a coach at practice and Dad over dinner? Does visuospatial information trump verbal information every time? Just how many words is a picture really worth? Do children formulate and test hypotheses in the same way that adults do? Is implicit learning really a constant in motor development? These questions about implicit motor learning by children, and many more, will require considerable hypothesis testing of our own!

REFERENCES

Alloway, T. P., Gathercole, S. E., & Pickering, S. J. (2006). Verbal and visuospatial short-term and working memory in children: Are they separable? *Child Development, 77*(6), 1698–1716.

Baddeley, A. D. (1966). The capacity for generating information by randomization. *Quarterly Journal of Experimental Psychology, 18*(2), 119–129.

Baddeley, A. D. (2003). Working memory: Looking back and looking forward. *Nature Reviews Neuroscience, 4,* 829–839.

Baddeley, A. D., & Hitch, G. (1974). Working memory. In G.A. Bower (Ed.), *Recent advances in learning and motivation* (Vol. 8). New York, NY: Academic Press.

Baddeley, A. D., & Wilson, B. A. (1994). When implicit learning fails: Amnesia and the problem of error elimination. *Neuropsychologia, 32*(1), 53–68.

Bandura, A. (1962). *Social learning through imitation.* Lincoln, NE: University of Nebraska Press.

Bandura, A., Grusec, J. E., & Menlove, F. L. (1966). Observational learning as a function of symbolization and incentive set. *Child Development, 37*(3), 499–506.

Barker, R. G. (1968). *Ecological psychology: Concepts and methods for studying the environment of human behavior.* Stanford, CA: Stanford University Press.

Berry, D. C., & Broadbent, D. E. (1988). Interactive tasks and the implicit explicit distinction. *British Journal of Psychology, 79*(2), 251–272.

Berry, D. C., & Dienes, Z. (1993). *Implicit learning: Theoretical and empirical issues.* Hove, UK: Erlbaum.

Capio, C. M., Poolton, J. M., Sit, C. H. P., Eguia, K. F., & Masters, R. S. W. (2012). Reduction of errors during practice facilitates fundamental movement skill learning in children with intellectual disabilities. *Journal of Intellectual Disability Research,* doi: 10.111/j.1365-2788.2012.01535.x

Capio, C. M., Poolton, J. M., Sit, C. H. P., Holmstrom, M., & Masters, R. S. W. (2011). Reducing errors benefits the field-based learning of a fundamental movement skill in children. *Scandinavian Journal of Medicine and Science in Sports.* doi: 10.1111/j.1600-0838.2011.01368.x

Chambaron, S., Ginhac, D., Ferrel-Chapus, C., & Perruchet, P. (2006). Implicit learning of a repeated segment in continuous tracking: A reappraisal. *Quarterly Journal of Experimental Psychology, 59*(5), 845–854.

Chandler, S. (1993). Are rules and modules really necessary for explaining language? *Journal of Psycholinguistic Research, 22*(6), 593–606.

Chauvel, G., Maquestiaux, F., Hartley, A., Joubert, S., Diderjean, A., & Masters, R. S. W. (2012). Age effects shrink when motor learning is predominantly supported by nondeclarative, automatic memory processes: Evidence from golf putting. *Quarterly Journal of Experimental Psychology, 65*(1), 25–38.

Chow, J. Y., Davids, K., Button, C., Shuttleworth, R., Renshaw, I., & Araujo, D. (2007). The role of nonlinear pedagogy in physical education. *Review of Educational Research, 77*(3), 251–278.

Clare, L., Wilson, B. A., Carter, G., Breen, K., Gosses, A., & Hodges, J. R. (2000). Intervening with everyday memory problems in dementia of Alzheimer type: An errorless learning condition approach. *Journal of Clinical and Experimental Neuropsychology, 22*(1), 132–146.

Cock, J. J., Berry, D. C., & Buchner, A. (2002). Negative priming and sequence learning. *European Journal of Cognitive Psychology, 14*(1), 27–48.

Cohen, A., Ivry, R., & Keele, S. W. (1990). Attention and structure in sequence learning. *Journal of Experimental Psychology: Learning, Memory, and Cognition, 16*(1), 17–30.

Dahl, R. (1980). *The Twits.* London, UK: Jonathan Cape.

Davids, K., Araujo, D., Shuttleworth, R., & Button, C. (2003). Acquiring skill in sport: A constraints-led perspective. *International Journal of Computer Sciences in Sport, 2*(2), 31–39.

Deci, E. L., & Ryan, R. M. (1985). *Intrinsic motivation and self-determination in human behavior.* New York, NY: Plenum.

Deroost, N., Zeischka, P., & Soetens, E. (2008). Negative priming in the SRT task: Learning of irrelevant sequences is enhanced by concurrent learning of relevant sequences. *European Journal of Cognitive Psychology, 20*(1), 47–68.

Didier, J-P., & Bigand, E. (2010). *Rethinking physical and rehabilitation medicine: New techniques induce new learning strategies.* Paris, France: Springer.

Donnelly, C. M., & McDaniel, M. A. (1993). Use of analogies in learning scientific concepts. *Journal of Experimental Psychology: Learning, Memory, and Cognition, 19*(4), 975–987.

Dweck, C. S., & Leggett, E. L. (1988). A social-cognitive approach to motivation and personality. *Psychological Review, 95*(2), 256–273.

Ferguson, A. N., & Bowey, J. A. (2005). Global processing speed as a mediator of developmental changes in children's auditory memory span. *Journal of Experimental Child Psychology, 91*(3), 89–112.

Fitts, P., & Posner, M. (1976). *Human performance.* Belmont, CA: Brooks/Cole.

Flavell, J. H., Green, F. L., & Flavell, E. R. (2000). Development of children's awareness of their own thoughts. *Journal of Cognitive Development, 1,* 97–112.

Fox, A. M., & Lent, B. (1996). Clumsy children. Primer on developmental coordination disorder. *Canadian Family Physician, 42,* 1965–1971.

French, R. M. (2007). The dynamics of the computational modeling of analogy-making. In P. Fishwick (Ed.), *The CRC handbook of dynamic systems modeling.* Boca Raton, FL: CRC Press LLC.

Frensch, P. A. (1998). One concept, multiple meanings: On how to define the concept of implicit learning. In M. A. Stadler & P. A. Frensch (Eds.), *Handbook of implicit learning* (pp. 47–104). Thousand Oaks, CA: Sage.

Gathercole, S. E. (2004). Working memory and learning during the school years. *Proceedings of the British Academy, 125,* 365–380.

Gathercole, S. E., & Alloway, T. P. (2006). Practitioner review: Short-term and working memory impairments in neurodevelopmental disorders: Diagnosis and remedial support. *Journal of Child Psychology and Psychiatry, 47*(1), 4–15.

Gathercole, S. E., Lamont, E., & Alloway, T. P. (2006). Working memory in the classroom. In S. J. Pickering (Ed.), *Working memory and education* (pp. 219-240). London, UK: Elsevier.

Gebauer, G. F., & Mackintosh, N. J. (2007). Psychometric intelligence dissociates implicit and explicit learning. *Journal of Experimental Psychology: Learning, Memory, and Cognition, 33*(1), 34–54.

Gentner, D. (1988). Metaphor as structure mapping: The relational shift. *Child Development, 59,* 47–59.

Gesell, A. (1954). The ontogenesis of infant behaviour. In C. Carmichael (Ed.), *Manual of child psychology* (2nd ed.) (pp. 335-373). New York, NY: Wiley.

Gibson, J. J. (1979). *The ecological approach to visual perception.* Boston, MA: Houghton Mifflin.

Gomez, R. L., & Gerkin, L. A. (1999). Artificial grammar learning by 1-year-olds leads to specific and abstract knowledge. *Cognition, 70,* 109–135.

Green, T. D., & Flowers, J. H. (1991). Implicit versus explicit learning processes in a probabilistic, continuous fine-motor catching task. *Journal of Motor Behavior, 23*(4), 293–300.

Greenbaum, J. L., & Graf, P. (1989). Preschool period development of implicit and explicit remembering. *Bulletin of the Psychonomic Society, 27*(5), 417–420.

Halliday, M. S., Hitch, G. J., Lennon, B., & Pettipher, C. (1990). Verbal short-term memory in children: The role of the articulatory loop. *European Journal of Cognitive Psychology, 2*(1), 23–38.

Hardy, L., Mullen, R., & Jones, G. (1996). Knowledge and conscious control of motor actions under stress. *British Journal of Psychology, 87,* 621–636.

Hayes, B. K., & Hennessy, R. (1996). The nature and development of nonverbal implicit memory. *Journal of Experimental Child Psychology, 63*(1), 22–43.

Hayes, N. A., & Broadbent, D. E. (1988). Two modes of learning for interactive tasks. *Cognition, 28*(3), 249–276.

Hitch, G. J., Halliday, M. S., Schaafstal, A. M., & Schraagen, J. M. C. (1988). Visual working memory in young children. *Memory & Cognition, 16*(2), 120–132.

Hofstadter, D. R. (2001). Analogy as the core of cognition. In D. Gentner, K. J. Holyoak, & B. N. Kokinov (Eds.), *The analogical mind: Perspectives from cognitive science* (pp. 499–538). Cambridge, MA: The MIT Press/Bradford Books,

Hulme, C., Thompson, N., Muir, C., & Lawrence, A. (1984). Speech rate and the development of spoken words: The role of rehearsal and item identification processes. *Journal of Experimental Child Psychology, 38,* 241–253.

Karmiloff-Smith, A. (1992) *Beyond modularity: A developmental perspective on cognitive science.* Cambridge, MA: MIT Press.

Kelso, J. A. S. (1982). Concepts and issues in human motor behavior: Coming to grips with the jargon. In J. A. S. Kelso (Ed.), *Human motor behavior: An introduction* (pp. 21–58). Hillsdale, NJ: Earlbaum Associates.

Koedijker, J. M., Poolton, J. M., Maxwell, J. P., Oudejans, R. R. D., Beek, P. J., Masters, R. S. W. (2011). Attention and time constraints in perceptual-motor performance: Instruction, analogy and skill level. *Consciousness and Cognition, 20*(2), 245–256

Krist, H., Fieberg, E. L., & Wilkening, F. (1993). Intuitive physics in action and judgment: The development of knowledge about projectile motion. *Journal of Experimental Psychology-Learning Memory and Cognition, 19*(4), 952–966.

Lam, W. K., Masters, R. S. W., & Maxwell, J. P. (2010). Cognitive demands of error processing associated with preparation and execution of complex movement. *Consciousness and Cognition, 19,* 1058–1061.

Lam, W. K., Maxwell, J. P., & Masters, R. S. W. (2009a). Analogy versus explicit learning of a modified basketball shooting task: Performance and kinematic outcomes. *Journal of Sports Sciences, 27*(2), 179–191.

Lam, W. K., Maxwell, J. P., & Masters, R. S. W. (2009b). Analogy learning and the performance of motor skills under pressure. *Journal of Sport and Exercise Psychology, 31*(3), 337–357.

Lam, W. K., Maxwell, J. P., & Masters, R. S. W. (2010). Probing the allocation of attention in implicit [motor] learning. *Journal of Sport Sciences, 28*(14), 1543–1554.

Liao, C-M., & Masters, R. S. W. (2001). Analogy learning: A means to implicit motor learning. *Journal of Sports Sciences, 19,* 307–319.

Luria, A. R. (1959). Experimental-analysis of the development of voluntary action in children. *Acta Psychologica, 15,* 460–461.

MacMahon, K. M. A., & Masters, R. S. W. (2002). The effects of a secondary task on implicit motor skill performance. *International Journal of Sport Psychology, 33*(3), 307–324.

Masters, R. S. W. (1992). Knowledge, knerves and know-how: The role of explicit versus implicit knowledge in the breakdown of a complex motor skill under pressure. *British Journal of Psychology, 83*(3), 343–358.

Masters, R. S. W. (2000). Theoretical aspects of implicit learning in sport. *International Journal of Sport Psychology, 31,* 530–541.

Masters, R. S. W., & Maxwell, J. (2008). The theory of reinvestment. *International Review of Sport and Exercise Psychology, 1*(2), 160–183.

Masters, R. S. W., & Poolton, J. (2012). Advances in implicit motor learning. In A. M. Williams & N. J. Hodges (Eds.), *Skill acquisition in sport: Research, theory and practice* (2nd ed.). London, UK: Routledge.

Masters, R. S. W., MacMahon. K. M. A., & Pall, H. S. (2004). Implicit motor learning in Parkinson's disease. *Rehabilitation Psychology, 49*(1), 79–82.

Masters, R. S. W., Maxwell, J. P., & Eves, F. F. (2009). Marginally perceptible outcome feedback, motor learning and implicit processes. *Consciousness and Cognition, 18*(3), 639–645.

Masters, R. S. W., Poolton, J. M., & Maxwell, J. P. (2008). Stable implicit motor processes despite aerobic locomotor fatigue. *Consciousness and Cognition, 17*(1), 335–338.

Masters, R. S. W., Lo, C. Y., Maxwell, J. P., & Patil, N. G. (2008). Implicit motor learning in surgery: Implications for multi-tasking. *Surgery, 143*(1), 140–145.

Masters, R. S. W., Poolton, J. M., Maxwell, J. P., & Raab, M. (2008). Implicit motor learning and complex decision making in time constrained environments. *Journal of Motor Behavior, 40*(1), 71–79.

Maxwell, J. P., Masters, R. S. W., & Eves, F. F. (2000). From novice to no know-how: A longitudinal study of implicit motor learning. *Journal of Sports Sciences, 18*(2), 111–120.

Maxwell, J. P., Masters, R. S. W., & Eves, F. F. (2003). The role of working memory in motor learning and performance. *Consciousness and Cognition, 12*(3), 376–402.

Maxwell, J. P., Masters, R. S. W., Kerr, E., & Weedon, E. (2001). The implicit benefit of learning without errors. *Quarterly Journal of Experimental Psychology Section a—Human Experimental Psychology, 54A*(4), 1049–1068.

Maybery, M., Taylor, M., & O'Brien-Malone, A. (1995). Implicit learning: Sensitive to age but not IQ. *Australian Journal of Psychology, 47*(1), 8–17.

McDaniel, M. A., & Donnelly, C. M. (1996). Learning with analogy and elaborative interrogation. *Journal of Educational Psychology, 88*(3), 508–519.

Meulemans, T., van der Linden, M., & Perruchet, P. (1998). Implicit sequence learning in children. *Journal of Experimental Child Psychology, 69,* 199–221.

Miyake, A., Friedman, N. P., Emerson, M. J., Witzki, A. H., & Howerter, A. (2000). The unity and diversity of executive functions and their contributions to complex "frontal lobe" tasks: A latent variable analysis. *Cognitive Psychology, 41,* 49–100.

Mullen, R., Hardy, L., & Oldham, A. (2007). Implicit and explicit control of motor actions: Revisiting some early evidence. *The British Journal of Psychology, 98*(1), 141–156.

Mulligan, N. W. (1997). Attention and implicit memory tests: The effects of varying attentional load on conceptual priming. *Memory & Cognition, 25*(1), 11–17.

Nemeth, D., Janacsek, K., Balogh, V., Londe, Z., Mingesz, R., Fazekas, M., Jambori, S., Danyi, I., & Vetro, A. (2010). Learning in autism: Implicitly superb. *PLoS One, 5*(7). doi:10.1371/journal.pone.0011731

Newell, K. M. (1986). Constraints on the development of coordination. In M. Wade & H. T. A. Whiting (Eds.), *Motor development in children: Aspects of coordination and control* (pp. 341–360). Amsterdam, Netherlands: Martinus Hijhoff.

Nicolson, R. I. (1981). The relationship between memory span and processing speed. In M. Friedman, J. P. Das, & N. O'Connor (Eds.), *Intelligence and learning* (pp. 179–184). New York, NY: Plenum.

Nissen, M. J., & Bullemer, P. (1987). Attentional requirements of learning: Evidence from performance measures. *Cognitive Psychology, 19*(1), 1–32.

Ohlsson, S. (1996). Learning from performance errors. *Psychological Review, 103*(2), 241–262.

Orrell, A. J., Eves, F. F., & Masters, R. S. W. (2006a). Implicit motor learning of a balancing task. *Gait & Posture, 23*(1), 9–16.

Orrell, A. J., Eves, F. F., & Masters, R. S. W. (2006b). Motor learning of a dynamic balancing task after stroke: Implicit implications for stroke rehabilitation. *Physical Therapy, 86*(3), 369–380.

Pacton, S., Perruchet, P., Fayol, M., & Cleeremans, A. (2001). Implicit learning out of the lab: The case of orthographic regularities. *Journal of Experimental Psychology: General, 130*(3), 401–426.

Pew, R. W. (1974). Human perceptuo-motor performance. In B. H. Kantowitz (Ed.), *Human information processing: Tutorials in performance and vognition.* New York, NY: Erlbaum.

Piaget, J. (1937/1954). *The construction of reality in the child.* New York, NY: Basic Books.

Poolton, J. M., Masters, R. S. W., & Maxwell, J. P. (2005). The relationship between initial errorless learning conditions and subsequent performance. *Human Movement Science, 24*(3), 362–378.

Poolton, J. M., Masters, R. S. W., & Maxwell, J. (2006). The influence of analogy learning on decision-making in table tennis: Evidence from behavioural data. *Psychology of Sport & Exercise, 7*(6), 677–688.

Poolton, J. M., Masters, R. S. W., & Maxwell, J. P. (2007a). Passing thoughts on the evolutionary stability of implicit motor behaviour: Performance retention under physiological fatigue. *Consciousness and Cognition, 16*(2), 456–468.

Poolton, J. M., Masters, R. S. W., & Maxwell, J. P. (2007b). Development of a culturally appropriate analogy for implicit motor learning in a Chinese population. *The Sport Psychologist, 21*(4), 375–382.

Reber, A. S. (1967). Implicit learning of artificial grammars. *Journal of Verbal Learning and Verbal Behavior, 6*(6), 855–863.

Reber, A. S. (1992). The cognitive unconscious: An evolutionary perspective. *Consciousness and Cognition, 1*(2), 93–133.

Reber, A. S. (1993). *Implicit learning and tacit knowledge: An essay on the cognitive unconsciousness.* New York, NY: Oxford University Press.

Reber, A. S., Walkenfeld, F. F., & Hernstadt, R. (1991). Implicit and explicit learning: Individual differences and IQ. *Journal of Experimental Psychology: Learning, Memory and Cognition, 17*(5), 888–896.

Rendell, M., Farrow, D., Masters, R. S. W., & Plummer, N. (2011). Implicit practice for technique adaptation in expert performers. *International Journal of Sports Science and Coaching, 6*(4), 553–566.

Renshaw, I., Chow, J. Y., Davids, K., & Hammond, J. (2010). A constraints-led perspective to understanding skill acquisition and game play: A basis for integration of motor learning theory and physical education praxis? *Physical Education & Sport Pedagogy, 15*(2), 117–137.

Richland, L. E., Morrison, R. G., & Holyoak, K. J. (2006). Children's development of analogical reasoning: Insights from scene analogy problems. *Journal of Experimental Child Psychology, 94*, 249–273.

Rosenbaum, P., Paneth, N., Leviton, A., Goldstein, M., Bax, M., Damiano, D., Dan, B., & Jacobsson, B. (2007). A report: The definition and classification of cerebral palsy April 2006. *Developmental Medicine and Child Neurology Supplement, 109*, 8–14.

Saffran, J. R., Aslin, R. N., & Newport, E. L. (1996). Statistical learning by 8-month-old infants. *Science, 274*, 1926–1928.

Schalock, R. L., Borthwick-Duffy, S. A., Bradley, V. J., Buntinx, W. H. E., Coulter, D. L., Craig, E. M., et al. (2010). *Intellectual disability: Definition, classification, and systems of supports* (11th ed.). Washington, DC: American Association of Intellectual and Developmental Disabilities.

Sidman, M., & Stoddard, L. T. (1967). The effectiveness of fading in programming a simultaneous form discrimination for retarded children. *Journal of the Experimental Analysis of Behavior, 10*(1), 3–15.

Spanò, M., Mercuri, E., Randò, T., Pantò, T., Gagliano, A., Henderson, S., & Guzzetta, F. (1999). Motor and perceptual-motor competence in children with Down syndrome: Variation in performance with age. *European Journal of Paediatric Neurology, 3*(1), 7–13.

Squires, E. J., Hunkin, N. M., & Parkin, A. J. (1997). Errorless learning of novel associations in amnesia. *Neuropsychologia, 35*(8), 1103–1111.

Sun, R., Merrill, E., & Peterson, T. (2001). From implicit skills to explicit knowledge: A bottom-up model of skill learning. *Cognitive Science, 25*(2), 203–244.

Terrace, H. S. (1963). Discrimination learning with and without "errors." *Journal of Experimental Analysis of Behavior, 6*(1), 1–27.

Thelen, E., & Smith, L. B. (1994). *A dynamic systems approach to the development of cognition and action.* Boston, MA: MIT Press.

Tse, A. C. Y., Masters, R. S. W., Whitehill, T., Ma, E. P. M. (2012). The use of analogy in speech motor learning. *International Journal of Speech-Language Pathology, 14*, 84–90.

Ulrich, B. D. (1987). Perceptions of physical competence, motor competence, and participation in organized sport: Their interrelationships in young children. *Research Quarterly for Exercise and Sport, 58*(1), 57–67.

Ulrich, D. (2000). *Test of gross motor development* (2nd ed.). Texas: Pro-Ed.

van der Kamp, J., Oudejans, R., & Savelsbergh, G. (2003). The development and learning of the visual control of movement: An ecological perspective. *Infant Behavior & Development, 26*, 495–515.

van Sommers, P. (1984). *Drawing and cognition: Descriptive and experimental studies of graphic production processes.* Cambridge, UK: Cambridge University Press.

Vinter, A., & Detable, C. (2008). Implicit and explicit motor learning in children with and without Down's syndrome. *British Journal of Developmental Psychology, 26*(4), 507–523.

Vinter, A., Pacton, S., Witt, A., & Perruchet, P. (2010). Implicit learning, development and education. In J-P. Didier, & E. Bigand (Eds.), *Rethinking physical and rehabilitation medicine* (pp. 111–127). Paris, France: Springer Verlag.

Vinter, A., & Perruchet, P. (1999). Isolating unconscious influences: The neutral parameter procedure. *Quarterly Journal of Experimental Psychology: Human Experimental Psychology, 52A*(4), 857–875.

Vinter, A., & Perruchet, P. (2000). Implicit learning in children is not related to age: Evidence from drawing behavior. *Child Development, 71*(5), 1223–1240.

Vinter, A., & Perruchet, P. (2002). Implicit motor learning through observational training in adults and children. *Memory & Cognition, 30*(2), 256–261.

White, R. W. (1959). Motivation reconsidered: The concept of competence. *Psychological Review, 66*(5), 297–333.

Wolters, G., & Prinsen, A. (1997). Full versus divided attention and implicit memory performance. *Memory & Cognition, 25*(6), 764–771.

Wulf, G., & Schmidt, R. A. (1997). Variability of practice and implicit motor learning. *Journal of Experimental Psychology: Learning, Memory and Cognition, 23*(4), 987–1006.

Xu, F., & Denison, S. (2009). Statistical inference and sensitivity to sampling in 11-month-old infants. *Cognition, 112,* 97–104.

Xu, F., & Garcia, V. (2008). Intuitive statistics by 8-month-old infants. *Proceedings of the National Academy of Sciences of the United States of America, 105*(13), 5012–5015.

Zelazo, P. D., Muller, U., Frye, D., & Marcovitch, S. (2003). The development of executive function in early childhood. *Monographs of the Society for Research in Child Development, 68*(3), vii–137.

Zelazo, P. D., Reznick, J. S., & Pinon, D. E. (1995). Response control and the execution of verbal rules. *Developmental Psychology, 31*(3), 508–517.

Zhu, F. F., Poolton, J. M., Wilson, M. R., Maxwell, J. P., & Masters, R. S. W. (2011). Implicit motor learning promotes low verbal-analytical involvement in motor performance: Neural co-activation as a yardstick of movement specific reinvestment. *Biological Psychology, 87*(1), 66–73.

Zhu, F. F., Poolton, J. M., Wilson, M. R., Hu, Y., Maxwell, J. P., & Masters, R. S. W. (2011). Implicit motor learning promotes neural efficiency during laparoscopy. *Surgical Endoscopy, 25,* 2950–2955.

CHAPTER 4

THE ACQUISITION OF MOVEMENT SKILL IN CHILDREN THROUGH NONLINEAR PEDAGOGY

Jia Yi Chow, Keith Davids, Ian Renshaw, and Chris Button

INTRODUCTION

The acquisition of effective movement skills can help an individual establish a sound foundation for performing and executing a myriad of movement behaviors. This is especially pertinent for children, who should be exposed to relevant and appropriate opportunities in the developmental years to acquire critical movement skills that can be specific or transferable to individual or a variety of contexts. Without doubt, the emphasis for practitioners such as teachers and coaches would be to establish and organize effective practice conditions that encourage children to acquire various movement skills. Particularly, the role of practice (informal and formal), as well as the delivery of instructions, are crucial in shaping the learning experiences of our children.

In this chapter, we will discuss and share insights on the design of pedagogical and training approaches underpinned by a nonlinear pedagogical perspective. Key theoretical principles underlying such an approach will be presented to highlight the focus on providing a learning environment that encourages children to search and explore movement solutions, based on their own individual constraints, and the way in which goal-directed coordination emerges as a consequence of the interaction among key constraints in the learning context. In addition, we discuss practical implications for organizing learning experiences for children based on such a nonlinear pedagogical approach. Particularly, we want to highlight that it may not be as simple as engaging the child in 10,000 hours of practice to enable them to become skilled athletes, and it is more important to create learning situations where the practice is appropriate and much of it can be informal, with the teacher or coach taking on a facilitative role in the transmission of skill acquisition (Phillips, Davids, Renshaw, & Portus, 2010).

Below, we begin our discussion on how we should view learning as occurring in situated settings that can account for the complex, dynamic, yet inherent interactions that are present in these situations.

ACQUISITION OF MOVEMENT SKILLS IN AN EMBODIED CONTEXT

It has been highlighted that neurobiological systems should be examined from a "situated" perspective in relation to learning, as this will provide valuable insights into the development of an embodied cognition (e.g., Clark, 1997, 1999, 2001; Varela, Thompson, & Rosch, 1995). The Cartesian view of separating cognition and body is considered reductive, requiring revision since the learner may be better conceptualized as an integrated, complex system (Kelso & Engström, 2006; Port & van Gelder, 1995, Tschacher & Dauwalder, 2003). Such a view on the mind and body working as separate entities within a human movement system is artificial and unrealistic. Undoubtedly, learning takes place in dynamic contexts and the acquisition of knowledge occurs as a consequence of indeterminate interactions between learners and the environment (Barab & Kirshner, 2001).

These advances in embodied cognition emphasize the learner-environment relationship. This systemic approach is harmonious with contemporary work on motor performance and skill acquisition, influenced by concepts in ecological psychology and nonlinear dynamics, such as information-action coupling, self-organization, constraints, emergence, variability, and stability of behavior in neurobiological systems (see Davids, Button, & Bennett, 2008; Handford, Davids, Bennett, & Button, 1997; Kelso, 1995; Newell, Liu, & Mayer-Kress, 2008; Warren, 2006). Alternative conceptualizations of processes of perception, cognition, decision making, and action have emerged for studying intentional behavior in complex, self-organizing, neurobiological systems functioning in dynamic environments (e.g., van Orden, Holden, & Turvey, 2003). This *ecological dynamics* rationale proposes that the most relevant information for performance and learning in dynamic environments arises from continuous performer-environment interactions (Araújo, Davids, & Hristovski, 2006; Raczaszek-Leonardi & Kelso, 2008; van Orden et al., 2003). In ecological dynamics, the coupling of perception and action subsystems is based on the close interaction between neurobiological systems and their environments. Under this synergy, insights from psychology, biology, and physics have been integrated to enhance the understanding of how neurobiological systems function adaptively in their eco-niches (e.g., Davids & Araújo, 2010; Davids, Button, Araújo, Renshaw, & Hristovski, 2006; Warren, 2006). Performance and learning are constrained by key features of the organism-environment system, including the structure and physics of the environment, biomechanics, and morphology of individual and specific task constraints. Adaptive, goal-directed behavior emerging as neurobiological systems attempt to satisfy these interacting constraints.

Undoubtedly, there is a need to adopt a systems-based approach to properly investigate and describe the processes underlying skill acquisition in children, since the path to developing functional movement behaviors for children is multifaceted and complex. Therefore, the first step in establishing a possible pedagogical approach to investigating and encouraging skill acquisition in children is to acknowledge that the human movement system is a complex neurobiological system. We highlight below some key concepts associated with the understanding that human neurobiological systems can indeed function as complex systems.

HUMAN BIOLOGICAL SYSTEMS AS COMPLEX SYSTEMS

Basis for a Complex System

Complex biological systems in nature are composed of many individual degrees of freedom (i.e., movement possibilities offered by the system's components), such as the individual organisms in a flock of birds, a school of fish, and a colony of insects. Research has established that individual organisms use relatively simple local behavioral rules to create structures and patterns at the collective level that are more complex than the behavior of each individual system agent. From the movements and interactions of individual components of a complex system (e.g., the movement trajectory of a single fish in a school), rich patterns of coordinated behavior can emerge (e.g., the dazzling, synchronized movements of the school in avoiding predators). The emergence of form under constraints in complex systems is an important area of study in the analysis of weather patterns, stock market fluctuations, coordinated activity in animal colonies, and the interactions of players in sports teams (Camazine et al., 2001). Emergence is a collective property of any open system, not uniquely possessed by any of the individual agents, which leads to the spontaneous appearance of coordinated patterns of behavior (Kauffman, 1995). Emergent coordination tendencies are a collective property of dynamic, open systems of interacting agents, such as attacker-defender dyads (or pairs) in team sports like basketball, rugby union, and futsal (Araújo, Davids, Bennet, Button, & Chapman, 2004; Passos et al., 2008; Vilar, Araújo, Davids, & Travassos, 2012). As Kauffmann (1995) pointed out, "No vital force or extra substance is present in the emergent, self-reproducing whole. But the collective system does possess a stunning property not possessed by any of its parts" (p. 24). That property is pattern-forming dynamics, in which rich patterns of functional behavior emerge from the spontaneous interactions between system components. This idea has been imported into human movement science from theoretical physics and physical biology, where scientists have long been interested in how living systems assemble, sustain, and disassemble the large-scale (or macroscopic) patterns between the huge number of system components (e.g., see Kugler & Turvey, 1987).

Evidence has shown that complex systems are able to exploit the constraints that surround them in order to allow functional patterns of behavior to emerge in specific contexts. Complex systems in nature are able to do this because they are often open systems that are sensitive to many factors or constraints acting on the system. Achieving and maintaining stability of action could be a problem for open, complex systems, such as neurobiological systems, because of the potential for interaction between the environment and the system. Physical processes of self-organization support biological systems in using environmental energy to sustain functional periods of action stability (see Prigogine & Stengers, 1984). Self-organization in complex neurobiological systems is not a random or completely "blind" process in which any pattern can result; rather it is partly determined and somewhat predictable. Typically, complex, dynamic systems adopt only a very few states of organization, and a neurobiological system only inhabits certain parts of the landscape of all the possibilities that it could hypothetically adopt (Kauffmann, 1993).

In human neurobiological systems, surrounding energy flows constitute a source of information shaping the patterns of cognitions and actions that emerge during task performance. Self-organization of neurobiological systems into different states of order occurs when the many micro components interact and begin to influence each other's behavior. These micro-level dynamics typically do not lead to large-scale changes in system behavior, but merely a lot of underlying fluctuation, which mildly disturbs system stability (Camazine et al., 2001). However, key events, such as critical changes in values of energy arrays surrounding the system (e.g., optical or acoustic energy sources gained from approaching objects), can alter the whole system structure leading to macroscopic level changes and reorganization into a different state.

CONSTRAINTS FOR THE EMERGENCE OF COORDINATION

Newell (1986) classified three primary constraints: task, organismic, and environmental (see Chow et al., 2006 for a detailed review of the different categories of constraints). These three classes of constraints do not influence the learning process independently, but rather form complex interacting configurations that shape the *perceptual-motor workspace* of each learner in specific directions (Kelso, Fink, DeLaplain, & Carson, 2001; Newell, 1996). The perceptual-motor workspace contains all the potential movement solutions for an individual learner that may exist. In nonlinear neurobiological systems, constraint configurations do not prescribe each learner's behavior, but simply guide it through interaction with his or her perceptual-motor systems. For example, in sport, a learning environment forms a perceptual-motor workspace for each child, to which each individual brings unique constraints such as physical capacities, psychological skills, genetic make-up, and previous experience with a task. These personal constraints interact with important task constraints such as space, equipment, objects, and other players, as well as environmental constraints such as weather conditions, ambient lighting, and the social pressure of coaches and of parents who are watching. From this description it is clear that quite variable movement solutions will emerge from individual learners as they attempt to satisfy the range of interacting constraints during learning. The distinctive configurations of constraints between learners are manifest in how each individual attempts to satisfy specific task constraints during practice. Therefore, in teaching a child to learn movement skills, it is incorrect to identify a common, idealized motor pattern towards which all learners should aspire (e.g., teaching every individual to perform a classical technique for an action in sport, such as a certain golf swing). Different individual constraints suggest that it is dysfunctional to seek to establish universal optimal learning pathways. Each child can often experience discontinuous, qualitative changes in his or her performance due to the presence of instabilities in his or her perceptual-motor landscape. These instabilities may be due to growth, development, maturation, training, or learning across the lifespan. The perceptual-motor landscape may undergo changes in stability, requiring learners to adapt quickly to a newly emerging, stable movement solution (i.e., on a much shorter time scale than the long-term learning process itself). For example, prolonged periods of training may alter limb properties (e.g., increasing stiffness or restricted power), requiring performers to change their movement responses. That is why successful aging athletes adapt their movement solutions and re-invent themselves as competitive performers. A nonlinear pedagogical approach frames the individuality of learning pathways and individuality of performance solutions for a given movement task. Furthermore, it is important to note that constraints act on learners along different timescales, from the immediate (at the timescale of perception and action) to the more long term (at the timescale of developmental change over months and years).

AFFORDANCES FOR ACTION

The importance of the perceptual-motor system for picking up and using information to guide actions in the perceptual-motor workspace is exemplified by Gibson's (1979) theory of direct perception in ecological psychology. This framework proposes that information from the environment can be obtained by learning to pick up invariant sources of information, which can be used to regulate a performer's intentions and actions directly. According to Gibson's (1979) ideas, patterns of sensory stimulation specific to the performance environment can be picked up by athletes to regulate actions. For example, patterns of light reflected from surfaces and objects in the performance environment can specify properties of those surfaces and objects for a performer, such as how fast an object or individual is moving or how wide the gap is between opponents. Patterns of stimulation from proprioceptors can also specify an object's haptic properties (e.g., its length and mass) during equipment selection, obtained through grasping, wielding, hefting, and other manipulatory activities in humans (Beak, Davids, & Bennett, 2002).

The direct coupling of perception and action is based on the mutuality and reciprocity of performers and their performance environment. Under this synergy, biology and physics come together with psychology to define a behavioral science at a new scale of analysis—the ecological scale (Turvey & Shaw, 1995). Gibson's (1979) theory of direct perception suggests that a performer and the performance environment are dynamical systems coupled by information. In these complementary systems, specific intentional behaviors, such as intercepting an object or diving into space, emerge from a process of exploration before being stabilized into functional action patterns (Warren, 2006). When a child performs an exploratory action, such as picking up a racquet to detect its merit for hitting a tennis ball, this wielding behavior reveals object properties perceived with respect to the environment. Exploratory movements in practice and performance environments are, therefore, essential for perception and action to become tightly coupled during learning in sport.

For example, racquet properties in tennis are not perceived in arbitrary metrics such as units for measuring distance. Equipment in sport affords different actions from different performers in relation to distinct physical properties, such as hand span or arm length. In order to perform successfully with equipment as extensions of their bodies, individual performers perceive affordances of racquets with respect to their morphological and biomechanical properties (Beak et al., 2002). Performers are able to solve particular problems in sport by picking up relevant body-scaled environmental properties, such as whether a specific racquet affords hitting a tennis ball to the back of the court or not, with respect to relevant physical organismic constraints such as hand span and arm strength during exploratory practice. In ecological psychology, *affordance* is a central concept that captures the complementary relationship of a performer and the performance environment. Affordances are the starting points for the study in ecological psychology of what individuals perceive, what they learn and know, and how they decide and act (Turvey & Shaw, 1999).

UNDERSTANDING ACQUISITION OF MOVEMENT COORDINATION

Controlling Movement Possibilities

In recent years studies of complex neurobiological systems have revealed insights into how nonlinear dynamical systems adapt to the environment (Davids, Button, & Bennett, 1999). This task poses an immense challenge, since there are close to 10^2 joints, 10^3 muscles, and 10^{14} cells that have to be functionally coordinated in human movement systems for goal-directed actions to occur (Kelso, 1995; Turvey, 1990). How humans select and control the numerous movement possibilities available to them has intrigued movement scientists for a long time, and has been captured in the well known "degrees of freedom problem" (see Bernstein, 1967). Nonlinear dynamicists have emphasized the need to examine individual variability and development of neurobiological systems when considering the dynamic interactions inherent in all movement contexts (Davids et al., 1999).

Insights of Bernstein (1967) provide a useful starting point for explaining how coordination occurs within neurobiological systems from the perspective of nonlinear dynamics. The adoption of a systems-based approach has become increasingly relevant in the study of human movement coordination and control. Coordination has been referred to as the process by which neurobiological system components are assembled and brought into proper relation with each other during a goal-directed activity (Turvey, 1990). Bernstein (1967) viewed the basic coordination problem in humans as the process of mastering redundant degrees of freedom of the moving organ into a controllable system. This conceptualization of coordination suggests that complex neurobiological systems need not be decomposed into biomechanical and neurophysiological building blocks for the purposes of study (Bongaardt, 1996). Bernstein's ideas have been harnessed by researchers in the field, such as Turvey and colleagues, and Warren, who emphasized the dynamics of perception and action, aligning with the work of Gibson (1979) in ecological psychology (see Turvey, 1977; Turvey, Fitch, & Tuller, 1982; Warren, 2006). There have also been a number of creative and insightful studies by Thelen and co-investigators providing dynamical explanations of change and development in human movement systems, highlighting the key role of variability and instabilities during that process (see Thelen, 1995; Thelen & Smith, 1994). As mentioned earlier in the chapter, Newell and co-workers have highlighted the constraints on perception and action across many different timescales in neurobiological performance, learning, and development (e.g., Newell, Liu, & Mayer-Kress, 2001; Newell & Vaillancourt, 2001; Stratton, Liu, Hong, Mayer-Kress, & Newell, 2007).

Particular impetus has been provided by the studies of Kelso and colleagues on bimanual coordination in identifying the role of key constructs of self-organization, attractors (i.e., preferred stable patterns of behaviors that a system will reside in), order parameter (i.e., a variable that describes the state of the system), and control parameter (i.e., a scaling parameter that can be manipulated to effect a change in the state of the system), as well as transitions between stable states of neurobiological organization (see Buchanan & Kelso, 1999; Kelso, 1984;

Schöner & Kelso, 1988). To exemplify, H2O can exist in three different states (i.e., attractors), but it can only reside in any one state at one point in time. The order parameter that describes H_2O would be the state (i.e., vapor, liquid, or solid). The control parameter is temperature since it can be scaled to effect a change in the state of H2O.

The construction and adaptation of movement patterns have been successfully modeled and investigated by means of synergetic theoretical concepts since Haken, Kelso, and Bunz first applied them in investigations of the brain and behavior (Haken, Kelso, & Bunz, 1985; Kelso, 2002). In their pioneering Haken-Kelso-Bunz (HKB) model (which adopted a finger-waggling task to examine key concepts in dynamical systems theory relating to human movement) and its subsequent development (Schöner, Haken, & Kelso, 1986), abrupt changes in bimanual and multilimb oscillatory movement patterns were explained by a loss-of-stability mechanism (Jeka & Kelso, 1995; Kelso & Jeka, 1992), which produced spontaneous phase transitions from less stable to more stable states of motor organization, with changes in critical control parameters.

Together, these theoretical and empirical advances have provided a sound rationale for a nonlinear dynamics explanation of how processes of perception, cognition, decision making, and action underpin intentional movement behaviors in dynamic environments (e.g., Turvey & Shaw, 1995, 1999; van Orden et al., 2003). This framework proposes that the most relevant information for decision making and regulating action in dynamic environments is emergent during performer-environment interactions (see Araújo et al., 2006; van Orden et al., 2003).

Traditional investigations of limited-degree-freedom actions have provided some useful models for understanding how control systems may operate during neurobiological action. But they have shed fewer insights on understanding how many biomechanical degrees of freedom are managed in complex actions prevalent in dynamic performance environments involving multiagent interactions in engineering, industrial, and sport complexes (Davids et al., 2006). Although many initial studies of movement organization from the perspective of nonlinear dynamics tended to favor analysis of actions involving a limited number of degrees of freedom, rather than multi-articular movement patterns (for a review of this body of work see Davids et al., 1999), investigation of complex multi-articular movements has proceeded rapidly in the last two decades (see, for example, Vereijken, Van Emmerik, Bongaardt, Beek, & Newell, 1997, in learning a ski-simulator task; Beek & Turvey, 1992, for juggling; Chen, Liu, Mayer-Kress, & Newell, 2005, in learning a pedalo task; Chow, Davids, Button, & Koh, 2008, in learning to kick a soccer ball; Balasubramaniam & Turvey, 2004, in hula hooping; and Broderick & Newell, 1999, in ball bouncing). Interesting issues in neurobiological coordination and control concern how the spatiotemporal diversity of interactions between motor system degrees of freedom emerges, and the nature of task, environmental, or personal constraints that shape its manifestation. In particular, it is unclear what behavioral information performers exploit for parameterization of their actions, given that performance diversity arises predominantly from the varying time of varying engagement and disengagement of motor system degrees of freedom.

Degeneracy in Neurobiological Systems
Some researchers (e.g., Braun & Wolpert, 2007) have proposed theories, such as *optimal control,* which use the term *redundancy* to explain how the motor system responds to perturbations

by finding different movement solutions to achieve the same task goal. However, the use of the term *degeneracy* is more appropriate than redundancy in examining coordination in neurobiological systems. Degeneracy exists at all levels of neurobiological systems and is technically defined as nonisomorphic components (dissimilar components) producing isofunctional (similar) outcomes, effects, or solutions (Tononi, Sporns, & Edelman, 1999). The concept of degeneracy subserves the capacity of neurobiological systems to achieve the same or different outcomes in varying situations, with structurally different components of the musculo-skeletal subsystem (Edelman & Gally, 2001; Hong & Newell, 2006). Degenerate systems demonstrate the flexibility and adaptability to organize themselves to fit continuously evolving task constraints in information-rich environments, so that global movement goals can be attained (Edelman & Gally, 2001). Tononi et al. (1999) argued that degeneracy is a more likely feature of neurobiological systems than the term redundancy, since neurobiological systems have a different solution for ensuring system robustness and functionality in nature.

The notion of functional degrees of freedom is not limited to anatomical degrees of freedom (see Bernstein, 1967), and it underlines how degeneracy serves as a more suitable framework for understanding the concept of neurobiological degrees of freedom. Degeneracy provides the theoretical basis to describe how adaptive functional behaviors are present in human movement, most obviously when examining multi-articular actions. Furthermore, researchers and practitioners need to design experimental tasks to study how degeneracy can play an important role in the acquisition of coordination. Representative experimental tasks need to capture how information from the environment can be used to guide movement and how the control and emergence of adaptive behavior arises from the coupling of perceptual and action systems in neurobiology.

In the subsequent section, we will highlight some of the key bases of a nonlinear pedagogy approach through the provision of some exemplar discussion on how it can be applied in a practical setting.

A PRACTICAL EXAMPLE OF NONLINEAR PEDAGOGY

Perhaps at this point in the chapter some detailed practical examples would be useful to contextualize the theoretical information discussed thus far. In a subsequent section we discuss the role of nonlinear pedagogy in unstructured practice and play. However, the first example will consider how a movement practitioner (e.g., a physical education [PE] teacher) may employ a nonlinear pedagogy philosophy within a structured, purposeful practice environment. The example describes a hypothetical soccer (association football) lesson taught by a PE teacher. For argument's sake the purpose or learning objective within this example is to develop defensive skills, such as marking and tackling, among a group of 25 10-year-old children.

An important initial task for our PE teacher is to establish the key constraints (boundary conditions) on learning within the practice environment that he or she is constructing (Davids et al., 2008). Environmental constraints include the practice location, weather conditions, and the influence of significant others (e.g., school friends, the teacher). Broader but perhaps less obvious environmental constraints on the learners include sociocultural values and expectations that can arise from factors such as gender typing, ethnicity, and body image. Such constraints interact with organismic or personal factors at an individual level, meaning that each learner brings differences in, for example, self-esteem and motivation, alongside the range of other anthropometric and physiological differences typical among children. Finally, a number of significant task constraints influence the coordination of learners, including the task goal, rules, playing area, and number of players involved in the practice activity. Constraints that are relatively stable over time can often act as rate limiters that may delay or even prevent functional movement solutions from emerging. For example, an obese child who is sensitive about his or her body image or motor competency may choose not to fully engage in practice activities, thereby potentially limiting his or her rate of progression (Jones, Okely, Caputi, & Cliff, 2010). Importantly, all of these constraints on movement behavior interact to produce a complex landscape of movement solutions that is dynamic and inherently nonlinear in its structure (Button, Chow, & Rein, 2008).

By identifying the most influential constraints on action, the teacher can begin to channel the learning process efficiently by creating practice activities in which the learners must discover and experiment with different movement solutions (Chow et al., 2006). Our group of early learners, predominantly at Newell's Coordination stage of learning (see Newell's model of learning), are still assembling primitive movement solutions that allow them to satisfy the task goal (Chow, Davids, Button, & Rein, 2008; Newell, 1986). Initially, the teacher may split the large group into small dyads (i.e., 1 vs. 1) to allow the children to experiment with and identify effective defensive strategies. Furthermore, by limiting the time and space available to the attacker a modified game can be created in which the defender can appreciate how his or her body position, movement, and proximity to the attacker influence the chances of making a block or tackle. By swapping roles and changing players in the dyads, the teacher can intermittently disrupt the stability of the learner's initial solutions and thereby increase the repertoire of defensive skills. Such simple practice activities with limited instruction and demonstration offered by the teacher allow each individual learner to exploit degeneracy and develop his or her own preferred set of actions within a game-like situation (Davids et al., 2008). For example, quick and agile players may realize that they can step back and allow the attacker a little more space if they have the speed to steal the ball as the attacker tries to dribble around them. Alternately, slower, bigger players may prefer to use their larger body as a shield to prevent the attacker from getting past them.

The teacher's role is to promote self-organization of effective movement solutions both at an individual and a team (or group) level. If novices receive no guidance, the emergent behavior one might expect in practice would be for the players to cluster around the ball and race after it as a group—the swarming phenomenon, commonly seen among young children in different team ball sports (Button, Chow, Dutt, Mazumder, & Vilar, 2011). As individuals improve their passing, dribbling, and defensive skills, and teams learn how best to cooperate, more structured and predictable patterns of movement become more predominant. Indeed elite sports teams dynamically change team formations during the course of games to create instability in their opponents' behaviors and to capitalize on their own strengths (Bourbousson, Poizat, Saury, & Seve, 2010).

Structured or formal practice is typically guided by a practitioner for several reasons. First, in schools and sports clubs practices are usually organized for groups of learners over specific periods of time (e.g., a school lesson or period). Indeed, our group of learners can be thought of as a collection of individuals, each acquiring skills at different rates within their soccer lesson. By focusing initially on one task goal (e.g., how to defend against an attacker) and by manipulating the difficulty of the task, the teacher can set temporary boundaries within which common solutions and learning rates are likely to quickly emerge (Newell, Mayer-Kress, Hong, & Liu, 2009). Without such organization the identification of an appropriate task goal and rate of progression are left to chance, resulting in a potentially less efficient process of self-organization (see next subsection on unstructured practice). A group of learners without any guidance can also lack a shared target or goal, and consequently communicate with each other less effectively. Despite a high level of complexity and potential for chaos, groups of animals (e.g., flocks, swarms, shoals, crowds) can achieve an incredible level of coordination simply by adhering to a few simple rules in pursuit of a common target (Passos et al., 2009). Furthermore, the guidance of the teacher can serve to reinforce certain functional behaviors that can emerge over other suboptimal solutions. For example, through praise, positive feedback, and targeted practice activities, the teacher can promote fair and legal defensive skills at the expense of unfair and dangerous behaviors.

Many learners swiftly move from the Coordination stage to the Control stage (see Newell's model of learning); indeed these phases can be nested together such that it is difficult to characterize one stage from the other (Chow et al., 2008). In terms of the 1 vs. 1 defending activity described above, the teacher should be looking for opportunities to inject variability into the practice in order to encourage the learners to modify their movement patterns appropriately with relevant environmental information. For example, research examining small-sided dyads has revealed that the relative distance and speed between the attacker and defenders are crucial variables that strongly influence the defender's chances of making a successful block (e.g., Araújo et al., 2004, for basketball; Correia, Araújo, Davids, Fernandes, & Fonseca, 2011, for team sports; Passos et al., 2008, for rugby). As such, the teacher might wish to attune the defender to such variables by manipulating them in a systematic fashion. Getting the attacker to move quickly by imposing a time limit for the task is one simple way to create instability between the dyads. The introduction of a second attacker to the drill (or 3 vs. 2, etc.) provides an additional challenge for the defender in terms of identifying the relevant opportunities (affordances) to intercept the ball. For example, one potential affordance may arise when the player in possession is "trapped" near the sideline, with no simple passing opportunity to his or her teammate. In a 2 vs. 1 dyad the defenders must now assess how they can prevent the attacker in possession from either dribbling along the sideline or creating space to pass to their teammate. Such situations are common to many team sports, and creating a modified version within practice promotes a suitable level of specificity and transferability to the game context.

Clearly, with a group of early learners it may appear wise to allow them sufficient (practice) time to discover appropriate defensive skills before moving on to more complex concepts, such as defending as a unit or creating an off-side trap for the attacking team. However, one of the obvious attractions of using modified games within which practice activities can be structured is that such progressions can be seamlessly built into the game by the teacher without dictating the same rate of progression for everyone. For example, introducing a rule that once the defender has successfully blocked his or her attacker on three consecutive occasions another attacker is added, meaning that the progression of learning is individual (not group) based and also sensitively attuned to the level of competency the learner has developed.

While it no doubt will always be challenging to teach large groups of learners within a restricted time frame, we believe that reconceptualizing learning as a nonlinear, dynamic process can empower the practitioner to create a more fruitful practice environment.

In brief, nonlinear pedagogy encompasses the view that game skill acquisition occurs in a nonlinear manner, and therefore the pedagogical approach undertaken should also be dynamic and nonlinear in nature. Specifically, based on some of the earlier discussions and examples shared, nonlinear pedagogy generally incorporates (a) manipulation of key constraints to channel learners to search for functional movement solutions in their individualized perceptual motor workspace—the manipulation of task constraints such as equipment, rules of the activity, and task goals can be easily undertaken, and the practitioner must also take into account the interaction with the performer and environmental constraints that allows the emergence of self-adjusted, goal-directed coordination for the learner; (b) the role of variability in allowing learners to acquire new movement patterns and such fluctuations in movement variability could be an important phenomenon for new movement patterns to emerge; and (c) instructions that allow learners to focus on the effect of their movement behavior such that the movement pattern underpinning the outcome may not be overly prescriptive for practitioners to accept the possibility of many or different movement solutions for achieving the same outcome (i.e., the idea of degeneracy). The emphasis here is therefore on the individual and the recognition that a nonlinear pedagogical approach can account for such individuality in the emergence of movement behaviors in learning (see Chow et al., 2007).

While the idea of what nonlinear pedagogy should entail is clear, empirical work to determine the extent of its effectiveness is scarce, and certainly investigations on its perceived relevance to game skill acquisition needs to be undertaken. Nevertheless, we further highlight the pertinent practical implications for skill acquisition with relation to children in the following section.

PRACTICAL IMPLICATIONS FOR CHILDREN: ROLE OF UNSTRUCTURED PRACTICE

Adopting a nonlinear pedagogical approach emphasizes the idea that practice and performance environments for children need to facilitate opportunities to

- Focus on the individual;
- Accept different developmental trajectories for children;
- Identify rate limiters in children;
- Attune to perceptual information in guiding action;
- Build functional intrinsic dynamics through purposeful practice.

Considering these factors in program planning will lead to intrinsically motivating environments that meet the needs of each individual child in different dimensions (e.g., skill acquisition, social and emotional, and physical and psychological). In this section we highlight how adopting a nonlinear pedagogical approach can underpin a range of strategies to enhance the learning and developmental experiences for children when playing sports.

THE ROLE OF UNSTRUCTURED PRACTICE IN CHILDREN'S SKILL DEVELOPMENT

An unstructured practice environment provides the necessary ingredients that fulfill all of our stated requirements for children's sport skill development. *Backyard games* (an Australian term meant to reflect games played by children in backyards, streets, and local parks) provide an ideal foundation for the development of expertise in sport. They allow learners to devote hours of unstructured, holistic practice that enables the acquisition of often unique skills, requisite mental toughness, and the physical conditioning that underpins their later expertise (Cannane, 2009; Cooper, 2010; Renshaw & Chappell, 2010). Unstructured practice opportunities, without the presence of adults, signify that children can try things and make mistakes without admonishments from coaches and parents. Learning in these fun environments leads to a lifelong love of games (Renshaw & Chappell, 2010). Through this romance with sport (see Bloom, 1985), players can develop the intrinsic motivation needed to undertake the significant amounts of play and practice necessary to develop high-level performance skills (Côté, 1999; Renshaw & Chappell, 2010).

Unstructured practice fires children's imagination, which seems to be an important component in developing the skills and creativity needed for excellence (Côté, 1999; Chappell, 2004; Cooper, 2010). It shows how the notion of optimal movement solutions for a specific performance task being generalizable to all sport performers is inappropriate, given the complex and degenerate nature of neurobiological systems (Glazier & Davids, 2010). The coach-free backyard provides children with the perfect environment to ensure that variability is an intrinsic feature of skilled motor performance, providing the flexibility to adapt performance in dynamic environments (Araújo, 2007). Adaptability is standard in children's backyard sport, as they have to assemble movement solutions to cope with often unique physical performance environments as well as devise rules and adaptations to games to ensure that everyone wants to continue to play. In the backyard, essentially no skill is ever repeated, but instead, as Sheets-Johnstone cited by Sutton (2008) describes, "a kinetic dynamics unfolds that is at once both familiar and yet quintessentially tailored kinetically to the particular situation at hand" (p. 765).

Unstructured play opportunities may be a very important part of the skill acquisition process, as they provide the building blocks for potential champions, offering many of the conditions that have been identified as being essential for ultimate high achievement (see Côté, Baker, & Abernethy, 2007). Many youngsters played in "big games" in the backyard or local park, and this is an activity that is perhaps of more value than just being fun. A number of former sporting stars in Australia have provided anecdotal support for the backyard as the breeding ground for future expertise. For example, former Australian Cricket Centre of Excellence Head Coach Greg Chappell strongly believes that these early experiences in backyard sports are a significant factor in providing a foundation upon which expertise can develop (Renshaw & Chappell, 2010):

> I mean those early years of where we played our make believe test matches in the
> back yard or whether we were an older brother or younger brother or whether it

was just me throwing the ball against the wall, the imagination was a really important part of it as well and I think many years later I used that experience in visualization sessions and so on. (p. 156)

A similar story is told by former Wallaby captain John Eales. Just like many other rugby-obsessed Australian boys, Eales spent many hours as a youngster in his backyard kicking goals in Bledisloe Cup matches (the annual challenge match between Australia and New Zealand). In 2000, when he was faced with the challenge of converting an injury time penalty to beat the All Blacks in a real life game, Eales was not fazed, as he "had kicked a 100 of those goals as a youngster" (http://www.youtube.com/watch?v=tcpasb1r_nY). In backyard games, the unique environments of individuals underpin the emergence of playing styles that are later often the signatures of experts (see Cannane, 2009).

In summary, backyard sport has far more to offer than just fun. For those responsible for skill acquisition programs, harnessing the ideas and principles of backyard games can provide holistic development of emotional, physical, technical, tactical, and mental skills (Berry, Abernethy, & Côté, 2008; Renshaw & Chappell, 2010), as well as the leadership and social skills needed for later success, both as athletes and as human beings (Cooper, 2010).

DESIGNING GAMES FOR CHILDREN IN SPORT

How then can we adapt the ideas of the backyard to the more structured sporting environments of children's sport? One argument would be to simply delay the onset of organized sport and provide an unstructured learning program at sporting clubs, where children can simply play without being exposed to potentially restrictive coaching practices. Another solution would be to take the benefits of the backyard and design games that meet the needs of children. A key consideration when designing practice and competitive games is making sure that the task dynamics are aligned with the intrinsic dynamics of the individual performers. Facilitating opportunities that lead to enhanced performance requires moving children into metastable regions of their perceptual-motor landscape. Some sports have been lucky (or astute?) enough to design games that create the intensity required to push athletes into these regions. For example, *futebol-de-salao* (futsal) serves this function for developing Brazilian footballers. A game originally played in the dance halls that required use of a small, heavy ball (for safety), futsal is a high-intensity 5 vs. 5 game played on a small court. Players have a high number of touches of the ball and are constrained to develop fast footwork and intricate ball skills. Additionally, because it is difficult to lift the ball over the defenders, players have to continuously move to create passing lanes to facilitate passing opportunities. Many of Brazil's great players initially learned their skills through futsal, and some believe that it is one of the key reasons behind the success of the Brazilian football team (Gladwell, 2008; Syed, 2010).

In other sports, coaches do not have tailor-made games to fall back on and have to use their own creativity to design high-intensity training opportunities. Coaches use many strategies to push players beyond their current boundaries, as world-class performance comes about by striving for a target that is just out of reach. In these challenging environments top performers attempt to stretch their limitations in every session (Syed, 2010). For example, in some racket sports coaches use multifeeds to force players to perceive and move faster, while in table tennis coaches increase the area a player has to defend by increasing the table width (at one side) to force improvement in their footwork. In gymnastics coaches use innovative supports to help young performers build the technique and strength required to do specific movements, such as two-legged circles on the pommel horse (Renshaw, Davids, Shuttleworth, & Chow, 2009)

A Formula for Controlling Game Intensity

The creativity of expert coaches described above highlights the challenges faced by less experienced coaches when attempting to design appropriate learning environments. For example, in invasion games coaches often struggle to decide on the appropriate pitch dimensions in training and practice games. When setting up small-sided games it is important to ensure that an appropriate level of challenge is provided, commensurate with the ability level of the group. For the less experienced coach the process is problematic and prone to guesswork as to the best fit between players and the available time/space. An interesting possibility is to use a mathematical model to control the time/space demands on players. This model, which we term the *Game Intensity Index* (GII), is a function of the pitch size and the number of players in the game. By dividing the pitch area by the number of players, we can calculate a GII (see Equation 1). This tool might be used to (a) create game demands representative of the competition environment, (b) compare game forms, (c) control the difficulty level for players, and (d) assess skill levels.

$$\text{Game Intensity Index (GII)} \quad = \quad \frac{\text{Pitch Area (m}^2)}{\text{Number of Players}}$$

Equation 1. GII is calculated by dividing the area of the pitch/court by the number of players playing in the game.

    Creating a representative game design. Consider the following hypothetical problem. In adult professional football, modern defensive strategies designed to deny time and space to attacking players result in the defensive side compressing play, and often the majority of players can be found in one quarter of the field. Taking a standard football field (e.g., Old Trafford, Manchester, is 105m x 68m), this would mean that if all outfield players were in a quarter of the pitch, the GII for a professional football game is calculated to be 89 (see (a) below).

    (a) Professional football:

$$\text{Game Intensity Index (GII)} \quad = \quad \frac{\frac{105}{2} \times \frac{68}{2}}{20} \quad = \quad \frac{1785}{20} \quad = 89$$

    If a coach then wished to design a small-sided game to replicate the GII of a professional footballer (or to assess a player's ability in games of this intensity), we would then need to manipulate pitch size and numbers to come up with a GII of 89. In (i) it can be seen that a 40m x 25m pitch for a typical 6 vs. 6 practice game gives a GII of 83, only slightly higher[1] than the demands of the real game.

    (i) A 6 vs. 6 small-sided game for professional football practice

$$(GII) = \frac{40 \times 25}{12} = \frac{1000}{12} = 83$$

Comparing game forms. The GII model can also be useful in comparing the relative intensity and representativeness of games that administrators have developed in junior sport. The Football Federation Australia recently introduced its new National Curriculum, and central to this initiative was the development of a small-sided game program in order to "allow all children to develop into the best players they can be" (FFA, 2010, p. 2). The program introduced games of 4 vs. 4 for U-6 & U-7, 7 vs. 7 for U-8 & U-9 and 9 vs. 9 for U-10 & U-11 games before the introduction of the adult 11 vs. 11 game at U-12. Table 4.1 provides the GII for each game format. The table raises some startling issues. For example, the games with the highest intensity were those for U-6 & U-7 players, when perhaps it is expected that the lowest intensity levels would be provided as young children grapple with the challenges of mastering the football. Similarly, it is interesting to note what a significant impact a different pitch size can have on GII for each game format. Changing pitch sizes for games with the same number of players can create up to a 67% change in the level of intensity in 7 vs. 7, and even bigger changes in 9 vs. 9. The significance of not playing off-side impacts on the intensity of the game, as it means that play becomes more spread out, and highlights that administrators need to carefully consider the impact of removing fundamental rules in creating games that are representative of the demands of the parent game. Given the earlier discussion of the importance of futsal on Brazilian soccer and its prominence in Australia, we also calculated the GII for futsal, revealing a GII of 70, a level much higher than any other game form, including professional football. Perhaps these data underpin the perceived merits of futsal for footballers?

Table 4.1. Australian Football Federation Small-Sided Game Guidelines

Playing Format	Numbers	Offside	Field Size	Game Intensity Index (GII)
Under 6 & 7	4 vs. 4	No	30m x 20m	75
		No	¼ Full Size Pitch (25m x 18m)	56
Under 8 & 9	7 vs. 7	No	40m x 30m (min)	100
		No	50m x 40m (max)	167
Under 10 & 11	9 vs. 9	No (informally)	½ Full Size Pitch (50m x 35m)	109
		No (informally)	60m x 40m (min)	150
		No (informally)	70m x 50m (max)	219
Futsal	5 vs. 5	No	35m x 20m	70
Under 12 +	11 vs. 11	Yes	105m x 68m (compression into ½ field)	178.5
Under 12 +	11 vs. 11	Yes	105m x 68m (compression into ¼ field)	89

The dimensions for futsal courts range from 25-42m x 15-25m.
In this example the middle range is taken to provide an exemplar.

Controlling the difficulty level for players and assessing skill levels. It should not be forgotten that the skill level of players is a major consideration in the level of intensity that should be set by a coach. It should be clear from the previous discussion that the GII provides coaches with a tool for carefully manipulating the intensity of games. By using the GII, the player's initial skill levels can be assessed in order to determine the appropriate GII for facilitating the emergence of enhanced performance. Then, the GII can be precisely manipulated, enabling players to adapt to specific game intensities. A final point concerns the potential of the GII as a developmental tool. The GII provides coaches and sport scientists with a tool for analyzing players at different stages of the development continuum and enables recommendations to be made for fitting playing pitch dimensions to the skill level of individuals rather than simply making decisions based on age or administrative factors.

In this section we have showcased some ideas for designing sports programs for children. An initial focus of providing opportunities for unstructured play opportunities was suggested as a way of creating the conditions for the optimal development of children's sporting ability. We discussed how these ideas could be adopted by coaches in the design of practice, before considering a potential formula that could lead to a more precise match between the developmental stages of individual children, as reflected in their current intrinsic dynamics and rate limiters, and the imposed task demands of games. Throughout this discussion we emphasized the value of playing "real" games as opposed to performing drills, since games enable the development of functional intrinsic dynamics and provide opportunities for learning to attune to key perceptual information sources during performance.

CONCLUSION

The acquisition of movement skills takes on a nonlinear pathway, and the application of a nonlinear pedagogy approach is an appropriate approach to understand, describe, and plan practices for learners. It is critical that practitioners harness the critical window of opportunity during a child's developmental years, in order to provide sound and relevant practice opportunities to engage our children so that they may acquire functional movement skills. The discussion of a nonlinear pedagogical approach in this chapter provides a possible theoretical and practical platform for teachers and coaches to plan effective learning activities for our children.

The challenge ahead is to undertake more empirical work in applied settings based on the concepts of nonlinear pedagogy, in order to examine the extent of the effectiveness of such a pedagogical approach. Ongoing empirical investigations will certainly provide more insights on how nonlinear pedagogy works in facilitating skill acquisition for our children.

In terms of practical implications for physical educators and coaches working with young athletes as well as children, the focus should be on encouraging them to explore and find individualized movement solutions that can be functional for the various specific performance contexts. Perhaps, we need to be more mindful of the need to be less prescriptive in our instructions and accept that we should play a facilitating role in the process of skill acquisition for our children.

REFERENCES

Araújo, D. (2007). Promoting ecologies where performers exhibit expert interactions. *International Journal of Sport Psychology, 38,* 73–77.

Araújo, D., Davids, K., Bennett, S., Button, C., & Chapman, G. (2004). Emergence of sport skills under constraint. In A. M. Williams & N. J. Hodges (Eds.), *Skill acquisition in sport: Research, theory and practice* (pp. 409–433). London, UK: Routledge, Taylor & Francis.

Araújo, D., Davids, K., & Hristovski, R. (2006). The ecological dynamics of decision making in sport. *Psychology of Sport and Exercise, 7*(6), 653–676.

Balasubramaniam, R., & Turvey, M. T. (2004). Coordination modes in the multisegmental dynamics of hula hooping. *Biological Cybernetics, 90,* 176–190.

Barab, S. A., & Kirshner, D. (2001). Guests editors' introduction: Rethinking methodologies in the learning sciences. *The Journal of the Learning Sciences, 10*(1&2), 5–15.

Beak, S., Davids, K., & Bennett, S. J. (2002). Child's play: Children's sensitivity to haptic information in perceiving affordances of rackets for striking a ball. In J. Clark & J. Humphrey (Eds.), *Motor development: Research and reviews* (pp. 120–141). Minnesota: NASPE.

Beek, P. J., & Turvey, M. T. (1992). Temporal patterning in cascade juggling. *Journal of Experimental Psychology: Human Perception and Performance, 18*(4), 934–947.

Bernstein, N. A. (1967). *The control and regulation of movements.* London, UK: Pergamon Press.

Berry, J., Abernethy, B., & Côté, J. (2008). The contribution of structured practice and deliberate play to the development of expert perceptual and decision-making skill. *Journal of Sport and Exercise Psychology, 30,* 685–708.

Bloom, B. S. (1985). *Developing talent in young people.* New York, NY: Ballantine.

Bongaardt, R. (1996). *Shifting focus. The Bernstein tradition in movement science.* Amsterdam, Netherlands: Druk 80.

Bourbousson, J., Poizat, G., Saury, J., & Seve, C. (2010). Team coordination in basketball: Description of the cognitive connections among teammates. *Journal of Applied Sport Psychology, 22,* 150–166.

Braun, D. A., & Wolpert, D. M. (2007). Optimal control: When redundancy matters. *Current Biology, 17*(22), R973–R975.

Broderick, M. P., & Newell, K. M. (1999). Coordination patterns in ball bouncing as a function of skill. *Journal of Motor Behavior, 31*(2), 165–188.

Buchanan, J. J., & Kelso, J. A. S. (1999). To switch or not to switch: Recruitment of degrees of freedom stabilizes biological coordination. *Journal of Motor Behavior, 31*(2), 126–144.

Button, C., Chow, J. Y., Dutt Mazumder, A., & Vilar, L. (2011, May). *Exploring the swarming effect in children's football.* Paper presented at the World Congress of Science and Football, Nagoya, Japan.

Button, C., Chow, J. Y., & Rein, R. (2008). Exploring the perceptual-motor workspace: New approaches to skill acquisition and training. In Y. Hong & R. Bartlett (Eds.), *Handbook of biomechanics and human movement science* (pp. 538–553). London, UK: Routledge.

Camazine, S., Deneubourg, J.-L., Franks, N. R., Sneyd, J., Theraulaz, G., & Bonabeau, E. (2001). *Self-organization in biological systems.* Princeton, NJ: Princeton University Press.

Cannane, S. (2009). *First tests: Great Australian cricketers and the backyards that made them.* Sydney, Australia: ABC Books.

Chappell, G. (2004). *Cricket: The making of champions.* Melbourne, Australia: Lothian Books.

Chen, H. H., Liu, Y. T., Mayer-Kress, G., & Newell, K. M., (2005). Learning the pedalo locomotion task. *Journal of Motor Behavior, 37*(3), 247–256.

Chow, J. Y., Davids, K., Button, C., & Koh, M. (2008). Coordination changes in a discrete multi-articular action as a function of practice. *Acta Psychologica, 127*(1), 163–176.

Chow, J. Y., Davids, K., Button, C., & Rein, R. (2008). Dynamics of movement patterning in learning a discrete multiarticular action. *Motor Control, 12*(3), 219–240.

Chow, J. Y., Davids, K., Button, C., Shuttleworth, R., Renshaw, I., & Araújo, D. (2006). Nonlinear pedagogy: A constraints-led framework to understand emergence of game play and skills. *Nonlinear Dynamics, Psychology and Life Sciences, 10*(1), 74–104.

Chow, J. Y., Davids, K., Button, C., Shuttleworth, R., Renshaw, I., & Araújo, D. (2007). The role of nonlinear pedagogy in physical education. *Review of Educational Research, 77,* 251–278.

Clark, A. (1997). *Being there: Putting brain, body and world together again.* Cambridge, MA: MIT Press.

Clark, A. (1999). An embodied cognitive science? *Trends in Cognitive Sciences, 3*(9), 345–351.

Clark, A. (2001). *Mindware. An introduction to the philosophy of cognitive science.* New York, NY: Oxford University Press.

Cooper, P. (2010). Play and children. In L. Kidman & B. J. Lombardo (Eds.), *Athlete-centred coaching* (pp. 37–151). Worcester, UK: IPC Print Resources.

Correia, V., Araújo, D., Davids, K., Fernandes, O., & Fonseca, S. (2011). Territorial gain dynamics regulates success in attacking sub-phases of team sports. *Psychology of Sport and Exercise, 12*(6), 662–669.

Côté, J. (1999). The influence of the family in the development of talent in sport. *The Sport Psychologist, 13,* 395–417.

Côté, J., Baker, J., & Abernethy, B. (2007). Practice and play in the development of sport expertise. In R. Eklund & G. Tenenbaum (Eds.), *Handbook of sport psychology* (3rd ed.) (pp. 184–202). Hoboken, NJ: Wiley.

Davids, K., & Araújo, D. (2010). Perception of affordances in multi-scale dynamics as an alternative explanation for equivalence of analogical and inferential reasoning in animals and humans. *Theory & Psychology, 20*(1), 125–134.

Davids, K., Button, C., Araújo, D., Renshaw, I., & Hristovski, R. (2006). Movement model from sports provide representative task constraints for studying adaptive behavior in human movement system. *Adaptive Behavior, 14*(1), 73–94.

Davids, K., Button, C., & Bennett, S. J. (1999). Modeling human motor systems in nonlinear dynamics: Intentionality and discrete movement behaviours. *Nonlinear Dynamics, Psychology, and Life Sciences, 3*(1), 3–30.

Davids, K., Button, C., & Bennett, S. J. (2008). *Coordination and control of movement in sport: An ecological approach.* Champaign, IL: Human Kinetics.

Edelman, G. M., & Gally, J. (2001). Degeneracy and complexity in biological systems. *Proceedings of the National Academy of Sciences, 98*(24), 13763–13768.

Football Federation Australia (FFA). (2010). *Small-sided football laws.* Sydney, Australia: Football Federation Australia.

Gladwell, M. (2008). *Outliers: The story of success.* Camberwell, Australia: Penguin Group.

Glazier, P., & Davids, K. (2010). Deconstructing neurobiological coordination: The role of the biomechanics-motor control nexus. *Exercise & Sport Science Reviews, 38*(2), 86–90.

Gibson, J. J. (1979). *An ecological approach to visual perception.* Boston, MA: Houghton-Mifflin.

Haken, H., Kelso, J. A. S., & Bunz, H. (1985). A theoretical model of phase-transitions in human hand movements. *Biological Cybernetics, 51*(5), 347–356.

Handford, C., Davids, K., Bennett, S., & Button, C. (1997). Skill acquisition in sport: Some applications of an evolving practice ecology. *Journal of Sports Sciences, 15*(6), 621–640.

Hong, S. L., & Newell, K. M. (2006). Practice effects on local and global dynamics of the ski-simulator task. *Experimental Brain Research, 169*(3), 350–360.

Jeka, J. J., & Kelso, J. A. S. (1995). Manipulating symmetry in the coordination dynamics of human movement. *Journal of Experimental Psychology: Human Perception and Performance, 21*(2), 360–374.

Jones, R. A., Okely, A. D., Caputi, P., & Cliff, D. P. (2010). Perceived and actual competence among overweight and non-overweight children. *Journal of Science and Medicine in Sport, 13*(6), 589–596.

Kauffmann, S. A. (1993). *The origins of order: Self-organization and selection in evolution.* New York, NY: Oxford.

Kauffmann, S. A. (1995). *At home in the universe: The search for laws of complexity.* London, UK: Viking.

Kelso, J. A. S. (1984). Phase transitions and critical behavior in human bimanual coordination. *American Journal of Physiology, 246*(6), R1000–R1004.

Kelso, J. A. S. (1995). *Dynamic patterns: the self-organization of brain and behavior.* Cambridge, MA: MIT.

Kelso, J. A. S. (2002). The complementary nature of the coordination dynamics. *Nonlinear Phenomena in Complex Systems, 5*(4), 364–371.

Kelso, J., & Engström, D. (2006). *The complementary nature.* Cambridge, MA: The MIT Press.

Kelso, J. A. S., & Jeka, J. J. (1992). Symmetry-breaking dynamics in human inter-limb coordination. *Journal of Experimental Psychology: Human Perception and Performance, 18*(3), 645–668.

Kelso, J. A. S., Fink, P., DeLaplain, C. R., & Carson, R. G. (2001). Haptic information stabilizes and destabilizes coordination dynamics. *Proceedings of the Royal Society B, 268*(1472), 1207–1213.

Kugler, P. N., & Turvey, M. T. (1987). *Information, natural law, and the self-assembly of rhythmic movement.* Hillsdale, NJ: Erlbaum.

Newell, K. M. (1986). Constraints on the development of coordination. In M. G. Wade & H. T. A. Whiting (Eds.), *Motor development in children. Aspects of coordination and control* (pp. 341–360). Dordrecht, Netherlands: Martinus Nijhoff.

Newell, K. M. (1996). Change in movement and skill: Learning, retention and transfer. In M. L. Latash & M. T. Turvey (Eds.), *Dexterity and its development* (pp. 393–430). Mahwah, NJ: Erlbaum.

Newell, K. M., Liu, Y. T., & Mayer-Kress, G. (2001). Time scales in motor learning and development. *Psychological Review, 108*(1), 57–82.

Newell, K. M., Liu, Y-T., & Mayer-Kress, G. (2008). Landscapes beyond the HKB Model. In A. Fuchs & V. K. Jirsa (Eds.), *Coordination: Neural, behavioral and social dynamics* (pp. 27–44). Berlin, Germany: Springer Verlag.

Newell, K. M., Mayer-Kress, G., Hong, S. L., & Liu, Y.-T. (2009). Adaptation and learning: Characteristic time scales of performance dynamics. *Human Movement Science, 28*(6), 655–687.

Newell, K. M., & Vaillancourt, D. E. (2001). Dimensional change in motor learning. *Human Movement Studies, 20*(4–5), 695–715.

Passos, P., Araújo, D., Davids, K., Gouveia, L., Milho, J., & Serpa, S. (2008). Information-governing dynamics of attacker-defender interactions in youth rugby union. *Journal of Sports Sciences, 26*(13), 1421–1429.

Passos, P., Araújo, D., Davids, K., Gouveia, L., Serpa, S., Milho, J., & Fonseca, S. (2009). Interpersonal pattern dynamics and adaptive behavior in multiagent neurobiological systems: Conceptual model and data. *Journal of Motor Behavior, 41*(5), 445–459.

Phillips, E., Davids, K., Renshaw, I., & Portus, M. (2010). Expert performance in sport and the dynamics of talent development. *Sports Medicine, 40*(4), 271–283.

Port, R. F., & van Gelder, T. (1995). *Mind as motion: Explorations in the dynamics of cognition.* Cambridge, MA: MIT Press.

Prigogine, I., & Stengers, I. (1984). *Order out of chaos.* New York, NY: Bantam Books.

Raczaszek-Leonardi, J., & Kelso, J. A. S. (2008). Reconciling symbolic and dynamic aspects of language: Toward a dynamic psycholinguistics. *New Ideas in Psychology, 26*(2), 193–207.

Renshaw, I., & Chappell, G. S. (2010). A constraints-led approach to talent development in cricket. In L. Kidman & B. Lombardo (Eds.), *Athlete-centred coaching: Developing decision makers* (2nd ed.) (pp. 151–173). Worcester, UK: IPC Print Resources.

Renshaw, I., Davids, K., Shuttleworth, R., & Chow (2009). Insights from ecological psychology and dynamical systems theory can underpin a philosophy of coaching. *International Journal of Sport Psychology, 40*(4), 580–602.

Schöner, G., Haken, H., & Kelso, J. A. S. (1986). A stochastic theory of phase transitions in human hand movement. *Biological Cybernetics, 53*(4), 442–452.

Schöner, G., & Kelso, J. A. S. (1988). Dynamic pattern generation in behavioural and neural systems. *Science, 239*(4847), 1513–1520.

Stratton, S. M., Liu, Y. T., Hong, S. L., Mayer-Kress, G., & Newell, K. M. (2007). Snoddy (1926) revisited: Time scales of motor learning. *Journal of Motor Behavior, 39*(6), 503–515.

Sutton, J. (2008). Batting, habit and memory: The embodied mind and the nature of skill. *Sport in Society, 10*(5), 763–786.

Syed, M. (2010). *Bounce: How champions are made.* London, UK: Fourth Estate.

Thelen, E. (1995). Motor development. A new synthesis. *American Psychologist, 50*(2), 79–95.

Thelen, E., & Smith, L. B. (1994). *A dynamic systems approach to the development of cognition and action.* London, UK: MIT Press.

Tononi, G., Sporns, O., & Edelman, G. M. (1999). Measures of degeneracy and redundancy in biological networks. *Proceedings of the National Academy of Science, 96*(6), 3257–3262.

Tschacher, W., & Dauwalder, J. P. (2003). *The dynamical systems approach to cognition.* Singapore: World Scientific.

Turvey, M. T. (1977). Preliminaries to a theory of action with reference to vision. In R. E. Shaw & J. Bransford (Eds.), *Perceiving, acting, and knowing: Toward an ecological psychology* (pp. 211–265). Hillsdale, NJ: Erlbaum.

Turvey, M. T. (1990). Coordination. *American Psychologist, 45*(8), 938–953.

Turvey, M. T., & Shaw, R. (1995). Toward an ecological physics and a physical psychology. In R. L. Solso & D. W. Massaro (Eds.), *The science of the mind: 2001 and beyond* (pp. 144–169). New York, NY: Oxford University Press.

Turvey, M. T., & Shaw, R. (1999). Ecological foundations of cognition: I. Symmetry and specificity of animal-environment systems. *Journal of Consciousness Studies, 6*(11–12), 95–110.

Turvey, M. T., Fitch, H. L., & Tuller, B. (1982). The Bernstein perspective: 1. The problems of degrees of freedom and context-conditioned variability. In J. A. S. Kelso (Ed.), *Human motor control* (pp. 239–252). Hillsdale, NJ: Erlbaum.

Van Orden, G., Holden, J. G., & Turvey, M. (2003). Self-organization of cognitive performance. *Journal of Experimental Psychology: General, 132,* 331–350.

Varela, F. J., Thompson, E., & Rosch, E. (1995). *The embodied mind: Cognitive science and human experience.* London, UK: MIT Press.

Vereijken, B., Van Emmerik, R. E. A., Bongaardt, R., Beek, W. J., & Newell, K. M. (1997). Changing coordinative structures in complex skill acquisition. *Human Movement Science, 16*(6), 823–844.

Vilar, L., Araújo, D., Davids, K., & Travassos, B. (2012). Constraints on competitive performance of attacker-defender dyads in team sports. *Journal of Sports Sciences, 30*(5), 459–469.

Warren, W. H. (2006). The dynamics of perception and action. *Psychological Review, 113*(2), 358–389.

ENDNOTE

[1] The lower the score, the higher the intensity.

CHAPTER 5

MOTOR DEVELOPMENT AND PERFORMANCE
Robert M. Malina

INTRODUCTION

Improvement of general and sport-specific skills is a primary objective of youth sports programs, from community levels through advanced sports schools and academies. Learning and improving sport skills are also primary motivations of children and adolescents for involvement in sport (Coelho e Silva, Sobral, & Malina, 2009; Ewing & Seefeldt, 1989; Siegel, Peña Reyes, Cárdenas Barahona, & Malina, 2009). Movement skills, including sport skills, do not exist in isolation. They are important dimensions of growing up as all youth pass from birth through adolescence. This chapter considers motor development and performance in general, as well as relative to sport in the framework of physical growth and biological maturation.

GROWING UP

The universal business of growing up includes three interrelated processes: growth, maturation, and development (Malina, Bouchard, & Bar-Or, 2004). Growth refers to the increase in the size of the body as a whole and its parts. As children grow, size increases, physique and body composition change, and different parts of the body grow at different rates and times, resulting in changes in proportions. Corresponding changes occur in specific organs and related structures. For example, heart mass and volume follow a growth pattern like that for body weight, while the lungs and lung functions follow a growth pattern like that for height.

Maturation refers to progress towards the biologically mature state, an operational concept as maturity varies with body systems. All tissues, organs, and systems mature. Maturation of the skeletal and reproductive systems is used most often in studies of children and adolescents, although parameters of the growth curve in height are also used. Maturation varies in timing and tempo within and among individuals. Timing refers to when specific maturational events occur, while tempo refers to the rate of their progress.

Development refers to the learning of behaviors expected by society, that is, behavioral competence that is culture specific. As children experience life at home, school, and church, and in sports, recreation, and other community activities, they develop cognitively, socially, emotionally, morally, and so on. They are learning to behave in a culturally appropriate manner. The development of competence in movement skills—the acquisition and refinement of skillful performance in a variety of movement activities, is an important dimension of development that straddles the biological and behavioral domains.

These three processes are discussed in more detail in subsequent sections. It is important to note, however, that physical growth, biological maturation, and behavioral development occur simultaneously and interact with each other. The interactions influence self-concept, self-esteem, body image, and perceived competence, as well as skills and behaviors related to a sport or sport discipline. The processes vary within and among individuals, especially during the adolescent growth spurt and sexual maturation. The demands of sport—for example intensive training, scrutiny of coaches and other adults, altered peer relationships, and so on—are superimposed upon those associated with normal growth, maturation, and development.

Growth and maturity characteristics have increasing importance for performance and, in turn, sport as the individual progresses through childhood and into and through adolescence. Components of performance, strength, power, speed, agility, endurance, and other elements have their own adolescent spurts that vary in timing relative to the spurt in height. Environmental conditions present added dimensions that influence opportunities to move, practice, and perform. These include the human environments, parents, siblings, play and school mates, peers, teammates, teachers, coaches, and sport organizations, among others. Natural environments are reasonably obvious—climate, altitude, and topography. Man-made environments and environmental alterations are increasingly important—expansion of urban settings, technological advances, pollution, and so on. Human, natural, and man-made environments are in many ways central to the development of movement and performance capabilities.

Interrelationships among growth, maturation, and development have been well documented in the longitudinal growth studies conducted at the University of California, Bekeley, which date to 1928 (see Jones, Bayley, MacFarlane, & Honzik, 1971, for a selection of papers from the studies). Of relevance to the present discussion, the studies not only described changes in growth, maturation, and development with age and sex, but also considered relationships between physical characteristics and psychosocial development during adolescence; self-conceptions, motivations, and social development of boys and girls at the extremes of the maturity continuum; and strength of boys and girls relative to biological maturity status, among other topics. Interest in relationships between growth and maturation on one hand and adolescent behavior on the other has continued, especially among girls (see Brooks-Gunn & Petersen, 1983), while the need for such an approach has been highlighted in reviews of age at menarche in athletes (Malina, 1983) and growth and maturation of young athletes (Malina, 2002). Research addressing interrelationships among growth, maturation, and behavior during adolescence has increased more recently in the sport sciences to include studies of physical activity (Cumming et al., 2011; Cumming, Standage, Gillison, & Malina, 2008; Sherar, Cumming, Eisenmann, Baxter-Jones, & Malina, 2010) and youth sport (Cumming, Battista, Standage, Ewing, & Malina, 2006; Cumming, Eisenmann, Smoll, Smith, & Malina, 2005).

OVERVIEW OF GROWTH, MATURATION, AND DEVELOPMENT

Essential elements in understanding physical growth and biological maturation are considered in this chapter and are discussed in depth in Malina, Bouchard, and Bar-Or (2004). Several aspects of behavioral development relevant to growth and maturation are also summarized. Motor development and performance are considered in a separate section.

Growth

Height and weight (body mass) are the two dimensions most commonly used to monitor growth status. Children are expected to become taller and heavier with age. By about 9–10 years in girls and 11–12 years in boys, the rate of growth in height accelerates, marking the transition into the adolescent growth spurt, a period of rapid growth that is highly variable among individuals. Rate of growth in height increases until it reaches a peak or maximum (peak height velocity), then gradually decreases and eventually ceases as mature (adult) height is reached. Girls, on average, start the growth spurt, reach peak velocity, and stop growing about two years earlier than boys. Nevertheless, ages at the initiation of the spurt, peak height velocity, and cessation of growth vary among individuals. Other linear body dimensions follow a growth pattern similar to height, though vary in the timing of their respective growth spurts. The growth spurt in the legs, for example, occurs earlier than that in the trunk (Malina, Bouchard, et al., 2004).

The growth spurt in body weight begins slightly later than the spurt in height. Weight is a composite of many tissues, but is most often partitioned in terms of its lean (fat-free) and fat components: body weight = fat-free mass + fat mass. Methods of estimating body composition are discussed elsewhere in more detail (see Malina, 2007a; Malina & Geithner, 2011).

Fat-free mass has a growth pattern similar to that of height and weight. Sex differences are negligible during childhood and become clearly established during the adolescent spurt. Males gain almost twice as much lean tissue as females across adolescence, while females gain about twice as much fat mass as males. A significant portion of the changes in body composition occurs during the interval of maximal growth in height. Fat-free mass is heterogeneous, but the two major components, skeletal muscle and bone mineral, have their own growth spurts. On average, the spurts in muscle tissue and bone mineral occur after peak height velocity in boys and girls, and the spurt in bone mineral occurs after that for muscle. Peak gains in lean tissue and bone mineral during the spurt are greater in boys than in girls (Iuliano-Burns, Mirwald, & Bailey, 2001).

Maturation

Studies of biological maturation have primarily used three indicators: skeletal age, secondary sex characteristics—pubic hair, genital and breast development, and menarche—and age at peak height velocity. Dental maturation has also been used, but it proceeds independently of the above indicators. Methods of assessment and limitations are summarized elsewhere (see Beunen, Rogol, & Malina, 2006; Malina, Bouchard, & Bar-Or, 2004). Skeletal age is applicable from childhood through adolescence, while secondary sex characteristics and age at peak height velocity are limited to the adolescent or pubertal years.

Three methods are commonly used to assess skeletal age—the Greulich-Pyle, Tanner-Whitehouse, and Fels methods (Malina, 2011; Malina, Bouchard, & Bar-Or, 2004). These methods vary in the criteria and scales of maturity from which a skeletal age is assigned. Skeletal ages with the three methods are related, but are not equivalent. A skeletal age corresponds to the level of skeletal maturity attained by a youngster relative to the reference sample of the method used. For example, a boy may have a chronological age of 10.5 years and a skeletal age of 12.3 years. The boy has attained the skeletal maturity equivalent to that of a boy of 12.3 years in the reference sample and is advanced in skeletal maturity. Another boy may have a chronological age of 10.5 years but a skeletal age of 9.0 years. He has attained the skeletal maturity of a child 9.0 years; this boy is delayed in skeletal maturity for his chronological age. Skeletal age is ordinarily expressed relative to chronological age in the majority of studies.

Indicators of sexual maturity are useful during puberty when they are overtly manifest. Genitals, breasts, and pubic hair are ordinarily assessed by a physician using the criteria of Tanner (1962) during clinical examination; some studies utilize self-assessments. The criteria define a youngster as being in a stage of genital, breast and/or pubic hair, ranging from 1 (pre-pubertal) to 5 (postpubertal or mature). Stage 2 represents initial, overt manifestation of the characteristic, while stages 3 and 4 represent progress through puberty. The stages, though useful, have limitations: (a) an assessment indicates stage at the time of observation and does not provide information on when a youngster entered the stage or how long he or she has been in the stage; (b) although genital and pubic hair maturation in boys and breast and pubic hair maturation in girls are related within each sex, stages are not equivalent, that is, genital 3 does not equal pubic hair 3, and moreover, genital 3 does not equal breast 3; (c) the duration of a stage and timing of transition from one stage to another are difficult to estimate; (d) the rate of transition through stages from early puberty to maturity is variable within and among individuals, but is not as well documented; and (e) youth in the same stage of puberty but of different chronological age can be quite different in growth status and behavioral development.

The first menstrual period, menarche, is an important indicator of pubertal timing. Age at menarche can be estimated with two methods in individuals, prospective and retrospective. The former follows individual girls longitudinally through puberty, while the latter asks girls to recall the age at which they attained menarche. The retrospective or recall method, with potential for error associated with memory, has limited utility with young girls about 9–14 years of age, since some girls in the sample will not have attained menarche and thus bias the estimated mean age.

Girls can also be classified as pre- or postmenarcheal, that is, whether or not they have attained menarche. This provides an indicator of menarcheal status. It is important to recognize, however, that pre- and postmenarcheal girls of different chronological ages vary considerably in physical characteristics, for example premenarcheal girls 11 and 14 years of age and post-menarcheal girls 11 and 14 years of age (Malina, Bouchard, & Bar-Or, 2004).

Longitudinal data beginning at about 9 or 10 years of age, and that span at least five to six years (preferably a broader span) during adolescence, are required to derive age at peak height velocity. It is an indicator of maturational timing and is usually derived by mathematically modeling longitudinal height records for individual children. Other variables of interest include age at take-off of the spurt, and size and velocity of growth at take-off and peak. Modeling can be done for weight, other linear dimensions, and performance variables.

A method for predicting the time before or after peak height velocity, labeled *maturity offset,* has been developed (Mirwald, Baxter-Jones, Bailey, & Beunen, 2002). It requires age, height, weight, sitting height, and estimated leg length. Subtracting maturity offset from chronological age provides a prediction of age at peak height velocity. This protocol has increasingly been used as an indicator of maturity timing with athletes (Malina, Claessens, et al., 2006; Nurmi-Lawton et al., 2004; Sherar, Baxter-Jones, Faulkner, & Russell, 2007; Till, Cobley, O'Hara, Chapman, & Cooke, 2010) and is viewed as central to the long-term athlete development (LTAD) model. Accordingly,

> LTAD requires the identification of early, average, and late maturers in order to help design appropriate training and competition programs in relation to optimal trainability and readiness. The beginning of the growth spurt and the peak of the growth spurt are very significant in LTAD applications.... (Balyi, Cardinal, Higgs, Norris, & Way, 2005, p. 23)

Maturity offset is indicated for use in this context, although there is a major lack of empirical evidence to support some contentions of the LTAD model (see Ford et al., 2011).

Percentage of mature (adult) height attained at a given age is also a maturity indicator that has been used primarily in analyses of longitudinal data (Bielicki, Koniarek, & Malina, 1984; Nicolson & Hanley, 1953). Height of a youngster is expressed as a percentage of mature height, usually height at 18 years of age. Two 12-year-old boys may have the same height, but one has reached 85% and the other 90% of their respective adult heights. The boy who has attained 90% of adult height is closer to maturity and thus more mature than the other. Percentage of predicted mature height has been used in several studies of young athletes (e.g., Cumming et al., 2006; Malina, Cumming, Morano, Barron, & Miller, 2005; Malina, Morano, et al., 2006). The protocol predicts mature height from age, height, and weight of a child, and midparent height—the average of the heights of the biological parents (Khamis & Roche, 1994). Current height is expressed as a percentage of predicted mature height.

Although the maturity offset protocol and percentage of predicted mature height are being used increasingly in research with young athletes, they have not been extensively cross-validated with established maturity indicators (Malina, Coelho e Silva, Figueiredo, Carling, & Beunen, 2012; Malina, Dompier, Powell, Barron, & Moore, 2007). Predicted ages at peak height velocity (PHV) from maturity offset tend to have reduced standard deviations compared to estimates in longitudinal studies, which are usually about one year (Malina & Beunen, 1996; Malina, Bouchard, & Bar-Or, 2004). The offset and percentage mature height protocols are based on samples of European ancestry, so that application to other ethnic groups requires caution. Ethnic variation in proportions of sitting height and leg length is a potential concern with the maturity offset method (Malina, Bouchard, & Bar-Or, 2004).

Development

The development of behavioral competence proceeds simultaneously in the cognitive, social, emotional, and moral domains. The development of competence in movement skills is also an important behavioral domain, but is considered in a separate section of this chapter. The subsequent discussion highlights several general features of behavioral development. The specifics are beyond the scope of this chapter and can be found in general texts of developmental psychology, while several aspects of behavioral development are covered in depth in other chapters of this book. Of relevance to the focus of the volume, many youngsters begin participation in organized sport at about 5–6 years of age and continue in sport through adolescence; those working with youth should be aware of behavioral changes that occur across this interval.

The period between the preschool years and adolescence is often called middle childhood. It approximately spans formal entrance into school (first grade) to the onset of puberty (which, as indicated above, is variable in timing among individuals). Competence gradually develops in several behavioral domains during middle childhood. However, two features are especially significant (Levine, 1983). First, the child gradually refines his or her self-concept: Who am I? How do I feel about myself? Where do I fit in? and so on. Second, the child learns many skills, including cognitive-related skills such as reading, writing, and number manipulation, as well as interpersonal behaviors and relationships that underlie social, emotional, and moral competence: for example, sharing, cooperation, honesty, and sensitivity to others. In the development of behavioral competence, the child often evaluates himself or herself. They very often ask, for example, Am I doing OK? Do you still love me? Two primary sources of feedback in this self-evaluative process are adults—specifically parents, teachers, and coaches—and peers—their playmates and teammates. It is essential that adults working with children be aware of their developing sense of self and the ongoing process of self-evaluation.

It is during middle childhood that the peer group emerges as a source of support, criticism, and comparison in handling the many challenges associated with an emerging sense of behavioral competence. Peer group activities occur in many settings, and children have multiple peer groups, both formal, as in school, church, and organized sport, and informal, as in neighborhoods and playgrounds. The significance and strength of peer groups increase with age during middle childhood. The organized sport setting is a major source of peer group experiences for many children. This is rather obvious in team sports, but in highly individual sports such as diving, gymnastics, figure skating, and swimming, coaches need to be especially sensitive to the child's need for group affiliation and the need to develop a sense of the group.

Middle childhood is followed by adolescence. The transition into adolescence and from adolescence to adulthood is a period of major changes physically and behaviorally (Brooks-Gunn & Petersen, 1983; Montemayor, Adams, & Gullotta, 1990). The developmental tasks of adolescence are many, but three stand out. First, it is a period of physiological learning as the youngster copes with the physical and physiological changes associated with the growth spurt and sexual maturation. The youngster must learn to understand and accept these changes, to accept his or her body, and to adapt to masculine and feminine roles. A major concern of adolescents during this time is their physical appearance. Second, it is a period of new relationships with age peers. During middle childhood, peer groups were largely the same sex. During adolescence, youngsters develop relationships with age peers of both sexes, so that social acceptance is a major concern. And, third, it is a period of striving for independence. The youngsters strive for emotional independence from parents and other adults as they prepare for adult roles. Hence, it is a time of emotional peaks and valleys, of self-doubt, of changes in self-esteem, and of changing interests. Many youngsters experience a decline in self-esteem as they go through the developmental tasks of adolescence, especially during the transition from childhood into adolescence. It is no surprise that many youngsters drop out of sport between 12 and 14 years of age. The demands of normal adolescence may play a role in this decision.

The preceding is based largely on the American cultural context, which tends to emphasize the individual and individual achievements. Developmental demands for children and adolescents vary among cultures. Some cultures, for example, have distinct and even formal rituals associated with adolescence and puberty; there is no such cultural or traditional rite in the United States, Canada, and Europe. Adolescence in the US is a seemingly drawn out process and a time of confusion and insecurity for many youth as they strive for independence on the path to adulthood.

MOTOR COMPETENCE: DEVELOPMENT AND PERFORMANCE

The acquisition and refinement of skillful performance in a variety of movement activities is an important dimension of development that straddles the biological and behavioral domains. Movement activities are often viewed in terms of patterns and skills. Pattern refers to the basic elements of a specific movement behavior: walking, running, jumping, overhand throwing, kicking a stationary ball, and so on. Skill refers to accuracy, economy, and efficiency of movements composing a pattern. Allowing for individual differences in development, children learn to run, jump, throw, skip, hop, etc., but all do not perform these movements with the same skill.

Motor Development

Children develop competence in a variety of movement patterns during the preschool years and extending into middle childhood. They are the foundation for other skills, combinations of skills, and sport-specific skills. Movement patterns are broadly labeled as locomotor (walking, running, jumping, hopping, galloping, skipping), nonlocomotor (bending, twisting, reaching), projection (throwing, kicking, striking), and reception (catching, fielding). These labels are arbitrary; combinations of patterns compose most movements, for example running long jump; trapping, dribbling, and shooting in soccer; running for a vault in gymnastics.

Temporal, spatial, and sequential elements in the development of several movement patterns during childhood have been described and summarized as a sequence of stages from immature to mature form. Stages are to some extent arbitrary, as they are superimposed on an ongoing process of development that is not necessarily continuous. Inter- and intra-individual variations in rate of progress through the sequence of changes for each movement pattern are considerable, although this issue has not received much attention in the motor development literature. Some children may show relatively long periods of stability or minimal change followed by a burst of progress; others may regress to a less mature stage before progressing to a more advanced stage; and still others may show seemingly continuous development.

The development of eight fundamental movement patterns has been described for children in the mixed-longitudinal Motor Performance Study at Michigan State University (Haubenstricker, Branta, & Seefeldt, 1999; Seefeldt & Haubenstricker, 1982). Boys tend to attain each stage of overhand throwing and kicking a stationary ball earlier than girls, whereas girls tend to attain each stage of hopping and skipping earlier than boys, which may be related to perceptions of the cultural appropriateness of activities that involve these movement patterns. Other patterns (running, standing long jump, catching, striking) show a similarity between boys and girls, but there is a variation in ages at which mature stages are reached. Comparisons by age and sex were not reported for two other movement patterns, galloping and punting.

Variation in the duration of intervals between specific stages has not been systematically evaluated. Attainment of mastery of each stage of a movement pattern varies among individuals. Attainment of mastery of different movement patterns also varies within individuals. The methodology is also a source of variation: for example, specified changes from one stage to the next may be too great, stage demands may be too difficult, and the intervals between observations in a longitudinal series may be too short or too long. As with any set of discrete stages, interpolating between stages also presents analytical problems.

Pattern development during childhood can be addressed in the context of several questions, but two are relevant to the present discussion. Progress in the development of movement proficiency in early and middle childhood is related to growth and maturation. Basic movement patterns develop during the first seven or eight years of life. The processes are dependent, in part, upon genotype, maturation of the neuromuscular system, residual effects of prior movement experiences, and current movement experiences including practice and learning. The processes are also dependent upon growth, which is often overlooked. During this interval, height and weight increase, weight-for-height (body mass index) and subcutaneous fatness decrease over five years and then increase, and proportions change, specifically relative lengthening of the extremities (Malina, Bouchard, & Bar-Or, 2004). The increase in the body mass index at 5–6–7 years of age is labeled as the adiposity rebound. An early rebound is related to later overweight and obesity (Rolland-Cachera et al., 1987), but its potential implications for motor development have not been addressed. Implications of changing body proportions for the changing position of the center of gravity are obvious.

The second context relates to the transition from basic movement patterns to more complex patterns and skills. In addition to genotype, growth, and neuromuscular maturation, the transition probably depends on earlier experiences, opportunities for movement, quality of instruction and practice, and other factors. A "proficiency barrier" during the transition has been hypothesized (Seefeldt, 1980). The barrier implies a critical level of competence, above which a youngster is likely to apply the skills in games and sports, and below which the youngster will not be involved. If a proficiency barrier exists, when does it emerge? It is likely to emerge in middle childhood when basic movement patterns and skills should be reasonably well in place. This is also the time when children often are enrolled in sport programs (although some parents enroll their children in developmental programs at 3–4 years; Malina, 2010). What are the correlates of the barrier? Can the barrier be remedied with appropriate instruction and practice? Do teachers/coaches of children entering a sport have sufficient understanding of developmental sequences and knowledge of how to provide an environment in which developing movement patterns can be nurtured and improved? What is the influence of specific instruction, practice, and adult modeling and/or entry into a sport on the developmental progress and integration of movement patterns into more complex sequences?

Motor Performance

Proficiency in basic movements is accompanied by improved levels of performance, which can usually be quantified in tasks done under specified conditions: for example, distance or height jumped (power), distance a ball is thrown (power), time elapsed in completing a 30m dash (speed) or a shuttle run (speed and agility), number of sit-ups performed in 20 seconds (abdominal strength), and force expressed against a fixed resistance (strength). Performances, on average, improve with age during childhood, and the overlap between sexes is considerable. With the onset of adolescence, performances of girls improve to about 13–14 years of age and then level off or improve only slightly, while those of boys accelerate sharply; sex differences are thus magnified (Malina, Bouchard, & Bar-Or, 2004).

Performances of boys show well-defined growth spurts in strength and power items that show peak gains, on average, after peak height velocity. On the other hand, speed of arm movement, running speed and agility, and lower back flexibility show peak gains in boys, on average, before peak height velocity (Beunen et al., 1988; Malina, Bouchard, & Bar-Or, 2004). The timing of peak gains in strength and power appear to be coincident with those for body mass and muscle mass. The earlier spurts for running speed and lower back flexibility may be related to growth of the lower extremities, which experience their adolescent spurt before that of the trunk. Boys have relatively longer legs early in the adolescent spurt, which may influence running speed and lower trunk flexibility.

Data relating performances of girls to the adolescent spurt are not extensive. Girls show adolescent spurts in static strength and power after maximum growth in height. The magnitude of the growth spurt in arm strength in girls, however, is only about one-half of the maximum gain in boys. Presently available data for flexibility and speed tasks contrast the trends for boys in that both show maximum gains after PHV in girls. When performances of girls are related to time before and after menarche, trends are not consistent (Malina, Bouchard, & Bar-Or, 2004). Menarche is a late maturational event and major gains in growth and performance have already occurred.

Individual differences in growth and maturity status influence performance; contributions of size and maturity to performance have been addressed with regression analysis. Among children 7–12 years of age, the variances in static strength (grip, push, pull), standing long jump, dash, and ball throw explained by chronological age and skeletal age, individually or in combination with height and weight, ranged from 4% to 46% in boys and 7% to 41% in girls (Katzmarzyk, Malina, & Beunen, 1997). The strongest predictor of strength was body weight. The influence of skeletal age on strength was expressed mainly through body size, whereas it had a more direct influence on the jump, run, and throw. In a similar analysis of Belgian boys 12–19 years, chronological age and skeletal age per se, or in combination with height and weight, explained small percentages of variation in several performance tasks (<17%), but a greater percentage of variance (33% to 58%) in static strength (Beunen, Ostyn, Simons, Renson, & Van Gerven, 1981). The largest percentages of variance in performances accounted for by chronological age, skeletal age, and body size occurred at 14 and 15 years. Chronological age, skeletal age, stature, and weight are all highly interrelated at these ages, so it is difficult to partition specific effects of maturation per se on strength and performance. A corresponding study of Belgian girls ages 6–16 years indicated a significant effect of skeletal age in interaction with body size on explained variance (up to 33%) in static strength, but little effect (<10%) on other performances (Beunen et al., 1997). With the exception of strength in adolescent boys, the evidence indicates that more than one-half of the variance in performances was not accounted for by chronological age, skeletal age, height, or weight. By inference, other factors influence performances of youth.

An alternative approach to maturity effects on performance is by comparing youth at the extremes of the maturation continuum. Youth are classified as late (delayed for chronological age), on time (average for chronological age), and early (advanced for chronological age) maturing. Height and weight show a gradient of early > on time > late during childhood and adolescence in both sexes; differences are most marked about the time of maximal growth in height and weight. In late adolescence, height differences among maturity groups are eliminated, while those for weight persist. The gradient of early > on time > late is also apparent in static and functional strength (arm pull, flexed arm hang), power (vertical and standing long jumps), and running speed in adolescent boys, but corresponding comparisons in girls indicate negligible differences (Malina, Bouchard, & Bar-Or, 2004). Data addressing variation in performance at the extremes of maturity during childhood are limited.

TRAINABILITY OF MOVEMENT SKILLS

Differential responsiveness of youth (trainability) to instructional, practice, and/or training programs at different ages is implicit in talent identification and development programs for sport (for example, Balyi et al., 2005; Bompa, 1985, 1995; Hartley, 1988; Petiot, Salmela, & Hoshizaki, 1987). The responsiveness of children and adolescents to training programs has been addressed primarily in the context of muscular strength (Blimkie & Sale, 1998; Malina, 2006; Sale, 1989) and aerobic capacity (Armstrong & Barker, 2011; Baquet, van Praagh, & Berthoin, 2003; Pfeiffer, Lobelo, Ward, & Pate, 2008). The responsiveness of youth to instructional practice and/or training programs for the development of movement skills in general and sport-specific skills has been less extensively studied.

Trainability of movement skills is related to the concept of readiness or the ability to successfully handle the demands of a structured learning situation, for example, specific instruction and practice of sport skills. The concept is implicit in youth sport, specifically the readiness of a child to handle the demands of a sport. Broadly speaking, readiness can be viewed as the match and/or interaction between two components—the characteristics of the child and the demands of the setting. Characteristics of the child include growth (size attained, physique, body composition), maturation (timing and tempo), and development (cognitive, social, emotional, motor behaviors). Demands of the setting include the instructional and practice situation, style and quality of teaching/coaching, individual or group activity, and specific skills, among others.

Trainability is also related to the concept of critical periods or specific intervals during which a youngster may be maximally sensitive to environmental influences, both positive and negative, in the development of movement behaviors and skills. Central to critical periods are two assumptions: changes occur rapidly, and organizational processes can be modified more effectively during the intervals (Bornstein, 1989; Scott, 1986). Critical periods may represent times of maximal readiness. However, evidence for critical periods in the development of motor and sport-specific skills is limited and not convincing (Anderson, 2002; Haubenstricker & Seefeldt, 2002).

Programs of talent identification and development often include an initial phase beginning at about 5–7 years (and perhaps earlier) for artistic gymnastics, figure skating, and diving. The initial phase emphasizes general skill development, especially overall dexterity and coordination, and balance between general and sport-specific skills. Increased emphasis on sport-specific skills occurs during the transition into adolescence (about 9–10 years in girls). Procedures for other sports vary but the underlying principles are similar. Specialization generally occurs in adolescence. Although individual differences in maturation are noted, little specific information is offered on how programs address the issue.

The theoretical framework of expert performance (Ericsson, 2003; Ericsson, Krampe, & Tesch-Römer, 1993), with a focus on deliberate practice over an extended period, emphasizes the quality of instruction and practice, as well as the ability of the individual to organize specific knowledge. The accumulation of experience is ultimately represented in the motor and cognitive neural substrates. Public discussion of this model may have contributed to an apparent increase in sport specialization at relatively early ages (Malina, 2010).

The primacy of explicit instruction and supervised practice, with corrections as necessary, in the expertise model represents formal learning. Many sport activities of youth in the not-too-distant past, and at present in many parts of the developing world, were/are carried out in informal settings under the generic label street games. They represent what is now labeled deliberate play (Côté, 1999). Street games involve frequent repetitions but not under the eye of a coach; trial and error; experimentation and repetition; variable settings; and exposure to different conditions, skills, and rules. Sport and sport-related skills are learned without awareness or explicit knowledge of the skills. Acquisition of skills under such circumstances represents informal or implicit learning (Cleermans, Destrebecqz, & Boyer, 1998). Skills learned informally may be adaptable to the variety of sports and sport circumstances. Research on implicit learning in sport is in its infancy but is expanding (see Masters, van der Kamp, and Capio, Chapter 3 in this text).

The responsiveness of youth to sport instruction and practice aimed at the development of proficiency in general as well as sport-specific skills obviously needs further study (Malina, 2008). The process is complex. Characteristics of the learner need to be included in the equation, especially individual differences in growth, maturation, and behavior. Although beyond the scope of this chapter, the trainability of motor skills, as well as responsiveness to strength and aerobic training programs, has a significant genotypic component (Bouchard, Malina, & Pérusse, 1997; Peeters, Thomis, Beunen, & Malina, 2009).

GROWTH AND MATURATION OF YOUNG ATHLETES

Trends in growth, maturation, and motor performance considered in the preceding sections characterize the general population. Applications to young athletes and talent development will be considered subsequently. Sport by its nature is exclusive. Definition and classification of sport participants as athletes are variable so that sampling is a major issue. Samples of athletes in childhood and early adolescence are very different from those in late adolescence, and even the latter can range from general participants to the relatively few select, elite, or junior national players.

Size Attained

Body size can influence self- and/or coach-selection for a sport. Strength and power advantages associated with earlier maturation are additional factors that may attract boys to sports and influence success and opportunity for selection. In contrast, maturity-associated variation in strength and power is not as clearly delineated in girls.

Athletes of both sexes and in most sports have, on the average, heights that equal or exceed reference medians. Gymnastics is the only sport that presents a profile of short height in both sexes. Figure skaters of both sexes also present shorter heights, although data are less extensive. Given the wide range of normal variation among individuals and in the timing and tempo of maturation, there are exceptions to the trends. Athletes also tend to have body weights that, on average, equal or exceed reference medians, but gymnasts, figure skaters, and ballet dancers of both sexes consistently show lighter weights. Gymnasts and figure skaters have appropriate weights for their heights, while female ballet dancers and distance runners of both sexes tend to have lower weights for their heights (Malina, 1994, 1998; Malina & Rogol, 2011).

Body Composition

Given the generally negative influence of elevated levels of fatness on performances in which the body is moved or projected through space (runs, jumps, vaults), studies of body composition often focus on the estimated percentage of body weight that is composed of body fat (percent fat). Athletes 9–18 years of age tend to have a lower percent fat than nonathletes of the same chronological age, but there is considerable overlap between athletes and the reference, more so in males than females (Malina & Geithner, 2011). Few samples of female athletes have a percent fat that approximates the reference, but higher estimates are typically observed in adolescents in throwing events (track and field). Estimates of percent fat also overlap considerably among athletes in different sports, but there is variability within a sport.

Bone mineral is the component of fat-free mass that is currently receiving major attention in athletes. Data consistently indicate higher bone mineral content and density in athletes of both sexes compared to youth in general (Malina & Geithner, 2011).

Biological Maturation

Trends in body size are related, in part, to variation in biological maturation. Skeletal age is the only maturity indicator that can be used in childhood and adolescence. Data for skeletal age in athletes less than 10 years of age are limited except for artistic gymnasts. Male gymnasts, swimmers, track athletes, and soccer and ice hockey players less than 10 years of age present skeletal and chronological ages that are, on average, equivalent. Late and early maturing boys are about equally represented among male athletes in several team and individual sports at 10–11 years of age. With increasing age during adolescence, the numbers of late maturing athletes decline, while those of early maturing and skeletally mature athletes increase. Adolescent gymnasts are the single exception; they have, on average, skeletal ages that lag behind their chronological ages (Malina, 1994, 2011).

Skeletal age data for female athletes are available primarily for artistic gymnasts and swimmers, with information more variably available for girls in other sports. Late and early maturing girls are about equally represented among artistic gymnasts and swimmers less than 10 years of age, and mean skeletal ages approximate chronological ages. During adolescence, girls late and on time in skeletal maturation dominate samples of gymnasts (especially the elite), while early maturing girls are a minority. Swimmers less than 14 years of age tend to be on time in skeletal age and samples include several more early than late maturers. At 14–15 years, equal numbers of swimmers are on time or mature, while most swimmers 16–17 years are skeletally mature (Malina, 2011).

Comparative data on the pubertal status of athletes in several sports are difficult to interpret largely due to the limitations of pubertal stages and lack of control for chronological age in analyses. The indicator of sexual maturation that has received most attention is age at menarche. Only prospective and status quo data deal with youth. Prospective data for athletes followed from prepuberty through puberty are limited to small, select samples; a potentially confounding issue is selective drop-out or exclusion. Status quo data for athletes provide sample estimates, and samples characteristically include athletes of variable skill levels at younger ages and more select athletes at older ages, which can bias median estimates. Nevertheless, the majority of mean/median ages at menarche for adolescent athletes in prospective and status quo samples approximate population averages, while artistic gymnasts, figure skaters, and ballet dancers are later maturing (Malina, 1983, 1998; Malina, Bouchard, & Bar-Or, 2004). Other data for athletes are retrospective and based on samples of mature (postmenarcheal) late adolescent and adult athletes, and as such have limited applicability to younger athletes.

MOTOR PERFORMANCE OF YOUNG ATHLETES

The visibility of talented young athletes in the media—for example female artistic gymnasts and figure skaters, female and male divers, and Little League baseball players, among others—highlights their performance skills. Of interest is how do young athletes compare to the general population in standard tests used in surveys or developmental programs? Do they show the same trends with age and sex? How do performances of young male and female athletes in the same sport compare?

Studies of young athletes often include measures of power (vertical jump, standing long jump), speed (sprints), flexibility (most often sit and reach), abdominal muscular strength and endurance (sit-ups), agility (shuttle run, quadrant jump), and static strength (grip), among others. Several studies including performance measures are highlighted in the subsequent discussion.

Data are more available for athletes in individual sports. Among team sports, performances of youth soccer players have been studied more often and also include tests of skills specific to the sport.

Athletes and the General Population

Compared to reference medians of the Michigan State University Motor Performance Study (Haubenstricker et al., 1999), elite youth distance runners (10K+) in Michigan were more flexible (sit and reach) from 10–17 years and had greater upper body functional strength (bent arm hang). Mean performances in the latter changed only slightly with age in boys, but declined in girls. Performances of runners of both sexes on the vertical and standing long jumps were similar to the respective reference between 10 and ~14 years and were below the reference in later adolescence. Jumping performances of boys increased across the age range while those of girls were rather stable after 14 years (Eisenmann & Malina, 2003).

Performance protocols for the vertical jump and sit and reach of Junior Olympic divers were the same as the Michigan State University study (Malina, 2007b). Divers of both sexes performed, on average, better than the reference in both tasks from 10–18 years. Similarly, boys and girls 11–15 years training in Polish sports schools (primarily in athletics) performed better than a national sample of youth in grip strength and standing long jump (Malina, Ignasiak, et al., 2011; Malina, Rożek, et al., 2012).

Performances of Belgian soccer players 12–15 years classified by competitive level as elite (1st and 2nd division clubs), subelite (3rd and 4th division clubs), and nonelite (regional teams) (Vaeyens et al., 2006) were compared to reference medians for Belgian (Flemish) boys (Steens, 2006). Items included sit and reach, standing long jump, sit-ups, flexed arm hang, and agility and endurance shuttle runs. On average, elite players performed better than the reference in all tasks. The subelite also performed better except in the sit and reach. The nonelite were more variable; they performed better on the agility and endurance shuttle runs and bent arm hang, but did not consistently differ from the reference in sit and reach, standing long jump, and sit-ups. Contrasts between players and reference were more marked at 14–15 than 12–13 years, which may reflect maturity differences between samples.

Limiting the comparisons to soccer players, the gradient for all performances was elite > subelite > nonelite. The gradient was most marked for the endurance shuttle run, standing long jump, and bent arm hang. Differences between the subelite and nonelite were small for the agility shuttle run. For sit-ups and sit and reach, differences among players by competitive level were more apparent at 14–15 than 11–12 years. In contrast, performance differences in four soccer skills (dribbling, lobbing, juggling, shooting) among players by competitive level were neither large nor consistent (Vaeyens et al., 2006).

Sex Differences Among Athletes in the Same Sport

Comparisons of male and female athletes participating in the same sports present interesting trends. Among elite youth distance runners (Eisenmann & Malina, 2003), males performed better in the bent arm hang and sit-ups, while females performed better in the sit and reach from 10–16 years. Sex differences in a figure-8 run (agility) and standing long and vertical jumps were negligible between 10–13 years; subsequently, performances of females did not change appreciably while those of males improved into later adolescence. The quadrant jump (agility), in contrast, showed negligible sex differences from 10–16 years.

Performances on several tests were compared between male and female Junior Olympic divers in three competitive age groups, < 13, 14–15, and 16–18 years (Malina, Geithner, O'Brien, & Tan, 2005). Within each age group, males and females did not differ in sit-ups and quadrant jump, males performed better in the vertical jump and females performed better in the sit and reach. Performances in a one kg medicine ball throw from a seated position did not differ between sexes in the two younger age groups, but were better in males 16–18 years.

Among participants in track and field sport schools in Poland, males performed better than females in grip strength, standing long jump, 2kg medicine ball throw from a standing position, and 20m sprint, but differences were more marked in athletes 14–15 years than 11–13 years (Malina et al., 2010). Results were generally similar in specific disciplines, though numbers of participants were smaller. The sex differences at 14–15 years reflected to a large extent the male adolescent growth spurt in body size, muscle mass, strength, and power.

Although data are limited, young athletes in the same sports or same events within a sport do not differ, on average, in motor performance during childhood. Males tend to perform better, on average, on tests of strength and power. Tests of flexibility tend to favor females, while sex differences in a test of coordination showed negligible differences.

Variation Between Sports

Studies of young athletes in different sports generally do not include the same test protocols. In the two studies of youth distance runners (Eisenmann & Malina, 2003) and divers (Malina, Cumming, et al., 2005) of both sexes, three performance items had the same protocol and thus permitted a comparison between sports. Within each sex, divers performed better than runners in flexibility (sit and reach) and power (vertical jump), while runners performed better in the test of coordination (quadrant jump).

Among Polish female track and field athletes 11–15 years, participants in sprints, middle distance and distance runs, jumps, and general athletics did not differ in grip strength, standing long jump, 2kg medicine ball throw, or 20m sprint (Malina, Ignasiak, et al., 2011). The track and field athletes as a group performed better in the standing long jump and 20m sprint compared to participants in primarily team sports. The groups did not differ in the medicine ball throw, while team sport participants were stronger (Malina, Ignasiak, et al., 2011).

Results were generally similar for male track and field athletes by discipline and between athletes in several team sports (Malina, Rożek, et al., 2011). Performances in the standing long jump and 20m sprint did not differ among track and field disciplines, and only two post hoc comparisons were significant for grip strength and medicine ball throw. Among team sport athletes, a combined sample of handball and volleyball players performed better in the medicine ball throw than soccer players; the other three items did not differ among the basketball, soccer, handball plus volleyball, or individual sport participants. The combined sample of track and field athletes performed better in the 20m sprint and jump than the combined sample of athletes in other sports, while grip strength and medicine ball throw did not differ (Malina, Rożek, et al., 2011).

It is possible that similar training protocols and perhaps selection criteria function to re-duce the magnitude of sex differences in performances in young athletes, especially the more elite. An exception is the male adolescent spurts in muscle mass, specifically upper body mus-culature, strength, and power that contribute to male performance advantages in these tasks.

MATURITY-ASSOCIATED VARIATION AMONG ATHLETES

The issue of maturity-associated variation in performances of young athletes has been ad-dressed primarily in soccer players. In the general population, performances in static and functional strength, power, and speed tasks show a maturity gradient of early > on time > late (Malina, Bouchard, & Bar-Or, 2004). Portuguese players 11–12 years of contrasting maturity status, however, did not differ in speed (sprint), agility (shuttle run), power (counter movement jump), and four soccer skills (ball control, dribbling, passing, shooting); only aerobic capacity (endurance shuttle run) differed, late > on time = early. Results were identical in players 13–14 years of age, with one exception: for the jump, early > on time > late (Figueiredo, Gonçalves, Coelho e Silva, & Malina, 2009a). Among elite French U-14 players, the vertical jump, 40m dash, anaerobic power, and strength of the preferred and nonpreferred legs differed among maturity groups, early > on time > late; the endurance shuttle run did not differ among groups (Carling, Le Gall, & Malina, 2012).

Multiple linear regressions were also used to estimate the relative contributions of chrono-logical age, skeletal age, stage of pubic hair, body size, adiposity, and years of training to performances and soccer skills in Portuguese players 11–15 years old (Figueiredo, Coelho e Silva, & Malina, 2011; Malina, Cumming, Kontos, et al., 2005; Malina, Eisenmann, Cumming, Ribeiro, & Aroso, 2004; Malina, Ribeiro, Aroso, & Cumming, 2007). Maturity status interacted with training history, body size, and/or adiposity to explain between 21% and 58% of varianc-es in tests speed, power, agility, and endurance. Maturity status was a more relevant predictor among players 13–15 years. Sport-specific skills, in contrast, were largely independent of the predictors that accounted for < 25% of the variance.

Other factors influence performances of athletes as in the general population. Individual differences in timing and tempo of maturation of neural control and perceptual-cognitive skills during adolescence, individual differences in responsiveness to instruction and training, and coach-athlete interactions are potential sources of variation, especially in sport-specific skills. Studies should be extended beyond growth and maturation to include perceptual-cognitive and behavioral characteristics of players and characteristics of coaches and training environ-ments. Conversely, studies of perceptual-cognitive and behavioral characteristics of young athletes should be extended to include indicators of physical growth and biological variation as potential covariates.

Corresponding data addressing maturity-associated variation in performances of adolescent female athletes are limited. Pre- and postmenarcheal 13-year-old athletes in the Polish sports schools did not differ in grip strength, standing long jump, 20m sprint, or medicine ball throw, while late and average plus early maturing 14–15 year old athletes differed in grip strength but not in the standing long jump, sprint, or medicine ball throw (Malina, Ignasiak, et al., 2011).

RELATIVE AGE EFFECT

The overrepresentation of players born in the first quarter of a selection year, or the relative age effect, is of interest in discussion of youth sport (see MacDonald and Baker, Chapter 12, in this text). Discussions of the relative age effect often invoke size variation within a single chronological year as a potential explanatory factor. Size per se may be a factor affecting success at young age levels when strength, speed, and power are often a premium, and may bring successful players to the attention of coaches. The success, in turn, may enhance opportunities for special attention, better coaching, and so on. As noted, however, size is confounded by variation in biological maturation. Behavioral characteristics associated with variation in size and maturation merit further consideration (Cumming, Standage, & Malina, 2004).

Data dealing with the relative age effect generally focus on records of birthdates within a selection year for relatively large samples. Field studies of young athletes, on the other hand, are generally based on relatively small samples, but may provide insights. Among 62 soccer players 11 years of age born in 1992 and observed in December 2003, skeletal age, body size, adiposity, speed, power, agility, endurance, and sport-specific skills did not differ by birth quarter. Similar results were noted among 50 players 13 years of age born in 1990 and observed in April 2004 (Figueiredo, Coelho e Silva, & Malina, in press). Consistent with the preceding, skeletal age, body size, percent fat, endurance, anaerobic power, vertical jump, speed, and strength did not differ by birth quarter among elite U-14 French soccer players (Carling, Le Gall, Reilly, & Williams, 2009). Height and weight, endurance, speed, power, and a composite soccer skill score showed no consistent trend from oldest to youngest among soccer players 14.0 to 14.99 years grouped by quartile of chronological age (Malina, Ribeiro, et al., 2007).

Studies of the relative age effect in performances of young athletes should be expanded to include indicators of biological maturation, growth status, functional performances, skills, and player behaviors, and perhaps more importantly, characteristics of development programs in specific sports.

SELECTION AND EXCLUSION

The issue of dropouts is also topic of discussion in youth sports, but systematic evaluations of those who drop out are rarely done. Changing interests are often indicated by youth in the United States (Ewing & Seefeldt, 1989), Portugal (Coelho e Silva et al., 2009), and Mexico (Siegel et al., 2009) as a primary reason for dropping out of sport. It is not known if the changing interests include interest in other sports. In addition to changing interests, systematic exclusion (cutting) as selection and competitive processes become more rigorous is an additional factor.

This topic has received some attention in artistic gymnastics. Among small samples of elite Polish gymnasts, females (n = 5) and males (n = 6) who persisted differed from those who dropped out (n = 4 females, 8 males) (Ziemilska, 1981). Girls dropped out between 14.5 and 15.5 years while boys dropped out between 13.5 and 15.0 years. Girls who persisted were shorter from 12–15 years than dropouts, but the groups did not differ in height at 16–17 years; in contrast, those who persisted were lighter through the age range. Among males, those who persisted were shorter than dropouts from 12–18 years, but the groups did not consistently differ in body weight. Gymnasts who persisted and those who dropped out also differed in ages at peak height velocity (Malina, 1999). Similar results were noted in elite Swiss female gymnasts (Tönz, Stronski, & Gmeiner, 1990). Dropouts were taller and heavier, average in skeletal age at the start of training, and earlier in menarche. Among Belgian female gymnasts, dropouts were chronologically older and more advanced in skeletal maturation (Claessens & Lefevre, 1998). Samples of artistic gymnasts in childhood, the transition into adolescence, and early adolescence are clearly quite different from samples in later adolescence. The sport appears to favor the shorter and later-maturing individual.

In contrast, soccer apparently excludes late maturing boys and favors biologically average and early maturing boys during the transition into and through adolescence (Malina, 2011). This may reflect the selection (self, coach), differential success of boys advanced in maturity status, nature of the game (more physical contact in older age groups), or some combination of these and other factors. It is also possible that late maturing boys selectively drop out.

Characteristics of youth players associated with dropping out or moving up in soccer have not been systematically addressed. Baseline growth, maturation, functional performances, and sport-specific skills of Portuguese players at 11–12 ($n = 87$) and 13–14 ($n = 72$) years were compared among those who at follow-up two years later had discontinued participation in the sport (dropout), continued at the same level (club player), or moved to a higher level (elite). The latter were selected for the regional team or by elite clubs that have national strategies for talent identification and development; transfer to a different club requires approval of both the sending and receiving clubs (Figueiredo, Gonçalves, Coelho e Silva, & Malina, 2009b). Among players 11–12 years at baseline, a gradient of elite ($n = 12$) > club ($n = 54$) > dropout ($n = 21$) was suggested for size, speed, power, agility, and endurance, although differences among groups were not consistent. Elite players performed better in only two of four skills, dribbling and ball control. The gradient of elite ($n = 21$) > club ($n = 36$) > dropout ($n = 21$) was more clearly defined among players 13–14 years at baseline. Elite players were older, more advanced in skeletal and sexual maturation, larger in body size, and performed better in functional tests and three skills than club players and dropouts. The results suggest a potentially important role for growth, maturity status, and performance as factors in attrition, persistence, and moving up in youth soccer.

The preceding studies focus primarily on physical and functional characteristics of youth who drop out and youth who persist in a sport. Associated behavioral characteristics are not often considered. Among female gymnasts, the primary factor that differentiated those who continued from those who dropped out was chronological age; dropouts were significantly older (Lindner, Caine, & Johns, 1991). These authors suggested that "social and psychological factors" associated with older ages in adolescent girls were the primary factors in discontinuing participation, though data were not presented.

Dropouts from competitive swimming (17.6 ± 4.1 years) and youth currently involved in the sport (18.7 ± 6.6 years) were compared on a variety of psychosocial and sport-specific developmental factors (Fraser-Thomas, Côté, & Deakin, 2008). Data were obtained with structure retrospective interviews. Samples were matched by gender (21 females, 4 males in each group), years of competitive swimming, competitive level (regional, provincial, national), familial characteristics, and urban or rural residence. Dropouts discontinued training and competition within the three years prior to the study. Currently active swimmers were taller (168.7 ± 7.4cm) than dropouts (164.1 ± 8.1cm), but the groups did not differ in body weight. By inference, at the time of study, the dropouts had, on average, more weight-for-height than currently active swimmers. Compared to currently active swimmers, dropouts began training and reached *top club* status earlier, had fewer extracurricular activities, and spent less time in unstructured play swimming time, specifically at younger ages. Dropouts also experienced less one-on-one coach time than active swimmers. On the other hand, several psychosocial factors related to family support and pressures, peer and sibling influences, and coach pressures did not differ between dropouts and active swimmers. Of interest, parents of dropouts were more likely to have been successful athletes as youngsters (Fraser-Thomas et al., 2008).

Available data on dropouts are limited to relatively few sports and by different methodological approaches. Nevertheless, the issue of dropping out and persisting in a sport is more complicated than meets the eye. The limited data suggest the potential relevance of physical growth, biological maturation, performance, and behavioral characteristics of the young athlete, and also the home and sport environments. There is obviously a need to extend studies to a variety of sports, as well as to youth athletes at different developmental levels within a sport. It would also be interesting to compare youth who voluntarily dropped out with those who were systematically excluded by a specific sport (cut).

CONCLUSION

The acquisition and refinement of skillful performance in a variety of movement activities, is an important dimension of development that straddles the biological and behavioral domains. Development of movement patterns for several basic skills has been reasonably well described, although factors that influence the processes have not been systematically considered. These include earlier experiences and opportunities, quality of instruction and practice, and individual differences in physical growth, biological maturation, and behavioral development. Genotype has been implicated in the development of movement skills, but data are relatively limited.

The transition from basic movement patterns to more complex sports skills is a different issue that has not been studied in depth. It is generally assumed that movement patterns and skills associated with specific sports can be refined and improved with appropriate instruction and practice. There is, however, relatively little systematic information on the role of specific instruction and practice in the improvement of specific sports skills at young ages. Evidence from studies of expertise, including on elite athletes, emphasizes the importance of early exposure and deliberate practice. The expertise data are limited to relatively few sports. Systematic data addressing the role of developmental play in the development of movement patterns and sports skills are also limited.

In contrast to the development and refinement of sports skills in young athletes, relatively more is known about their physical growth and biological maturation, and general physical fitness and performance. There is a need for research that systematically addresses the interactions of biological growth and maturation, and behavioral development, in the refinement of sport skills and related performances in young athletes. Issues related to physical growth, biological maturation, and behavioral development, and their interactions, also need systematic consideration in studies of selection and exclusion (dropout) in youth sports and of the relative age effect among young athletes.

REFERENCES

Anderson, D. I. (2002). Do critical periods determine when to initiate sport skill training? In F. L. Smoll & R. E. Smith (Eds.), *Children and youth in sport: A biopsychosocial perspective* (2nd ed.) (pp. 105–148). Dubuque, IA: Kendall/Hunt.

Armstrong, N., & Barker, A. R. (2011). Endurance training and elite young athletes. *Medicine and Sport Science, 56,* 59–83.

Baquet, G., van Praagh, E., & Berthoin, S. (2003). Endurance training and aerobic fitness in young people. *Sports Medicine, 33*(15), 1127–1143.

Balyi, I., Cardinal, C., Higgs. C., Norris, S., & Way, R. (2005). Canadian sport for life: Long-term athlete development resource paper V2. Vancouver, British Columbia: Canadian Sport Centres. Retrieved from http://www.canadiansportforlife.ca/default.aspx?PageID=1076&LangID=en

Beunen, G. P., Rogol, A. D., & Malina, R. M. (2006). Indicators of biological maturation and secular changes in biological maturation. *Food and Nutrition Bulletin, 27*(4), S244–S256.

Beunen, G. P., Ostyn, M., Simons, J., Renson, R., & Van Gerven, D. (1981). Chronological and biological age as related to physical fitness in boys 12 to 19 years. *Annals of Human Biology, 8*(4), 321–331.

Beunen, G. P., Malina, R. M., Van't Hof, M. A., Simons, J., Ostyn, M., Renson, R., & Van Gerven, D. (1988). *Adolescent growth and motor performance: A longitudinal study of Belgian boys.* Champaign, IL: Human Kinetics.

Beunen, G. P., Malina, R. M., Lefevre, J., Claessens, A. L., Renson, R., Kanden Eynde, B., Vanreusel, B., & Simons, J. (1997). Skeletal maturation, somatic growth and physical fitness in girls 6–16 years of age. *International Journal of Sports Medicine, 18*(6), 413–419.

Bielicki, T., Koniarek, J., & Malina, R. M. (1984). Interrelationships among certain measures of growth and maturation rate in boys during adolescence. *Annals of Human Biology, 11*(3), 201–210.

Blimkie, C. J., & Sale, D. G. (1998). Strength development and trainability during childhood. In E. Van Praagh (Ed.), *Pediatric anaerobic performance* (pp. 193–224). Champaign, IL: Human Kinetics.

Bompa, T. O. (1985). *Talent identification. Sports science periodical on research and technology in sport—Physical testing GN-1.* Ottawa, Canada: The Coaching Association of Canada.

Bompa, T. O. (1995). *From childhood to champion athlete.* Toronto, Canada: Veritas Publishing.

Bornstein, M. H. (1989). Sensitive periods in development: Structural characteristics and causal interpretations. *Psychological Bulletin, 105*(2), 1–19.

Bouchard, C., Malina, R. M., & Pérusse, L. (1997). *Genetics of fitness and physical performance.* Champaign, IL: Human Kinetics.

Brooks-Gunn, J., & Petersen, A. C. (1983). *Girls at puberty: Biological and psychosocial perspectives.* New York, NY: Plenum.

Carling, C., Le Gall, F., & Malina, R. M. (2012). Body size, skeletal maturity and functional characteristics of elite U-14 academy soccer players between 1992 and 2003. *Journal of Sports Sciences,* in press.

Carling, C., Le Gall, F., Reilly, T., & Williams, A. M. (2009). Do anthropometric and fitness characteristics vary according to birth date distribution in elite youth academy soccer players? *Scandinavian Journal of Medicine and Science in Sports, 19*(1), 3–9.

Claessens, A. L., & Lefevre, J. (1998). Morphological and performance characteristics as drop-out indicators in female gymnasts. *Journal of Sports Medicine and Physical Fitness, 38*(4), 305–309.

Cleeremans, A., Destrebecqz, A., & Boyer, M. (1998). Implicit learning: News from the front. *Trends in Cognitive Sciences, 2*(10), 406–416.

Coelho e Silva, M. J., Sobral, F., & Malina, R. M. (2009). Motivation for sport in Portuguese youth–biological and social dimensions. In M. J. Coelho e Silva, A. J. Figueiredo, M. T. Elferink-Gemser, & R. M. Malina (Eds.), *Youth sports: Participation, trainability and readiness* (pp. 49–61). Coimbra, Portugal: University of Coimbra Press.

Côté, J. (1999). The influence of the family in the development of talent in sport. *The Sport Psychologist, 13,* 395–417.

Cumming, S. P., Standage, M., & Malina, R. M. (2004). Youth soccer: A biocultural perspective. In M. J. Coelho e Silva & R. M. Malina (Eds.), *Children and youth in organized sport* (pp. 209–221). Coimbra, Portugal: University of Coimbra Press.

Cumming, S. P., Standage, M., Gillison, F., & Malina, R. M. (2008). Sex differences in exercise behavior during adolescence: Is biological maturation a confounding factor? *Journal of Adolescent Health, 42*(5), 480–485.

Cumming, S. P., Battista, R. A., Standage, M., Ewing, M. E., & Malina, R. M. (2006). Estimated maturity status and perceptions of adult autonomy support in youth soccer players. *Journal of Sports Sciences, 24*(10), 1039–1046.

Cumming, S. P., Eisenmann, J. C., Smoll, F. L., Smith, R. E., & Malina, R. M. (2005). Body size and perceptions of coaching behaviors by adolescent female athletes. *Psychology of Sport and Exercise, 6*(6), 693–705.

Cumming, S. P., Standage, M., Loney, T., Gammon, C., Neville, H., Sherar, L. B., & Malina, R. M. (2011). The mediating role of physical self-concept on relations between biological maturity status and physical activity in adolescent females. *Journal of Adolescence, 34*(3), 465–473.

Eisenmann, J. C., & Malina, R. M. (2003). Age- and sex-associated variation in neuromuscular capacities of adolescent distance runners. *Journal of Sports Sciences, 21*(7), 551–557.

Ericsson, K. A. (2003). The development of elite performance and deliberate practice: An update from the perspective of the expert-performance approach. In J. Starkes & K. A. Ericsson (Eds.), *Expert performance in sport: Recent advances in research on sport expertise* (pp. 49–81). Champaign, IL: Human Kinetics.

Ericsson, K. A., Krampe, R. T., & Tesch-Römer, C. (1993). The role of deliberate practice in the acquisition of expert performance. *Psychological Review, 100*(3), 363–406.

Ewing, M. E., & Seefeldt, V. (1989). *American youth and sports participation.* North Palm Beach, FL: American Footwear Association.

Figueiredo, A. J., Coelho e Silva, M. J., & Malina, R. M. (2011). Predictors of functional capacity and skill in youth soccer players. *Scandinavian Journal of Medicine and Science in Sports, 21*(3), 446–454.

Figueiredo, A. J., Coelho e Silva, M. J., & Malina, R. M. (in press). *Relative age effect: Size, maturity, function, skill and goal orientation of youth soccer players by birth quarter.*

Figueiredo, A. J., Gonçalves. C. E., Coelho e Silva, M. J., & Malina, R. M. (2009a). Youth soccer players, 11–14 years: Maturity, size, function, skill and goal orientation. *Annals of Human Biology, 36*(1), 60–73.

Figueiredo, A. J., Gonçalves, C. E., Coelho e Silva, M. J., & Malina, R. M. (2009b). Characteristics of youth soccer players who drop out, persist or move up. *Journal of Sports Sciences, 27*(9), 883–891.

Ford, P., de Ste. Croix, M., Lloyd, R., Meyers, R., Moosavi, M., Oliver, J., Till, K., & Williams, C. (2011). The long-term athlete development model: Physiological evidence and application. *Journal of Sports Sciences, 29*(4), 389–402.

Fraser-Thomas, J., Côté, J., & Deakin, J. (2008). Examining adolescent sport dropout and prolonged engagement from a developmental perspective. *Journal of Applied Sport Psychology, 20,* 318–333.

Hartley, G. L. (1988). A comparative view of talent selection for sport in two socialist states—the USSR and the GDR—with particular reference to gymnastics. In *The growing child in competitive sport: The 1987 BANC international proceedings* (pp. 50–56). Leeds, UK: National Coaching Foundation.

Haubenstricker, J. L., & Seefeldt, V. (2002). The concept of readiness applied to the acquisition of motor skills. In F. L. Smoll & R. E. Smith (Eds.), *Children and youth in sport: A biopsychosocial perspective* (2nd ed.) (pp. 61–81). Dubuque, IA: Kendall/Hunt.

Haubenstricker, J. L., Branta, C. F., & Seefeldt, V. D. (1999). History of the motor performance study and related programs. In J. L. Haubenstricker & D. L. Feltz (Eds.), *100 years of kinesiology: History, research, and reflections* (pp. 103–125). East Lansing, MI: Department of Kinesiology, Michigan State University.

Iuliano-Burns, S., Mirwald, R. L., & Bailey, D. A. (2001). The timing and magnitude of peak height velocity and peak tissue velocities for early, average and late maturing boys and girls. *American Journal of Human Biology, 13*(1), 1–8.

Jones, M. C., Bayley, N., MacFarlane, J. W., & Honzik, M. P. (1971). *The course of human development: Selected papers from the longitudinal studies, Institute of Human Development, the University of California, Berkeley.* Waltham, MA: Xerox College Publishing.

Katzmarzyk, P. T., Malina, R. M., & Beunen, G. P. (1997). The contribution of biological maturation to the strength and motor fitness of children. *Annals of Human Biology, 24*(6), 493–505.

Khamis, H. J., & Roche, A. F. (1994). Predicting adult stature without using skeletal age: The Khamis-Roche method. *Pediatrics, 94*(4), 504–507. (erratum in Pediatrics 1995 Mar; 95(3): 457 for the corrected version of the tables).

Levine, M. D. (1983). Middle childhood. In M. D. Levine, W. B. Carey, A. C. Crocker, & R. T. Gross (Eds.). *Developmental pediatrics* (pp. 108–132). Philadelphia, PA: Saunders.

Lindner, K. J., Caine, D. J., & Johns, D. P. (1991). Withdrawal predictors among physical and performance characteristics of female competitive gymnasts. *Journal of Sports Sciences, 9*(3), 259–272.

Malina, R. M. (1983). Menarche in athletes: A synthesis and hypothesis. *Annals of Human Biology, 10*(1), 1–24.

Malina, R. M. (1994). Physical growth and biological maturation of young athletes. Exercise and Sport Sciences Reviews, 22, 389–433.

Malina, R. M. (1998). Growth and maturation of young athletes: Is training for sport a factor? In K-M. Chan & L. J. Micheli (Eds.), *Sports and children* (pp. 133–161). Hong Kong, China: Williams and Wilkins Asia.

Malina, R. M. (1999). Growth and maturation of elite female gymnasts: Is training a factor? In F. E. Johnston, B. Zemel, & P. B. Eveleth (Eds.), *Human growth in context* (pp. 291–301). London, UK: Smith-Gordon.

Malina, R. M. (2002). The young athlete: Biological growth and maturation in a biocultural context. In F. L. Smoll & R. E. Smith (Eds.), *Children and youth in sport: A biopsychosocial perspective* (2nd ed.) (pp. 261–292). Dubuque, IA: Kendall/Hunt.

Malina, R. M. (2006). Weight training in youth—growth, maturation, and safety: An evidence-based review. *Clinical Journal of Sports Medicine, 16*(6), 478–487.

Malina, R. M. (2007a). Body composition in athletes: Assessment and estimated fatness. *Clinics in Sports Medicine, 26*(1), 37–68.

Malina, R. M. (2007b). Growth, maturation and development: Applications to young athletes and in particular to divers. In R. M. Malina & J. L. Gabriel (Eds.), *USA diving: Coach development reference manual* (pp. 3–29). Indianapolis, IN: USA Diving Publications.

Malina, R. M. (2008). Skill: Acquisition and trainability. In O. Bar-Or & H. Hebestreit (Eds.), *The young athlete* (pp. 96–111). Oxford, UK: Blackwell Publications.

Malina, R. M. (2010). Early sport specialization: Roots, effectiveness, risks. *Current Sports Medicine Reports, 9*(6), 364–371.

Malina, R. M. (2011). Skeletal age and age verification in youth sport. *Sports Medicine, 41*(11), 925–947.

Malina, R. M., & Beunen, G. (1996). Monitoring growth and maturation. In O. Bar-Or (Ed.), *The child and adolescent athlete* (pp. 647–672). Oxford, UK: Blackwell Science.

Malina, R. M., & Geithner, C. A. (2011). Body composition of young athletes. *American Journal of Lifestyle Medicine, 5*(3), 262–278.

Malina, R. M., & Rogol, A. D. (2011). Sport training and the growth and pubertal maturation of young athletes. *Pediatric Endocrinology Reviews, 9,* 440–454.

Malina, R. M., Bouchard, C., & Bar-Or, O. (2004). *Growth, maturation, and physical activity* (2nd ed.). Champaign, IL: Human Kinetics.

Malina, R. M., Geithner, C. A., O'Brien, R., & Tan, S. K. (2005). Sex differences in the motor performances of elite young divers. *Italian Journal of Sport Sciences, 12,* 18–23.

Malina, R. M., Ribeiro, B., Aroso, J., & Cumming, S. P. (2007). Characteristics of youth soccer players aged 13–15 years classified by skill level. *British Journal of Sports Medicine, 41*(5), 290–295.

Malina, R. M., Coelho e Silva, M. J., Figueiredo, A. J., Carling, C., & Beunen, G. P. (2012). Interrelationships among invasive and non-invasive indicators of biological maturation in adolescent male soccer players. *Journal of Sports Sciences,* in press.

Malina, R. M., Cumming, S. P., Morano, P. J., Barron, M., & Miller, S. J. (2005). Maturity status of youth football players: A non-invasive estimate. *Medicine and Science in Sports and Exercise, 37*(6), 1044–1052.

Malina, R. M., Dompier, T. P., Powell, J. W., Barron, M. J., & Moore, M. T. (2007). Validation of a non-invasive maturity estimate relative to skeletal age in youth football players. *Clinical Journal of Sports Medicine, 17*(5), 362–368.

Malina, R. M., Eisenmann, J. C., Cumming, S. P., Ribeiro, B., & Aroso, J. (2004). Maturity-associated variation in the growth and functional capacities of youth football (soccer) players 13–15 years. *European Journal of Applied Physiology, 91*(5–6), 555–562.

Malina, R. M., Cumming, S. P., Kontos, A. P., Eisenmann, J. C., Ribeiro, B., & Aroso, J. (2005). Maturity-associated variation in sport-specific skills of youth soccer players aged 13-15 years. *Journal of Sports Sciences, 23*(5), 515–522.

Malina, R. M., Morano, P. J., Barron, M., Miller, S. J., Cumming, S. P., & Kontos, A. P. (2006). Incidence and player risk factors for injury in youth football. *Clinical Journal of Sports Medicine, 16*(3), 214–222.

Malina, R. M., Claessens, A. L., Van Aken, K., Thomis, M., Lefevre, J., Philippaerts, R., & Beunen, G. P. (2006). Maturity offset in gymnasts: Application of a prediction equation. *Medicine and Science in Sports and Exercise, 38*(7), 1342–1347.

Malina, R. M., Ignasiak, Z., Rożek, K., Sławinska, T., Domaradzki, J., Fugiel, J., & Kochan, K. (2011). Growth, maturity and functional characteristics of female athletes 11–15 years. *Human Movement, 12,* 31–40.

Malina, R. M., Rożek,, K., Ignasiak, Z., Sławinska, T., Fugiel, J., Kochan, K., & Domaradzki, J. (2011). Growth and functional characteristics of male athletes 11–15 years of age. *Human Movement, 12,* 180–187.

Malina, R. M., Sławinska, T., Ignasiak, Z., Rożek,, K., Kochan, K., Domaradzki, J., & Fugiel, J. (2010). Sex differences in growth and performance of track and field athletes 11–15 years. *Journal of Human Kinetics, 24,* 79–85.

Mirwald, R. L., Baxter-Jones, A. D. G., Bailey, D. A., & Beunen, G. P. (2002). An assessment of maturity from anthropometric measurements. *Medicine and Science in Sports and Exercise, 34*(4), 689–694.

Montemayor, R., Adams, G. R., & Gullotta, T. P. (Eds.). (1990). *From childhood to adolescence: A transitional period?* Newbury Park, CA: Sage Publications.

Nicolson, A. B., & Hanley, C. (1953). Indices of physiological maturity: Derivation and interrelationships. *Child Development, 24*(1), 3–38.

Nurmi-Lawton, J. A., Baxter-Jones, A. D., Mirwald, R. L., Bishop, J. A., Taylor, R., Cooper, C., & New, S. A. (2004).

Evidence of sustained skeletal benefits from impact-loading exercise in young females: A 3-year longitudinal study. *Journal of Bone Mineral Research, 19*(2), 314–322.

Peeters, M. W., Thomis, M. A. I., Beunen, G. P., & Malina, R. M. (2009). Genetics and sports: An overview of the pre-molecular biology era. *Medicine and Sport Science, 54,* 28–42.

Petiot, B., Salmela, J. H., & Hoshizaki, T. B. (Eds.). (1987). *World identification systems for gymnastics talent.* Montreal, Canada: Sport Psyche Editions.

Pfeiffer, K. A., Lobelo, F., Ward, D., & Pate, R. R. (2008). Endurance trainability of children and youth. In O. Bar-Or & H. Hebestreit (Eds.), *The young athlete* (pp. 84–95). Oxford, UK: Blackwell Science.

Rolland-Cachera, M. F., Deheeger, M., Guilloud-Bataille, M., Avons, P., Patois, E., & Sempe, M. (1987). Tracking the development of adiposity from one month of age to adulthood. *Annals of Human Biology, 14*(3), 219–229.

Sale, D. (1989). Strength and power training during youth. In C. V. Gisolfi & D. R. Lamb (Eds.). *Perspectives in exercise science and sports medicine* (Vol. II). *Youth, exercise, and sport* (pp. 165–216). Indianapolis, IN: Benchmark Press.

Scott, J. P. (1986). Critical periods in organization processes. In F. Falkner & J. M. Tanner (Eds.), *Human growth* (Vol. 1), *Developmental biology, prenatal growth* (pp. 181–196). New York, NY: Plenum.

Seefeldt, V. D. (1980). Developmental motor patterns: Implications for elementary school physical education. In C. Nadeau, W. Holliwell, K. Newell, & G. Roberts (Eds.), *Psychology of motor behavior and sport* (pp. 314–323). Champaign, IL: Human Kinetics.

Seefeldt, V. D., & Haubenstricker, J. (1982). Patterns, phases, or stages: An analytical model for the study of developmental movement. In J. A. S. Kelso & J. E. Clark (Eds.), *The development of movement control and co-ordination* (pp. 309–319). New York, NY: Wiley.

Sherar, L. B., Baxter-Jones, A. D. G., Faulkner, R. A., & Russell, K. W. (2007). Do physical maturity and birth date predict talent in male youth ice hockey players? *Journal of Sports Sciences, 25*(8), 879–886.

Sherar, L. B., Cumming, S. P., Eisenmann, J. C., Baxter-Jones, A. D. G., & Malina, R. M. (2010). Adolescent biological maturity and physical activity: Biology meets behavior. *Pediatric Exercise Science, 22*(3), 332–349.

Siegel, S. R., Peña Reyes, M. E., Cárdenas Barahona, E. E., & Malina, R. M. (2009). Participation in organized sport among urban Mexican youth. In M. J. Coelho e Silva, A. J. Figueiredo, M. T. Elferink-Gemser, & R. M. Malina (Eds.), *Youth sports: Participation, trainability and readiness* (pp. 38–48). Coimbra, Portugal: University of Coimbra Press.

Steens, G. (Ed.). (2006). *Moet er nog sport zijn? Sport, beweging en gezondheid in Vlaanderen 2002–2006* (Vol. 1). Antwerp, Belgium: F & G Partners.

Tanner, J. M. (1962). *Growth at adolescence* (2nd ed.). Oxford, UK: Blackwell Scientific Publications.

Till, K., Cobley, S., O'Hara, J., Chapman, C., & Cooke, C. (2010). Anthropometric, physiological and selection characteristics in high performance UK junior rugby league players. *Talent Development and Excellence, 2*(2), 193–207.

Tönz, O., Stronski, S. M., & Gmeiner, C. Y. K. (1990). Wachstum und pubertät bei 7- bis 16 jahrigen kunstturneirinnen: Eine prospektive studie. *Schweizerische Medizinische Wochenschrift, 120,* 10–20.

Vaeyens, R., Malina, R. M., Janssens, M., Van Renterghem, B., Bourgois, J., & Vrijens, J. (2006). A multidisciplinary selection model for youth soccer: The Ghent Youth Soccer Project. *British Journal of Sports Medicine, 40*(11), 928–934.

Ziemilska, A. (1981). Wpływ intensywnego treningu gymnastycznego na rozwój somatyczny I dojrzewanie dzieci (Influence of intensive gymnastics training on growth and sexual maturation of children). *Studia i Monografie Akademia Wychowania Fizycznego* (Studies and Monographs of the Academy of Physical Education), Warsaw, Poland.

CHAPTER 6

PHYSICAL AND SKILL TESTING IN EARLY PHASES OF TALENT DEVELOPMENT

Ronnie Lidor and Gal Ziv

INTRODUCTION

Researchers in the area of talent identification and early development in sport mostly consider the age of 14 to be the final year of an athlete's *developmental years* (see Baker, Schorer, Cobley, Schimmer, & Wattie, 2009; Côté, Macdonald, Baker, & Abernethy, 2006), a phase reflecting his or her early involvement in sports. After the age of 14, talented athletes typically begin their *specialization years,* namely the years during which they focus solely on one sport activity and devote a considerable amount of practice to refining specific athletic skills. Coaches who work with athletes of ages up to 14 typically ask themselves questions related to the physical ability, skill level, and psychological-emotional profile of their athletes: How fast is this kid? Is he quick enough to move on the court? How high can she jump? Does this child have the commitment to be part of our competitive training program? Will he be able to handle the pressure in his first championship game?

In order to provide answers to the above questions, coaches regularly use designated tests in their work with young athletes (see, for example, Reiman & Manske, 2009; Strand & Wilson, 1993). Tests assessing physical characteristics, physiological attributes, sport-specific skills, and psychological-emotional profiles are commonly used in studies on athletes under the age of 14 who are in their early phases of talent development (Brown, 2001; Lidor, Côté, & Hackfort, 2009). In addition, measurements of anthropometrics in this age group are also frequently performed.

In this chapter, we focus on two aspects of testing—physical and skill. The physical and skill aspects are considered to be the most important foundations of a typical training program aimed at developing talent in young athletes (Bompa, 1999); therefore, coaches prefer to use physical and skill tests, and not other tests such as those assessing athletes' psychological-emotional attributes. In our chapter, the term *physical test* is used to refer to those tests given to athletes at early phases of talent development to assess their motor, physical, and physiological abilities. For example, in order to assess the explosive power of their athletes, coaches use a vertical jump test or a standing long jump test. To assess their athletes' speed ability, coaches use tests of short sprints (e.g., 5 to 30m). In these tests, coaches aim at assessing the general physical abilities of the athletes.

The term *skill test* is used in this chapter to describe those tests that specifically assess the skill level of an athlete in a given task. Skills tests are task oriented, and typically refer to a highly developed specific sequence of responses. For example, a dribbling test in basketball or team handball assesses the level of the player's competence in dribbling the ball, a skill he or she is expected to exhibit in practices and games. A defensive maneuver test in judo assesses a specific defensive skill that the judoka is required to perform in combats.

Assessment of physical abilities and skill levels is only one of the main objectives of the use of physical and skill tests in early phases of talent development. Among the other objectives of the physical and skill tests are (a) to identify individual strengths and weaknesses of the young athlete, (b) to assess the effectiveness of a specific training program aimed at improving performances in young athletes, (c) to monitor the health status of the young athlete, (d) to enable the prediction of future performances, and (e) to provide feedback to athletes on their performances in order to encourage them to further improve (Carling, Reilly, & Williams, 2009). Coaches who work with athletes of ages up to 14 should obtain relevant information associated with physical and skill tests, in order to benefit from their use throughout the different phases of the training programs. Coaches should be aware of the appropriate use of the data of the physical and skill tests; they should realize what can and cannot be done with the obtained data.

The purpose of this chapter is threefold: (a) to review a series of studies ($n = 26$) focusing on the role of physical and skill tests in early phases of talent development in sport, (b) to discuss a number of benefits associated with the use of physical and skill tests in the early phases of talent development, and (c) to suggest a number of practical implications for coaches who administer tests in the early phases of talent development.

We conducted a computerized search for peer-reviewed articles published in English in three databases: PubMed, SPORTDiscus, and Google Scholar. Search terms included *talent identification, talent development, talent detection,* and *talent selection*; and *physical test, physiological test,* and *motor test*. In addition, we manually searched library holdings and the lists of references of the studies that came up in the computerized search. The search yielded 26 studies, and these are included in our review.

PHYSICAL AND SKILL TESTING IN TEAM AND INDIVIDUAL SPORTS

Studies are presented for each sport separately, allowing researchers and practitioners in each sport to easily access relevant information. Team sports included rugby, soccer, team handball, volleyball, and water-polo. Individual sports included tennis, combat sports, rowing, swimming, and running.

Team Sports

Rugby. A model for identifying talent in rugby was proposed by a group of researchers in South Africa (Pienaar, Spamer, & Steyn, 1998). In their study, 14 physical and motor tests and 14 anthropometric measurements were performed on 173 ten-year-old boys with no rugby experience and on 45 rugby league players under the age of eleven. The rugby players performed better than the nonrugby players on all rugby skill, motor, and physical tests except for the sit-and-reach test. The rugby players were also taller and heavier, although no differences in percent body fat were observed. Based on the obtained data, a discriminant analysis was able to differentiate between potential rugby players and nonplayers based on sprint time, passing accuracy, and static and dynamic strength. The researchers also developed equations for potential and nonpotential rugby players based on four anthropometric (femur width, arm girth corrected for percent fat, calf girth corrected for percent fat, and height-to-mass ratio) and four motor and physical (7m passing accuracy, sprint time, flexed arm-hang, and vertical jump) tests. Based on these variables, 93.8% of the boys were classified correctly. It appears that such a model may have practical value. However, as the authors of the study suggested, more research and a longitudinal approach are needed in order to replicate these findings and validate them.

Soccer. We found four studies on young soccer players in which a number of physical and skill tests were used. In one study, differences between skill levels in anthropometric measurements and functional capacity were examined in a group of 69 male soccer players between the ages of 13–15 years competing at the highest level in Portugal (Malina, Ribeiro, Aroso, & Cumming, 2007). Maturation was assessed by stage of pubic hair. The players were divided into quintiles of soccer skill level based on six soccer-specific tests (ball control with the body [keeping ball in air without using arms or hands], ball control with the head, slalom dribbling with a pass, slalom dribbling, passing accuracy, and shooting accuracy). Three functional tests were administered: 30m dash, vertical jump, and yo-yo endurance run. In addition, height, body mass, age, and soccer experience were recorded. The only difference between skill levels was in the yo-yo endurance run, which was statistically significant only between the 1st and the 5th quintiles. Maturational status and height accounted for 21% of the variance in skill level. This was increased to 29% when the yo-yo endurance run was added.

The role of maturation in the performance of general and specific physical and motor tests should be recognized as a covariate that can explain some of the differences between players in the preadolescent and those in the adolescent stages of development (for more information on the relationships between maturation and performance in young athletes, see Chapter 5 in this volume). For example, in the same sample of 69 male players, physical maturity and training experience explained 21% of the variance in aerobic capacity. In addition, body mass and maturity explained 50% of the variance in the 30m sprint, and height and maturity explained 41% of the variance in vertical jump performance (Malina, Eisenmann, Cumming, Ribeiro, & Aroso, 2004).

While physical maturity, height, and body mass appear to contribute significantly to the performance of general physiological tests, they contribute to a lesser degree to the performance of soccer-specific skills. This was observed in a study of the same 69 players (Malina et al., 2005). In this study, 21% of the variance in dribbling the ball and passing was explained by age and maturity, and 14% of the variance in ball control with the head (i.e., the player has to keep the ball in the air using only the head within a 9 x 9 meter square) was explained by maturity, height, and height x mass interaction (this was calculated as the product of the residuals of height and body mass in order to reduce collinearity between height and body mass, as they are highly related). In addition, 13% of the variance in ball control with the body was explained by maturity and years of training, and 8% of the variance in shooting accuracy was explained by maturity and height. As the authors of this study suggested, unlike physiological tests, skill tests are affected by many more variables than body mass and maturity status. These variables include, among others, neural control of movement and perceptual-cognitive skills.

While maturational status can account for some of the variance in the performance of several physical and motor tests, it does not account for all of it. One study examined the differences between elite, subelite, and nonelite young soccer players in anthropometric, physical, physiological, and soccer-specific skill tests (Vaeyens et al., 2006). In this study, 232 players between the ages of 12–16 years were tested over a period of five years. An analysis of covariance was used with maturational status as the covariate. It was found that in the under-13 and under-14 age groups, better running speeds and technical abilities were found in the elite players when compared to the nonelite players. In addition, a discriminant analysis based on two technical, two endurance, and two speed tests correctly classified approximately 70% of the players into one of the three skill groups. The importance of this study is in its multidisciplinary approach to talent identification, and in its finding that talent can be identified through a combination of tests from a number of disciplines.

Team handball. Anthropometric data and results of a number of motor tests were acquired from male ($n = 279$) and female ($n = 126$) under-14 team handball players (Lidor, Falk, et al., 2005). The testing was part of the selection process for the Junior National Team in Israel. The motor tests included an agility test, standing long jump, medicine ball throw, 20m sprint from a standing position, 20m sprint with a flying start, and a slalom dribbling test. The results showed no differences in height and body mass between selected and nonselected players. In addition, in most cases no differences were found in the motor tests between selected and nonselected players. In fact, out of a total of 59 t-tests that were performed, only 13 (22%) were found to be significant, and even in those a wide overlap was found between the selected and nonselected players. It should be noted that a correction for multiple comparisons was not made. If such a correction had been used, most of the statistically significant results would have been invalidated. The only test that showed some consistent results between selected and non-selected players was the dribbling slalom test. This test requires agility, speed, and ball-handling skill, and it is possible that due to its game-specific nature, it was able, at least in some cases, to differentiate between selected and nonselected players.

In another study, of 12- to 14-year-old team handball players in Belgium, it was found that compared to a reference sample of boys, the players performed better in tests of speed, power, and strength (Mohamed et al., 2009). However, there were no comparisons between players of different skill levels within this age group. The fact that better performance was demonstrated by the players when compared to the sample group is not necessarily specific to team handball.

Volleyball. A number of anthropometric measurements and the results of physiological and motor tests were collected from a group of 32 twelve- to thirteen-year-old female volleyball players in Croatia (Grgantov, Katic, & Jankovic, 2006). Players' performance was scored based on both team quality and each player's ability within the team, as assessed by the coaches. The better players had higher standing reach, greater height, and longer foot length compared to the other players. In addition, the better players were superior at serving, setting, and blocking the ball when compared to the other players. Specifically, serving the volleyball was the best predictor of performance ($r = .49$). These data can be used to help decide which tests can best predict success in volleyball at this age.

Water-polo. A two-year longitudinal study of 24 male water-polo players (age = 12–14 years) examined the differences in physical and motor abilities between those selected to the Junior National Team and those not selected (Falk, Lidor, Lander, & Lang, 2004). The swimming tests included freestyle swimming for 50m, 100m, 200m, and 400m; breast-stroke for 100m; a modified butterfly style (i.e., butterfly motion in arms, breast-stroke motion in legs) for 100m; and ball handling for 50m. The players' vertical jump from the water, throwing accuracy, and strength were also tested. The selected players performed better in some of the swimming tests (i.e., freestyle for 100m, 200m, and 400m; modified butterfly; and handling the ball for 50m). Effect sizes of all observed differences were high. In addition, over the two-year period the players who were selected to the National Team improved more on the distance throw than the players who were not selected. The fact that no differences were found between groups in throwing accuracy and distance could be due to the fact that the task included throwing to the goal from a set point and without the presence of a goalkeeper. Future research should try to create more realistic testing conditions. Lastly, it should be noted that maturational age was not reported in this study.

Individual Sports

Tennis. A battery of physical tests was performed on a group of 12 male tennis players (mean chronological age = 13.6 ± 1.4 years; maturational age = Tanner stages III-IV) to examine their relationship to players' tournament rankings (Girard & Millet, 2009). The tests included sprints, various vertical jump protocols (e.g., countermovement jump, squat jump), grip strength, and planter flexors torque. It was found that sprint ability, vertical jump, and strength of the dominant limbs were good predictors of tennis performance. For example, a correlation of .74 was found between 20m sprints and players' ranking, a correlation of -.8 was found between countermovement jump and players' ranking, and a correlation of -.73 was found between planter flexor torque of the dominant leg and players' ranking.

In contrast to the findings that emerged from Girard and Millet's (2009) study, a study of 83 male players between the ages of eight and twelve found no relationships between the results of several physical tests that examined speed, agility, strength, jumping ability, and tennis playing ability (Roetert, Garrett, Brown, & Camaione, 1992). In fact, the only statistically significant correlation was low ($r = .23$), and was found between an agility test and player ranking. However, tennis stroke quality, which was rated by three tennis professionals, correlated significantly with player ranking. For example, a correlation of .68, .59, and .57 was found between the forehand, backhand, and service, respectively, and national player ranking.

The differences between these studies in the ability of physical tests to predict playing ability can be explained, at least in part, by the maturational age of the participants. As Girard and Millet (2009) suggested, the progressive increase in strength and speed during puberty may have resulted in more distinct relationships in their study, due to the relatively higher maturational age of the participants when compared to the study by Roetert et al. (1992). Indeed, Roetert et al. (1992) suggested that physical abilities may begin to transfer to playing ability with maturation or with specific training.

The idea that in later maturational stages, physical tests can better predict performance is supported by findings of a study that conducted a discriminant analysis on a series of physical tests in an attempt to differentiate between three groups of male and female tennis players: United States Tennis Association (USTA) national team players (mean age = 15.4 years), USTA development camp players (mean age = 13.6 years), and USTA area training center players (age not available) (Roetert, Brown, Piorkowski, & Woods, 1996). It was found that on the basis of an agility side shuffle test, vertical jump, sit-and-reach test, and push-ups, 67.65% of the cases were classified correctly into the three groups. The model that differentiated between groups did not include gender or age. The chronological ages of the participants in this study suggested that most were of later maturational stages.

Lastly, it appears that ability in tennis-specific skills can predict tennis performance. This was demonstrated in a study of 531 male and female players (age = 11.9 ± 1.2) who underwent a series of anthropometric, physiological, and tennis-specific skill tests (Birrer, Levine, Gallippi, & Tischler, 1986). The tennis-specific skills were assessed by three coaches. Strong correlations were found between tournament play and forehand ($r = .89$), backhand ($r = .91$), volley ($r = .91$), smash ($r = .85$), and number of leg moves ($r = .86$). However, these were examined in the tournament itself, and therefore the strong relationships are not surprising. Weak correlations were found between anthropometric and physiological tests and tournament play.

Combat sports. Intuitively, sport-specific skill tests should be able to predict sport performance. However, in one study of young judokas, judo-specific physical tests failed to predict the judokas' rankings (Lidor, Melnik, Bilkevitz, Arnon, & Falk, 2005). Ten judokas between the ages of 12–15 years underwent a general 3-minute physical test and a 10-station judo-specific physical test, three times over a period of two years. The 3-minute general test included sit-ups, push-ups, and a maximal test of side-to-side jumps over a 30cm bench. The judo-specific test included specific judo exercises, as well as agility and strength tests. The results showed that the judo-specific test failed to predict judokas' rankings as given by coaches in 1995 and in 2003. In contrast, correlations of .58 to .69 were found between the 3-minute general physical test and the judokas' rankings. In fact, the test that best predicted the 2003 ranking was the side-to-side jump test, which explained 43% of the variance in ranking. Still, almost 60% of the variance was unaccounted for. The rest of the variance can be explained by a number of factors, among them psychological (e.g., personality, motivation), social (e.g., peer and parental support), environmental (e.g., nutrition), and genetic factors. According to this study, physical tests alone cannot accurately predict who will become a good judoka.

Anthropometric and physiological characteristics of young wrestlers were reported in three studies (Camic et al., 2009; Sady, Thomson, Berg, & Savage, 1984; Sady, Thomson, Savage, & Petratis, 1982). In one study of 253 wrestlers (age = 11.1 ± 1.6 years), nine anthropometric measurements (mass; height; body mass index; circumferences of waist mid-arm, calf, and mid-thigh; and two skinfolds—subscapular and triceps) were compared to those in a national sample of boys (Camic et al., 2009). Comparisons were made between six independent age groups: age 8, 9, 10, 11, 12, and 13. The results showed similarities between the wrestlers and the national sample group in most comparisons of height and mass, and no differences between groups in yearly changes in mass and height. However, wrestlers did have lower circumferences and lower body fat. In another study (Sady et al., 1982), 7% less body fat was found in a group of 23 wrestlers between the ages of 8.8–12.8 years when compared to that found in 23 nonwrestlers of the same ages. However, both groups had similar skeletal structure and lean body mass.

Lastly, physiological characteristics of 15 prepubescent wrestlers (age = 11.3 ± .3 years) were compared to those in a group of active boys of a similar age (Sady et al., 1984). The participants underwent a series of physiological tests that included a graded treadmill test to exhaustion, a modified Wingate anaerobic test that was conducted twice on two consecutive days, and body composition measurements using skinfold calipers. The wrestlers had higher VO_2max values (54.0 ± 1.15 mlO_2·min^{-1}·kg^{-1}) than the nonwrestlers (45.6 ± 2.1 mlO_2·min^{-1}·kg^{-1}). In addition, wrestlers had higher anaerobic power values, which improved from Day 1 (225 ± 13.5 W) to Day 2 (257 ± 12.7 W) when compared to those of the comparison group (187 ± 13.8 and 189 ± 16.8 W for Day 1 and Day 2, respectively). Lastly, percent body fat was much lower in wrestlers (12.7 ± 1.03%) when compared to that of the comparison group (22.9 ± 2.28%). Clearly, wrestlers have more favorable body fat values and aerobic and anaerobic capabilities when compared to those of regular active boys. However, the data on wrestlers do not allow us to determine whether differences exist between elite and nonelite wrestlers.

Rowing. In one study, 12 anthropometric and 6 physiological variables were used to predict 1,000m rowing ergometer performance in 12.0- to 13.9-year-old rowers (Mikulic & Ruzic, 2008). The rowing ergometer results were recorded at an indoor rowing championship in Zagreb. This competition was the most important winter competition for these rowers. The results revealed 11 anthropometric variables and 4 physiological attributes that correlated significantly with rowing performance. For example, significant correlations were found between rowing performance and height ($r = -.79$), body mass ($r = -.6$), lean body mass ($r = -.82$), leg length ($r = -.72$), arm length ($r = -.71$), absolute VO_2max ($r = -.89$), relative VO_2max ($r = -.36$), and maximal ventilation ($r = -.77$). A regressional model based on both anthropometric and physiological variables resulted in an R^2 of .84. The variables in this model were VO_2max, biacromial diameter, thigh girth, and body height. The fact that absolute VO_2max was more important than relative VO_2max is not surprising. Absolute VO_2max is the maximum amount of oxygen that a person can consume in one minute. Relative VO_2max is the maximum amount of oxygen that can be consumed in one minute relative to one's body mass (e.g., per kg of body mass). While relative VO_2max better represents the aerobic capacity when work is being performed against body mass (e.g., running, race walking), absolute VO_2max better represents aerobic capacity when work is being performed against an external force (e.g., rowing—force is applied against the drag of the water). According to this study, better rowers have a taller stature, higher absolute VO_2max, and higher muscle mass.

In another study of 12- to 14-year-old rowers, a modified Wingate anaerobic test conducted on a rowing ergometer was used to test anaerobic power (Mikulic, Ruzic, & Markovic, 2009). A total of 128 rowers participated in the study: 12-year-old ($n = 37$), 13-year-old ($n = 31$), and 14-year-old (n = 30) rowers. Tanner stage was 2.3, 3.3, and 3.9 for the three age groups, respectively. The test included two trials of 30 seconds of all-out effort, separated by 15 minutes. The results showed that the 14-year-old group had higher peak power and mean power (both absolute and relative to body mass) when compared to the 12-year-old and 13-year-old groups. The authors of this study used allometric scaling to account for the differences in body height and mass. The differences between groups in anaerobic power were still significant after this scaling, suggesting that there are other factors besides body size that affect anaerobic performance (e.g., training status, nutrition, technical skills).

Swimming. The relationship between anthropometric and physiological characteristics and swimming performance was examined in a group of 12 swimmers between the ages of nine and twelve (Klika & Thorland, 1994). Anthropometric tests included height, body mass, body density, and arm length. Physiological tests included leg power, arm-stroke force, leg-kick force, peak VO_2, and stroke rate. Performance was measured as the swimming velocity for 100 yards. The results showed that the swimming velocity correlated significantly with body density (r = -.65), fat mass (r = .61), peak VO_2 (r = .58), and stroke rate (r = .65). In addition, discriminant analysis correctly classified all participants into two groups—faster swimmers and slower swimmers—based on four variables: leg-kick force, peak VO_2, stroke efficiency (m·stroke^{-1}), and muscularity (kg·m^{-3}). Out of those four variables, one is purely anthropometric (muscularity), one relates to both anthropometric and physiological characteristics (stroke efficiency), and two are mainly physiological (leg-kick force and peak VO_2). Therefore, it appears that a combination of anthropometric and physiological data can differentiate between faster and slower young swimmers.

In another study, of 24 swimmers between the ages of 12–14, the relationships between several anthropometric and physiological variables and the 100m freestyle swimming performance were examined (Vitor & Böhme, 2010). A swim-specific anaerobic power test was conducted. This test was based on eight repetitions of maximal effort freestyle swimming for 25m (8 x 25m). Other physiological variables included stroke rate, distance per stroke (m·swim cycle^{-1}), swimming index (multiplying swimming speed by distance per stroke—higher values suggest a more efficient swimming technique), and critical speed (the greatest velocity that can be maintained without fatigue). Multiple regression analysis revealed that anaerobic power, critical speed, and swimming index explained 88% of the variance in the 100m freestyle performance. Unlike the study of Klika and Thorland (1994), the anthropometric data did not predict swimming performance. However, it should be noted that the swimming index is based on the multiplication of swimming speed and distance per stroke. Distance per stroke can increase when arm and leg power increase, but also when arm and leg length increase. Hence, at least in part, anthropometric variables are likely to underlie an improvement in the swimming index.

Both a multiple regression analysis and a discriminant analysis were conducted to assess the relationships between anthropometric, physiological, and technical variables and swimming performance in 66 male (age = 13.6 ± .6 years) and 67 female (age = 11.5 ± .6 years) swimmers (Saavedra, Escalante, & Rodríguez, 2010). Both general and specific fitness tests were conducted. Age, sitting height, 30-min test (a swimming aerobic endurance test), 6 x 50m at 1:30 test (a test assessing speed endurance and including 6 sets of a 50m swim at 1.5-minute intervals), and swimming index explained 82.4% of the variance in swimming performance in male swimmers. In female swimmers, age, 30-min test, 6 x 50m at 1:30 test, and velocity in a 50m all-out swim explained 84.5% of the variance in swimming performance. A discriminant analysis correctly classified 94.1% of the best male swimmers based on age, 30-min test, 6 x 50m at 1:30 test, shoulder extension, arm span, and height. In female swimmers, 71.0% of the participants were correctly classified based on a 30-min test, horizontal floating, velocity at a 50m all-out swim, and age. It is interesting to note that only specific fitness tests entered the prediction formulas, and that none of the general fitness tests predicted swimming performance. In addition, age was the most important predictor and therefore, as the authors suggested, competitions should be based on birth date rather than age categories.

A critical speed test appears to be a good predictor of swimming endurance in young swimmers. In one study, critical speed was determined from maximal freestyle swimming for 100m, 200m, and 400m in 10–12-year-old and 13–15-year-old boys and girls (Greco & De-nadai, 2005). The critical speed was determined from the regression equation between swimming distance and the time needed to complete the distance. The participants then performed a 30-min endurance swimming test. During this test, participants swam at 95% of their critical speed, and the test ended when they reached voluntary exhaustion. If the participants were able to complete the 30 min, swimming velocity was increased by 1–2% and another 30-min swim was conducted on another day. This procedure was repeated until voluntary exhaustion occurred. Correlations between critical speed and maximal speed for the 30-min endurance test were between .87 and .97 based on chronological age, and between .93 and .98 based on sexual maturation. As the authors suggested, critical speed is an important variable for assessing aerobic performance in swimmers, regardless of their age or gender.

Running. Anthropometrics, isokinetic torque, and power were examined in a group of 12 male sprinters (age = 11.9 ± .3 years) and a group of 12 male distance runners (age = 12.0 ± .3 years; Thorland, Johnson, Cisar, Housh, & Tharp, 1990). Isokinetic testing included leg extension in velocities of 30, 60, 120, 180, 240, and 300 $°·s^{-1}$, and power was measured using the Wingate anaerobic test. It was found that sprinters were taller than distance runners (154.0 ± 3.0 vs. 149.7 ± 2.1cm, respectively), and the peak power of sprinters (384 ± 76 W) was higher than that of distance runners (314 ± 47 W). In fact, the peak power values of distance runners were not higher than those found in nonrunners of similar age. Isokinetic torque values of both sprinters and distance runners were similar to those found in nonrunners of similar age. However, sprinters were stronger than distance runners in the velocities of 180 and 300 $°·s^{-1}$.

A similar study examined isokinetic torque values and anaerobic power in a group of 12 female sprinters (age = 11.1 ± .2 years) and 12 female distance runners (age = 10.9±.2 years) (Thorland, Johnson, Cisar, Housh, & Tharp, 1987). Isokinetic torque values of sprinters were higher than those of distance runners at velocities above 180 $°·s-1$. However, no differences between groups were found in anaerobic power. From these two studies it appears that, at least in males, the Wingate anaerobic test can differentiate between young sprinters, distance runners, and nonrunners. This cannot be said for isokinetic testing in either males or females or for the Wingate anaerobic test in females.

Lastly, anaerobic power was tested by using the Wingate anaerobic test in a group of young male and female runners (Tharp, Johnson, & Thorland, 1984). When divided by body mass, anaerobic power was higher in the male sprinters (age = 13.7 ± 1.7 years) when compared to the male distance runners (age = 13.8 + 2.1). No differences in anaerobic power were found between female sprinters and distance runners.

BENEFITS ASSOCIATED WITH THE USE OF PHYSICAL AND SKILL TESTS

Based on the studies reviewed in this chapter, three benefits associated with the use of physical and skill tests in early phases of talent development are discussed.

Assessment and feedback. Physical and skill tests have been found to be effective instructional tools for assessing athletic ability and skill level in athletes up to the age of 14. Physical and skill tests have been used in sports such as rugby, soccer, team handball, volleyball, waterpolo, tennis, combat sports, rowing, swimming, and running. The physical tests used in the studies reviewed in our chapter are presented in Table 6.1. As can be seen, coaches can use tests to measure anthropometrics and to assess abilities such as aerobic capacity, anaerobic power and strength, speed and agility, and flexibility in the young athlete. For each of these abilities, a number of tests can be performed. In addition, a variety of skill tests can be found in the reviewed studies according to the given sport.

Coaches can use the outcomes of the physical and skill tests not only to assess the abilities and skill level of their young athletes, but also to provide them with feedback information on their progress in the training program. Coaches can also use the outcomes of the tests to assess the contribution of the training program to the improvement (or lack of improvement) of the young athlete. If necessary, coaches can re-plan the training program and carry out a new program that better reflects the specialized needs of the individual athlete.

Educational value. In a number of studies, the physical and skill tests were administered once (e.g., Pienaar et al., 1998; Roetert et al., 1992), and in others several times (e.g., Falk et al., 2004; Lidor, Falk, et al., 2005). The provision of the physical and skill tests, either once or a number of times during the annual training program, should serve as a learning experience for the young athlete. This experience will benefit young athletes in (a) teaching them more about their own physical abilities, strengths and limitations when performing the executed acts/tasks, and the physical/skill variables assessed (Lacy, 2011), (b) increasing their knowledge about how to perform under testing conditions in which they are assessed quantitatively by objective devices (e.g., timer, distance recorder, video), and (c) motivating them to devote more time to practicing those acts/skills that were scored low in the given tests. The more relevant the physical and skill tests are to the young athletes, the more the athletes benefit from their use. If the physical and skill tests authentically reflect what the athletes are actually required to do during practice sessions and games, the athletes will probably be more motivated to prepare themselves for the test in order to improve their achievements.

Prediction. An attempt was made in a number of studies discussed in our review to predict future performance of the young athlete (e.g., Grgantov et al., 2006; Lidor, Falk, et al., 2005; Saavedra et al., 2010). It can be observed from the reviewed studies that no clear-cut evidence has been found to support the predictive value of physical and skill tests in early phases of talent development in sport. However, there are some data indicating that some tests given to young athletes can serve as good predictors for performance in actual games or final

Table 6.1. Physical Tests Used in Early Phases of Talent Development

Measure	Test	Sport
Anthropometrics	Height, body mass, percent fat, various circumferences, etc.	All sports
Aerobic capacity	Yo-yo endurance run	Soccer
	Maximal aerobic capacity (VO_2max) and other cardiorespiratory measures (e.g., ventilation)	All sports
	Specific swimming endurance test	Swimming
Anaerobic power and strength	Standing long jump	Team handball
	Vertical jump*	Rugby, soccer, tennis
	Wingate anaerobic test	Wrestling, rowing, running
	Medicine ball throw	Team handball
	Hand grip	Tennis
	Flexed arm hang	Rugby
	Planter flexors torque	Tennis
	Sit-ups	Judo
	Push-ups	Tennis
	Side-to-side jumps over bench	Judo
	Leg power, arm stroke force, leg kick force, swim-specific anaerobic tests	Swimming
	Isokinetic testing	Running
Speed and agility	5–30m sprints	Soccer, team handball
	100–400m swims	Water polo, swimming
	Agility (e.g., T-test, side shuffle test)	Tennis
Flexibility	Sit and reach test	Rugby

* There are a number of vertical jump protocols. The two most common are the counter-movement jump, in which the athlete squats and immediately leaps back up, and the squat jump, in which the athlete starts the jump from a static squat position.

rankings of athletes/players (e.g., Grgantov et al., 2006). On the other hand, we also found data indicating no correlation of achievements of physical and skill tests with final selection and ranking of athletes/players (e.g., Lidor, Falk, et al., 2005).

In addition, physical maturation was not taken into account in most of the reviewed studies. It has been found that maturation can affect anthropometric measures as well as body composition (see Malina et al., 2004, and Chapter 5 in this text). Achievements in physical and skill tests can be substantially influenced by early or late maturation. In the reviewed studies, it is possible that the athletes/players were more physically mature during the period of data collection than the less-talented athletes/players. In order to accurately distinguish between talented and less-talented individuals, data on their maturation level should be included as well.

If the aim of coaches is to use the data obtained in the physical and skill tests given to their athletes to predict the athletes' future performances, then they should adopt a cautious approach. Since it is less effective to rely only on the achievements of the athletes in the physical and skill tests when their aim is to predict future performance of their young athletes, it is recommended that coaches minimize the use of physical and skill tests. It is assumed that more parameters are involved in the prediction formula of future performance in sport, among them the quality of coaching, the physical conditions of the learning environments, and the support the young athlete is provided by his or her family, school, and the community at large. Therefore, not only should data from physical and skill tests be collected for prediction of future success, but also qualitative data associated with the feelings, perceptions, and thoughts of the young athletes on different aspects related to their training program. In addition, verbal reports collected from the athlete's family members, particularly the parents, and his or her friends and teachers concerning the involvement of the young athlete in the training program should be obtained. Only a multifaceted set of data from different sources will enable the coach to objectively assess the chances of the young athlete to attain a high level of proficiency.

PRACTICAL IMPLICATIONS FOR COACHES

Four practical implications for coaches who work with athletes in early phases of talent development are discussed:

First, coaches are recommended to select the most relevant and authentic physical and skill tests to be given in the training program. Various physical and skill tests can be found in the literature, and therefore coaches should first analyze the objectives of each test, its protocol and specific requirements, and only then select the one that most fits the objectives of the training program.

Second, physical and skill tests should be an integral instructional foundation of the training program. Taking the tests should serve as a learning experience for the young athlete, and therefore it is recommended that the selected tests be administered more than once during the annual program. For example, coaches can give the tests in the preparation, competition, and transition phases of the annual training program.

Third, coaches are advised not to count on the outcomes of the physical and skill tests if their aim is to predict future performance of the young athlete. Strong support has not been found for the predictive value of physical and skill tests in early phases of talent development.

Fourth, it is recommended that coaches use alternative approaches to measurement for assessing the physical attributes and skill level of the young athlete. Among the alternative assessment techniques are systematic observations, interviews, and rubrics (a ranked set of descriptors that specifies the components of a skill; Bishop, 2008). These approaches can complement the physical and skill tests that are already used by coaches, and can also be used effectively when working with young athletes.

REFERENCES

Baker, J., Schorer, J., Cobley, S., Schimmer, G., & Wattie, N. (2009). Circumstantial development and athletic excellence: The role of date of birth and birthplace. *European Journal of Sport Science, 9*(6), 329–339.

Birrer, R. B., Levine, R., Gallippi, L., & Tischler, H. (1986). The correlation of performance variables in preadolescent tennis players. *Journal of Sports Medicine & Physical Fitness, 26*(2), 137–139.

Bishop, P. A. (2008). *Measurement and evaluation in physical activity applications.* Scottsdale, AZ: Holcomb Hathaway.

Bompa, T. (1999). *Periodization: The theory and methodology of training* (4th ed.). Champaign, IL: Human Kinetics.

Brown, J. (2001). *Sports talent: How to identify and develop outstanding athletes.* Champaign, IL: Human Kinetics.

Camic, C. L., Housh, T. J., Mielke, M., Hendrix, C. R., Zuniga, J. M., Johnson, G. O., Housh, D. J., & Schmidt, R. J. (2009). Age-related patterns of anthropometric characteristics in young wrestlers. *Medicine and Science in Sports and Exercise, 41*(5), 1014–1019.

Carling, C., Reilly, T., & Williams, A. M. (2009). *Performance assessment for field sports.* London, UK: Routledge.

Côté, J., Macdonald, D. J., Baker, J., & Abernethy, B. (2006). When "where" is more important than "when": Birthplace and birthdate effects on the achievement of sporting expertise. *Journal of Sports Sciences, 24*(10), 1065–1073.

Falk, B., Lidor, R., Lander, Y., & Lang, B. (2004). Talent identification and early development of elite water-polo players: A 2-year follow-up study. *Journal of Sports Sciences, 22*(4), 347–355.

Girard, O., & Millet, G. P. (2009). Physical determinants of tennis performance in competitive teenage players. *Journal of Strength and Conditioning Research, 23*(6), 1867–1872.

Greco, C. C., & Denadai, B. S. (2005). Critical speed and endurance capacity in young swimmers: Effects of gender and age. *Pediatric Exercise Science, 17*(4), 353–363.

Grgantov, Z., Katic, R., & Jankovic, V. (2006). Morphological characteristics, technical and situation efficacy of young female volleyball players. *Collegium Antropologicum, 30*(1), 87–96.

Klika, R. J., & Thorland, W. G. (1994). Physiological determinants of sprint swimming performance in children and young adults. *Pediatric Exercise Science, 6*(1), 59–68.

Lacy, A. C. (2011). *Measurement and evaluation in physical education and exercise science* (6th ed.). Boston, MA: Benjamin Cummings.

Lidor, R., Côté, J., & Hackfort, D. (2009). ISSP position stand: To test or not to test? The use of physical skill tests in talent detection and in early phases of sport development. *International Journal of Sport and Exercise Psychology, 7*(2), 131–146.

Lidor, R., Falk, B., Arnon, M., Cohen, Y., Segal, G., & Lander, Y. (2005). Measurement of talent in team handball: The questionable use of motor and physical tests. *Journal of Strength & Conditioning Research, 19*(2), 318–325.

Lidor, R., Melnik, Y., Bilkevitz, A., Arnon, M., & Falk, B. (2005). Measurement of talent in judo using a unique, judo-specific ability test. *Journal of Sports Medicine and Physical Fitness, 45*(1), 32–37.

Malina, R. M., Cumming, S. P., Kontos, A. P., Eisenmann, J. C., Ribeiro, B., & Aroso, J. (2005). Maturity-associated variation in sport-specific skills of youth soccer players aged 13–15 years. *Journal of Sports Sciences, 23*(5), 515–522.

Malina, R. M., Eisenmann, J. C., Cumming, S. P., Ribeiro, B., & Aroso, J. (2004). Maturity-associated variation in the growth and functional capacities of youth football (soccer) players 13–15 years. *European Journal of Applied Physiology, 91*(5–6), 555–562.

Malina, R. M., Ribeiro, B., Aroso, J., & Cumming, S. P. (2007). Characteristics of youth soccer players aged 13–15 years classified by skill level. *British Journal of Sports Medicine, 41*(5), 290–295.

Mikulic, P., & Ruzic, L. (2008). Predicting the 1000m rowing ergometer performance in 12–13-year-old rowers: The basis for selection process? *Journal of Science and Medicine in Sport, 11*(2), 218–226.

Mikulic, P., Ruzic, L., & Markovic, G. (2009). Evaluation of specific anaerobic power in 12–14-year-old male rowers. *Journal of Science and Medicine in Sport, 12*(6), 662–666.

Mohamed, H., Vaeyens, R., Matthys, S., Multael, M., Lefevre, J., Lenoir, M., & Philippaerts, R. (2009). Anthropometric and performance measures for the development of a talent detection and identification model in youth handball. *Journal of Sports Sciences, 27*(3), 257–266.

Pienaar, A. E., Spamer, M. J., & Steyn, H. S. (1998). Identifying and developing rugby talent among 10-year-old boys: A practical model. *Journal of Sports Sciences, 16*(8), 691–699.

Reiman, M. P., & Manske, R. C. (2009). *Functional testing in human performance.* Champaign, IL: Human Kinetics.

Roetert, E. P., Brown, S. W., Piorkowski, P. A., & Woods, R. B. (1996). Fitness comparisons among three different levels of elite tennis players. *Journal of Strength and Conditioning Research, 10*(3), 139–143.

Roetert, E. P., Garrett, G. E., Brown, S. W., & Camaione, D. N. (1992). Performance profiles of nationally ranked junior tennis players. *Journal of Applied Sport Science Research, 6*(4), 225–231.

Saavedra, J. M., Escalante, Y., & Rodríguez, F. A. (2010). A multivariate analysis of performance in young swimmers. *Pediatric Exercise Science, 22*(1), 135–151.

Sady, S. P., Thomson, W. H., Berg, K., & Savage, M. (1984). Physiological characteristics of high-ability prepubescent wrestlers. *Medicine and Science in Sports and Exercise, 16*(1), 72–76.

Sady, S. P., Thomson, W. H., Savage, M., & Petratis, M. (1982). The body-composition and physical dimensions of 9- to 12-year-old experienced wrestlers. *Medicine and Science in Sports and Exercise, 14*(3), 244–248.

Strand, B. N., & Wilson, R. (1993). *Assessing sport skills.* Champaign, IL: Human Kinetics.

Tharp, G. D., Johnson, G. O., & Thorland, W. G. (1984). Measurement of anaerobic power and capacity in elite young track athletes using the Wingate test. *Journal of Sports Medicine & Physical Fitness, 24*(2), 100–106.

Thorland, W. G., Johnson, G. O., Cisar, C. J., Housh, T. J., & Tharp, G. D. (1987). Strength and anaerobic responses of elite young female sprint and distance runners. *Medicine and Science in Sports and Exercise, 19*(1), 56–61.

Thorland, W. G., Johnson, G. O., Cisar, C. J., Housh, T. J., & Tharp, G. D. (1990). Muscular strength and power in elite young male runners. *Pediatric Exercise Science, 2*(1), 73–82.

Vaeyens, R., Malina, R. M., Janssens, M., Van Renterghem, B., Bourgois, J., Vrijens, J., & Philippaerts, R. M. (2006). A multidisciplinary selection model for youth soccer: The Ghent Youth Soccer Project. *British Journal of Sports Medicine, 40*(11), 928–934.

Vitor, F., & Böhme, M. (2010). Performance of young male swimmers in the 100-meters front crawl. *Pediatric Exercise Science, 22*(2), 928–934.

CHAPTER 7

SELF-EFFICACY

Melissa A. Chase and Scott W. Pierce

INTRODUCTION

"I always believed I'd be a great athlete, whether I wanted to be one or not." In his book *Open: An Autobiography,* retired professional tennis player Andre Agassi points to his confidence as an important factor in his tennis success (Agassi, 2009, p. 105). Agassi's story of his talent development in tennis, from the time of his birth to his retirement, is unique and tumultuous. When Agassi was age two, his father made him run around with a racket taped to his hand and sleep with a tennis ball over his bed. His father's continued intensity and obsession with Andre becoming the best tennis player in the world dominated his childhood and led to a "love-hate" relationship with tennis that he did not reconcile with until very late in his career. Through all the highs and lows of Agassi's tennis career, his performance mirrored his confidence. When Agassi doubted his ability he dropped to a world ranking of 141. He would later make the decision to rededicate himself to tennis and through hard work and diligent preparation, Agassi was able to rebuild his confidence and go on to achieve renewed success. Andre Agassi's story does not represent the optimal learning environment for talent development in children, however it does illustrate the importance of believing in yourself and your athletic ability.

Most people believe that athletes with high self-confidence are more likely to be successful in their chosen sport. Coaches try to instill greater confidence in their athletes because they know these self-beliefs are related to better performance, higher motivation, and in the end, greater enjoyment. The theoretical foundation for these assumptions is based in part upon Bandura's work on self-efficacy theory (1977, 1986, 1997). Self-efficacy and self-confidence are often used interchangeably, with confidence being the more common term among athletes and practitioners. Self-efficacy refers to people's judgments of their capability to successfully perform a task or activity in a specific situation or context (e.g., free throw in a basketball game, golf putt during match play). Bandura (1997) stresses that self-efficacy beliefs are judgments that athletes have about what they can accomplish with the skills they have. For example, the statement "I have great jumping ability in basketball" explains which skills the athlete possesses but not what he can accomplish. A statement referring to self-efficacy would be "I think I can out-jump and get more rebounds than my opponent."

Self-confidence is defined as a more global perception of ability, or individuals' beliefs about their abilities to achieve success based on these abilities (Vealey & Chase, 2007). When athletes make statements about qualities they have (i.e., I have great running speed) or statements that describe who they are (i.e., I am a great runner), they are referring more to self-confidence than self-efficacy. While the study of more global perceptions of ability has in many ways contributed to the understanding of the relationship between self-belief and performance, this chapter will focus on the importance of self-efficacy to children's talent development in sport and how self-efficacy develops in optimal learning environments. The first section of the chapter describes self-efficacy theory (e.g., sources, types, consequences, and factors related to children's self-efficacy). The next section provides an overview of the research in self-efficacy, focusing on implications for talent development, and the last section describes how to create an optimal learning environment for enhancing self-efficacy and talent development.

SELF-EFFICACY THEORY

Self-efficacy theory was originally developed from Bandura's work in social cognitive theory (1977, 1986). He proposed that self-referent thought mediates the relationship between knowledge and behavior. Therefore, how individuals evaluate their capabilities and their self-perceptions of efficacy will affect their thought patterns, motivation, emotional reactions, and behavior. Bandura defined self-efficacy as "beliefs in one's capabilities to organize and execute the courses of action required to produce given attainments" (Bandura, 1997, p. 3). This suggests that efficacy judgments are not based on what those skills are; rather, they are based on what one can do with whatever skills one possesses. For example, talented athletes may understand and have strong beliefs about their ability to use their highly developed skills in the context of their sport. An efficacious ice hockey player believes he can skate with the puck, react to the defense, and score a goal in the closing minutes of a game.

In the sport psychology literature, self-efficacy expectations are not the only influence on thoughts and behavior; however, they are consistently found to be an important and necessary cognitive mechanism (Bandura, 1997). These expectations include not only regulating one's physical performance execution (e.g., ability to successfully complete a cross-country race), but also regulating the thought processes, emotional states, and actions needed in relation to changing environmental conditions. An athlete might believe she has the ability to run a cross-country race successfully, but her self-efficacy about running might differ under competitive conditions if she has experienced difficulty in recent training runs, is feeling anxious, or is being pushed by the competition to run faster than her normal pace. Self-efficacy is dynamic and involves the control of physical performance execution, disruptive thinking (e.g., negative thoughts, worries), and affective states (e.g., anxiety, fear). Therefore, specific types of efficacy beliefs in the sport domain include task efficacy, self-regulatory efficacy, competitive efficacy, learning efficacy, preparatory efficacy, ameliorative or coping efficacy, and performance efficacy. Task efficacy is defined as athletes' belief in their ability to perform a particular task. Self-regulatory efficacy is defined as athletes' belief in their ability to adhere to or have control over their motivation, thoughts, emotions, and behavior. Competitive efficacy focuses on athletes' belief in their ability to perform successfully against an opponent or win in competitive situations. Learning efficacy and preparatory efficacy both involve the learning of new skills but they are considered to be slightly different types of efficacy (Bandura, 1997). Learning efficacy is the belief athletes have in their ability to learn a new skill, whereas preparatory efficacy is the belief athletes have that they can successfully perform the skill while preparing for competition (or acquiring new skills) in practice. Ameliorative or coping efficacy is defined as the belief athletes have in their ability to control diverse threats such as negative thoughts, pain, or stress. Finally, performance efficacy refers to the athletes' belief that they can be successful at the time of a performance or competition (Feltz, Short, & Sullivan, 2008).

SOURCES OF SELF-EFFICACY

Self-efficacy theory (Bandura, 1986) suggests that there are four sources of efficacy information: past performance, vicarious experience, verbal persuasion, and physiological/affective states. Maddux (1995) proposed two additional determinants of self-efficacy—emotional states and imaginal experiences, which have often been included in the literature. These six sources influence one's efficacy expectations, which in turn influence one's behavior patterns (e.g., choice, effort, persistence) and thought patterns (e.g., goals, worry, attributions) (see Figure 7.1). Individuals may depend upon one or more of these sources to form their efficacy expectations. The cognitive processing of efficacy information involves (a) determining the types of information attended to and used, and (b) the combination rules or heuristics used for weighting and integrating various pieces of efficacy information (Bandura, 1986). Often forgotten is the fact that the importance of an individual's efficacy sources can vary across situations and domains. That is, to enhance their self-efficacy, athletes may use different sources in different ways in different situations. For example, an elite tennis player may depend upon his parents for positive comments and encouragement early in the tennis season; they have always been very encouraging and their support adds to his self-efficacy beliefs. As the season progresses and he gains some wins and good performances, he then relies more on this good performance for his self-efficacy. At the end of the season, in preparation for the tournament, he chooses to rely more on his coach for self-efficacy information. He views the coach's opinion and advice as an important source at this stage of the season. All of these sources of information are important to his efficacy beliefs, with a slight shift in importance as the demands of tennis change throughout the season.

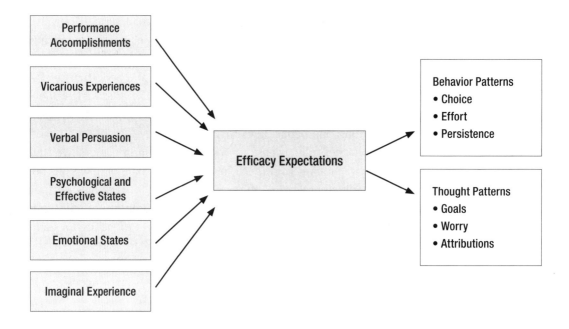

Figure 7.1. Relationship between sources of self-efficacy, efficacy expectations, and behavior/thought patterns

Past Performance

Sources of past performance are based upon one's mastery experiences or accomplishments. This source is believed to be the most influential in determining efficacy beliefs. Typically, if past performances are successful, efficacy expectations will increase; if performances are unsuccessful, efficacy expectations will be lowered. Bandura (1997) has also stated that the temporal pattern of success and failure will affect performance experiences and efficacy expectations. Too many failed early attempts without success might lead to task avoidance and lower efficacy. Children benefit the most when the task is modified to produce successful attempts, with occasional failures at first, and then with the task difficulty and effort required for success gradually increased (Chase, Ewing, Lirgg, & George, 1994). For example, a child learning to play basketball may have higher efficacy if she makes a lot of baskets when first learning to shoot. However, if she continues to miss shot after shot, her efficacy may be lowered. One way to modify the task to help ensure greater success is to lower the basket height from 10 feet to 9 feet and to use an intermediate size basketball.

There is some debate about the effect of task difficulty and amount of effort needed to succeed on self-efficacy beliefs. Not yet supported with research, it is hypothesized that self-efficacy should increase following success with low effort on difficult tasks (Bandura, 1997). In turn, efficacy will decrease following failure or even success on difficult tasks that require so much effort that the performer cannot foresee being able to sustain the needed effort in future attempts.

Vicarious Experience

This source of information involves observation and comparison of others' performance on a task. Watching other people perform successfully can increase self-efficacy, while seeing others perform unsuccessfully can lower expectations. These modeling effects are more potent when one is similar to the model (George, Feltz, & Chase, 1992). For example, the athlete might compare her or his body size, age, or gender with the model. Self-efficacy can also be determined by making social comparisons with the performance of others. Children may watch other athletes perform and learn from the positive and negative consequences of their performance, and thus form their own efficacy judgments. While vicarious experiences are believed to be weaker than performance accomplishments, they can be an influential source. The most salient information to vicariously increase one's efficacy would come from models that are of slightly higher ability level and provide a challenge to perform better.

Verbal Persuasion

Verbal persuasion is usually found in the form of instruction or persuasive techniques from significant others (e.g., parents, coaches, peers), self-talk, and other cognitive strategies. Bandura (1986) states that it is more difficult to raise efficacy beliefs with this source than it is to lower beliefs; however, sustained positive verbal persuasion may serve as a strong motivator for children. Verbal messages directed toward performance must be realistic, and the extent of the influence will depend upon the credibility and trustworthiness of the person providing the message. Self-talk and affirmation statements are examples of the ways in which athletes can persuade themselves that they have the capacity to successfully perform. Verbal persuasion that focuses on the process and progress toward improvement will lead to higher self-efficacy than comments focusing on product and errors in competition (Bandura, 1997). An example of this is Coach Smith, who focuses on the fundamentals and techniques of hitting a baseball, and provides suggestions on how to improve the athlete's swing, as opposed to Coach Jones, who focuses only on whether the athlete hit the baseball. The athlete with Coach Smith will have higher efficacy over time than the athlete with Coach Jones.

Physiological States

Information from this source is the result of the cognitive appraisal of a physiological condition or state. They include affective states, autonomic arousal, levels of pain, and fatigue. Typically, negative physiological states will lower efficacy expectations, and positive states or the absence of negative states will increase efficacy expectations. The level and quality of these states must be evaluated and interpreted individually within the context of the situation and meaning assigned to the response. For example, children may perceive "butterflies in their stomach" as a sign that they are feeling ill or, in a more positive way, that they are excited about the competition.

Emotional States

Emotional states can be described as the mood of the individual. Happiness, stress, or fear derived from involvement in a sport or physical activity might impact the development of efficacy expectations (Chase, Magyar, & Drake, 2005; Kavanagh & Hausfeld, 1986; Maddux,

1995). Bandura (1997) suggests that athletes cognitively appraise emotions and this affects their behavior. They often make judgments about whether they can cope with an emotional state such as stress or fear and still reach their performance goals. When children experience happiness or positive moods and success, they are more likely to increase their efficacy beliefs, while children who experience sadness and failure are more likely to decrease their efficacy beliefs.

Imaginal Experiences

Maddux (1995) refers to the use of mental imagery and how those images and feelings influence one's self-efficacy and improve performance as a separate source of self-efficacy. Bandura (1997) referred to this source as self-modeling under vicarious experiences. Despite how it is categorized, imaginal experiences can increase self-efficacy beliefs if the images are successful and decrease self-efficacy if the images are a failure (Vealey & Walter, 1993). Talented athletes who hit the winning shot, score the overtime goal, or become a hero when the match is on the line, often describe the numerous times they have practiced the competition's deciding moment in their dreams or imagination.

All six of these determinants are cognitively appraised, within the context of the situation, to develop one's efficacy expectations. The key to developing optimal learning environments is to incorporate all of these sources in age-appropriate ways that fit the context of the situation and individual (Chase, 1998).

CONSEQUENCES OF SELF-EFFICACY

Self-efficacy beliefs contribute to psychosocial behavior in distinct ways. These beliefs will influence how people behave (e.g., choice, effort, persistence), how they perform, their thought patterns (e.g., goals, worry, attributions), and their emotional reactions (e.g., happiness, sadness) in various situations. For example, children tend to avoid situations in which they believe they are not capable of performing. Their level of efficacy will determine how much effort they put forth and how long they will persist in the face of failure. Thoughts and emotional reactions are affected by one's efficacy in regard to stress and attentional demands. Children with high self-efficacy can focus their attention on the task at hand and expend more effort than children with low self-efficacy, who may be stressed and tend to divert attention from possible solutions.

Self-efficacy also influences how people cognitively decode things that happen to them. A strong sense of self-efficacy fosters optimism, belief in opportunities for improvement, and effective courses of action. People with stronger self-efficacy set higher goals and commit to their goals more strongly (Bandura & Wood, 1989) than do people with weaker beliefs about their abilities. Also, people who believe strongly in their problem-solving abilities are highly efficient and highly effective problem solvers and decision makers, while those who doubt their abilities are cognitively inefficient and ineffective in solving problems and making decisions (Bandura & Jourden, 1991).

Overall, studies have consistently found that self-efficacy is an essential and meaningful cognitive mechanism in predicting, explaining, and describing performance, whether in the laboratory or in competitive sport situations (Bandura, 1997; Feltz et al., 2008). We know that performance success raises efficacy beliefs and failures tend to lower beliefs. In turn, given that an individual has the proper incentives and requisite skills, self-efficacy will be a major determinant of behavior (Bandura, 1977). Specific to the purpose of this chapter, the next section focuses on factors related to children's self-efficacy.

FACTORS RELATED TO CHILDREN'S SELF-EFFICACY

Too often in sport children are assumed to take on the characteristics of adults in their perceptions, actions, and performance capabilities. Consideration must be made of the differences between adults and children, and to what extent appropriate action and accurate interpretation of results can be made for children in sport. Several factors that relate specifically to children are accuracy of beliefs, conceptions of ability, attributions, understanding effort and ability, and gender differences in self-efficacy.

Accuracy of Beliefs
An important issue within the study of children's self-efficacy is the accuracy with which they appraise their own physical ability. Bandura (1986) refers to one's overestimation of ability as similar to a resilient sense of efficacy. Resilient efficacy expectations, if not unrealistically exaggerated, can be advantageous (Bandura, 1986). However, misjudgment of one's ability has consequences. Individuals who overestimate their ability may try activities in which they cannot succeed and may subsequently experience needless failures. For example, an elite gymnast who attempts a double back-handspring when she is still having difficulty with a back-handspring may fail or even get injured because she is not ready for the more advanced skill. These failures may undermine their development of efficacy or present potentially dangerous situations that result in injury (Bandura, 1986). Underestimators of their ability may become self-limiting and restrict the activities that they experience. Therefore, the degree to which children are accurate in their self-appraisal is crucial information that will affect their motivation (choice, effort, and persistence) and future efficacy beliefs.

Research in perceptions of competence has found that as children get older they become more accurate in their estimates of competence (Benenson & Dweck, 1986; Harter, 1982; Nicholls, 1978; Stipek, 1981; Stipek & Tannatt, 1984). Horn and Weiss (1991) examined ability judgments in children aged 8 to 13 years. They found that accuracy judgments of physical competence were low in 8- to 9-year-olds, and increased with age. Feltz and Brown (1984) investigated the accuracy of perception of competence in soccer players aged 9 to 13 years. They found that children were more accurate in their perceptions of soccer competence as their age increased. When Chase and colleagues (1994) examined basketball shooting efficacy in children aged 9 to 11, they found that the children in their study tended to drastically overestimate their basketball shooting efficacy in relation to actual shooting performance, regardless of their age. Chase (2001a) examined age and gender differences in children's self-appraisal of ability in physical education and sport to determine how those estimates relate to their motivational intentions. She found an age and gender interaction, as 8- and 9-year-old boys overestimated their ability more so than 8- to 9-year-old girls; however, 12- to 13-year-old girls overestimated their ability more so than 12- to 13-year-old boys. Surprisingly, there were low correlations between accuracy scores and intended effort. In summary, children under 10 or 11 years typically are not accurate in estimating their ability. After age 11 or 12 they become more accurate in their beliefs, due to developmental changes in their conception of ability and understanding of effort and ability.

Conception of Ability

Research has shown that preexisting belief systems, such as implicit theories of intelligence or conception of ability, may affect self-efficacy (Jourden, Bandura, & Banfield, 1991; Kanfer, 1990; Wood & Bandura, 1989). In general, people with an incremental conception of ability (i.e., believe that ability level is changeable) will have higher self-efficacy, whereas people with a fixed entity conception of ability (i.e., believe that ability level is not changeable) tend to have lower self-efficacy.

Dweck's research for the past 20 years has demonstrated that how children view their abilities profoundly affects the way they live their lives (Dweck, 2006). Her research has examined how two mindsets (a fixed mindset or a growth mindset) affect school achievement, friendships, athletic performance, and motivation. Specifically, if children believe that their abilities are fixed or unchangeable (similar to a fixed entity belief), they tend to believe they either have what it takes to succeed or they don't. A fixed mindset affects children's effort because they believe that those who have the ability don't have to work hard, that things come easily to them. When they do encounter failure they tend to give up, or they only seek out opportunities where there is no risk of failure. Children with a growth mindset think just the opposite. They believe that their ability is changeable and that they can improve with effort (similar to an incremental belief). Failure is not threatening to them because it is a part of learning and of working hard to accomplish something. A review of the literature in this area has found clear and consistent findings that children with a growth mindset (as opposed to a fixed mindset) will have higher self-efficacy (Kanfer, 1990), persist longer and put forth more effort (Jourden et al., 1991), perform better in physical activities (Lirgg, George, Chase, & Ferguson, 1996), and have higher school grades and achievement test scores (Dweck, 2006).

Understanding Effort and Ability

Nicholl's (1984) work in achievement motivation theory also suggests that conceptions of ability, task difficulty, and effort will vary in meaning for children of different cognitive maturity levels, and this influences self-beliefs and motivation. Children 5 to 6 years old have a self-referenced conception of task difficulty and are considered egocentric. They make decisions about the difficulty of the task based upon how hard the task was for them to complete. They typically are not capable of differentiating between effort, luck, or ability, so that children who are viewed as putting forth the most effort possess the most ability. Children 7 to 11 years old tend to have a norm-referenced conception of task difficulty or are considered to be at a normative level. They may be able to partially differentiate between conceptions of effort, luck, ability, and task difficulty, although they sometimes equate putting forth less effort with having high ability. Children 12 years and older can typically differentiate ability from effort, luck, and task difficulty. They understand that ability is a capacity, so that when an individual performs better than a friend and an equal amount of effort was put forth, or performs as well without putting forth much effort, the outcome is due to higher ability.

Fry and Duda (1997) extended Nicholls' theory of achievement motivation by examining children's understanding of effort and ability aspects in the sporting and academic domains. One hundred and forty students between the ages of 5 and 13, including eight boys and eight girls from each age group, completed two film sessions and an interview. Each of the film sessions showed two children applying unequal effort in a task (physical and academic), with the outcome being: the children achieving the same score, and the lazier child achieving a higher score. A positive and strong relationship in relation to effort and ability emerged between physical and academic tasks. This provided support for the levels of understanding of effort and ability in the physical task, as identified by Nicholls. Additionally, support was found for the hierarchical nature of reasoning, with conceptions of effort and ability building over time. No gender differences were evident in understanding effort and ability in either physical or academic contexts. Nicholls' theory and subsequent research suggests that understanding the difference between ability, effort, luck, and task difficulty is a developmental factor (associated with but not determined by age) that impacts how children perceive their self-beliefs.

Attributions

Bandura (1986) states that there is a reciprocal relationship between causal attributions and self-efficacy expectations. He suggests that individuals with high self-efficacy who experience failure tend to attribute that failure to lack of effort, whereas individuals with low self-efficacy who experience failure attribute that failure to low ability (Bandura, 1990; Collins, 1986). In turn, success will increase self-efficacy if the attribution is due to ability rather than luck. Failure can result if attributions for previous failures are thought to be due to lack of ability rather than low effort or bad luck.

Only a few studies have examined children's causal attributions for performance in a sport situation (e.g., Bird & Williams, 1980; Bukowski & Moore, 1980; Weiss, McAuley, Ebbeck, & Wiese, 1990). Bird and Williams (1980) examined age differences in 7- to 18-year-old children. They found that 7 to 9 year olds attributed success mainly to effort and luck. Children 10- to 15 years old attributed performance to effort, whereas 16- to 18-year-old males attributed performance to effort and females of this age attributed performance to luck. Bukowski and Moore (1980) investigated perceived causes for success and failure among boys 7 to 16 years of age. They found that attributions for luck and task difficulty had little importance for boys. Ability was found to be an important attribute only for success, whereas effort was viewed as important for success and failure. Chase (2001b), in her research with 8- to 14-year-old children, found that high efficacy children attributed their failure more to lack of effort, whereas low efficacy children attributed failure to lack of ability.

Overall, the attributions that children make for their failures are very important to future self-efficacy, performance, and motivation. If children believe that they fail because of lack of ability and that their ability will never change, meaning their performance will never improve, why should they continue to try? Failure is neither enjoyable nor viewed as acceptable in most situations. Attributions of low ability could certainly lead to lower self-efficacy and discontinuation from the activity. Therefore, children should attribute their failures to lack of effort or preparation (Schunk, 1995) and successes to effort and ability (Bandura, 1990).

Gender Differences in Children's Self-Efficacy

Initial research on gender differences in self-beliefs was conducted from a self-confidence perspective, which informs subsequent research in self-efficacy. Early research suggested that males had higher self-confidence than females in all achievement situations (Maccoby & Jacklin, 1974). Lenney (1977) suggested that gender differences in self-confidence were due to specific achievement situations: when tasks were competitive, when ambiguous feedback was given, and/or when the task was sex-typed as male or masculine. Several studies examined gender differences in the self-confidence of children performing various motor tasks, and mixed results were found (e.g., Corbin, Landers, Feltz, & Senior, 1983; Corbin & Nix, 1979; Lewko & Ewing, 1980). In Lirgg's (1991) meta-analysis of self-confidence studies, she found that when studies incorporated masculine tasks (e.g., tasks that are typically done by males only or are viewed by society as more appropriate for males), this contributed to males having higher confidence than females in some situations. When these results were examined by age, she found that self-confidence decreased by age while gender differences in self-confidence increased, with males having higher confidence than females. This suggests that boys and girls under 12 to 13 years old tend to be similar in levels of self-confidence; however, boys have higher confidence than girls when they are over 13 years old. Lirgg suggested that these results should be interpreted with caution, because the studies were conducted with small sample sizes.

In the Chase et al. (1994) study, which examined self-efficacy, results indicated that boys and girls did not differ in their self-efficacy by gender on a basketball-shooting task. The explanation provided was that basketball was perceived as a gender-neutral task. In a study with 8- to 14-year-old boys and girls, Chase (2001b) found that when children were allowed to select their own sport or physical activity and then report on their efficacy beliefs, there were no gender differences. Overall, it is important to note that "males do not always have higher self-efficacy scores than females" (Feltz et al., 2008. p. 114). There are a host of variables that could interact with perceptions of self-efficacy for girls and boys as they develop and mature into confident athletes.

SUMMARY OF RESEARCH ON CHILDREN'S SELF-EFFICACY AND RECOMMENDATIONS FOR FUTURE RESEARCH

Sport participation is important in developing and validating children's self-efficacy (Bandura, 1997) and determining their social status among their peers (Chase & Dummer, 1992; Chase & Machida, 2011). Most of the previous research has examined sources of self-efficacy and associated factors in children, but there have been only a few studies examining the consequences of self-efficacy in children (e.g., behavior, thought patterns, emotional reactions). Those studies found, for example, that youth wrestlers who remained in the sport had higher self-efficacy than wrestlers who dropped out (Burton & Martens, 1986), that children with higher efficacy chose to participate in sport in the future more than children with lower efficacy (Chase,

2001b), and that runners with higher self-efficacy chose more difficult tasks than those with lower self-efficacy (Escartí & Guzmán, 1999). Research has often drawn from the results of studies with adults or adolescents and applied the findings to children. Developmental factors suggest that this is not appropriate, and more research is needed with children. See Table 7.1 for an overview of self-efficacy research conclusions.

Table 7.1. Overview of Self-Efficacy Research Conclusions

1. Accurate self-beliefs will positively affect motivation (choice, effort, and persistence) and future efficacy beliefs.
2. Children become more accurate in their estimates of competence as they age.
3. Children who believe performance can improve will have higher self-efficacy, persist longer, put forth more effort, and perform better in physical activities.
4. Task difficulty and effort will vary in meaning for children of different cognitive maturity levels, and this influences self-beliefs and motivation.
5. Children should attribute their failures to lack of effort or preparation and successes to effort and ability.
6. Boys tend to have higher efficacy beliefs in sport than girls, but not always.
7. Children with higher efficacy choose to participate in sport in the future more than children with lower efficacy.

Future research related to talent development in children should focus on the role of self-efficacy and the development and maintenance of these beliefs over time as children develop. Ericsson (2003) suggests that expert performers have the acquired ability to use mental representations to anticipate, plan, and decide upon alternative paths of action. These mental representations add to the control of complex mechanisms such as attention, memory, and perceptions. Ericsson goes on to suggest that "most amateurs do not improve their performance only because they have reached (in their minds) an acceptable level" (Ericsson, 2003, p. 63). Perhaps in children, perceptions of ability, conceptions of ability, and understanding of effort or task difficulty as related to self-efficacy tend to influence how they define acceptable levels and assess their motivation to become better performers. Future research might examine in greater depth children's goals and their definition of acceptable levels.

Future research might also focus on the role of self-perceptions (self-efficacy or self-confidence) in promoting deliberate practice in children. Self-efficacy research would suggest that one's willingness to put forth effort, choose to stay with the task, and persist in the face of failure are predicted by the level of self-efficacy (Bardura, 1997; Chase, 2001b). For example, Gould and Carson (2004) stated their concern that without developing a love of the game, children will not have the motivation to sustain the effort needed to pursue excellence and to put forth as many as 10,000 hours or 10 years of deliberate practice to develop into expert performers, as suggested by Ericsson (1996). The love of the game often comes from and is associated with the perception that one is good at the game.

The structure of youth sports, especially in the United States, has increasingly become more about specializing in one sport at an early age than about diversification across many sports (Wiersma, 2000). Research by Côté and colleagues (Côté, 1999; Côté & Fraser-Thomas, 2008) on the Developmental Model of Sport Participation (DMSP) highlights the importance of physical training and psychosocial influences through three stages of athlete development. See Chapter 11 for more information about these stages: the first stage (the sampling years), the second stage (the specializing years), and the third stage (the investment years).

Côté and Fraser-Thomas (2008) suggest that in the sampling years children should be provided with sampling opportunities that will influence perceptions of competence (e.g., self-efficacy), and in turn, motivation. Future research might examine how children's self-efficacy influences the sports which they choose to sample, and their decision to continue with or drop out of these sports in the years to come. Which sources of information between the ages of 6 and 13 years are most salient for children as they sample new sports and decide whether to specialize? See Table 7.2 for a summary of future research suggestions.

Table 7.2. A Summary of Future Research Suggestions

1. How do children's perceptions of ability, conceptions of ability, and understanding of effort or task difficulty as related to self-efficacy influence the ways they define acceptable levels of performance and their motivation to become better performers?
2. How do self-perceptions (self-efficacy or self-confidence) promote deliberate practice in children?
3. How does children's self-efficacy influence the sports they choose to sample?
4. How does children's self-efficacy influence their decision to continue with or drop out of these sports?
5. Which sources of information between the ages of 6 and 13 years are most salient for children as they sample new sports and decide whether to specialize?

CREATING THE OPTIMAL LEARNING ENVIRONMENT FOR SELF-EFFICACY

There is a popular myth that some children are natural-born athletes, born with special qualities that naturally lead them to become exceptional athletes. Nevertheless, research would suggest that these athletes are not innately athletically gifted; they developed their talents after countless hours of deliberate play (Côté & Fraser-Thomas, 2008), deliberate practice (Ericsson, Krampe, & Tesch-Romen, 1993), and numerous athletic competitions. Along with skill development and thousands of hours of preparation, a strong belief in their abilities was constructed. For talented children hoping to become world-class athletes, efficacious beliefs can result from optimal learning environments in which they develop their athletic talent. The last section of this chapter suggests ways to create a learning environment conducive to enhancing self-efficacy beliefs.

The context of any situation has to be considered, and a one-size-fits-all approach never works well. Especially with children, when applying techniques to enhance self-efficacy, it is important to consider the individual, his or her developmental level and experience, influence of significant others, and situation-specific aspects of his or her sport. In general, efficacy-enhancing techniques often focus on the six sources of self-efficacy and how to build and maintain these beliefs. For example, Feltz et al. (2008) provide a list of 14 efficacy-enhancing techniques specific to novice and to experienced athletes, which are comprehensive and stem from (a) performance accomplishments, (b) vicarious experiences, (c) verbal persuasion, (d) physiological states, (e) emotional states, and (f) imaginal experiences. Chase (2010) also describes several methods for improving self-efficacy in children with mental skills training, revealing the importance of using a developmental perspective that encompasses the influences of psychological, biological, social, and physical factors within the social context of their sport.

We propose six recommendations for creating an optimal learning environment, which focus on the key factors influencing self-efficacy (see Figure 7.2). These are described individually in the following section, and include the recommendations to (a) understand, integrate, and weigh all the sources of self-efficacy information; (b) modify the task for early success; (c) include challenges to overcome adversity; (d) use effort attributions for success and failure; (e) view conception of ability as incremental; and (f) provide unconditional support by significant others regardless of the outcome.

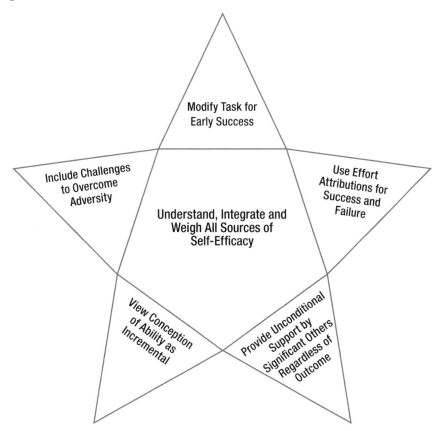

Figure 7.2. Creating an optimal learning environment.

Using the illustration of a star, at the center of the recommendations is the child's ability to *understand, integrate, and weigh all the sources of self-efficacy information.* As children develop, they will be able to simultaneously attend to multiple sources of efficacy information and start to distinguish between important and less important information (Bandura, 1997). Their ability to process multiple sources of efficacy information, as well as their improved self-appraisal skills, will help them form accurate judgments about abilities and task demands. An optimal learning environment would encourage multiple sources of efficacy information and boost proficient self-appraisal skills. For example, it is important to help children understand the demands of the task through explanation (verbal), demonstration (nonverbal), and modeling (similar others). Repetition of skills and tactics should be provided so they can integrate efficacy information from successful and unsuccessful attempts over time (Bandura, 1997). Assisting children with setting realistic goals is beneficial in limiting the discrepancy between their goal and performance, so that they will not become discouraged or set their goals too low so that they become bored. The ability to characterize and retain efficacy information derived from frequent prior experiences and situations provides a stable sense of efficacy and resilience.

Since past performance is such a strong determinant of efficacy beliefs and future success, an optimal learning environment ensures that children will experience success. One of the best ways to create successful performance accomplishments is to *modify the task for early success.* It is important to incorporate Bandura's (1986) recommendation for a temporal pattern of success and failure by seeking early success with a few failures, as opposed to early failure with a few successes. Modification of sport skills can be accomplished by changing the equipment, the rules, the playing field, the opponent (e.g., defense or no defense), or the target goals. For example, Chase et al. (1994) examined equipment modification in youth basketball and found that modifications such as lowering the basket height and decreasing the basketball size could influence efficacy beliefs and shooting performance. An optimal learning environment for talented children would modify the task or situation so that the children would experience success with some failure, and as they improve and gain confidence the level of difficulty could increase.

Monitor the modification closely so that the task does not become too easy, causing the children to lose interest. Interviews with professional athletes reflecting upon their own childhood experiences and talent development suggested that an optimal learning environment also includes *challenges to overcome adversity* (Chase, Pierce, Byrd, & Roethlisberger, 2010). All of the professional athletes interviewed in this study stated that overcoming challenges helped them gain confidence and become better performers. They recalled family members (e.g., older siblings, parents) competing hard with them and not letting them win in games as a key influence in their development. Overcoming adversity also teaches children resiliency and the importance of self-belief. Therefore, the balance between success and challenge is important. For some talented athletes this may mean that she or he will play with children a year or so older on a more competitive team than that available at her or his own age level. Or, the coach should provide more challenging practices and competitions to enhance the skill level of the athlete.

Another recommendation for creating an optimal learning environment is to encourage the child, parents, and coaches to use *effort attributions for success and failure.* When children are learning a new skill it often takes some time and practice before the skill is acquired. If the child quits directly after a failure occurs, without trying hard or persisting, then learning is unlikely. Changing children's beliefs about their ability to be successful should provide them with the motivation to continue past that learning curve. One of the most important tenets of self-efficacy theory is that efficacy beliefs will sustain effort, persistence, and choice in the face of failure. When individuals are successful, not as much intervention is required. However, in situations where failure occurs, then that is when motivational intentions may become critical, so that with time individuals can overcome mistakes, learn new skills, and improve performance. Using effort attributions for failure encourages children to believe that with hard work they will improve and eventually master the skill. Using effort attributions for success can also reinforce the importance of hard work and persistence. As children learn the difference between effort and ability, at around the age of 11 to 12 years, attributions to effort become even more important in an optimal learning environment.

Similar to using effort attributions is the recommendation that children *view conception of ability as incremental.* Children who view ability as changeable and not as a set entity will more likely be motivated to put forth effort to improve. If the learning environment is set up so that children are taught that their ability is innate or less likely to change, they may develop a belief that working hard to improve would not change their performance. An optimal learning environment for talent and self-efficacy development would stress that ability to perform at the highest levels comes from practice and hard work. As parents and coaches, it is sometimes difficult to work with talented young athletes and avoid comments and behavior that reinforces the notion they are innately talented, because performing new skills can come very easy to talented children. Nevertheless, as they get older and performance demands increase, children will reach a point where practice and hard work and the motivation to continue are needed for them to develop to their full potential.

Unconditional support provided by significant others regardless of the outcome is placed at the base of the star, to represent this recommendation as a foundation for an optimal learning environment. There are two keys to this recommendation. First, significant others typically are parents or other family members. Csikszentmihalyi, Rathunde, Whalen, and Wong (1993) suggest that no child succeeds unless he or she is supported by caring adults or significant others. Côté (1999) found that families, particularly the parents, play a crucial role in elite athlete development as the athletes progress through the sampling, specializing, and investment years. Bloom's (1985) talent development research has also demonstrated the important role parents play in athletic talent development. The second key is that support is unconditional regardless of the outcome. This suggests that whether the child wins or loses, plays well or plays poorly, the support from his or her significant others is the same and is positive. Optimal learning environments should provide consistent, unconditional support as well. For example, Kate scored the winning goal in the championship game. Her teammates and fans showered her with hugs and admiration for days. Her parents treated Kate the same as they always did after a game and the same as if she had missed the winning goal in the championship game. Their unconditional support of Kate will enhance her self-efficacy and become a source she depends on in the future.

Creating the optimal learning environment for self-efficacy development and improved performance will help foster talent development in children. The optimal learning environment is one in which a developmental perspective that includes the influences of psychological, biological, social, and physical factors within the social context of the sport is considered. Self-efficacy expectations are not the only influence on performance and talent development; however, they are consistently found to be an important and necessary cognitive mechanism for success (Bandura, 1997).

CONCLUSION

Coaches, physical educators, and other practitioners may want to implement the following suggestions when attempting to create the optimal learning environment for children:

- Keep in mind that performance accomplishments are important for enhancing efficacy.

- Teach or coach children at their appropriate developmental levels, both cognitive and physical.

- Provide a balanced mixture of success and challenge to improve performance when designing their practice experiences. This can include modifying the practice situation for early success, providing a large number of practice repetitions, and keeping the practice challenging and fun.

- Be positive in verbal and nonverbal communication with children.

- Provide children with information about how to improve their performance and encourage attributions that suggest children can improve with good effort.

This chapter proposes that children at all levels of talent development need to encounter an optimal learning environment in which they can improve their performance, enjoy participation at appropriate developmental levels, and utilize various sources of efficacy information.

REFERENCES

Agassi, A. (2009). *Open: An autobiography*. New York, NY: Knopf Doubleday.

Bandura, A. (1977). Self-efficacy: Toward a unifying theory of behavioral change. *Psychological Review, 84*(2), 191–215.

Bandura, A. (1986). *Social foundations of thought and action: A social cognitive theory*. Englewood Cliffs, NJ: Prentice-Hall.

Bandura, A. (1990). Perceived self-efficacy in the exercise of personal agency. *Applied Sport Psychology, 2*(2), 128–163.

Bandura, A. (1997). *Self-efficacy: The exercise of control*. New York, NY: Freeman.

Bandura, A., & Jourden, F. J. (1991). Self-regulatory mechanisms governing the impact of social comparison on complex decision making. *Journal of Personality and Social Psychology, 60*(6), 941–951.

Bandura, A., & Wood, R. (1989). Effect of perceived controllability and performance standards on self-regulation of complex decision making. *Journal of Personality and Social Psychology, 56*, 805–814.

Benenson, J., & Dweck, C. (1986). The development of trait explanations and self-evaluations in the academic and social domains. *Child Development, 57*(5), 1179–1187.

Bird, A. M., & Williams, J. M. (1980). A developmental-attributional analysis of sex role stereotypes for sport performance. *Developmental Psychology, 16*(4), 319–322.

Bloom, B. S. (Ed.). (1985). *Developing talent in young people.* New York, NY: Ballantine.

Bukowski, W. M., & Moore, D. (1980). Winners' and losers' attributions for success and failure in a series of athletic events. *Journal of Sport and Exercise Psychology, 2*(3), 195–210.

Burton, D., & Martens, R. (1986). Pinned by their own goals: An exploratory investigation into why kids drop out of wrestling. *Journal of Sport Psychology, 8*(3), 183–197.

Chase, M. A. (1998). Sources of self-efficacy in physical education and sport. *Journal of Teaching in Physical Education, 18*(1), 76–89.

Chase, M. A. (2001a). Children's accuracy of self-appraisal of ability and motivational beliefs in physical education. *The Physical Educator, 58,* 103–112.

Chase, M. A. (2001b). Children's self-efficacy, motivational intentions, and attributions in physical education and sport. *Research Quarterly for Sport and Exercise, 72*(1), 47–54.

Chase, M. A. (2010). Children and applied sport psychology. In S. Hanrahan & M. Andersen (Eds.), *Handbook of applied sport psychology* (pp. 377-386). London, UK: Routledge.

Chase, M. A., & Dummer, G. M. (1992). The role of sport as a social status determinant for children. *Research Quarterly for Exercise and Sport, 63*(4), 418–424.

Chase, M. A., & Machida, M. (2011). The role of sports as a social status determinant for children and adolescents: Thirty years later. *Research Quarterly for Exercise and Sport, 82,* 593–601.

Chase, M. A., Magyar, T. M., & Drake, B. (2005). Fear of injury in gymnastics: Self-efficacy and psychological strategies to keep on tumbling. *Journal of Sports Sciences, 23*(5), 465–475.

Chase, M. A., Ewing, M. E., Lirgg, C. D., & George, T. R. (1994). The effects of equipment modification on children's self-efficacy and basketball shooting performance. *Research Quarterly for Exercise and Sport, 65*(2), 159–168.

Chase, M. A., Pierce, S. W., Byrd, M., & Roethlisberger, B. (2010). *Talent development in youth sports: Reflections from professional athletes.* Paper presented at the Association of Applied Sport Psychology Conference, Providence, RI.

Collins, J. (1986). Self-efficacy and ability in achievement behavior. In A. Bandura (Ed.), *Social foundations of thought and action: A social cognitive theory.* Englewood Cliffs, NJ: Prentice-Hall.

Corbin, C. B., Landers, D. M., Feltz, D. L., & Senior, K. (1983). Sex differences in performance estimates: Female lack of confidence vs. male boastfulness. *Research Quarterly for Exercise and Sport, 54*(4), 407–410.

Corbin, C. B., & Nix, C. (1979). Sex-typing of physical activities and success predictions of children before and after cross-sex competition. *Journal of Sport Psychology, 1*(1), 43–52.

Côté, J. (1999). The influence of the family in the development of talent in sport. *The Sport Psychologist, 13,* 395–417.

Côté, J., & Fraser-Thomas, J. (2008). Play, practice, and athlete development. In D. Farrow, J. Baker, & C. MacMahon (Eds.), *Developing sport expertise* (pp. 17–25). London, UK: Routledge.

Csikszentmihalyi, M., Rathunde, K., Whalen, S., & Wong, M. (1993). *Talented teenagers: The roots of success and failure.* New York, NY: Cambridge University Press.

Dweck, C. S. (2006). *Mindset: The new psychology of success.* New York, NY: Random House.

Ericsson, K. A. (1996). *The road to excellence: The acquisition of expert performance in the arts and sciences, sports, and games.* Mahwah, NJ: Erlbaum.

Ericsson, K. A. (2003). The development of elite performance and deliberate practice: An update from the perspective of the expert-performance approach. In J. Starkes & K. A. Ericsson (Eds.), *Expert performance in sport: Recent advances in research on sport expertise* (pp. 49–81). Champaign, IL: Human Kinetics

Ericsson, K. A., Krampe, R. T., & Tesch-Romen, C. (1993). The role of deliberate practice in the acquisition of expert performance. *Psychological Review, 100*(3), 363–406.

Escartí, A., & Guzmán, J. F. (1999). Effects of feedback on self-efficacy, performance, and choice in an athletic task. *Journal of Applied Sport Psychology, 11,* 83–96.

Feltz, D. L., & Brown, E. (1984). Perceived competence in soccer skills among young soccer players. *Journal of Sport Psychology, 6*(4), 385–394.

Feltz, D. L., Short, S. E., & Sullivan, P. J. (2008) *Self-efficacy in sport.* Champaign, IL: Human Kinetics.

Fry, M. D., & Duda, J. L. (1997). A developmental examination of children's understanding of effort and ability in the physical and academic domains. *Research Quarterly for Exercise and Sport, 68*(4), 331–344.

George, T. R., Feltz, D. L., & Chase, M. A. (1992). The effects of model similarity on self-efficacy and muscular endurance: A second look. *Journal of Sport and Exercise Psychology, 14*(3), 237–248.

Gould, D., & Carson, S. (2004). Myths surrounding the role of youth sports in developing Olympic champions. *Youth Studies Australia, 23*(1), 19–26.

Harter, S. (1982). The perceived competence scale for children. *Child Development, 53*(1), 87–97.

Horn, T. S., & Weiss, M. R. (1991). A developmental analysis of children's self-ability judgments in the physical domain. *Pediatric Exercise Science, 3*(4), 310–326.

Jourden, F. J., Bandura, A., & Banfield, J. T. (1991). The impact of conception of ability on self-regulatory factors and motor skill acquisition. *Journal of Sport and Exercise Psychology, 13*(3), 213–226.

Kanfer, R. (1990). Motivation and individual differences in learning: An integration of developmental differential and cognitive perspectives. *Learning and Individual Differences, 2*(2), 221–239.

Kavanagh, D., & Hausfeld, S. (1986). Physical performance and self-efficacy under happy and sad moods, *Journal of Sport Psychology, 8*(2), 112–123.

Lenney, E. (1977). Women's self-confidence in achievement settings. *Psychological Bulletin, 84*(1), 1–13.

Lewko, J. H., & Ewing, M. E. (1980). Sex differences and parental influences in the sport involvement of children. *Journal of Sport Psychology, 2*(1), 62–68.

Lirgg, C. D. (1991). Gender differences in self-confidence in physical activity: A meta-analysis of recent studies. *Journal of Sport and Exercise Psychology, 13*(3), 294–310.

Lirgg, C. D., George, T. R., Chase, M. A., & Ferguson, R. H. (1996). Impact of conception of ability and sex-type of task on male and female physical self-efficacy. *Journal of Sport and Exercise Psychology, 18*(4), 426–434.

Maccoby, E. E., & Jacklin, C. N. (1974). *The psychology of sex differences.* Palo Alto, CA: Stanford University Press.

Maddux, J. E. (1995). Self-efficacy theory: An introduction. In J. E. Maddux (Ed.), *Self-efficacy, adaptation, and adjustment* (pp. 3–33). New York, NY: Plenum.

Nicholls, J. G. (1978). The development of the concepts of effort and ability, perception of academic attainment, and the understanding that difficult tasks require more ability. *Child Development, 49*(3), 800–814.

Nicholls, J. G. (1984). Achievement motivation: Conception of ability, subjective experience, task choice and performance. *Psychological Review, 91*(3), 328–346.

Schunk, D. H. (1995). Self-efficacy, motivation, and performance. *Journal of Applied Sport Psychology, 7*(2), 109–134.

Stipek, D. (1981). Children's perceptions of their own and their classmates ability. *Journal of Educational Psychology, 73*(3), 404–410.

Stipek, D., & Tannatt, L. (1984). Children's judgments of their own and their peers' academic competence. *Journal of Educational Psychology, 76*(1), 75–84.

Vealey. R. S., & Chase, M. A. (2007). Self-confidence in sports. In T. S. Horn (Ed.), *Advances in sport and exercise psychology* (pp. 65–98). Champaign, IL: Human Kinetics.

Vealey, R. S., & Walter, S. M. (1993). Imagery training for performance enhancement. In J. M. Williams (Ed.), *Applied sport psychology* (2nd ed.) (pp. 200–224). Palo Alto, CA: Mayfield.

Weiss, M. R., McAuley, E., Ebbeck, V., & Wiese, D. M. (1990). Self-esteem and causal attributions for children's physical and social competence in sport. *Journal of Sport and Exercise Psychology, 12*(1), 21–36.

Wiersma, L. D. (2000). Risks and benefits of youth sport specialization: perspectives and recommendations. *Pediatric Exercise Science, 12*(1), 13–22.

Wood, R., & Bandura, A. (1989). Impact of conception of ability on self-regulatory mechanisms and complex decision-making. *Journal of Personality and Social Psychology, 56*(3), 407–415.

CHAPTER 8

PERFECTIONISM: ITS DEVELOPMENT AND INFLUENCE ON EMERGING TALENT IN YOUTH

Howard K. Hall, Andrew P. Hill, and Paul R. Appleton

INTRODUCTION

In almost every achievement domain, the pursuit of high personal standards is considered to be a distinguishing feature of exceptional performers. This is because the action reflects an array of seemingly adaptive behaviors that, when exhibited with sufficient intensity over a sustained period, will·lead to heightened performance. In sport, it has been reported that elite athletes who appear disposed toward perfectionism exhibit a similar pattern of relentless achievement striving that contributes to their outstanding accomplishments. This has led to speculation that perfectionism may be a hallmark quality of elite sport performance, because it gives rise to the sort of motivational blueprint that is considered to be essential for both long-term athlete development and sporting success (Gould, Dieffenbach, & Moffett, 2002). Caution must be exercised before endorsing such a view, however, as perfectionism incorporates a wide range of distinguishing characteristics. While striving to accomplish exceedingly high standards may be one core defining feature of perfectionism, this particular personality disposition can reflect other, more debilitating, characteristics. These activate psychological processes that not only undermine the quality of motivation demonstrated by young athletes but may ultimately inhibit adaptive achievement striving. The paradoxical nature of perfectionistic striving (Flett & Hewitt, 2005) clearly raises questions about claims that perfectionism may be a defining characteristic of elite sport performers and suggests that its debilitating qualities must be managed and its underlying cognitions modified if perfectionistic young athletes are to fulfill their potential, perform at exceptionally high levels, and maintain psychological health.

While numerous websites designed to support budding athletes offer advice on avoiding the perils of perfectionism, comparatively little is known about the effects of perfectionism in youth sport. Much of the evidence that informs our understanding of perfectionism has been generalized from social, educational, and clinical contexts, and from recent sporting research that has tended to employ adult samples. However, in order to make sense of the findings from this research, which has begun to examine both the influence of perfectionism upon young athletes and its development during childhood and adolescence, it is necessary to first explore what is meant by the term *perfectionism* in order to understand the specific nature of the personality characteristic and its defining features. This will enable those with either a theoretical or an applied interest in athlete perfectionism to (a) differentiate perfectionistic striving from other forms of achievement behavior, (b) understand the psychological processes to which it gives rise, (c) make sense of the extant literature on perfectionism in sport, and (d) formulate strategies that will help individuals to cope effectively with its potentially debilitating consequences.

This chapter will draw upon different approaches to the study of perfectionism in order to define the construct. It will provide an analysis of various approaches to the measurement of perfectionism and identify possible motivational mechanisms that explain its influence on patterns of achievement related cognition, affect, and behavior. It will then provide a brief synthesis of what we currently know about the influence of perfectionism on youth sport participants and examine its origins in parental interactions. Finally, the chapter will examine how the sporting environment and the climate created by coaches may act to reinforce distorted views about achievement and perpetuate the dysfunctional cognitive style with which perfectionism seems to be associated.

WHAT CONSTITUTES PERFECTIONISM?

Because perfectionism is a commonly used term in the modern lexicon, it appears to be a behavioral characteristic that is colloquially understood, with which some are able to identify, but that few in sport are capable of defining precisely. Even in the field of psychology there is considerable disagreement about the exact meaning of the term. A decade ago, Flett and Hewitt (2002) reported that a search of the literature had uncovered 21 separate terms that had been used to describe the construct. While there was some evidence of conceptual overlap among the different expressions, there appeared to be divergent opinion about which features might best represent the construct beyond the pursuit of exceedingly high personal standards. This is largely due to an inability to agree on its defining qualities and that the distinction between perfectionism and other forms of achievement striving has become blurred; this has led some researchers to conclude that perfectionism may present in either adaptive or maladaptive forms (Rice & Lapsley, 2001; Slade & Owens, 1998; Stoeber, 2011).

Other researchers clearly reject the notion that perfectionism in any form can be a universally positive quality, arguing that when viewed as a broad multidimensional construct, perfectionism is a fundamentally debilitating characteristic (Flett & Hewitt, 2002; Greenspon, 2000; Hall, Hill, & Appleton, 2012). Although they consider that perfectionism energizes relentlessly striving, they propose that it comprises other defining core qualities that reflect a harsh self-critical style. These act collectively to generate a fundamentally maladaptive pattern of cognition and achievement behavior that, when sustained, will lead to considerable impairment and distress (Flett & Hewitt, 2002; Hall, in press). This perspective considers that while some core features of perfectionism may, in isolation, be associated with positive outcomes, when considered in conjunction with other more insidious qualities of the construct, their collective influence impedes adaptive performance appraisal and sets in motion a debilitating process that may undermine psychological well-being.

Although its core features are often the subject of considerable debate, there is almost universal agreement that one important characteristic of perfectionism is a strong psychological commitment to the pursuit of excessively high standards (Burns, 1980; Hamachek, 1978; Hollender, 1965; Pacht, 1984). However, while many athletes exhibit this motivational quality, not all are perfectionists. Of note is the fact that perfectionists are not just devoted to exceptionally lofty goals but remain rigidly committed to the pursuit of these standards regardless of any evidence that suggests that such action may contribute to deleterious effects (Burns, 1980; Hamachek, 1978; Hollender, 1965). This is because perfectionists firmly believe that without relentless striving toward excessive and inflexible standards they will be unable to gain the benefits from achieving valued goals that not only reflect positively on themselves but contribute to their self-definition.

Perfectionism, therefore, cannot simply be defined by the act of striving to meet exceedingly high standards. It is a more complex personality characteristic that represents a way of thinking about achievement that is governed by a constellation of seemingly irrational beliefs and potentially dysfunctional attitudes (Ellis, 1962; Hamachek, 1978; Jones, 1968, Weissman & Beck, 1978). Together they distort both the meaning of success and failure and the criteria against which achievement is evaluated. It is important to note that perfectionists are not characteristically driven to pursue exceptional performance standards because there is inherent worth in the process of achievement striving or because they exhibit a pure intrinsic interest in the activity. Rather, their achievement striving is governed by the fact that goal accomplishment carries instrumental value in the form of perceived social acceptance, recognition, or enhanced self-esteem (Burns, 1980; Hamachek, 1978; Hollender, 1965; Pacht, 1984). Thus, it is evident that an inherent pressure to establish a sense of contingent self-worth becomes a principal source of maladaptive achievement striving in many perfectionists (Campbell & DiPaula, 2002; Flett & Hewitt, 2006; Hill, Hall, Appleton, & Kozub, 2008).

Beyond the establishment and validation of contingent self-worth, there are other core defining features of perfectionism that will also contribute to undermining the quality of achievement striving. Therefore, understanding the psychological processes that these qualities engender is important, as they may help to explain why this particular personality characteristic becomes routinely debilitating. For example, the criteria used by perfectionists to evaluate success and failure will tend to be both rigid and inflexible, because it is believed that desirable outcomes will only be forthcoming when high standards are accomplished. As a result, perfectionists will tend to consider success and failure in a dichotomous, all-or-nothing manner (Burns, 1980; Hollender, 1965), and due to the irrational significance that is assigned to achievement, falling short will almost certainly bring about distressing emotional consequences as it acts to undermine self-definition. Unfortunately, for perfectionists perceived failure tends to be a recurrent experience, and because the standards to which perfectionists aspire are habitually excessive, the probability of failure is increased. This only contributes to the generation of further emotional distress, as any performance that is appraised as less than flawless will be subject to considerable self-censure and condemned as inadequate.

Perfectionists realize that when appraising achievement in this manner there is little scope for error and this heightens their concern about making mistakes. Their hypervigilance with avoiding errors and their sensitivity to negative evaluation from others render it difficult to maintain a sense of contingent self-worth. Moreover, because irrational importance is often attached to achievement in a specific domain, sensitivity to failure and external criticism may not only undermine self-esteem in that domain, but may overgeneralize to impact negatively on global self-worth (Burns, 1980; Frost, Marten, Lahart, & Rosenblate, 1990; Hamachek, 1978). This preoccupation with avoiding inadequacy and maintaining a contingent self-worth also interferes with any objective evaluation of investment requirements and contributes to perfectionistic individuals exhibiting vague doubts about whether sufficient competence, preparation, or effort can be demonstrated to bring about successful goal accomplishment (Frost et al., 1990). Thus, in order to compensate for this perceived inadequacy and reduce the possibility that criticism or disapproval will be directed toward them, achievement striving becomes characteristically compulsive (Frost et al., 1990).

The defining features of perfectionism that have been described are believed to underpin a range of personal and interpersonal processes that not only explain the nature and direction of this potentially debilitating pattern of cognition and behavior, but help to distinguish between subtly different forms of this characteristic. Hewitt and Flett (1991) argue that when individuals strive to accomplish their own self-imposed high standards and direct their harsh self-evaluative processes inward, it reflects self-oriented perfectionism. This is thought to render individuals vulnerable because of the irrational importance that is attached to meeting excessively high personal standards, as well as the distorted belief that meeting one's own perfectionistic ideals should always be possible (Campbell & DiPaula, 2002). Hewitt and Flett (1991) further argue that when the direction of the harsh critical evaluation is inward but the source of evaluation is perceived to be external, it reflects socially prescribed perfectionism. Individuals exhibiting this form of perfectionism strive to reach standards that they perceive are imposed upon them by others. This renders them vulnerable because they adhere to a belief that only through accomplishment of the perceived standards of others will they gain the necessary recognition, reinforcement, or approval to bring about a sense of worth (Campbell & DiPaula, 2002). In contrast to self-oriented and socially prescribed perfectionism, Hewitt and Flett (1991) suggest that when perfectionism is targeted outwards its direct effects go beyond the individual, as it contributes to a number of debilitating interpersonal rather than intrapersonal processes. They argue that when others are the focus of an individual's unrealistically high expectations and harsh critical evaluations it reflects other-oriented perfectionism. This form of perfectionism has debilitating consequences and may undermine interpersonal trust, create conflict, and induce interpersonal hostility, because the critical nature of other-oriented perfectionists means that they are rarely satisfied with the efforts or accomplishment of others (Hewitt & Flett, 1991).

Whether directed inwards or targeted outwards, perfectionism is collectively represented by the core defining qualities described above. When considered in combination, these qualities underpin perfectionistic thinking, regulate perfectionistic striving, and govern the mechanisms that render individuals psychologically vulnerable. Unfortunately, research on perfectionism in sport and other domains has not always employed a consistent definition, and on occasion multidimensional components of perfectionism have been disaggregated to create perfectionism variants. These often contain some necessary core qualities, but in their disaggregated form they are insufficient to constitute perfectionism (Hall, in press; Hall et al., 2012). An awareness of the strengths and weaknesses of common measures that have been employed may aid in the interpretation of what often appears to be contradictory literature examining perfectionism in youth sport.

THE MEASUREMENT OF PERFECTIONISM IN SPORT

In recognition that perfectionism is a multidimensional construct, sport research has employed a number of established measures and a variety of strategies to try to capture the core defining characteristics of the disposition. The measurement of perfectionism remains a source of considerable debate, however, and the degree to which approaches vary makes consistent interpretation of research findings a challenge. An important factor that consistently hinders interpretation of the perfectionism literature is that with little consideration of the qualities necessary to define the construct, various combinations of individual elements have emerged as the basis for the creation of derivative forms perfectionism, the validity of which some in the field have challenged (e.g., Greenspon, 2000; Hall et al., 2012). A proliferation of terms such as *positive, healthy,* or *adaptive perfectionism,* which appear to describe individuals who exhibit a few of the core qualities of the personality characteristic means that those wishing to understand perfectionism in sport must be cognizant of what is being captured when different measures or constellations of subscales are employed.

One of the most commonly adopted measures of perfectionism in sport research has been the Frost Multidimensional Perfectonism Scale (F-MPS). The F-MPS comprises six subscales that are considered to reflect both the nature and origin of the personality characteristic. Four dimensions are designed to assess key intrapersonal qualities, including the pursuit of high personal standards, concern about mistakes, vague doubts about action, and a preoccupation with precision and order. Two further dimensions measure interpersonal qualities and reflect the perceived expectations and perceived critical evaluation of parents. While Frost et al. (1990) argue that summing up the scores on the subscales will produce a total perfectionism score, they advocate examining individual profiles to determine whether individuals exhibit the core dimensions of the construct. The Frost MPS has acted as a template for the development of a sport specific version of the instrument (Sport MPS), which has recently been validated by Gotwals and Dunn (2009). The principal difference between the two measures is that the interpersonal dimensions on the Sport MPS reflect different antecedents of perfectionism in the form of perceived parental pressure and perceived coach pressure.

While both of these instruments assess the broad multidimensional nature of the construct, their employment in sporting contexts has raised concerns about the best way to interpret the data that they generate. For example, there has been a tendency for researchers to ignore the composite profile and to disaggregate the various subscales when employing the instruments for research purposes. As a consequence, researchers have either examined the effects of individual dimensions or compared clusters of individual athletes exhibiting high scores on either adaptive features, the self-critical features, or low scores on all features.

It seems illogical, however, to consider perfectionism as a broad multidimensional construct with specific core defining qualities, and then focus upon the effects of its individual component parts. It also seems conceptually questionable to sum up the scores of the various subscales and consider the total score as an indication of the strength of perfectionism, without determining whether the self-critical components make a significant contribution to the overall total. Moreover, it appears to be a dubious strategy to consider the positive components in isolation from the self-critical elements. When constrained in this manner, neither combination of subscales may be sufficient to represent perfectionism, and the strategy fails to consider that it is the underlying reason behind the pursuit of the high standards that give rise to self-criticism for perfectionists. Therefore, it makes little sense to compare the effects of positive and self-critical dimensions in isolation from the other defining qualities, or statistically partial out the effects of self-critical dimensions from the pursuit of high standards, as some researchers have attempted (see, for example, Stoeber, 2011).

Another measure that has been employed on a regular basis in sport research is the Hewitt and Flett (1991) Multidimensional Perfectionism Scale (H-MPS). This instrument measures self-oriented, socially prescribed, and other-oriented perfectionism. Unlike the F-MPS, the H-MPS does not easily lend itself to disaggregation. This is because all of the core perfectionism qualities are broadly represented in each of the three subscales. While all three dimensions are considered to represent debilitating forms of perfectionism, self-oriented perfectionism is often found to be associated with positive outcomes. Factor analysis of both the F-MPS and the H-MPS by Frost, Heimberg, Holt, Mattia, and Neubauer (1993) revealed that self-oriented perfectionism contributed to a latent factor that included the personal standards and organization dimensions of the F-MPS, and was labeled *positive achievement striving*. However, to consider self-oriented perfectionism as a positive form of perfectionism fails to recognize that it is a source of vulnerability that will likely result in debilitating outcomes when difficulties are experienced and important goals are thwarted (Flett & Hewitt, 2002, 2006; Hewitt & Flett, 1991). That is, it creates a way of thinking about success and failure that becomes debilitating at the point when performances are perceived as discrepant from desired standards and the cognitive and behavioral strategies that are employed to overcome the discrepancies are perceived to be ineffective.

A recent addition to the measurement of sport-related perfectionism is the Multidimensional Inventory for Perfectionism in Sport (MIPS), developed by Stoeber, Otto, Pesheck, Becker, and Stoll, (2007). This instrument captures what Stoeber (2011) believes to be the dual nature of perfectionism. That is, one subscale reflects perfectionistic striving while the other represents negative reactions to imperfection, although neither variant alone captures the broader meaning of perfectionism. A narrative review of perfectionism in sport by Stoeber (2011) has argued that perfectionism in this context may best be assessed using a dual approach, which considers that perfectionism may manifest in both positive and negative forms. Stoeber claims that when perfectionism is defined in a constrained manner to reflect perfectionistic strivings, it appears to be motivationally adaptive and emotionally uplifting, and may even be consistent with a healthy pursuit of excellence. However, he also recognizes that perfectionistic striving is only healthy in the absence of perfectionistic concerns. When combined with this more debilitating component, perfectionistic striving not only undermines the quality of motivation but may pose a risk to both mental and physical health.

The dual approach promoted by Stoeber (2011) and others (e.g., Owens & Slade, 2008; Rice, Ashby, & Slaney, 1998; Slade & Owens, 1998) has one significant drawback in that the measures themselves appear to define the variants of the construct. The strategy is inherently problematic because it is possible that, in isolation, neither perfectionistic striving nor perfectionistic concerns represent the broad multidimensional construct described by early theorists, and therefore neither facet of the dualistic model represents perfectionism. If sport psychologists are to understand the etiology of perfectionism in youth sport, then researchers must aim for increased precision and consistency in the measurement of this personality characteristic. For youth sport participants to be regarded as perfectionists they must exhibit the requisite motivational intensity and a tendency toward self-critical appraisal. At this point evidence would confirm that while adaptive achievement striving may be a highly desirable quality to foster in young sport participants, perfectionism is not.

MOTIVATIONAL MECHANISMS UNDERPINNING PERFECTIONISM

Understanding how perfectionism is defined and measured provides various clues for helping to explain why individuals exhibiting this personality characteristic are motivated to pursue excessively high standards. However, it is important to note that the motivational qualities of perfectionism are not only reflected in the criteria against which accomplishments are evaluated, but in the way its core defining features convey both meaning and significance to the appraisal of achievement striving. While there is currently no definitive explanation of the psychological processes underlying the motivation of perfectionists, a number of authors have employed contemporary theories of motivation to speculate on the reasons why perfectionism may energize extraordinary effort and persistence, yet simultaneously trigger mechanisms that appear to undermine motivational quality and lead to psychological impairment.

Some researchers (e.g., Flett & Hewitt, 2006; Hall, in press; Hall et al., 2012; Hill & Appleton, 2012; Hall, Kerr & Matthews, 1998) have employed an approach to achievement motivation, described by Covington (Covington, 1992; Covington & Mueller, 2001), to explain the motivational mechanisms that may underlie perfectionistic striving. Covington and Mueller (2001) adopt the term *overstrivers* to describe those individuals whose motivation to strive compulsively appears energized by a combination of approach and avoidance tendencies. These individuals are believed to be simultaneously attracted to and repelled by thoughts about the consequences of their achievement striving. That is, they not only display a profound desire to succeed, but they harbor intense fears about the consequences of failure and the impact of aversive outcomes on their self-worth (Hall et al., 2012). Self-worth is thus perceived to be largely dependent on successful outcomes emerging from relentless striving. It has been noted that while individuals adopting this cognitive framework may experience considerable personal satisfaction and recognition from others as a result of successful achievement, perceived success tends to be fleeting and offers no more than temporary respite against the potentially aversive consequences of failure. This is because the pressure to achieve is perceived to be unrelenting when self-worth is contingent on the accomplishment of excessively high and often narrowly defined standards. Even periods of sustained success are unlikely to translate into enduring self-confidence for these individuals, as isolated failure is sufficient to stimulate underlying doubts about ability.

What this means for sustained motivation in young athletes is that despite any success that perfectionistic striving may bring, perfectionistic athletes are rendered characteristically vulnerable because of the meaning they ascribe to achievement. Moreover, there is a growing body of evidence to support this contention, with a number of studies demonstrating that perfectionism is underpinned by a combination of both approach and avoidance motives (see Dunn, Causgrove Dunn, & Syrotuik, 2002; Hall et al., 1998; Stoeber, Stoll, Pesheck, & Otto, 2008; Stoeber, Uphill, & Hotham, 2009; Van Yperen, 2006; Verner-Filion & Gaudreau, 2010). These studies all suggest that in its more debilitating manifestation, perfectionistic striving is regulated by avoidance goals, and it falls within a motivational framework where athletes feel that they must achieve exceedingly high standards in order to avoid perceived failure that renders perfectionism dysfunctional.

An analysis of perfectionistic striving that is grounded in self-determination theory offers a somewhat different explanation of the possible motivational processes underpinning perfectionism. When employing self-determination theory it may be argued that perfectionistic striving appears largely underpinned by less self-determined and more controlled forms of regulation, such as introjection (internal pressure and guilt) and external regulation (external pressure for social reinforcement or recognition). The regulatory style employed by perfectionistic individuals helps to create the perceived environment in which achievement striving takes place and frames how achievement information is appraised (Ryan & Deci, 2007). This appraisal process contributes significantly to a thwarting of rather than a facilitation of basic needs for autonomy, competence, and relatedness, and it is the failure to fulfill these basic needs that subsequently gives rise to debilitating cognitive and affective responses and acts to sustain dysfunctional achievement striving. It is apparent that for perfectionists, the quality of motivation may not only be undermined when the meaning of achievement is governed by failure avoidance, but also when the perception of internal control over the fulfillment of one's goals becomes diminished. The roots of this argument can be traced to the early theorizing of Hewitt and Flett (1991), who proposed differential motivational processes to explain variability in the strength of association between both self-oriented perfectionism and socially prescribed perfectionism, and a range of cognitive, affective, and behavioral outcomes.

Hewitt and Flett (1991) speculated that self-oriented perfectionism may be associated with a greater degree of self-determined behavior in comparison to socially prescribed perfectionism. Underlying this argument is a view that while the achievement striving for those exhibiting self-oriented perfectionism often contains an element of internal regulation, it is by no means completely self-determined, as it tends to be introjected and reflect what Hewitt and Flett (1991) consider to be an intrinsic need to be perfect. This means that while self-oriented perfectionists may not strive to achieve because they have an inherent interest in the activity, they do so out of a sense of volition, without the need for external reward, and because the activities in which they are invested have personal value. Need fulfillment is to a large extent under personal control, and this may explain why self-oriented perfectionism is often associated with positive outcomes when success is perceived and basic needs are fulfilled. However, with perceived failure these individuals may become psychologically vulnerable due to a self-imposed pressure to be perfect and internally imposed constraints. When failure to meet perfectionistic standards results in basic needs being thwarted, individuals may begin to experience shame, anxiety, and guilt, which collectively undermine self-worth and encourage the use of maladaptive behavioral strategies to protect the self (Ryan & Deci, 2007).

While self-oriented perfectionism may render individuals vulnerable at those times when performances are perceived to be discrepant from desired standards, socially prescribed perfectionism seems to be universally debilitating. This is because motivation is externally regulated through individuals striving to reach standards that they believe others impose upon them. These perceived external constraints undermine self-determined motivation and may subsequently lead to a diminished sense of need fulfillment and more frequent perceptions of need thwarting, as performances are frequently judged to be discrepant from desired standards. A combination of low perceived autonomy and a frequent perception that competence is being undermined may explain why socially prescribed perfectionism often leads to debilitating patterns of cognition and affect, as well as a range of maladaptive achievement behaviors. Empirical support that demonstrates that self-determination theory offers a framework to explain the achievement behavior of perfectionists has begun to emerge. For example, Van Yperen (2006) and Miquelon, Vallerand, Grouzet, and Cardinal (2005) have both reported that self-oriented perfectionism is associated with more, and socially prescribed perfectionism with less self-determined forms of motivation. More recently, Gaudreau and Antl (2008) confirmed that these relationships appear to hold when self-oriented perfectionism and socially prescribed perfectionism are included as components of composite measures of both personal standards and evaluative concerns perfectionism, respectively. Furthermore, in a followup study by Gaudreau and Thompson (2010), in comparison to those who only exhibit high personal standards perfectionism, self-determined motivation appears reduced when individuals exhibit both high personal standards and evaluative concerns perfectionism. That is, when perfectionism is considered in its broadest sense and captures all of the core qualities of the personality characteristic, motivational regulation exhibits a complex structure that appears reflective of diminished self-determination.

CORRELATES OF PERFECTIONISM IN YOUTH SPORT

Although we can only speculate at present on the motivational processes that underpin perfectionism, empirical evidence is beginning to emerge from studies in youth sport to confirm that the pursuit of exceptionally high standards appears problematic when accompanied by heightened evaluative concerns (e.g., Stoll, Lau, & Stoeber, 2008). It is worth acknowledging that regardless of the nature of perfectionism, when athletes perceive success and recognize that their efforts are a principal source of their accomplishments, the debilitating evaluative processes that may undermine sustained performance are unlikely to be activated. However, a more complex picture of the perfectionism-performance relationship emerges when perfectionistic athletes experience ongoing performance difficulties. For example, it has been found that when perfectionistic young athletes encounter perceived failure, their performance may deteriorate over time, through cognitive distraction, self-handicapping, or other failure-avoidant processes (see Anshel & Mansouri, 2005; Hill, Hall, Duda, & Appleton, 2011). The available research suggests that any immediate performance benefits of perfectionism that result from the energizing of achievement striving may only serve to mask the potentially debilitating psychological processes that begin to emerge as junior athletes struggle to meet their own high standards and perceive that their performances are discrepant from important goals.

Perfectionism appears to predispose junior athletes to potentially debilitating patterns of cognition and affect, and it is these, in conjunction with the employment of maladaptive achievement strategies, which ultimately undermine sustained performance. As previously noted, perfectionism has been found to be associated with a combination of both approach and avoidance goals in youth sport participants. This creates a mindset by which perfectionistic young athletes tend to appraise sporting contexts as threatening and respond with, among other things, elevated cognitive anxiety in the lead-up to performance (Hall et al., 1998; Stoeber et al., 2007), and with high levels of trait anger and mistake induced anger during competition (Vallance, Dunn, & Causgrove Dunn, 2006). Moreover, when these symptoms become acute, perfectionistic athletes begin to experience athlete burnout (Hall, in press; Hall et al., 2012). A growing body of evidence supports this contention, finding that when performance is constantly perceived to be falling short, it leaves perfectionistic athletes with a chronic sense of personal inadequacy and a growing cynicism toward their sport, because goal achievement appears constantly blocked, leaving their heightened expectations unfulfilled (see Gould, Udry, Tuffey, & Loehr, 1996; Hill & Appleton, 2011; Hill et al., 2008; Lemyre, Hall, & Roberts, 2008).

Other research (e.g., McArdle & Duda, 2004; Mouratidis & Michou, 2011) has found multidimensional perfectionism to be associated with combinations of both autonomous and controlled forms of motivational regulation, which again may collectively underpin the propensity to appraise achievement contexts as threatening and render perfectionistic young athletes susceptible to burnout. In attempting to determine some of the psychological mechanisms that underpin burnout in perfectionistic young athletes and explain why those experiencing self-oriented perfectionism may also be vulnerable, Hill, Hall, and Appleton (2010) found that self-oriented perfectionism had specific characteristics that differentiate it from conscientious achievement striving. These included concern over mistakes, negative reactions to mistakes, and fear of failure. This suggests that instead of considering self-oriented perfectionism to be a characteristic that is synonymous with conscientious achievement striving, those interested in youth sport should begin to focus their attention on the long term rather than the immediate influence of perfectionism. This is because there is a propensity to look at it cross-sectionally and to consider self-oriented perfectionism as an adaptive quality that has a sustained positive impact, rather than considering it a vulnerability factor that may lead to debilitation when goals are blocked and fundamental needs are thwarted.

From the emerging literature it is also evident that the debilitating consequences of perfectionism may extend far beyond the immediate sporting context and may have an insidious influence on the overall psychological and physical health of some young athletes. For example, research suggests that perfectionism has an aversive impact on the development and maintenance of good interpersonal relations (Ommundsen, Roberts, Lemyre, & Miller, 2005).

Looking at the context of children's soccer, Ommundsen et al. found that perfectionism was associated with a variety of problematic interpersonal outcomes, such as lower peer acceptance, perceptions of poor quality peer relations, and greater levels of conflict with friends and teammates. At its most extreme, perfectionism may contribute to serious health problems in athletes. Research that has found perfectionism to relate to both unhealthy attitudes towards body image (Dunn, Craft, Causgrove Dunn, & Gotwals, 2011) and disturbed eating attitudes (Haase, Prapavessis, & Owens, 2002). This provides worrying evidence of the potentially damaging nature of this construct on young athletes. Clearly, these findings suggest that perfectionism not only has the potential to engender debilitating patterns of cognition, affect, and behavior, but in some instances it may induce more destructive psychological processes that can threaten the physical health and well-being of youth sport participants.

Based upon the extant literature it is apparent that empirical research on the influence of perfectionism in youth sport contexts is still in its infancy. More research is clearly necessary before there is a sufficient weight of evidence to determine the true extent of its impact on young athletes. However, current findings reveal that a considerable number of youth sport participants exhibit many of the core defining qualities of perfectionism, and it is likely that unless steps are taken to manage their influence, the debilitating consequences of this personality characteristic will become more prominent as these young athletes mature. While an understanding of the developmental process by which perfectionism emerges in youth sport participants is also in its infancy, it is believed that the roots of perfectionism may lie in childhood.

HOW DOES PERFECTIONISM DEVELOP IN THE YOUTH SPORT PARTICIPANT?

Comparatively little is known about the development of perfectionism, although researchers maintain that the characteristics of this disposition may result from a combination of genetic inheritance and a process of acquired learning (Flett, Hewitt, Oliver, & McDonald, 2002). There is a limited body of empirical evidence that has been gleaned from both twin studies and research investigating the development of disordered eating that has established that some aspects of perfectionism may be genetically inherited (e.g., Lilenfield et al., 1998; Tozzi et al., 2004; Woodside et al., 2002). While it is not yet possible to put a precise figure on the hereditary component of perfectionism, it has been argued that somewhere between 24% and 49% of perfectionism characteristics may be a consequence of genetic inheritance (Shafran, Egan, & Wade, 2010). These figures suggest, however, that it is environmental factors that have the greatest influence on the development of perfectionism. While there are many features of the environment that may contribute to the overall development of the disposition, there appears to be universal agreement that the origins of perfectionism are to be found in childhood (see Flett et al., 2002 for a review), and that the family environment is a critical antecedent of the disposition because children begin to demonstrate various characteristics of perfectionism as a consequence of the interactions with their parents.

Although Flett et al. (2002) argue that numerous parental factors contribute to the development of perfectionism, they suggest that there is no one single route by which the disposition materializes in children. Instead, they propose that perfectionism may emerge by way of various developmental pathways, each of which is characterized by explicit psychological processes. One approach that considers that perfectionism may be a consequence of children modeling their parents' perfectionistic qualities is grounded in social learning (Bandura, 1977). A fundamental premise underlying this approach is that children's perfectionistic beliefs are learned either through imitation and subsequent internalization of parental evaluative standards or through imitation of idealized parental images. Some empirical evidence supports a social-learning approach. For example, Frost et al. (1993) found that in a sample of university students, perfectionism in daughters corresponded directly with perfectionism in mothers. Vieth and Trull (2004) also reported evidence for a same-sex association between parental perfectionism and perfectionism in their offspring. The development of perfectionism may not always be associated with any one parent, however, as Chang (2000) found that children's perfectionism was associated with the perfectionistic characteristics of both parents and that its source may lie beyond the primary care giver. One qualitative study (Spiers Neumeister, Williams, & Cross, 2009) has provided further support for a social-learning model by confirming that children not only model specific characteristics of perfectionism displayed by their parents, but they deliberately attempt to emulate an image of one or both parents because of a desire to be like them. Despite this support, one inherent weakness in this research is that most studies have utilized adult samples to establish these relationships. Few studies have tested for the existence of a modeling effect in youth samples. However, one investigation (Cook & Kearney, 2009) found evidence to support a modeling effect in parents and their teenage offspring. In explanation, the authors speculated that mothers may inadvertently model perfectionistic behavior to their children by taking extra precautions, expressing intolerance with imperfect situations, and avoiding activities where there is a probability of making mistakes.

A second approach that outlines how perfectionism might develop within family contexts reflects a social expectations model (Flett et al., 2002). Central to this approach is the contention that children's perfectionism is a direct consequence of contingent approval given by parents. Proponents of this model (Burns, 1980; Hamachek, 1978; Misseldine, 1963) argue that children's perfectionistic striving emerges because perfectionistic parents may be characteristically reluctant to reward and recognize their children's efforts and may appear indifferent unless achievements are outstanding. Moreover, because perfectionistic parents place considerable value on accomplishing extraordinarily high standards and often espouse rigid threshold criteria for success, they will tend to acknowledge only the most exceptional performance. As a consequence, children feel obliged to display a pattern of excessive achievement striving because they perceive that performing beyond a socially prescribed threshold criterion may be an effective way to obtain recognition and approval from their parents.

Some have argued that it is not only contingent approval from parents that engenders perfectionism in children (Hamachek, 1978). They have suggested that when parents' behavioral expectations are ambiguous or insufficient, children may choose to strive toward exceptional standards because they perceive that the resultant outcomes will reduce uncertainty about whether parents will be approving of their efforts. A further related mechanism by which parents may transmit their perfectionistic expectations is through nonapproval or disappointment when their child's performance appears discrepant from one that is desired (Burns, 1980; Hamachek, 1978). Through either the indifferent or disapproving responses of their parents, children learn that falling short is something to be avoided and that flawless and error-free performances will significantly increase the likelihood that parents will respond with acceptance or approval.

Over time, this pattern of parental reinforcement will not only cultivate perfectionistic striving but will also promote contingent self-worth in children. It is evident, however, that parental pressure on their children to achieve may be conveyed in an altogether more subtle manner. For example, research into children's motivation (Dweck, 2006; Kamins & Dweck, 1999) suggests that when parental feedback is directed toward personal attributes such as ability or intelligence rather than toward specific achievement behaviors, it reinforces what is termed an *entity belief* in the children, which conveys that these qualities are fixed rather than malleable and must be demonstrated in order to validate one's worth. With an entity belief, even positive reinforcement can be problematic because children receiving well-intentioned feedback that they are bright or able may begin to feel pressure that they must demonstrate these attributes in order to receive parental approval and validate a sense of self.

It is believed that when children use perfectionistic striving as a means of self-validation, they become psychologically vulnerable, as feedback that performance is discrepant has important implications for perceived worth. This is the principle reason why Flett et al. (2002) believe that despite empirical evidence linking it with numerous positive correlates, self-oriented perfectionism will *always* render individuals vulnerable. When performance is discrepant it threatens self-worth, and over time this will engender self-defeating patterns of behavior (Dweck, 1999).

A third approach, labeled a social reactions model (Flett et al., 2002), considers that a harsh, affectionless parenting style or chaotic family environments may engender perfectionism because this form of achievement striving provides children with a strategy for coping with the aversive consequences of parental behaviors. It is thought that when parents engage in harsh evaluation, manipulate children's behavior by inducing guilt and shame, or withdraw love to shape desirable behavior, these strategies intrude upon children's thoughts and feelings, inhibit the development of autonomy, and undermine the acquisition of a secure sense of self (Barber & Harmon, 2002). Children may become increasingly perfectionistic as a reaction to this intrusive and controlling parenting process because they perceive that the accomplishment of exceptional standards will not only result in achievement, but will diminish the source of aversion and elicit approval.

Empirical evidence to support a social reactions approach has been reported by Soenens and colleagues (Soenens, Vansteenkiste, et al., 2005; Soenens, Elliot, et al., 2005; Soenens et al., 2008). For example, Soenens, Vansteenkiste, et al. (2005) reported that maladaptive dimensions of perfectionism in adolescents were associated with a perceived controlling parenting style. In an extension of this study, Soenens, Elliot, et al. (2005) found that parental perfectionism was a critical antecedent of perceived psychological control, which in turn fully mediated maladaptive perfectionism in children. More recently, Soenens et al. (2008) reported the findings of a two-year longitudinal followup study, and found that perceived psychological control measured at time one, contributed directly to maladaptive perfectionism in teenagers a year later, and this directly predicted elevated symptoms of depression at the end of year two.

AN INTEGRATED APPROACH TO THE DEVELOPMENT OF PERFECTIONISM

Based on the three models described above, Flett et al. (2002) put forth an integrative, trans-actional model of perfectionism development that encapsulates an array of processes emanating from within and outside the child. These processes can be broadly grouped into three categories: parental factors, environmental pressures, and factors originating from within the self (Flett et al., 2002). Parental factors include specific practices and general styles adopted by caregivers when rearing their offspring. Flett and colleagues argued that parents of perfectionistic children are overly critical of mistakes, highly controlling, and engage in specific behaviors designed to encourage exceptional performance (e.g., placing the child in environments that expect perfection). The model also highlights parents' goals and values as key antecedents of children's perfectionism; parents that have ego-involving goals for the child and expect unrealistically high standards from their offspring will contribute to a family environment that is conducive to perfectionism development. Finally, Flett et al. (2002) suggested that a parent's personality is important in the development of children's perfectionism. According to the model, children have a natural tendency to emulate the personality characteristics of their parents, including the parent's perfectionism.

The model of perfectionism development also outlines a number of environmental pathways, including pressures emanating from cultures, occupations/activities, and significant others (e.g., teachers, peers). Regarding cultures, Flett et al. (2002) provide the example of pressures experienced by many women (and more recently men) to conform to an ideal body image. These pressures not only encourage striving towards the perfect body, but also promote a range of eating behaviors and exercise habits that are highly debilitating for physical health and psychological well-being. No less important is the role of significant others. Peers, for example, may be especially influential in maintaining the perfectionism of older children, because adolescence is a time when parental influence is replaced by pressures from other children (Flett et al., 2002). In the context of sport, the influence of additional social actors in the development of children's perfectionism may also extend to coaches (Anshel & Eom, 2003; Dunn et al., 2006; Gotwals & Dunn, 2009). Although coaches were excluded from Flett et al.'s (2002) model, their potential role in perfectionism development makes theoretical sense given that coaches may set unrealistic standards and produce punitive evaluations of athletes.

Child factors constitute a final developmental pathway towards perfectionism. According to the model, children are especially vulnerable to the development of perfectionism when their temperament is characterised by a combination of high fearfulness and high persistence (Flett et al., 2002). A study by Randles, Flett, Nash, McGregor, and Hewitt (2010) supports this hypothesised pathway. Using two samples of undergraduate students, Randles et al. (2010) reported that self-oriented and socially prescribed perfectionism were positively correlated with a fearful and frustrated temperament, while self-oriented perfectionism was also positively associated with a temperament that values persistence and effort, as well as a positive response to goal achievement. The findings of Randles and colleagues show that a child's temperament may contribute to a fear of failure, concerns regarding the implications of errors, a desire for approval, and persistent achievement striving: all of which define the perfectionism construct (Flett et al., 2002).

In addition to identifying an array of pathways towards perfectionism, Flett et al.'s (2002) model explains why children develop different types of perfectionism. The role of parental and cultural pressures is clearly central to the development of interpersonal dimensions such as socially prescribed perfectionism, but what about intrapersonal dimensions such as self-oriented perfectionism? Flett et al. (2002) argued that self-oriented perfectionism is partly the result of the child internalizing pressures from external sources, which are subsequently used to form internal beliefs regarding performance standards and self-worth. The process of internalizing socially imposed standards is highly dependent upon a number of factors, including the child's openness to socialization. While some children may choose to reject externally determined pressures, other children are open to, and highly influenced by, parental and societal demands. Flett et al. (2002) argued that children characterized by high openness will likely develop self-oriented perfectionism as a result of internalizing socially imposed pressures. A second key factor that determines whether socially imposed pressures develop into self-oriented perfectionism is the child's previous accomplishments in a particular domain. According to the model, children may internalize the pressures of significant others in domains where they have previously demonstrated competence on a regular basis, and where the attainment of self-imposed perfectionistic standards is seemingly possible. A final factor that encourages the internalization of socially imposed standards is the persistent exposure to, and subsequent desire to model, other self-oriented perfectionists.

EMPIRICAL TESTS OF FLETT ET AL.'S MODEL IN SPORTING CONTEXTS

A number of studies have begun to test Flett et al.'s (2002) model of perfectionism development. The findings lend support for children's sporting perfectionism being a function of both social learning and social expectations. Social learning was found to be a critical mechanism in research conducted by Appleton, Hall, and Hill (2010), which examined the relationship between dimensions of perfectionism exhibited by parents and elite junior athletes' using Hewitt and Flett's (1991) multidimensional scale. Regression analyses revealed support for the social learning explanation of perfectionism development, a finding that was consistent across the perfectionism dimensions. Parents' self-oriented perfectionism was the strongest predictor of athletes' self-oriented perfectionism, and parents' socially prescribed perfectionism was the strongest predictor of athletes' socially prescribed perfectionism. Appleton and colleagues' findings also provided initial evidence that the crossgenerational transmission of perfectionism dimensions is not limited to parent-child dyads of the same sex (e.g., father and son). Using a moderated regression analysis, athletes' gender failed to emerge as a significant moderator of the parent-athlete perfectionism relationship. The findings from this study reinforce Flett et al.'s (2002) proposal that imitation is highly influential in the development of children's perfectionism in sport. They also suggest that junior athletes may be susceptible to modelling the characteristics of perfectionism exhibited by both parents, who may have a constant presence as the child participates in sport (Appleton et al., 2010).

Although social learning provides one explanation of perfectionism development in young athletes, it is important to remain cognizant of the wider parenting literature, which suggests that the intergenerational transmission of personality characteristics may be mediated by crucial parenting styles and behaviors (e.g., Darling & Steinberg, 1993). Building upon the work of Soenens, Vansteenkiste, et al. (2005) and Soenens, Elliot, et al. (2005), a recent study by Appleton, Hall, and Hill (2009) tested the mediating role of parenting styles in the relationship between parents' and junior athletes' perfectionism. Using a sample of elite junior gymnasts and football players, Appleton et al. (2009) found a direct link between parents' and athletes' corresponding perfectionism dimensions, supporting the social-learning explanation of perfectionism development. However, Appleton et al. (2009) also reported that the relationship between parents' and athletes' socially prescribed perfectionism was partially mediated by parental empathy and psychological control. This latter finding suggests that parents reporting higher levels of socially prescribed perfectionism lack sensitivity and empathic concern towards their child because they may have an unhealthy preoccupation with their own socially imposed standards. Moreover, because the perfectionistic parent is less attuned to the developmental and empathetic needs of their child, he or she may resort to autonomy-inhibiting and intrusive behaviors when interacting with their offspring. In turn, this affectionless controlling parenting style may contribute to the development of socially prescribed perfectionism in the young athletic child, as he or she internalizes and subsequently strives toward parentally determined standards in a desperate attempt to gain the recognition and acceptance of their caregiver.

In addition to the parental factors examined by Appleton et al. (2009), a number of other studies from the sports literature indicate that harsh, punitive parenting styles and behaviors contribute to the development of athletes' perfectionism. McArdle and Duda (2004), for example, examined the relationships between adolescence athletes' perfectionism and their perceptions of parents' expectations, criticism, goal orientations, and degree of flexibility in the family home in terms of power structures (e.g., degree of assertiveness, control, and discipline), role relationships, and rules. The results of a cluster analysis revealed that athletes demonstrated an unhealthy profile of perfectionism (i.e., high personal standards, concern over mistakes, and doubts about action) when their primary caregiver was perceived as demanding higher standards and engaging in overly critical appraisals of their athletic child. In contrast, athletes reported a more adaptive profile of achievement striving (i.e., high personal standards, low concern over mistakes and doubts about action) when their parent was primarily task-oriented and contributed to a flexible family environment, combined with lower scores on the expectations, criticism, and ego orientation subscales. In a followup study, McArdle and Duda (2008) confirmed that perceived parental criticism was a significant predictor of athletes' concern over mistakes and doubts about actions, while parents' high expectations for their athletic child emerged as a significant predictor of athletes' self-reported personal standards in sport. Finally, a more recent study by Sapieja, Dunn, and Holt (2011) examined whether parental authoritativeness, a parenting style characterized by realistically high standards, emotional responsiveness, and autonomy support (Darling & Steinberg, 1993), differed as a function of youth soccer players' perfectionistic orientations. As hypothesized, healthy perfectionists reported significantly higher perceptions of maternal and paternal authoritativeness than a group of unhealthy perfectionists. In sum, there is a growing body of evidence that supports the parental-factors pathway of Flett et al.'s (2002) model of perfectionism development. It seems that unhealthy, dysfunctional perfectionism emerges in athletic children as a result of maladaptive parenting styles and behaviors characterized by unrealistically high expectations, combined with critical performance evaluations and conditional approval based on the attainment of athletic perfection.

The literature also supports the role of alternative environmental pressures in the development of junior athletes' perfectionistic cognitions. As identified above, the coach-created climate may be especially important in predicting athletes' perfectionism, and this assumption was recently tested by Appleton, Hall, and Hill (2011) with a sample of elite junior athletes. The authors hypothesized that the motivational climate created by the coach would predict additional variance in elite junior athletes' perfectionistic cognitions beyond the effects associated with the parent-initiated motivational climate. Overall, the hypothesis was supported. Regression analyses revealed that after controlling for the effects of the parent-initiated climate, the coach-created motivational climate predicted an additional 4% in male athletes' and 11% in female athletes' perfectionistic cognitions. One explanation for the findings concerns the level at which athletes' perfectionism was measured. Perfectionistic cognitions represent state-like thoughts that occur during participation. When junior athletes participate in sport, they are constantly enveloped by the coach-created motivational climate that reinforces the standard upon which competence is evaluated and that provides immediate performance-related feedback. These coach-created, achievement-related structures may therefore be responsible for directing the athlete's immediate thoughts towards perfectionistic themes.

It is evident from the available literature that the development of perfectionism in junior athletes involves a multitude of interwoven pathways, and clearly further research is now required to clarify the influence of additional processes (e.g., peers, child factors). However, the reported studies do reveal a number of specific parental and coaching pressures that are associated with athletes' perfectionism. These processes are highly destructive and suggest the resulting perfectionism may harm emerging talent in sport.

SUMMARY AND CONCLUSIONS

The principal aims of this chapter were to raise awareness of an emergent literature on perfectionism in youth sport, to examine the influence of this personality characteristic on youth sport participants, and to consider how perfectionism may be inadvertently cultivated through parental and coach interactions. Various approaches to understanding the construct were brought together to inform a precise definition of perfectionism and differentiate it from adaptive achievement striving. Contemporary motivational theories were employed to identify the psychological processes that perfectionism appears to engender in young athletes, and empirical evidence from youth sport was provided to support the contention that perfectionism had a largely debilitating influence on participants. Finally, various psychological models outlining the ways in which perfectionism is thought to develop were described, and empirical evidence was presented from recent research that articulates the processes by which parents and coaches are influential in the development of perfectionism in children involved in youth sport.

From the evidence presented, it is possible to draw some broad conclusions that may aid those working with youth sport participants. First, perfectionism should be considered as a debilitating multidimensional personality characteristic that incorporates both excessive achievement striving and a harsh, self-critical evaluative style. Second, perfectionism may energize heightened achievement striving, but over time its corrosive effects not only undermine the motivation of youth sport participants but may inflict considerable damage on both their psychological and physical health. Third, because there is a tendency in sport to define perfectionism by its measures rather than its core defining qualities, perfectionism may erroneously be viewed as positive when dimensions that refer to the pursuit of high standards are disaggregated from its more self-critical features. Fourth, there is evidence to suggest that the corrosive effects of perfectionism are prevalent in youth sport settings, especially when striving for sporting achievement becomes synonymous with self-validation. As youth sport is currently an underexplored context for examining the influence of perfectionism, further empirical research is necessary before it is possible to provide a comprehensive picture of the consequences of this personality disposition. Finally, empirical evidence is emerging to suggest that while the development of perfectionism begins in childhood it may also be perpetuated within the youth sport environment, and specifically through interactions that children have with both coaches and fellow participants. The challenge for youth sport researchers, however, is not only to understand the etiology of perfectionism but to begin to apply their understanding to influence parent and coach education, so that interventions to counter what Flett and Hewitt (2005) call the perils of perfectionism may help to prevent the development of perfectionistic thinking and promote more adaptive patterns of achievement striving.

REFERENCES

Anshel, M. H., & Eom, H. (2002). Exploring the dimensions of perfectionism in sport. *International Journal of Sport Psychology, 34*(3), 255–271.

Anshel, M. H., & Mansouri, H. (2005). Influences of perfectionism on motor performance, affect, and causal attributions in response to critical information feedback. *Journal of Sport Behavior, 28,* 99–124.

Appleton, P. R., Hall, H. K., & Hill, A. P. (2009). *The intergenerational transmission of perfectionism in elite junior sport. Parents psychological control and empathy as intervening variables.* Paper presented at the ISSP World Congress, Marakesh, Morocco.

Appleton, P. R., Hall, H. K., & Hill, A. P. (2010). Family patterns of perfectionism: An examination of elite junior athletes and their parents. *Psychology of Sport and Exercise, 11,* 363–371.

Appleton, P. R., Hall, H. K., & Hill, A. P. (2011). Examining the influence of the parent-initiated and coach-created motivational climate upon athletes' perfectionistic cognitions. *Journal of Sports Sciences, 29*(7), 661–671.

Bandura, A. (1977). Self-efficacy: Toward a unifying theory of behavioral change. *Psychological Review, 84*(2), 191–215.

Barber, B. K., & Harmon, E. L. (2002). Violating the self: Parental psychological control of children and adolescents. In B. K. Barber (Ed.), *Intrusive parenting* (pp. 15–52). Washington, DC: American Psychological Association.

Burns, D. D. (1980). The perfectionists script for self-defeat. *Psychology Today, 14*(November), 34–51.

Campbell, J. D., & Di Paula, A. (2002). Perfectionistic self-beliefs: Their relation to personality and goal pursuit. In G. L. Flett & P. L. Hewitt (Eds.), *Perfectionism: Theory, research, and treatment* (pp. 181–198). Washington, DC: American Psychological Association.

Chang, E. C. (2000). Perfectionism as a predictor of positive and negative psychological outcomes: Examining a mediation model in younger and older adults. *Journal of Counseling Psychology, 47*(1), 18–26.

Cook, L. C., & Kearney, C. A. (2009). Parent and youth perfectionism and internalizing psychopathology. *Personality and Individual Differences, 46*(3), 325–330.

Covington, M. V. (1992). *Making the grade: A self-worth perspective on motivation and school reform.* Cambridge, UK: Cambridge University Press.

Covington, M. V., & Mueller, K. J. (2001). Intrinsic versus extrinsic motivation: An approach/avoidance reformulation. *Educational Psychology Review, 13*(2), 157–176.

Darling, N., & Steinberg, L. (1993). Parenting style as context: An integrative model. *Psychological Bulletin, 113*(3), 487–496.

Dunn, J. C., Causgrove Dunn, J., Gotwals, J. K., Vallance, J. K. H., Craft, J. M., & Syrotuik, D. G. (2006). Establishing the construct validity evidence for the Sport Multidimensional Perfectionsism Scale. *Psychology of Sport and Exercise, 7*(1), 57–79.

Dunn, J. G. H., Causgrove Dunn, J., & Syrotuik, D. G. (2002). Relationship between multidimensional perfectionism and goal orientations in sport. *Journal of Sport and Exercise Psychology, 24*(4), 376–395.

Dunn, J. C., Craft, J. M., Causgrove Dunn, J., & Gotwals, J. K. (2011). Comparing a domain specific and global measure of perfectionism in competitive female figure skaters. *Journal of Sport Behavior, 34*(1), 25–46.

Dweck, C. S. (1999). *Self-theories: Their role in motivation personality and development.* Philadelphia, PA: Psychology Press.

Dweck, C. S. (2006). *Mindset: The new psychology of success.* New York, NY: Random House.

Ellis, A. (1962). *Reason and emotion in psychotherapy.* New York, NY: Lyle Stuart.

Flett, G. L., & Hewitt, P. L. (2002). Perfectionism and maladjustment: An overview of theoretical, definitional and treatment issues. In G. L. Flett & P. L. Hewitt (Eds.), *Perfectionism: Theory, research and treatment* (pp. 8–31). Washington, DC: American Psychological Association.

Flett, G. L., & Hewitt, P. L. (2005). The perils of perfectionism in sports and exercise. *Current Directions in Psychological Science, 14*(1), 14–18.

Flett, G. L., & Hewitt, P. L. (2006). Positive versus negative perfectionism in psychopathology: A comment on Slade and Owen's dual process model. *Behavior Modification, 30*(4), 472–495.

Flett, G. L., Hewitt, P. L., Oliver, J. M., & McDonald, S. (2002). Perfectionism in children and their parents: A developmental analysis. In G. L. Flett & P. L. Hewitt (Eds.), *Perfectionism: Theory, research and treatment* (pp. 89–132). Washington, DC: American Psychological Association.

Frost, R. O., Marten, P. A., Lahart, C., & Rosenblate, R. (1990). The dimensions of perfectionism. *Cognitive Therapy and Research, 14*(5), 449–468.

Frost, R. O., Heimberg, R. G., Holt, C. S., Mattia, J. I., & Neubauer, A. L. (1993). A comparison of two measures of perfection. *Personality and Individual Differences, 14*(1), 119–126.

Gaudreau, P., & Antl, S. (2008). Athletes broad dimensions of dispositional perfectionism: Examining change in life-satisfaction and the mediating role of sport-related motivation and coping. *Journal of Sport and Exercise Psychology, 30*(3), 356–382.

Gaudreau, P., & Thompson, A. (2010). Testing a 2 x 2 model of dispositional perfectionism. *Personality and Individual Differences, 48*(5), 532–537.

Gotwals, J. K., & Dunn, J. C. (2009). A multi method multi-analytic approach to establishing internal construct validity evidence: The sport multidimensional perfectionism scale 2. *Measurement in Physical Education and Exercise Science, 13*(2), 71–92.

Gould, D. R., Dieffenbach, K., & Moffett, A. (2002). Psychological characteristics and their development in Olympic champions. *Journal of Applied Sport Psychology, 14,* 172–204.

Gould, D., Udry, E., Tuffey, S., & Loehr, J. (1996). Burnout in competitive junior tennis players: I. A quantitative psychological assessment. *The Sport Psychologist, 10*(4), 332–340.

Greenspon, T. S. (2000). "Healthy perfectionism" is an oxymoron!: Reflections on the psychology of perfectionism and the sociology of science. *The Journal of Secondary Gifted Education, 11*(4), 197–208.

Haase, A. M., Prapavessis, H., & Owens, R. G. (2002). Perfectionism, social physique anxiety and disordered eating: A comparison of male and female elite athletes. *Psychology of Sport and Exercise, 3*(3), 209–222.

Hall, H. K. (in press). From adaptive achievement striving to athletic burnout: The debilitating influence of perfectionism. In D. Hackfort & A. Baria (Eds.), *Keynote addresses from the ISSP World Congress 2009.*

Hall, H. K., Hill, A. P., & Appleton, P. R. (2012). Perfectionism: A foundation for sporting excellence or an uneasy pathway to purgatory? In G. C. Roberts & D. C. Treasure (Eds.), *Advances in motivation in sport and exercise* (Vol. 3) (pp. 129–168). Champaign, IL: Human Kinetics.

Hall, H. K., Kerr, A. W., & Matthews, J. (1998). Precompetitive anxiety in sport: The contribution of achievement goals and perfectionism. *Journal of Sport and Exercise Psychology, 20*(2), 194–217.

Hamachek. (1978). Psychodynamics of normal and neurotic perfectionism. *Psychology, 15*(1), 27–33.

Hewitt, P. L., & Flett, G. L. (1991). Perfectionism in the self and social contexts: Conceptualization, assessment, and association with psychopathology. *Journal of Personality and Social Psychology, 60*(3), 456–470.

Hill, A. P., & Appleton, P. R. (2011). The predictive ability of the frequency of perfectionistic cognitions, self-oriented perfectionism, and socially prescribed perfectionism in relation to symptoms of burnout in youth rugby players. *Journal of Sports Sciences, 29*(7), 695–703.

Hill, A. P., Hall, H. K., & Appleton, P. R. (2010). A comparative examination of the correlates of self-oriented perfectionism and conscientious achievement striving in male academy cricketers. *Psychololgy of Sport and Exercise, 11*(2), 162–168.

Hill, A. P., Hall, H. K., Appleton, P. R., & Kozub, S. A. (2008). Perfectionism and burnout in junior elite soccer players: The mediating influence of unconditional self-acceptance. *Psychology of Sport and Exercise, 9*(5), 630–644.

Hill, A. P., Hall, H. K., Duda, J. D., & Appleton, P. R. (2011). The cognitive, affective and behavioural response of self-oriented perfectionists following three successive failures on a cycle ergometer task. *International Journal of Sport and Exercise Psychology, 9,* 189–207.

Hollender, M. H. (1965). Perfectionism. *Comprehensive Psychiatry, 6*(2), 94–103.

Jones, R. G. (1968). A factorial measure of Ellis's irrational belief system, with personality and maladjustment correlates. *Dissertation Abstracts International, 29,* 4379B–4380B.

Kamins, M., & Dweck, C. S. (1999). Person vs. process praise and criticism: Implications for contingent self-worth and coping. *Developmental Psychology, 35*(3), 835–847.

Lemyre, P. N., Hall, H. K., & Roberts, G. C. (2008). A social cognitive approach to burnout in elite athletes. *Scandinavian Journal of Medicine & Science in Sports, 18*(2), 221–224. doi: 10.1111/j.1600-0838.2007.00671.x

Lilenfeld, L. R., Kaye, W. H., Greeno, C. G., Merikangas, K. R., Plotnicov, K., Pollice, C., Rao, R., Strober, M., Bulik, C. M., & Nagy, L. (1998). A controlled family study of anorexia nervosa and bulimia nervosa: Psychiatric disorders in first-degree relatives and effects of proband comorbidity. *Archives of General Psychiatry, 55*(7), 603–610.

McArdle, S., & Duda, J. L. (2004). Exploring the social contextual correlates of perfectionism in adolescents: A multivariate perspective. *Cognitive Therapy and Research, 28*(6), 765–788.

McArdle, S., & Duda, J. D. (2008). Exploring the etiology of perfectionism and perceptions of self-worth in young athletes. *Social Development, 17*(4), 980–997.

Miquelon, P., Vallerand, R. J., Grouzet, F. M. E., & Cardinal, G. (2005). Perfectionism, academic motivation, and psychological adjustment: An integrative model. *Personality and Social Psychology Bulletin, 31*(7), 913–924.

Mouratidis, A., & Michou, A. (2011). Perfectionism and coping among adolescent athletes: The mediating role of self-determined motivation. *Psychololgy of Sport and Exercise, 12*(4), 355–367.

Ommundsen, Y., Roberts, G. C., Lemyre, P. N., & Miller, B. W. (2005). Peer relationships in adolescent competitive soccer: Associations to perceived motivational climate, achievement goals and perfectionism. *Journal of Sports Sciences, 23*(9), 977–989.

Owens, R. G., & Slade, P. D. (2008). So perfect it's positively harmful? Reflections on the adaptiveness and maladaptiveness of positive and negative perfectionism. *Behaviour Modification, 32*(6), 928–397.

Pacht, A. J. (1984). Reflections on perfection. *American Psychologist, 39*(4), 386–390.

Randles, D., Flett, G. L., Nash, K. A., McGregor, I. D., & Hewitt, P. L. (2010). Dimensions of perfectionism, behavioral inhibition, and rumination. *Personality and Individual Differences, 49*(2), 83–87.

Rice, K. G., Ashby, J. S., & Slaney, R. B. (1998). Self-esteem as a mediator between perfectionism and depression: A structural equations analysis. *Journal of Counseling Psychology, 45*(3), 304–314.

Rice, K. G., & Lapsley, D. K. (2001). Perfectionism, coping and emotional adjustment. *Journal of College Student Development, 42*(2), 157–168.

Ryan, R. M., & Deci, E. L. (2007). Active human nature: Self determination theory and the promotion and maintenance of sport, exercise and health. In M. S. Hagger & N. L. D. Chatzisarantis (Eds.), *Intrinsic motivation and self-determination in exercise and sport* (pp. 1–20). Champaign, IL: Human Kinetics.

Sapieja, K. M., Dunn, J. G. H., & Holt, N. L. (2011). Perfectionism and perceptions of parenting styles in male youth soccer players. *Journal of Sport and Exercise Psychology, 33*(1), 20–39.

Shafran, R., Egan, S., & Wade, T. (2010). *Overcoming perfectionism: A self-help guide using cognitive behavioural techniques.* London, UK: Robinson.

Slade, P. D., & Owens, R. G. (1998). A dual process model of perfectionism based on reinforcement theory. *Behavior Modification, 22*(3), 372–390.

Soenens, B., Vansteenkiste, M., Luyten, P., Duriez, B., & Goossens, L. (2005). Maladaptive perfectionistic self-representations: The mediational link between psychological control and adjustment. *Personality and Individual Differences, 38*(2), 487–498.

Soenens, B., Elliot, A. J., Goossens, L., Vansteenkiste, M., Luyten, P., & Duriez, B. (2005). The intergenerational transmission of perfectionism: Parents' psychological control as an intervening variable. *Journal of Family Psychology, 19*(3), 358–366.

Soenens, B., Luyckx, K., Vansteenkiste, M., Luyten, P., Duriez, B., & Goossens, L. (2008). Maladaptive perfectionism as an intervening variable between psychological control and adolescent depressive feelings: A three-wave longitudinal study. *Journal of Family Psychology, 22*(3), 465–474.

Speirs Neumeister, K. L., Williams, K. K., & Cross, T. L. (2004). Gifted high school students' perspectives on the development of perfectionism. *Roeper Review, 31*(4), 198–206.

Stoeber, J. (2011). The dual nature of perfectionism: Relationships with emotion, motivation and performance. *International Review of Sport and Exercise Psychology, 4*(2), 128–145.

Stoeber, J., Stoll, O., Pesheck, E., & Otto, K. (2008). Perfectionism and goal orientations in athletes: Relations with approach and avoidance orientations in mastery and performance goals. *Psychology of Sport and Exercise, 9*(2), 102–121.

Stoeber, J., Otto, K., Pesheck, E., Becker, C., & Stoll, O. (2007). Perfectionism and competitive anxiety in athletes: Differentiating striving for perfection and negative reactions to imperfection. *Personality and Individual Differences, 42*(6), 959–969.

Stoll, O., Lau, A., & Stoeber, J. (2008). Perfectionism and performance in a new basketball training task: Does striving for perfection enhance or undermine performance? *Psychology of Sport and Exercise, 9*(5), 620–629.

Tozzi, F., Aggen, S. H., Neale, B. M., Anderson, C. B., Mazzeo, S. E., Neale, M. C., & Bulik, C. M. (2004). The structure of perfectionism: a twin study. [Research Support, US Gov't, P.H.S.Twin Study]. *Behavior Genetics, 34*(5), 483–494. doi: 10.1023/B:BEGE.0000038486.47219.76

Vallance, J. K. H., Dunn, J. G. H., & Causgrove Dunn, J. L. (2006). Perfectionism, anger, and situation criticality in competitive youth ice hockey. *Journal of Sport and Exercise Psychology, 28*(3), 383–406.

Van Yperen, N. W. (2006). A novel approach to assessing achievement goals in the context of the 2 x 2 framework: Identifying distinct profiles of individuals with different dominant achievement goals. *Personality and Social Psychology Bulletin, 32*(11), 1432–1445.

Verner-Filion, J., & Gaudreau, P. (2010). From perfectionism to academic adjustment: The mediating role of achievement goals. *Personality and Indivual Differences, 49*(3), 181–186.

Vieth., A. Z., & Trull, T. (1999). Family patterns of perfectionism: An examination of college students and their parents. *Journal of Personality Assessment, 72*(1), 49–67.

Weissman, A. N., & Beck, A. T. (1978). *Development and validation of the dysfunctional attitudes scale.* Paper presented at the Association for the Advancement of Behavior Therapy, Chicago, Illinois.

Woodside, D. B., Bulik, C. M., Halmi, K. A., Fichter, M. M., Kaplan, A., Berrettini, W. H., Strober, M., Treasure, J., Lilenfeld, L., Klump, K., & Kaye, W. H. (2002). Personality, perfectionism, and attitudes toward eating in parents of individuals with eating disorders. *International Journal of Eating Disorders, 31*(3), 290–299.

CHAPTER 9

COACH-ATHLETE INTERACTIONS IN CHILDREN'S SPORT

Karl Erickson and Wade Gilbert

INTRODUCTION

Coaching has long been known to influence children's experiences in sport, in terms of both skill development and psychosocial outcomes (Horn, 2008; Smith & Smoll, 2007). But coaching does not exist in a vacuum; coaches exert this influence on athletes through their behaviors, primarily their interactive/communicative behavior. For the purposes of this chapter, such interactive/communicative behavior directed at athletes will be referred to as coach-athlete interaction. In fact, it could be argued that coach-athlete interaction is central to the coaching process; in order to influence athlete behavior, most other aspects of coaching (e.g., planning, practice structure, observation and analysis) must at some point be communicated through direct interaction between coach and athlete.

In our treatment of coach-athlete interaction, we begin by situating these interactions in their relationship to coaching effectiveness. We then review existing literature on coach-athlete interactions in children's sport, differentiated into descriptive and intervention studies of coach-athlete interactions. From this review, we generate a profile of effective coaching in children's sport and offer recommendations for practice. We finish by highlighting limitations of the current body of literature and propose several areas for future research considerations.

COACH-ATHLETE INTERACTIONS IN RELATION TO COACHING EFFECTIVENESS

A definition of coaching effectiveness was proposed by Côté and Gilbert (2009), whereby effective coaching is "the consistent application of integrated professional, interpersonal, and intrapersonal knowledge to improve athletes' competence, confidence, connection, and character in specific coaching contexts" (p. 316). Two elements of this definition are particularly relevant for the present chapter. First, the coaching process is directed at specific athlete outcomes (the 4 Cs—competence, confidence, connection, and character), and these outcomes refer to a holistic picture of athlete development. Second, the promotion of these outcomes occurs within a specific context. These two elements interact to outline important considerations for effective youth sport coaching and, more specifically, effective coach-athlete interaction in children's sport.

By acknowledging the fundamental priority of athlete development, this conceptualization places the young athlete at the center of the coaching process. Doing so provides tangible, athlete-driven targets for coach-led children's sport activities. The 4 Cs, adapted for sport from the work of Lerner and colleagues (e.g., Lerner et al., 2005), outline a series of sport and psychosocial outcomes reflective of holistic positive development as an athlete and as a person (Côté, Bruner, Erickson, Strachan, & Fraser-Thomas, 2010). The first C, *competence*, is defined as proficiency within a specific domain (i.e., the sport in question). *Confidence* reflects an individual's general perceptions of self-worth and self-efficacy within the sport domain. *Connection* refers to positive bonds with other people in the sport context, in which both parties contribute to the relationship. Finally, *character* refers to both moral or ethical development and empathic understanding of others: that is, an individual's sense of right and wrong for both his or her own actions and in regards to other people in sport. These outcomes are vital indicators of both sport and personal development. The coach-athlete interactions that play a foundational role in the coaching process can then be seen as a mechanism to promote the 4 Cs of holistic athlete development. Thus, effective coaching requires coach-athlete interactions that best promote the 4 Cs. Inherent in this goal-directed view is the notion that some coach-athlete interactions will be more conducive to promotion of the 4 Cs than others. But what determines the qualities of effective interactions? It is in consideration of this point that the differentiation of specific coaching contexts becomes most relevant.

Integrating the work of Lyle (2002) and Trudel and Gilbert (2006), four specific coaching contexts are identified in the integrated definition of coaching effectiveness (Côté & Gilbert, 2009; Côté, Young, Duffy, & North, 2007): (a) participation coaching for children, (b) participation coaching for adolescents and adults, (c) performance coaching for young adolescents, and (d) performance coaching for older adolescents and adults. These contexts are an integration of typically recognized coaching roles within the stages of athlete development proposed in the Developmental Model of Sport Participation (DMSP: Côté, 1999; Côté, Baker, & Abernethy, 2007). Of these, three collectively compose what we refer to as children's sport: participation coaches for children, participation coaches for young adolescents, and performance coaches for young adolescents. The central premise of identifying coaching contexts by athlete age and competitive level is that these two dimensions reflect differences in the athletes' cognitive, social, emotional, and sport development. Given the intended goal of coaching as promoting the 4 Cs, the different ages and competitive levels of athletes (and resultant differences in psychosocial and sport development needs) imply that these critical athlete outcomes are manifested differently in the different coaching contexts (Côté et al., 2010). For example, competence means a very different thing to a 7-year-old just learning soccer and to a 21-year-old university athlete. These variations therefore require different coaching strategies to best promote the 4 Cs in each context. Thus, the types or qualities of coach-athlete interactions that are effective will be determined by the specific coaching context in which they occur, as defined by the athletes' developmental needs in relation to age and competitive level.

In sum, effective coaching results in development or improvement of holistic athlete outcomes as defined by the 4 Cs framework. The expression of these 4 Cs, and by extension the coaching strategies that most effectively develop them, differ in relation to the age and competitive level of the athletes. Given that coaching strategies are expressed through coaches' interactive communication with their athletes, effective coaching then requires coach-athlete interactions directed at promoting the 4 Cs, tailored to the specific coaching context. With this consideration in mind, we now turn to the existing literature to review what is currently known about effective coach-athlete interactions in children's sport.

REVIEW OF RESEARCH ON COACH-ATHLETE INTERACTIONS IN YOUTH SPORT

For the purpose of this chapter we review the research on coach-athlete interactions in children's sport settings according to two broad classifications—descriptive research and intervention research. Research conducted from a descriptive perspective aims to identify how children's sport coaches interact with their athletes in real-world sport settings. Intervention research, on the other hand, examines the influence and effectiveness of attempts to modify these interactions between coaches and athletes, which typically take the form of training or feedback for the coach. The present discussion does not intend to serve as an exhaustive review of the general coach-athlete interaction research across all contexts, as several comprehensive reviews already exist (Cushion, 2010; Gilbert & Trudel, 2004; Jones, 1997; Kahan, 1999; Trudel & Gilbert, 1995). Instead, our intent is to identify key studies and findings of coach-athlete interaction research specifically in children's sport settings. Furthermore, although we will describe several measurement instruments in this chapter, readers interested in learning more about the wide range of instruments available for measuring coach-athlete interactions should refer to Horn (2008) and Darst, Zakrajsek, and Mancini (1989).

Descriptive Research on Coach-Athlete Interactions in Children's Sport
General profile. At the most basic level, a number of studies have provided a general profile of the coach-athlete interaction patterns typically exhibited by children's sport coaches. This research has shown that during games at least, coach-athlete interactions are grounded in extensive amounts of coach observation. For example, Lombardo (1984) completed a study with 38 youth sport coaches across a range of youth sports in the United States. Coaches evenly split their time during games between interacting with their athletes and observing their

athletes. Another observation study conducted over a decade later in a completely different setting (youth ice hockey in Canada) found almost identical results (Trudel, Côté, & Bernard, 1996). Observing 14 ice hockey coaches of 14–15 year olds across 32 games, Trudel and colleagues found an almost even split between coach observation (51.2%) and coach-participant interaction (48.8%). When the coaches did interact with the athletes during the game, most of these interactions occurred when the athletes were either in action (40.9%), on the bench (30.4%), or in transition between the two (22.3%).

Another important aspect of youth sport coaches' interaction with their athletes is to whom the interaction is directed. Lombardo (1984) reported that when coaches chose to interact with their athletes, much of the time it was with groups of athletes (70%) compared to individual athletes (30%). In contrast, however, two small-scale studies conducted with ice hockey coaches of 10 to 15 year olds in games and practices (Gilbert & Trudel, 1999; Seaborn, Trudel, & Gilbert, 1998) showed that the coaches' interactive behaviors were primarily directed at individual athletes in action. Thus, children's sport coaches as a group appear to vary in their relative emphasis on group versus individual communication.

In order to analyze the content of coaches' interactive behaviors, researchers have most often relied on systematic observation, which is the classification of observed behaviors according to a predetermined set of explicitly defined categories. The late 1970s produced the Coaching Behavior Assessment System (CBAS: Smith, Smoll, & Hunt, 1977), which was created using data from a wide range of youth team sports and is now one of the most widely used systematic observation systems in coaching research (Kahan, 1999). The CBAS classifies coaches' interactions into 12 specific behavioral categories, which are separated into two broad categories—spontaneous (coach self-initiated) behaviors and reactive behaviors (direct response to athlete behavior). The CBAS was first used to examine the behaviors of coaches of 10- to 15-year-old male baseball players during games over the course of a season (Smith, Smoll, & Curtis, 1978; Smoll, Smith, Curtis, & Hunt, 1978). Results from this landmark youth baseball coaching study showed that the vast majority of the coach behaviors were spontaneous (63.2%) as opposed to reactive (36.8%). In other words, most of what coaches did during games was initiated by the coach preceding athlete behavior as opposed to a reaction to something done by an athlete. A very similar split between spontaneous and reactive behaviors, with a much higher frequency of spontaneous behaviors, was also found in a later study with children's basketball coaches of athletes aged 9 to 12 years who were observed using the CBAS across 110 games (Smith, Zane, Smoll, & Coppel, 1983).

More specifically, the content of youth sport coaches' interactions with their athletes is typically characterized by high amounts of three primary behaviors: instruction, support and encouragement, and management. The two observational studies (Gilbert & Trudel, 1999; Seaborn, Trudel, & Gilbert, 1998) conducted with children's ice hockey coaches documented four dimensions of coach verbal behavior: (a) the content, (b) the timing, (c) the form, and (d) the intended target. Results from these exploratory studies showed that the five coaches exhibited similar behavioral profiles during games, with a high focus on team tactics and instruction. Similarly, in examining the coaching behaviors of English youth soccer coaches (including coaches of under-9 and under-13 age groups) at a variety of competitive levels, Ford, Yates, and Williams (2010) noted instruction was the most frequently recorded behavior across all age and skill groupings, accounting for approximately 30% of all coach behaviors. Segrave and Ciancio (1990) analyzed the behavior of a successful children's (ages 12–14) American-football coach and found a corresponding emphasis on instruction as the dominant behavior. The original studies using the CBAS with coaches of boys' baseball (ages 8–15: Curtis, Smith, & Smoll, 1979) and boys' basketball (ages 9–12: Smith et al., 1983) also found that instruction was the most frequently observed coaching behavior.

These same studies (Curtis et al., 1979; Ford et al., 2010; Gilbert & Trudel, 1999; Seaborn et al., 1998; Segrave & Ciancio, 1990; Smith et al., 1983) also noted that after instruction, the combination of praise, support, and encouragement consistently accounted for the next largest proportion of coaches' behaviors directed at their athletes. Of particular note is the study conducted by Segrave and Cianci (1990), who compared the profile of their targeted successful children's football coach with the profiles of successful university coaches presented in previous case study research. While coaches in both contexts similarly prioritized instruction, the children's coach was distinguished by a much greater emphasis on positive-focused reinforcement and encouragement behaviors, exhibiting a notable lack of the more negatively oriented scolds and hustles characterizing the university coaches' interactions. Finally, from these studies across a range of sports, it appears that youth sport coaches also frequently employ management or organizational behaviors (i.e., telling athletes where to go and what to do, structuring the sport environment), but less than instruction or praise and encouragement.

Thus it appears that coaches of children as a group typically exhibit a similar general profile with respect to the relative occurrence of instruction, support and encouragement, and management, regardless of the specific sport being coached. This profile is characterized by a high degree of instruction accompanied by a significant emphasis on positive reinforcement and encouragement. These instructive and supportive behaviors are given structure within the training or game situation through moderate usage of management and organizational interactions.

Influence of coach, athlete, and situational characteristics. Although the previously reviewed studies provide an overall behavioral profile of children's coaches in general, a number of studies have also examined potential differences in coach-athlete interactions according to individual characteristics of the coaches or their athletes, as well as contextual features of the sport setting. These characteristics include coach gender, coach experience, athlete age, expected athlete ability, competitive level, and game situation.

Several observational studies have explored coach gender differences with regard to interactive behavior differences. For example, Lacy and Goldston (1990) found that although male and female coaches do show some variance in behavioral profiles, they appear to be more alike than dissimilar in how they interact with their athletes. In contrast, a study using a different observation instrument comparing male and female coaches across a range of youth sports (Lombardo, 1984) found that coach behavioral patterns did vary widely, with male coaches offering much higher amounts of positive feedback than female coaches.

As an additional coach characteristic, Jones, Housner, and Kornspan (1997) examined the influence of different amounts of coaching experience on coaching behaviors with a standard sample of middle school athletes (i.e., upper-year elementary school). These authors reported that more experienced coaches exhibited higher frequencies of technical instruction, while less experienced coaches exhibited higher frequencies of silent observation. However, in this study the amount of experience was confounded with competitive level, as the more experienced coaches all coached at the high school level while the less experienced coaches were drawn from junior high school and middle school levels. So, the reported differences may have more do with the competitive level of the athletes typically coached than the coaches' degree of previous experience. In a more direct examination of the potential influence of competitive level, Ford and colleagues (2010) noted few differences in coaching behavior between coaches of under-9, under-13, and under-16 age groups at elite, subelite, and nonelite levels of English youth soccer. Similarly, Jones (1990) examined coach-athlete interactions of youth soccer coaches in different age-groups (5–7 and 9–12) during practices. No significant differences were found between the groups in their coach behavioral profiles; both groups provided high rates of direct instruction and created what the authors labeled a positive learning environment (high praise, low criticism).

Another noteworthy factor that has been identified within the larger body of coach behavior research is the *expectancy effect.* Also known as the *Pygmalion effect,* expectancy refers to the tendency of coaches' perceptions of individual athletes' ability to differentially influence the performance of those athletes, regardless of their objective ability. Differences in coach behaviors directed at individual athletes are posited as a possible mechanism through which expectancy effects may be manifested and have been noted in a number of different contexts (e.g., Solomon & Buscombe, in press). However, as with other coach or athlete individual difference variables, results in the children's sport context have been inconsistent. In the earliest study of the expectancy effect in children's sport, Rejeski, Darracott, and Hutslar (1979) used the CBAS to explore how coach behaviors vary among high and low expectancy 8- to 12-year-old basketball participants in the United States. The behaviors of 14 coaches were observed, and following data collection the coaches were asked to rank their athletes. Only those behaviors directed at the top three ranked athletes (high expectancy) and bottom three ranked athletes (low expectancy) were then coded using the CBAS. The primary significant difference was that coaches provided much more reinforcement to high expectancy athletes. However, in similar investigations Horn (1984) found the reverse pattern, with low expectancy athletes receiving more feedback, while Solomon (2008) noted no differences in the feedback given to high and low expectancy athletes. Thus there appears to be no uniform expectancy effect in children's sport, at least with respect to moderation via interactive coach behavior.

While the data regarding individual coach and athlete characteristics are notably inconsistent in children's sport, the influence of situational context on coaches' behavior is a promising but relatively underexplored topic. In an intriguing development in this area, Smith's (2006; Smith & Smoll, 2007) notion of behavioral signatures provided an important initial framework for analyzing the dynamic influence of situation. The basic premise of behavioral signatures is that coaches are not defined by their behavior alone, but by how their behavior varies across different situations. For example, in re-analyzing older CBAS-derived behavioral data, Smith (2006) was able to examine the behavioral profiles of individual youth baseball coaches in reference to specific game situations (i.e., winning, tied, losing). Data for two coaches were presented, both exhibiting similar overall levels of supportive, instructive, and punitive behaviors. However, when linked to game situation, the coaches showed notable differences in their situation-behavior profiles. One coach greatly increased supportive behavior in tied game situations and decreased instructional behavior when not winning, whereas the other did not. Additionally, both coaches became more punitive when their team was losing, in contrast to other coaches in the sample who became more supportive in losing situations. Further, Smith calculated stability coefficients for each coach in their situation-behavior profiles (i.e., how consistently the coach exhibited the same behaviors in the same game situation). Interestingly, significant variability was noted across the sample of coaches, suggesting that degree of consistency in situational patterning may be an important individual coach characteristic.

Effects on athlete outcomes. While the descriptive research reviewed thus far provides an overall picture of naturally occurring coach-athlete interactions in children's sport, it provides little information regarding the effectiveness of the reported behaviors—how well these interactions foster positive athlete development within the specific context of children's sport. Returning to the definition of coaching effectiveness outlined at the beginning of this chapter, in order to optimize children's development in sport we must understand the range of outcomes associated with different coach-athlete interactions for the children themselves. In contrast to the undifferentiated interaction profiles generated for children's sport coaches in general, a body of research has examined how differences in coaches' interactive behavior influence children's experience in sport.

Revisiting the pioneering work by Smith, Smoll and colleagues (Curtis et al., 1979; Smith et al., 1983; Smith & Smoll, 1990, 2007), a number of observational studies using the CBAS have noted relatively consistent associations between certain dimensions of coach behavior during games and children's attitudes toward the coach and their sport experience. Instruction, support (e.g., positive reinforcement after successes and encouragement after mistakes), and punishment appear to represent distinct behavioral dimensions. In general, athletes of coaches who are more instructive and supportive report liking their coach and their sport more than athletes of coaches who use these behaviors less often. This effect seems particularly strong for children with low self-esteem, whereby their sport experience is more greatly influenced by high or low frequencies of these two behavioral classes (Smith & Smoll, 1990). In contrast, punitive and punishment-oriented coaching behaviors demonstrate a consistently negative relationship with children's sport experience—the more punitive behavior observed, the lower the athletes' ratings of their coach and liking for the sport. Horn (1985) reported similar findings in her analysis of changes in children's perceptions of competence. Results of this unique longitudinal study, also using the CBAS, suggested that coaches' evaluative behaviors are key to changes in athletes' self-perceptions; supportiveness in response to successful performances and lack of punishment in response to mistakes were linked to improvements in perceived competence over the course of a middle school softball season. Using athletes' perceptions of the CBAS coaching behaviors rather than direct observation, Black and Weiss (1992) found that instructional and encouragement behaviors were the best predictors of 12- to 14-year-old swimmers' motivation for swimming and self-perceptions of ability. However, even small differences in athlete age may moderate the relative influence of each of these behavioral dimensions. For example, Smith and colleagues (1978) noted that younger athletes (aged 8–12) relied primarily on perceived levels of punitive behaviors and positive reinforcement/encouragement in differentiating their coaches. Older youth athletes (13–15), on the other hand, made more reference to the amount and quality of skill instruction.

When considering these general associations, however, it should be noted that the original baseball coaching study (Curtis et al, 1979) that combined coach behavior data, collected with the CBAS and from athlete reports, also showed considerable variance between observed frequencies of coaching behaviors and athlete perceptions of their occurrence. This initial examination of correspondence between coaching behaviors and athlete perceptions of those behaviors suggested that correspondence was very low for the majority of behaviors, but was quite high for behaviors classified as punitive. While these punitive behaviors occurred relatively infrequently, their independent association with negative athlete outcomes and the high accuracy of athlete perceptions of their occurrence points to a particularly salient negative effect in the children's sport context.

While not directly targeting specific coaching behaviors, a number of studies have examined the influence of the general tone or climate created by coaches' interactions with their athletes. One focus of this work is perceived autonomy support, a construct based on the self-determination theory of motivation (SDT: Ryan & Deci, 2000), which represents the degree to which athletes perceive their coach as recognizing and encouraging their capacity as independent decision makers, capable of contributing to the sport environment of their own volition (e.g., acknowledging and accepting athlete opinions, offering choice and participation in decision making, etc.). Two questionnaire studies with young swimmers (aged 10–17: Coatsworth & Conroy, 2009) and soccer players (aged 11–18: Adie, Duda, & Ntoumanis, 2012) examined the influence of perceived autonomy support on a number of athlete outcomes. Coatsworth and Conroy (2009) reported that athletes' perceptions of autonomy supportive coaching directly predicted their self-perceived competence and feelings of attachment to others in the sport environment, while indirectly predicting identity reflection and initiative as mediated by increases in perceived competence and self-esteem. Adie and colleagues (2012) conducted a longitudinal analysis over two seasons and found that perceptions of autonomy support from the coach accounted for differences between individual athletes in their subjective well-being, feelings of autonomy, self-perceived competence, and relationships with others, as well as reductions in physical and emotional exhaustion. Additionally, the degree of perceived coach autonomy support positively predicted changes within individual athletes in all these outcomes over time. Taken together, the results of these studies suggest that more autonomy supportive coach behaviors (at least as perceived by athletes) directly facilitate the development of a range of positive personal and social outcomes in young athletes. This broad range of outcomes is consistent with the holistic conceptualization of athlete development outlined in the definition of effective coaching.

In a similar vein, researchers have also examined the motivational climate created by coaches' evaluative communication with their young athletes. For example, Conroy, Kaye, and Coatsworth (2006) studied 7- to 18-year-old swimmers and found that athlete perceptions of a mastery-avoidance climate from the coach (i.e., emphasizing avoiding poor self-referenced performance, rather than striving for good performance) positively predicted the development of the athletes' own mastery-avoidance goal orientation. The development of these avoidance-based goals in turn led to demotivation and/or made the athletes' motivation for swimming more externally regulated. Using a similar questionnaire methodology, Cervelló, Santos-Rosa, García-Calvo, Jiménez, and Iglesias (2007) examined the influence of coach-initiated motivational climate in competition with 12- to 16-year-old tennis players. Athletes who perceived their coach as emphasizing self-referenced improvement, learning, and effort reported more task goal involvement during competition (i.e., focusing on their own standards and effort, rather than comparison with others) and were also rated as performing better by themselves and their coach. Thus, the manner in which coaches communicate their evaluations of their athletes' performances appears to play a significant role in children's approach to sport competition and even in their competitive success.

In addition to the independent effects of the specific coaching behaviors or their motivational tone, some evidence exists to suggest that more complex qualities of coach-athlete interactions also influence the resulting athlete outcomes. For example, Smith and colleagues (Smith, Shoda, Cumming, & Smoll, 2009) expanded on their earlier notion of situationally linked behavioral signatures by examining the relationships between changes in coach behavior with respect to game situation (i.e., winning, tied, or losing) for coaches of 10- to 15-year-old baseball players and the athletes' attitudes toward their coach. The authors found that although the overall rates of instructional, supportive, and punitive behaviors accounted for a small proportion of the variance in athletes' liking for their coach, particular situation-behavior contingencies (i.e., *if* situation, *then* behavior) demonstrated much stronger relationships with attitude toward the coach. Specifically, coaches who were highly supportive when winning and avoided punitive behaviors when losing were rated much more positively than coaches who displayed the opposite pattern. In general, coaches who become more punitive when their team started losing were rated poorly, while supportiveness while winning was significantly related to higher liking scores. Emphasizing the importance of situational specificity, both these behavioral dimensions lost their predictive value in the opposite game situation (i.e., punishment while winning and supportiveness while losing).

With the tendency of coaching research to focus exclusively on the behavior of the coach, another often overlooked element of coach-athlete interactions is the contribution of the athletes themselves. Although not labeled as such, evidence for the importance of reciprocal involvement in coach-athlete interactions was discussed at least as early as 1982 by Fisher and colleagues, based on their study of 50 youth basketball coaches and athletes (Fisher, Mancini, Hirsch, Proulx, & Staurowsky, 1982). The Fisher et al. study is noteworthy because it appears to be the first published example of research in a children's sport setting using a true coach-athlete interaction observational system, where both coach and athlete behavior was recorded. The Cheffers' Adaptation of Flanders' Interaction Analysis System (CAFAIS; Cheffers & Mancini, 1989), in combination with a measure of team climate, was used to explore potential relationships between coach-athlete interaction and team climates. Fisher and colleagues found distinctly different coach-athlete behavioral patterns in satisfied and less satisfied team climates. Coach-athlete interactions in satisfied team climates were characterized by concurrent instruction by the coach followed by positive behavioral adjustments made by the athletes, referred to as "learning by listening and doing" (Fisher et al., 1982, p. 397). In satisfied team climates coaches provided more acceptance and praise, and athletes initiated more interaction with their coaches and spent more time actively involved in playing basketball. In less satisfied team climates coaches offered low levels of acceptance and praise, athletes seldom initiated interaction with coaches, and the flow of athlete behavior was often interrupted for extended coach-initiated instruction. In fact, coaches in less satisfied team climates provided 70% more instructional information than coaches in satisfied team climates. In sum, coach-athlete interaction in satisfied team climates seems to represent an active learning environment where coaches and athletes regularly exchange control, compared to a passive learning environment in less satisfied team climates.

Building on the initial work of Fisher et al. (1982), two small-sample studies (Erickson, Côté, Hollenstein, & Deakin, 2011; Murphy-Mills, Vierimaa, Côté, & Deakin, 2010) were recently conducted with several effective youth sport coaches, using a dynamic systems-based approach for analyzing paired observational data called state space grids (SSGs: Lewis, Lamey, & Douglas, 1999). By collecting continuous time-series behavioral data for both the coach and the athletes, these studies were able to analyze the coach-athlete interaction as mutually defined by both coach and athlete behavior at any given moment. Both studies suggested that the coach-athlete interactions of effective coaches are characterized by a high degree of inter-activity between coach and athlete, even in situations predominantly focused on prescriptive technical instruction from the coach. Consistent with the findings of Fisher and colleagues (1982), this interaction characteristic differentiated the more effective from the less effective coaching environments in the Erickson et al. (2011) study. However, this work is in its early stages and much of the reciprocally interdependent quality of effective coach-athlete interactions remains to be examined.

In general, descriptive research on coach-athlete interactions in children's sport suggests a relatively consistent interactive behavioral profile for these coaches. While no clear differences based solely on coach or athlete characteristics have emerged, the collected literature demonstrates a significant impact on the outcomes young athletes experience from relatively subtle changes in the content or tone of coaches' behavior. What coaches say and how they say it can greatly influence the quality of children's sport experiences. Finally, the situational specificity and the individualized responses of the athletes to whom these behaviors are targeted may play key roles in determining the nature of the athlete outcomes produced by these interactions, and thus the overall effectiveness of children's sport coaching.

Intervention Research on Coach-Athlete Interactions in Children's Sport

While descriptive research on coach-athlete interactions aims to identify how coaches interact with their athletes, intervention research examines whether these interactions can be changed positively through training. The primary behavioral intervention strategy within the youth sport coaching literature is based on the a priori generation of effective coaching behavior principles, typically derived from descriptive interaction research examining athlete outcomes. Interventions are then targeted at increasing the coaches' adoption and frequency of utilization of these researcher-specified behaviors thought to lead to positive athlete outcomes.

The most enduring and comprehensive example of this intervention approach to studying coach-athlete interactions in youth sport settings is the work of Smith, Smoll and colleagues. Earlier in this chapter we described the origins of this work and the creation of the CBAS observational instrument. Descriptive studies using the CBAS with children's baseball and basketball coaches (Smith & Smoll 1990; Smith et al., 1978; Smith et al., 1983) provided the foundation for a behavior modification program initially referred to as Coach Effectiveness Training (CET). This brief (2.5 hours) workshop was designed to improve coach-athlete interactions in youth sport settings by teaching coaches to create a positive and mastery-oriented teaching environment. The CET format has subsequently been revised to incorporate some motivational climate aspects of coaching, although the message has remained fairly consistent, and is now referred to as MAC (Mastery Approach to Coaching: Smoll, Smith, & Cumming, 2007).

A number of studies have been conducted to measure the impact of CET on coach-athlete interactions with coaches of both male and female athletes between the ages of 10 and 15 in baseball and basketball (e.g., Barnett, Smoll, & Smith, 1992; Smith et al., 2007; Smith, Smoll, & Barnett, 1995; Smoll, Smith, Barnett, & Everett, 1993; Smith, Smoll, & Curtis, 1979; Smoll et al., 2007). Results across these studies show consistent improvements in the quality of coach-athlete interactions. CET-trained coaches exhibited more positive reinforcement, encouragement, and instruction (the behavioral targets of CET) as perceived by their athletes than untrained coaches, while athletes of trained coaches believed their coaches created a more positive, mastery-oriented team climate. Furthermore, athletes of trained coaches reported higher enjoyment, increased self-esteem (especially those with low initial self-esteem), and reduced performance anxiety, and dropped out less than athletes of untrained coaches. Results from a similar intervention based on CET with 7- to 18-year-old swimmers (Coatsworth & Conroy, 2006; Conroy & Coatsworth, 2004), however, reported less dramatic main effects with regard to athlete outcomes as a result of participation in the intervention. While trained coaches used more positive reinforcement and instruction and less punishment, increases in self-esteem were only significant for younger children (younger than age 11) and girls with low initial self-esteem, and there was no reduction in the athletes' fear of failure. This divergent finding highlights another issue salient to the study and modification of coach-athlete interactions. This last intervention was the only one conducted in an individual sport setting (swimming), whereas the other studies were completed with team sport coaches and athletes (baseball and basketball).

Another noteworthy example of a predefined behavioral target intervention approach in children's sport is a study designed to reduce athlete violence through modification of coaching behavior (Trudel, Bernard, Boileau, & Marcotte, 2000). A three-part intervention was employed with 28 ice hockey coaches of 14- to 15-year-old males in Canada to improve the way coaches taught body-checking, with particular emphasis placed on evaluating the intervention process. Despite a comprehensive multimethod approach to modifying coach and athlete behaviors (e.g., fewer incorrect body checks as measured by penalties during games), no significant differences were found pre- and postintervention. The coaches reported satisfaction with the intervention, but also indicated they did not fully adhere to the self-supervision component of the intervention. The authors concluded that coach interactive behavior would be resistant to change unless more regular and formal support and feedback were provided to the coaches. Also, the authors noted issues with the validity of using game performance indicators as measures of athlete behavior change due to the unpredictable and dynamic nature of youth sport competitions.

In contrast to the behavioral targets predefined by researchers characterizing the previously reviewed intervention research, there are several examples of studies using a collaborative action research approach to improving coaching effectiveness. In this approach, coaches (or the coach and researchers together) set their own behavioral targets that they feel are most relevant to their individual coaching experience. In a study by Komaki and Barnett (1977), the researchers and a competitive youth football coach jointly created 5-stage behavioral checklists for three specific football plays. In the intervention the coach was instructed to rate the athletes' (9- to 10-year-old males) execution of the plays using the behavioral checklist, and then to provide immediate feedback to the athletes during practices. After a baseline of at least 10 observations (games and practices), the coach implemented the behavior checklist feedback strategy across 14 observations (games and practices). Results showed notable improvement in the consistency of the successful completion of each of the three plays. This study provided initial evidence for the effectiveness of a self-selected behavioral specification and feedback modification approach to changing coach-athlete interactions in a children's sport setting. Similarly, Rushall and Smith (1979) reported on a case study designed to change an age-group swim coach's behavioral patterns during practice sessions. Following an initial pre-intervention observation period, the researchers and the swim coach collaborated on the selection of three behaviors targeted for change: (a) reward, (b) feedback, and (c) a reward + feedback combination. Over a period of 28 practice sessions, the swim coach used behavior checklists to self-record frequencies of the three targeted behaviors. Self-recording and knowledge of results were gradually reduced (fading/leaning) across the 28 sessions. Results showed that the fading/leaning approach used in the intervention was effective in increasing the frequency of all three self-selected coaching behaviors from pre- to postintervention. However, their study also showed that the quantity of the coach's overall verbal behaviors remained stable across the 6-month observation period. So although frequencies of the three targeted behaviors were increased as intended, this behavioral change resulted in an associated decrease in other positive coaching behaviors such as questioning, directing, and explaining. Another key finding from the intervention was an increase in the coach's verbal repertoire—in essence the coach had expanded his toolbox of feedback and reward terms. In the pre-intervention period the word "good" comprised 50% of the coach's feedback and reward, whereas in the postintervention period the coach expanded his verbal repertoire to 36 different words.

A final example of a collaborative intervention approach to studying coach-athlete interactions is an intervention designed to modify four youth soccer coaches' practice behaviors using the Computerized Coaching Analysis System (CCAS) (More & Franks, 1996; More, McGarry, Partridge, & Franks, 1996). The CCAS is used to collect data on three interrelated components during practice sessions—coach verbal comments, athlete technical success, and coach time management skills. Each coach was videotaped during practices and three of the four coaches received the results of the CCAS analysis of their behaviors, which were used to collaboratively discuss individualized strategies to move toward self-selected behavioral goals. The fourth coach was simply provided with copies of the videotapes to view at his own discretion. Results showed that the three coaches who received behavioral feedback made substantial improvements in moving toward their behavioral targets. The fourth coach (discretionary viewing of video tapes) did not exhibit targeted behavioral change.

One of the key findings of this intervention study was the situated nature of coach-athlete interactions. Even in the relatively controlled environment of this study (coaches were instructed to teach the same content in a 20-minute section of each observed practice), the behavioral profile of each coach varied across the observations. The authors cautioned that behavior modification efforts in sport coaching must be sensitive to the fact that each practice is "essentially a different learning context" (More & Franks, 1996, p. 541). As has been noted elsewhere across the coach-athlete interaction literature, perhaps an important benefit of coach-athlete interaction intervention research lies in providing practitioners with data to stimulate awareness and self-reflection on their idiosyncratic behavioral tendencies, upon which context-specific desirable behavioral change can be targeted (De Marco, Mancini, Wuest, & Schempp, 1996; Lacy & Darst, 1985; Rushall, 1977). The CCAS is noteworthy, however, because of its attempt to contextualize behavioral patterns while simultaneously providing instant feedback on a coach's progress toward behavioral targets. Despite showing promise as a tool for studying and modifying coach-athlete interactions in youth sport settings, no published reports of research with the CCAS can be found other than the original study published in 1996.

To summarize, the combined intervention research on coach-athlete interactions in children's sport suggests that coaches' interactive behavior can be changed through training, if they are provided with the necessary resources and attention. Further, these changes can lead to increased positive psychosocial outcomes for the athletes of trained coaches; thus, coaches can increase their effectiveness through behavioral training. The studies incorporating coach-selected behavioral goals also suggest that rather than simply acquiring knowledge from experts, coaches can be active participants in their own learning and are often willing to think critically about their own behavior in order to become more effective as coaches. However, care must be taken to ensure that the behavioral targets of any intervention appropriately fit individual coaches and the contexts in which they work.

CONCLUSIONS

In summarizing this chapter, it is important to remember that coaching effectiveness is defined by the promotion of a holistic range of athlete outcomes within a specific context. We have argued that these outcomes are produced largely through coach-athlete interactions appropriately tailored to the athlete-defined context.

Based on our review of the research literature, coach-athlete interactions in children's sport in general tend to be coach-initiated and are typically characterized by high amounts of instruction, support and encouragement, and management behaviors with an overall positive focus. No definite trends emerged with regard to differences related to coach (e.g., gender, experience) or athlete (i.e., age, ability, competitive level) characteristics. More influential in shaping coaches' behavior are situational characteristics, such as game situation (i.e., winning, tied, losing). While overall levels of the specific behaviors are typically consistent between coaches, individual coaches differ in their patterns of behavior change across different game situations.

Of particular interest are the characteristics of effective coaches of children's sport—those linked to positive performance and psychosocial outcomes in their athletes (see Table 9.1 for a summary). In general, coaches who are more instructive and supportive in the interactions with their athletes while avoiding punitive behaviors facilitate a range of positive outcomes in their athletes. Beyond specific behaviors, children appear to respond best to coaches who are autonomy-supportive, who evaluate performance with respect to self-referenced improvement, learning, and effort, and who promote an atmosphere of striving for personal mastery rather than avoiding incompetence. These motivational qualities have all been linked to a number of positive outcomes consistent with holistic athlete development. Finally, in enacting the recommended behaviors and creating the desirable motivational climate, effective children's coaches encourage active participation of their athletes and create a truly interactive environment rather than one defined by an autocratic, one-way flow of information from coach to athlete.

Studies employing interventions targeting coach-athlete interactions suggest that it is possible to shift children's coaches' behaviors toward those more facilitative of positive athlete

Table 9.1. Qualities of Effective Coaching in Children's Sport

Construct	Characteristics of effective coaching	Practical examples
Dominant behaviors	Instruction, support, lack of punishment	– Praise for desirable efforts – Encouragement and relevant technical instruction after mistakes
Motivational tone	Autonomy-supportive	– Inclusion of athletes in decision-making process – Providing justification for coaching decisions – Requesting athletes' perspectives
Goal orientation	Mastery/learning climate	– Evaluation of athlete performance based on self-referenced improvement, learning, and effort
Athlete interactivity	Encouraged	– Asking questions to athletes – Promoting discussion – Verbally confirming athletes' understanding of concepts/instructions

outcomes, thereby increasing coaches' effectiveness. In doing so, we may be able to indirectly influence children's talent development through the training of coaches. However, in order for coach training interventions to be most useful, the reviewed research implies that several considerations should be addressed. In particular, coaches require substantial training resources, time, and support for an intervention to have any effect on behavior. As well, the targeted behaviors must be tailored for the specific coaching context (i.e., individual athletes and organizational/cultural setting) and be appropriately incorporated into the coaches' overall pedagogical process.

LIMITATIONS AND FUTURE DIRECTIONS

While the reviewed literature provides a working profile of effective coaches of children's sport that hopefully can be used to improve the facilitation of talent development in children, a number of limitations should be kept in mind. First, while our intention was to review research on children, few studies limited their sample only to children, with the vast majority including older adolescent-age athletes (i.e., 14–18 years) as well. Thus, the majority of resulting conclusions may be reflective of the broader categorization of "youth" athletes, including but not limited to children, and particularly unique characteristics of younger children may not have clearly emerged. The amount of available research including children under the age of 14 appears to be relatively limited compared to the body of literature employing samples consisting entirely of athletes aged 14 years and older. A similar limitation applies to any potential distinctions between competitive and recreational levels (with some exceptions). Future research would do well to keep the context-specificity (defined by athlete age and competitive level) of coaching effectiveness in mind. Second, it is often difficult to discern possible differential effects of objectively observed coach behaviors in comparison to athlete reported measures (or the nature of relationships between the two). Studies thus far of autonomy-supportive coaching, and coach-created motivational climate in particular, show an almost total reliance on athlete-reported questionnaire methods. This is entirely appropriate, given the noted importance of athlete perceptions of coach behavior, but may limit our ability to translate this descriptive research into contextually appropriate behavioral targets for interventions.

Future research is needed to rectify the noted limitations of the current body of literature, as well as to continue to explore a number of promising areas of understanding. For example, the work of Smith and colleagues (2006; 2009) on situationally defined behavioral variation accounts for vital additional complexity in our understanding of effective coach-athlete interactions, and the limited initial work has already revealed useful new knowledge. Future work might look to incorporate the temporal sequencing of this variation in order to explore potential order and timing effects (i.e., past behavior influencing the effects of future behavior). Dynamic systems and related perspectives may offer insight into these potential nonlinear effects (Erickson & Côté, in press). Finally, not only are coach-athlete interactions patterned through time and situational changes, but the course of this patterning is determined by the mutual interaction of both coach and athlete over time rather than simply by the coach in isolation. Since Fisher and colleagues' (1982) study pairing observation and analysis of both coach and athlete behavior, there have been numerous calls for empirical recognition of the interdependence of coach and athlete behavior (e.g., Bowes & Jones, 2006; Jowett, 2007). To date this remains a relatively unexplored aspect of coach-athlete interactions, particularly in children's sport. In conclusion, the existing literature has generated a wealth of useful knowledge regarding effective coach-athlete interactions in children's sport. By building on this research, future work can extend our understanding of this critical interpersonal process in order to best promote talent development in children.

REFERENCES

Adie, J. W., Duda, J. L., & Ntoumanis, N. (2012). Perceived coach-autonomy support, basic need satisfaction and the well- and ill-being of elite youth soccer players: A longitudinal investigation. *Psychology of Sport and Exercise, 13*(1), 51–59.

Barnett, N. P., Smoll, F. L., & Smith, R. E. (1992). Effects of enhancing coach-athlete relationships on youth sport attrition. *The Sport Psychologist, 6*(2), 111–127.

Black, S. J., & Weiss, M. R. (1992). The relationship among perceived coaching behaviors, perceptions of ability, and motivation in competitive age-group swimmers. *Journal of Sport & Exercise Psychology, 14*(3), 309–325.

Bowes, I., & Jones, R. L. (2006). Working at the edge of chaos: Understanding coaching as a complex, interpersonal system. *The Sport Psychologist, 20*(2), 235–245.

Cervelló, E., Santos-Rosa, F. J., García-Calvo, T., Jiménez, R., & Iglesias, D. (2007). Young tennis players' competitive task involvement and performance: The role of goal orientations, contextual motivational climate, and coach-initiated motivational climate. *Journal of Applied Sport Psychology, 19*, 304–321.

Cheffers, J. T. F., & Mancini, V. H. (1989). Cheffers' Adaptation of Flanders' Interaction Analysis System (CAFIAS). In P. W. Darst, D. B. Zakrajsek, & V. H. Mancini (Eds.), *Analyzing physical education and sport instruction* (2nd ed.) (pp. 119–135). Champaign, IL: Human Kinetics.

Coatsworth, J. D., & Conroy, D. E. (2006). Enhancing the self-esteem of youth swimmers through coach training: Gender and age effects. *Psychology of Sport and Exercise, 7*(2), 173–192.

Coatsworth, J. D., & Conroy, D. E. (2009). The effects of autonomy-supportive coaching, need satisfaction, and self-perceptions on initiative and identity in youth swimmers. *Developmental Psychology, 45*(2), 320–328.

Conroy, D. E., & Coatsworth, J. D. (2004). The effects of coach training on fear of failure in youth swimmers: A latent growth curve analysis from a randomized, controlled trial. *Applied Developmental Psychology, 25*(2), 193–214.

Conroy, D. E., Kaye, M. P., & Coatsworth, J. D. (2006). Coaching climates and the destructive effects of mastery-avoidance achievement goals on situational motivation. *Journal of Sport & Exercise Psychology, 28*(1), 69–92.

Côté, J. (1999). The influence of the family in the development of talent in sports. *The Sport Psychologist, 13*, 395–417.

Côté, J., & Gilbert, W. (2009). An integrative definition of coaching effectiveness and expertise. *International Journal of Sport Science & Coaching, 4*(3), 307–323.

Côté, J., Baker, J., & Abernethy, B. (2007). Practice and play in the development of sport expertise. In R. Eklund & G. Tenenbaum (Eds.), *Handbook of sport psychology* (3rd ed.) (pp. 184–202). Hoboken, NJ: John Wiley.

Côté, J., Young, B., Duffy, P., & North, J. (2007). Towards a definition of excellence in sport coaching. *International Journal of Coaching Science, 1*, 3–17.

Côté, J., Bruner, M. W., Erickson, K., Strachan, L., & Fraser-Thomas, J. (2010). Athlete development and coaching. In J. Lyle & C. Cushion (Eds.), *Sport coaching: Professionalization and practice* (pp. 63–84). Oxford, UK: Elsevier.

Curtis, B., Smith, R. E., & Smoll, F. L. (1979). Scrutinizing the skipper: A study of leadership behaviors in the dugout. *Journal of Applied Psychology, 64*(4), 391–400.

Cushion, C. (2010). Coach behavior. In J. Lyle & C. Cushion (Eds.), *Sports coaching: Professionalisation and practice* (pp. 43–61). London, UK: Eslevier.

Darst, P. W., Zakrajsek, D. B., & Mancini V. H. (Eds.). (1989). *Analyzing physical education and sport instruction.* Champaign, IL: Human Kinetics.

De Marco, G. M., Mancini, V. H., Wuest, D. A., & Schempp, P. G. (1996). Becoming reacquainted with a once familiar and still valuable tool: Systematic observation methodology revisited. *International Journal of Physical Education, 32*, 17–26.

Erickson, K., & Côté, J. (in press). Observing the dynamics of coach-athlete interactions in real time: The state space grid method. In J. Denison, W. Gilbert, & P. Potrac (Eds.), *The handbook of sports coaching.* London, UK: Routledge.

Erickson, K., Côté, J., Hollenstein, T., & Deakin, J. (2011). Examining coach-athlete interactions using state space grids: An observational analysis in competitive youth sport. *Psychology of Sport and Exercise, 12*(6), 645–654.

Fisher, A. C., Mancini, V. H., Hirsch, R. L., Proulx, T. J., & Staurowsky, E. J. (1982). Coach-athlete interactions and team climate. *Journal of Sport Psychology, 4*(4), 388–404.

Ford, P. R., Yates, I., & Williams, A. M. (2010). An analysis of practice activities and instructional behaviours used by youth soccer coaches during practice: Exploring the link between science and application. *Journal of Sport Sciences, 28*(5), 483–495.

Gilbert, W., & Trudel, P. (1999). An evaluation strategy for coach education programs. *Journal of Sport Behavior, 22*, 234–250.

Gilbert, W. D., & Trudel, P. (2004). Analysis of coaching science research published from 1970–2001. *Research Quarterly for Exercise and Sport, 75*(4), 388–399.

Horn, T. (1984). Expectancy effects in the interscholastic setting: Methodological considerations. *Journal of Sport Psychology, 6*(1), 60–76.

Horn, T. (1985). Coaches' feedback and changes in children's perceptions of their physical competence. *Journal of Educational Psychology, 77*(2), 174–186.

Horn, T. (2008). Coaching effectiveness in the sport domain. In T. S. Horn (Ed.), *Advances in sport psychology* (3rd ed.) (pp. 239–267). Champaign, IL: Human Kinetics.

Jones, R. (1990). Coach-player interaction: A descriptive analysis of certified football association coaches' teaching basic techniques at the youth sport level. *Research Supplement: Physical Education Association of Great Britain and Northern Ireland, 7*, 6–10.

Jones, R. L. (1997). Effective instructional coaching behavior: A review of the literature. *International Journal of Physical Education, 24*(1), 27–32.

Jones, D. F., Housner, L. D., & Kornspan, A. S. (1997). Interactive decision making and behavior of experienced and inexperienced basketball coaches during practice. *Journal of Teaching in Physical Education, 16*(4), 454–468.

Jowett, S. (2007). Interdependence analysis and the 3+1 C's in the coach-athlete relationship. In S. Jowett & D. Lavallee (Eds.), *Social psychology in sport* (pp. 15–28). Champaign, IL: Human Kinetics.

Kahan, D. (1999). Coaching behaviour: A review of the systematic observation research literature. *Applied Research in Coaching and Athletics Annual, 14*, 17–58.

Komaki, J., & Barnett, F. T. (1977). A behavioral approach to coaching football: Improving the play execution of the offensive backfield on a youth football team. *Journal of Applied Behavior Analysis, 10*(4), 657–664.

Lacy, A. C., & Darst, P. W. (1985). Systematic observation of behaviors of winning high school head football coaches. *Journal of Teaching in Physical Education, 4*(4), 256–270.

Lacy, A. C., & Goldston, P. D. (1990). Behavior analysis of male and female coaches in high school girls' basketball. *Journal of Sport Behavior, 13*(1), 29–40.

Lerner, R. M., Lerner, J. V., Almerigi, J., Theokas, C., Phelps, E., Gestsdottir, S., et al. (2005). Positive youth development, participation in community youth development programs, and community contributions of fifth grade adolescents: Findings from the first wave of the 4-H Study of Positive Youth Development. *Journal of Early Adolescence, 25*(1), 17–71.

Lewis, M. D., Lamey, A. V., & Douglas, L. (1999). A new dynamic system method for the analysis of early socioemotional development. *Developmental Science, 2*(4), 457–475.

Lombardo, B. J. (1984). The coach in action: A descriptive analysis. *FIEP Bulletin, 54*, 9–15.

Lyle, J. (2002). *Sports coaching concepts: A framework for coaches' behavior.* London, UK: Routledge.

More, K. G., & Franks, I. M. (1996). Analysis and modification of verbal coaching behavior: The usefulness of a data-driven intervention strategy. *Journal of Sports Sciences, 14*(6), 523–543.

More, K. G., McGarry, T., Partridge, D., & Franks, I. M. (1996). A computer-assisted analysis of verbal coaching behavior in soccer. *Journal of Sport Behavior, 19*, 319–337.

Murphy-Mills, J., Vierimaa, Côté, J., & Deakin, J. (2010) *An examination of coach-athlete interactions in a highly successful youth sport program for athletes with disabilities.* Presented at Coaching Association of Canada's Sport Leadership Sportif Conference. Ottawa, ON, Canada.

Rejeski, W., Darracott, C., & Hutslar, S. (1979). Pygmalion in youth sport: A field study. *Journal of Sport Psychology, 1*(4), 311–319.

Rushall, B. S. (1977). Two observation schedules for sporting and physical education environments. *Canadian Journal of Applied Sports Sciences, 2*, 15–21.

Rushall, B. S., & Smith, K. C. (1979). The modification of the quality and quantity of behavior categories in a swimming coach. *Journal of Sport Psychology, 1*, 138–150.

Ryan, R. M., & Deci, E. L. (2000). Self-determination theory and the facilitation of intrinsic motivation, social development, and well-being. *American Psychologist, 55*(1), 68–78.

Seaborn, P., Trudel, P., & Gilbert, W. (1998). Instructional content provided to female ice hockey players during games. *Applied Research in Coaching and Athletics Annual, 13*, 119–141.

Segrave, J. O., & Ciancio, C. A. (1990). An observational study of a successful Pop Warner football coach. *Journal of Teaching in Physical Education, 9*(4), 294–306.

Smith, R. E. (2006). Understanding sport behavior: A cognitive-affective processing systems approach. *Journal of Applied Sport Psychology, 18*, 1–27.

Smith, R. E., Shoda, Y., Cumming, S. P., & Smoll, F. L. (2009). Behavioral signatures at the ballpark: Intraindividual consistency of adults' situation-behavior patterns and their interpersonal consequences. *Journal of Research in Personality, 43*(2), 187–195.

Smith, R. E., & Smoll, F. L. (1990). Self-esteem and children's reactions to youth sport coaching behaviors: A field study of self-enhancement processes. *Developmental Psychology, 26*(6), 987–993.

Smith, R. E., & Smoll, F. L. (2007). Social-cognitive approach to coaching behaviors. In S. Jowett & D. Lavallee (Eds.), *Social psychology in sport* (pp. 75–89). Champaign, IL: Human Kinetics.

Smith, R. E., Smoll, F. L., & Barnett, N. P. (1995). Reduction of children's sport performance anxiety through social support and stress-reduction training for coaches. *Journal of Applied Developmental Psychology, 16*(1), 125–142.

Smith, R. E., Smoll, F. L., & Curtis, B. (1978). Coaching behaviors in Little League Baseball. In F. L. Smoll & R. E. Smith (Eds.), *Psychological perspectives in youth sports* (pp. 173–201). Washington, DC: Hemisphere.

Smith, R. E., Smoll, F. L., & Curtis, B. (1979). Coach effectiveness training: A cognitive-behavioral approach to enhancing relationship skills in youth sport coaches. *Journal of Sport Psychology, 1*(1), 59–75.

Smith, R. E., Smoll, F. L., & Hunt, E. (1977). A system for the behavioral assessment of athletic coaches. *The Research Quarterly, 48*(2), 401–407.

Smith, R. E., Zane, N. W. S., Smoll, F. L., & Coppel, D. B. (1983). Behavioral assessment in youth sports: Coaching behaviors and children's attitudes. *Medicine and Science in Sports and Exercise, 15*(3), 208–214.

Smoll, F. L., Smith, R. E., Barnett, N. P., & Everett, J. J. (1993). Enhancement of children's self-esteem through social support training for youth sport coaches. *Journal of Applied Psychology, 78*(4), 602–610.

Smoll, F. L., Smith, R. E., & Cumming, S. P. (2007). Effects of a motivational climate intervention for coaches on changes in young athletes' achievement goal orientations. *Journal of Clinical Sport Psychology, 1*(1), 23–46.

Smoll, F. L., Smith, R. E., Curtis, B., & Hunt, E. (1978). Toward a mediational model of coach-player relationships. *Research Quarterly, 49*(4), 528–541.

Solomon, G. B. (2008). Expectations and perceptions as predictors of coaches' feedback in three competitive contexts. *Journal for the Study of Sports and Athletics in Education, 2*(2), 161–179.

Solomon, G. B., & Buscombe, R. M. (in press). Expectancy effects in coaching. In J. Denison, W. Gilbert, & P. Potrac (Eds.), *The handbook of sports coaching*. London, UK: Routledge.

Trudel, P., Bernard, D., Boileau, R., & Marcotte, G. (2000). Effects of an intervention strategy on penalties, body checking and injuries in ice hockey. In A. B. Ashare (Ed.), *Safety in ice hockey: Third volume ASTM 1341* (pp. 237–249). Philadelphia, PA: American Society for Testing and Materials.

Trudel, P., Côté, J., & Bernard, D. (1996). Systematic observation of youth ice hockey coaches during games. *Journal of Sport Behavior, 19,* 50–65.

Trudel, P., & Gilbert, W. (1995). Research on coaches' behaviors: Looking beyond the refereed journals. *Avante, 1*(2), 94–106.

Trudel, P., & Gilbert, W. D. (2006) Coaching and coach education. In D. Kirk, M. O'Sullivan, & D. McDonald (Eds.), *Handbook of physical education* (pp. 516–539). London, UK: Sage.

CHAPTER 10

PEER AND GROUP INFLUENCES IN YOUTH SPORT

Mark W. Bruner, Mark A. Eys, and Jennifer Turnnidge

INTRODUCTION

S port is a social context that provides rich opportunities for interpersonal interaction. Children are often drawn to sport for social reasons, including a desire for affiliation, social recognition, or wanting to be with friends (Allen, 2003). While sport fosters both social interactions and relationships with parents, coaches, and peers, it is the bond with peers that may have the most significant influence on children's motivation to participate in sport and, consequently, their personal and athletic development. Peers can also contribute to the quality of a youth's sport experiences through their companionship and support (Smith, 1999). Of equal importance, it is through their peer experiences that children can (a) explore the physical and social world; (b) acquire a wide range of behaviors, skills, attitudes, and experiences; (c) develop cognitive, social, and emotional functioning; (d) develop an ability to understand other's thoughts, emotions, and intentions; (e) develop a personal identity; and (f) develop moral values and attitudes (see Azmitia, Lippman, & Ittel, 1999; Gunnar, Senior, & Hartup, 1984; Hartup & Laursen, 1999; Kindermann, 2003; Light & Glachan, 1985; Rubin, Bukowski, & Parker, 2006).

Despite the consistent evidence that relations with peers are important for youth development, the overwhelming majority of research on social influence in a sport context focuses upon the role and social influence of coaches and parents in facilitating youth's physical and psychosocial outcomes (Smith, 2007). Far less research has focused on youth personal and athletic talent development through peer interactions and relationships in sport (Holt, Black,

Tamminen, Fox, & Mandigo, 2008). This is unfortunate, given the increasing recognition of peers in models of athlete development. In one of the earlier models of expertise development, Bloom (1985) examined experts in disciplines such as mathematics, art, science, and sport. Bloom utilized qualitative, retrospective interviews to describe the life story of these talented individuals. From these interviews, Bloom inferred that there were several significant persons who help shape the talent development process. Bloom believed that around the ages of 10–14, peers become more involved in the individual's talent areas, both as friends and competitors, and encourage the individuals to master relevant skills. More recently, models by Wylleman and Lavallee (2004) and Bailey and Morley (2006) proposed that talent development needs to be viewed as a multidimensional construct that stems from the emergence of a wide range of abilities, including interpersonal skills. As such, youth's ability to positively interact with peers may help to foster the development of sport expertise.

Although the association between peers and talent development in sport is not yet clearly understood, peers have been shown to play a key role in the development of expertise in other areas. For example, research within the education literature has established a significant link between peer experiences and youth's academic achievement (Wentzel & Caldwell, 1997). This line of research has consistently demonstrated that a relationship exists between high levels of peer acceptance and successful academic performance (e.g., Berghout-Austin & Draper, 1984; Wentzel, 1991). Friendships and group membership have also been related to academic achievement (e.g., Berndt & Keefe, 1995). Given these findings, it would be informative to determine if sport-based peer interactions can similarly facilitate athletic achievement.

Thus, the objectives of this chapter are to (a) provide an orientation for a guiding conceptual framework to better understand the multiple interrelated levels of social organization that underpin peer experiences; (b) explore the influence of peers on children's motivation to participate in sport, their athletic experiences, and their talent development; (c) delve deeper into the theory and empirical evidence within three levels of social complexity (interactions, relationship, groups) among peers in sport; and (d) highlight important avenues of future research.

CONCEPTUAL FRAMEWORK

Rubin, Bukowski, and Parker (1998, 2006) proposed that youth's experiences with peers can be conceptualized on three different levels of social complexity: interactions, relationships, and groups. This conceptualization was based upon earlier work by Hinde (1987) in child and social psychology. Figure 10.1 represents a conceptual framework of youth's experiences in sport based upon the previous work of Rubin et al. (1998, 2006) and Hinde (1987). Within this framework, the simplest level of complexity of peer experiences involves *interactions*. Interactions stem from the behavior of two individuals in a social exchange of some duration. The term interaction is typically reserved for dyadic behaviors that require interdependence between the two participants (Rubin et al., 2006). A comprehensive description of interactions requires understanding not only the content of what the individuals are doing, but also the qualities of the interaction (Hinde, 1976a). These interaction qualities emerge as a result of the combination of the participants' behaviors, and thus have properties that are not present in the behaviors alone (Hinde, 1976b). Positive peer interactions have been shown to be an

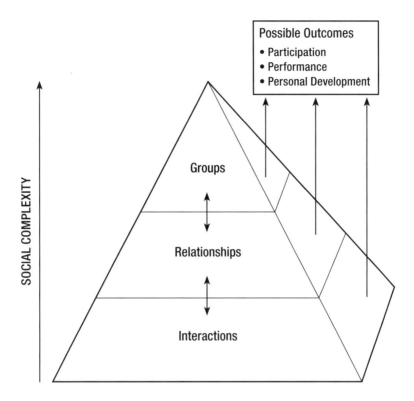

Note: Framework adapted from Rubin et al.'s (1998, 2006) and Hinde's (1987) previous work/conceptualizations of youth's experiences with peers.

Figure 10.1. Conceptual framework of youth's experiences with peers in sport.

important context for youth's social, cognitive, and emotional development (e.g., Hartup & Laursen, 1999; Kindermann, 2003).

Relationships represent a higher level of complexity of youth's experiences with peers (see Figure 10.1). Relationships are comprised of a succession of interactions between individuals who are known to each other (Rubin et al., 2006). According to Hinde (1995), relationships can be described across ten dimensions, such as the diversity of interactions within a relationship, the reciprocity of these interactions, and the individuals' commitment to the relationship. One dyadic relationship that is particularly salient for peer research in sport is friendship. Friendships are bidirectional relationships in which both parties share a sense of membership and belonging (Moran & Weiss, 2006). Previous research suggests that friendships in childhood can serve several important functions, such as providing support, affection, and instrumental and informational assistance (Newcomb & Bagwell, 1995).

Finally, relationships are further embedded in, and influenced by, a higher level of social complexity: *groups* (see Figure 10.1). Groups are a collection of interacting individuals who have some degree of reciprocal influence on each other (Rubin et al., 2006) and who interact with each other on a regular basis (Wentzel & Caldwell, 1997). Furthermore, groups can be defined by the characteristics of their participants, their types of interactions, and their constituent relationships. However, peer groups are more than simple aggregates of their interactions and relationships (Chen, Chen, & Kaspar, 2001). Groups can possess specific properties, such as group norms, processes, and structure, that are not necessarily found in lower-order peer experiences (Holt et al., 2008). Since groups can shape the type and range of interactions and relationships that can occur within them, they can have a significant influence on peer experiences. The latter half of the chapter will pay particular attention to the significant influence of groups on peers.

PEER INTERACTIONS IN SPORT

Within the developmental psychology literature, there is growing support for the notion that real-time interactions can be viewed as the raw materials of development (e.g., Fogel, 1993; Thelen & Smith, 1994), which are of great importance to psychological well-being (Steenbeek & van Geert, 2006). In line with this contention, Granic (2005) proposed that an individual's day-to-day interactive experiences can play an integral role in facilitating their developmental outcomes. The significance of investigating the behavioral patterns that shape peer interactions is further underscored by the fact that youth's interaction patterns and acceptance by the peer group are related (Steenbeck & van Geert, 2006). Asher and Coie (1990), for instance, found that children whose social behaviors led to maladaptive interaction patterns were more likely to be rejected by their peer group. Previous research has also consistently demonstrated that prosocial interactive behaviors are positively linked with peer acceptance (e.g.,Wentzel & Caldwell, 1997). Furthermore, the social skills that youth acquire through their interaction with peers may foster their ability to develop and maintain dyadic relationships, such as friendships (Rubin, Chen, Coplan, Buskirk, & Wojslawowicz, 2005). Drawing upon these studies, it is evident that peer interactions may have an important influence on youth's peer experiences at both the relationship and group levels.

Although there are a limited number of studies investigating peer interactions in sport, evidence exists to suggest that peer interactions may help to shape youth's skill acquisition. For example, d'Arripe-Longueville, Gernigon, Huet, Winnykamen, and Cadopi (2002) qualitatively assessed the role of peers in learning a swimming skill. The two purposes of this study were to examine the use of peer-assisted learning methods and to explore the effects of dyad type (symmetrical vs. asymmetrical) and gender on peer interaction modes. Symmetrical pairs consisted of two novice peers with similar competence levels, whereas asymmetrical pairs consisted of a novice peer paired with a skilled peer. Results indicated that the peer interactions in this study consisted of four key behaviors: guidance-tutoring, imitation, co-operation, and parallel activity. The results also illustrated that tutoring and imitation were exhibited more in asymmetrical dyads, while co-operation and parallel activity were manifested more in symmetrical dyads. Further, boys tended to engage in individual behaviors (parallel activity), whereas girls more frequently exhibited socially oriented behaviors such as cooperation and guidance-tutoring. Regarding performance, boys in asymmetrical dyads performed significantly better than all other groups. Overall, these findings provide some valuable insight into how the characteristics of one's peers may shape the content of peer interactions, and in doing so, may influence youth's skill development.

Peer interactions may also contribute to youth's motivation to participate in sport. Keegan, Harwood, Spray, and Lavallee (2009) conducted interviews with 40 youth sport participants in order to investigate the roles of coaches, parents, and peers in influencing athlete motivation. Results revealed that peers influenced participants' motivation through a wide range of behaviors, including competitive behaviors, collaborative behaviors, and evaluative communication. Participants also reported that behaviors that had a positive influence on motivation, such as patting one on the back, were perceived as acts of friendship. These results help to demonstrate the impact of peer behaviors on youth's sport motivation. In addition, they illustrate the interdependent nature of peer interactions and relationships.

Holt and colleagues' (2008) investigation of female soccer players' perceptions of their peer experiences is another study that evaluated peer interactions in sport. They conducted in-depth interviews with 34 girls from two youth soccer teams. Results indicated that players' short-term interactions provided opportunities to integrate new team members into the existing team structure. The results also suggested that participants recognized the importance of integrating new members in relation to the team's success. In addition, Holt et al. (2008) found that through their soccer experience, the youth learned to interact with different types of peers (i.e., youth who were perceived to have different interests, personalities, etc). More specifically, since the youth did not choose their teammates, they had to learn to cooperate and get along with peers who weren't necessarily their friends.

Overall, these studies provide some initial insight into how peer interactions may influence youth's sport experiences. However, there is still a lack of studies investigating the behaviors that make up peer interactions in sport. For example, it is unclear how behaviors that are directly sport related, such as providing technical feedback or discussing team strategies, may contribute to youth's talent development. Further, studies that fully capture the complex and reciprocal nature of peer interactions are limited (Murphy-Mills, Bruner, Erickson, & Côté, 2011). There is thus a need to continue to explore the interactions that occur between peers within the sport environment.

PEER RELATIONSHIPS IN SPORT

As noted previously, the primary construct at the relationship level is friendship. Research on friendship within the developmental psychology literature proposed that three distinct aspects of friendship are important to youth's psychosocial outcomes: (a) whether or not a child has friends, (b) who these friends are, and (c) the quality of these friendships (Bukowski, Newcomb, & Hartup, 1996; Newcomb & Bagwell, 1995). Each of these characteristics of friendship can play a unique role in facilitating development. This is supported by the fact that friendships can promote the acquisition of interpersonal skills, enhance self-concept and self-esteem, and produce feelings of personal well-being (Gifford-Smith & Brownell, 2003). Furthermore, friendships can serve as an important source of emotional security and can act as a protective cushion against some of the stresses and challenges that youth experience (Criss, Pettit, Bates, Dodge, & Lapp, 2002). Based on these contentions, it is reasonable to suggest that peer friendships may influence both youth's motivation to participate in sport and their expertise development.

Within the sport context, evidence exists to suggest that there is an important connection between sport participation and the development of friendship (e.g., Bigelow, Lewko, & Salhani, 1989; Weiss & Smith, 2002). In addition, studies have shown that a best friend's participation in sport can be a significant predictor of a youth's sport commitment and involvement (e.g., Wold & Anderssen, 1992). Patrick et al. (1999) examined the role of peer relationships in adolescents' continued involvement in the sports and the arts. They conducted semistructured interviews with 41 students in grades 9–12 and their parents in order to explore how the participants themselves viewed the association between peer experiences and activity participation. Of these 41 participants, 27 were involved in sport-related activities. Results suggested that adolescents perceived sport activities to be a particularly salient context in which to develop friendships. In fact, over half of the participants reported that their involvement in activities provided them with a significant opportunity to make friends and led to an increase in the number of friends they had. Furthermore, over one-third of the participants indicated that their activity involvement enhanced their social skills and improved their confidence in relating to peers.

In addition to reporting that participation in activities helped to extend the breadth of their social networks, adolescents also commented that their activity involvement helped to enhance the *quality* of the relationships within these networks (Patrick et al., 1999). This is supported by the fact that more than half of the adolescents described the friendships they formed in the activities as more intense and intimate than other friendships. Finally, the adolescents also reported that when they experienced positive activity-related friendships, their enjoyment of, and their commitment to, the activity was considerably enhanced. Based on these reports, Patrick and colleagues (1999) proposed that the benefits accrued through peer relationships were a significant factor influencing continued activity engagement. This is consistent with previous research that identifies the importance of social support with regard to participation in youth sport (Scanlan, Carpenter, Schmidt, Simons, & Keeler, 1993).

In an effort to further examine friendship in the sport context, Weiss and Smith (2002) explored age and gender differences in the quality of sport friendship and assessed the relationship between friendship quality and motivation-related variables. They distributed the Sport Friendship Quality Scale (SFQS; Weiss & Smith, 1999) to 191 tennis players ranging in age from 10 to 18 years. The participants also completed measures to assess their perceived tennis competence and perceived peer acceptance, as well as their tennis enjoyment and commitment. The results indicated that developmental and gender preferences for certain friendship qualities exist. This was supported by the finding that older athletes (14–18 years) rated loyalty, intimacy, things in common, and conflict higher than younger participants (10–13 years). Conversely, younger athletes rated companionship and pleasant play higher. Gender differences also emerged as girls rated self-esteem enhancement and supportiveness, loyalty and intimacy, and things in common higher than boys, who rated conflict resolution higher. The results revealed that the friendship qualities of companionship and pleasant play, conflict resolution, and things in common predicted higher tennis enjoyment and commitment. Furthermore, this research demonstrated that friendship quality is linked to athlete perceptions of enjoyment, competence, and sport commitment.

Finally, Ullrich-French and Smith (2006) investigated how youth's perceptions of their relationships with parents and peers predict motivational outcomes in youth sport. One hundred and eighty-six youth soccer players (10–14 years) completed surveys assessing friendship quality, parent-child relationship quality, peer acceptance, and motivational outcomes, including enjoyment, stress, perceived competence, and self-determined motivation. Findings indicated that friendship quality contributed to the prediction of enjoyment, perceived competence, and self-determined motivation. Based on these results, Ullrich-French and Smith (2006) posited that peers are important socializing agents for youth. This is in line with previous research that identified peers as key contributors to motivational outcomes in sport (e.g., Weiss & Smith, 2002).

GROUP PROCESSES IN SPORT

The previous two sections highlighted research and concepts pertaining to interactions and relationships among peers within the sport environment. Researchers suggested that the patterning of these interactions and relationships combine to produce the more complex entity of the group (Hinde, 1979; Rubin et al., 2006). Indeed, the definition of a group provided earlier in this chapter (i.e., interacting individuals who have reciprocal influence on one another) reflects this conception. However, in the sport environment, Carron and Eys (2012) provided a definition of a *sport team* (i.e., a specific type of group) that appears to reflect an even greater level of complexity:

> A collection of two or more individuals who possess a common identity, have common goals and objectives, share a common fate, exhibit structured patterns of interaction and modes of communication, hold common perceptions about group structure, are personally and instrumentally interdependent, reciprocate interpersonal attraction, and consider themselves to be a group. (p. 14)

Carron and Eys (2012) provided a comprehensive discussion about the derivation of this definition of a sport team (not to be reiterated in this chapter), which was based on the work of numerous group dynamics theorists. The definition does, however, underlie a set of concepts thought to be of importance in the study of sport teams that ultimately affects both individual and group outcomes. These concepts include the attributes of group members, the group's environment, group structure (e.g., status, roles), group cohesion, and other group processes (e.g., cooperation, cohesion, competition, goal setting). There is some overlap between these concepts and those highlighted as important to consider at the group level by Rubin et al. (2006) and Holt et al. (2008). For example, both teams of researchers identified *cohesion* as an important property to consider within groups. Furthermore, elements of group *structure* were also highlighted within these works; Rubin et al. (2006) briefly discussed the hierarchy or ordering of individuals within the group, while Holt and colleagues (2008) found the emergence of peer leaders and social hierarchy to be particularly relevant to female high school soccer teams.

Two issues pertaining to the links between group properties and the objectives of the present chapter and book (i.e., identifying conditions that underpin children's investment in sport and their talent development) need to be highlighted. First, is there evidence to suggest that these group properties play a role in the degree to which individuals invest themselves in sport? Drawing from research with adult participants, it is reasonable to conclude that the answer to this question is an unqualified yes. For example, individuals who perceive their team as highly cohesive are more likely to attend and to be on time for practices and games (Carron, Widmeyer, & Brawley, 1988), in addition to expending more effort in the process (Prapavessis & Carron, 1997). Other researchers found evidence between group perceptions and both intended and actual future participation in sport. In the case of the former, Eys, Carron, Bray, and Beauchamp (2005) found that athletes who perceived greater ambiguity related to their role responsibilities (i.e., a structural component of a group) had lower intentions to return to their team the following season. With respect to actual participation, Spink, Wilson, and Odnokon's (2010) results supported their hypothesis that those athletes in their study (i.e., elite hockey players) returning to play their sport held stronger perceptions of group cohesion the previous year (compared to those who did not return).

Clearly, talent development requires ongoing participation and investment in the chosen activity, and, as the previous paragraph communicates, group concepts are related to continued and future participation. However, a second issue related to the subject under examination in the present chapter is whether the links between group properties and sport investment are specifically demonstrated with *younger* populations. Overall, there remains a dearth of sport literature relating to the group's properties. This seems to reflect the larger body of literature, as Rubin et al. (2006) noted:

> In spite of the importance of the group, there has been, until recently, little attention paid to the assessment of group phenomena…. This is surprising because researchers often cite experiences with peers with reference to the "peer group." [This] could be attributed to the complex conceptual and methodological issues related to the study of group structure and organization. (p. 579)

The remainder of this section focuses on five concepts that have received recent research attention with younger populations in the sport environment. These include cohesion, role perceptions, group norms, social identity, and interdependence. Each section will include a definition of the concept, discuss issues pertaining to its conceptualization, and briefly highlight relevant literature (see Table 10.1 for an overview of each concept).

Group Cohesion

Carron, Brawley, and Widmeyer (1998) defined cohesion as "a dynamic process which is reflected in the tendency for a group to stick together and remain united in the pursuit of instrumental objectives and/or for the satisfaction of member affective needs" (p. 213). A conceptualization of cohesion (Carron, Widmeyer, & Brawley, 1985) devised with adults as the target population highlighted four dimensions, including (a) individual attractions to the group-task (i.e., individuals' perceptions of personal involvement toward the group's task aspects), (b) individual attractions to the group-social (i.e., individuals' perceptions of personal involvement toward the group's social aspects), (c) group integration-task (i.e., individuals' perceptions of the level of unity possessed by the group around task aspects), and (d) group integration-social

Table 10.1. Summary of Group Processes in Youth Sport

	Definition	Conceptualization	General Findings
Cohesion	"Dynamic process which is reflected in the tendency for a group to stick together and remain united in the pursuit of instrumental objectives and /or for the satisfaction of member affective needs." (Carron et al., 1998, p. 213)	Two dimensions of cohesion (task and social) assessed in children and youth.	1. Youth athletes' perceptions of coach-initiated motivational climate associated with group cohesion. Specifically, task-oriented motivational climate was positively related to perceptions of both task and social cohesion, while perceptions of an ego-oriented motivational climate were negatively related to perceptions of task cohesion. 2. Youth participating on sport teams reporting greater overall personal and social development perceived task and social cohesion to be higher throughout the season. 3. Task cohesion was found to be positively related to psychological need satisfaction that, in turn, was related to athletes' perceptions of developmental experiences, such as increased opportunities for leadership, emotional regulation, and goal setting, as well as decreased social exclusion.
Role Perceptions	Expectations for behaviors for a position in a social context (Biddle & Thomas, 1966).	Athletes need to understand (a) the scope of their responsibilities, (b) the behaviors necessary to fulfill their responsibilities, (c) how they will be evaluated with respect to role performance, and (d) the consequences should they not fulfill their role responsibilities.	1. Negative links were found between perceptions of role ambiguity and role performance. 2. Perceptions of social cohesion mid season were predictive of changes in role ambiguity (i.e., ambiguity surrounding scope of responsibilities and role behaviors) between mid and late season.
Group Norms	"Standards for behavior expected of group members." (Carron et al., 2005, p. 171)	Different types of norms identified: productive, social support, attendance, social inclusion, performance, and moral (e.g., cheating, aggression) in different situations: (a) during competitions, (b) at practices, (c) in social situations, and (d) during the off-season.	1. Team norms (productive norms, role involvement, social support) predicted perceptions of social loafing. 2. Group cohesion significantly and positively related to performance norms. 3. Coach leadership style significantly related to collective team norms for cheating and aggression. Specifically, autocratic coach behavior positively linked to the team norms for cheating and aggression. 4. Coach-athlete behaviors predicted norms in practice and social settings.

Table 10.1. Summary of Group Processes in Youth Sport (continued)

Social Identity	"That part of an individual's self concept which derives from his/her knowledge of his/her membership of a social group (or groups) together with the value and emotional significance attached to that membership." (Tajfel, 1981, p. 255)	Three dimensions: (a) cognitive centrality (the importance of being a group member); (b) in-group affect (the positive feelings associated with group membership); (c) in-group ties (perceptions of similarity, bonding, and belongingness with other group members) (Cameron, 2004).	1. Youth on winning teams identified more strongly and emphasized team unity significantly more than players on teams with losing records. 2. Social identity was a predictor of increased prosocial behavior toward teammates.
Interdependence	Actions of one individual within a group have implications for the next member, and ultimately the group as a whole (Johnson, 2003).	Multidimensional (task and outcome).	1. Outcome interdependence was a significant predictor of developmental experiences in youth sport (including identity exploration, initiative, emotional regulation, positive relationships, teamwork and social skills, and adult network and social capital). 2. Interdependence of the youth sport setting predicted a young athlete's enjoyment and burnout.

(i.e., individuals' perceptions of the level of unity possessed by the group regarding social aspects).

In more recent studies, Eys and colleagues (Eys, Loughead, Bray, & Carron, 2009a; 2009b) found support for their contention that the multidimensional conceptual model of cohesion outlined in the previous paragraph may lack relevance for a younger age group. Citing a review by Rubin et al. (2006) that discussed developmental differences with respect to how individuals view their interrelationships with others (e.g., friendships, group membership), Eys et al. (2009a) proposed that youth may view their group in less complex terms. They found empirical evidence through the development of the Youth Sport Environment Questionnaire (YSEQ) to suggest that examining cohesion via task versus social dimensions (compared to the four dimensions previously outlined) was most appropriate. The YSEQ is a questionnaire designed to assess perceptions of cohesion from youth aged 13–17 years. A similar structure (i.e., two-dimensional structure; task vs. social cohesion) was supported by Martin, Carron, Eys, and Loughead (2012) in the development of their questionnaire designed for children 9–12 years of age.

Given that the development of these two inventories is quite recent, a comprehensive set of literature has yet to be developed regarding cohesion perceptions with younger groups. However, a few studies highlighted some interesting findings. For example, Jewitt, Eys, Loughead, and Bruner (2010) communicated links between youth athletes' perceptions of the coach-initiated motivational climate and cohesion. Specifically, a task-oriented motivational climate was positively related to perceptions of both task and social cohesion, while perceptions of an ego-oriented motivational climate were negatively related to perceptions of task cohesion. Furthermore, Jewitt (2011) found that veteran (vs. first-year athletes) and team-sport athletes (vs. individual-sport athletes) had stronger perceptions of social cohesion, and recommended that particular attention be paid to the social environment in youth sport groups.

Finally, two recent studies examined cohesion as it relates specifically to developmental experiences. Bruner, Eys, and Côté (2011) found that those individuals participating on teams reporting greater overall personal and social development perceived task and social cohesion to be higher throughout the season. In a related fashion within a study by Taylor and Bruner (2012), task cohesion was found to be positively related to psychological need satisfaction, that in turn was related to athletes' perceptions of developmental experiences, such as increased opportunities for leadership, emotional regulation, and goal setting, and decreased social exclusion.

Role Perceptions

The concept of roles within groups falls under the general umbrella of group structure (Carron & Eys, 2012) and represents the expectations for behaviors for a position in a social context (Biddle & Thomas, 1966). Eys, Beauchamp, and Bray (2006) provided a comprehensive overview of literature devoted to understanding role involvement in sport. Their review shed light on the complexity of both the transmission and execution of role responsibilities. Furthermore, they noted a number of elements that are necessary to consider when examining roles. These include cognitive elements such as role ambiguity (i.e., a lack of clear information regarding one's role responsibilities), role acceptance (i.e., the degree to which an athlete agrees with his or her role responsibilities), role efficacy (i.e., the degree to which an athlete believes he or she can successfully execute interdependent role functions), and role conflict (i.e., the presence of incongruent or conflicting expectations for an individual), as well as affective (e.g., role satisfaction) and behavioral (i.e., role performance) elements.

Without question, role ambiguity has received the most research attention within the sport environment. In fact, initial support for Beauchamp and colleagues' conceptualization of role ambiguity (Beauchamp, Bray, Eys, & Carron, 2002) was based on responses from youth participants (mean age approximately 15 years). This conceptual model highlights the need for athletes to understand (a) the general scope of their responsibilities, (b) the behaviors necessary to fulfill their responsibilities, (c) how they will be evaluated with respect to role performance, and (d) the consequences should they not fulfill their role responsibilities. Within this same study, which has implications toward the development of talent, Beauchamp et al. (2002) found both direct and negative links between perceptions of role ambiguity and role performance.

A more recent longitudinal examination conducted by Bosselut, McLaren, Eys, and Heuzé (2012) with youth interdependent sport team athletes ties together the last two sections (i.e., role ambiguity and cohesion); they examined perceptions of these two group constructs at two time periods during a competitive season (mid- and late season). Their findings suggested that perceptions of social cohesion at midseason were predictive of changes in perceptions of two dimensions of role ambiguity (i.e., ambiguity surrounding scope of responsibilities and role behaviors) between mid- and late season.

Group Norms

Group norms comprise "the standards for behavior expected of group members" (Carron & Eys, 2012, p. 205). Norms are characterized as being descriptive, evaluative, unobtrusive, flexible, internalized, and stable in nature (Forsyth, 1983). In addition, norms outline what behavior in the group is considered acceptable (i.e., prescriptive norms) and unacceptable (i.e., proscriptive norms) (Munroe, Estabrooks, Dennis, & Carron, 1999), and they serve to both inform members about group standards and to integrate those members within the larger entity (Colman & Carron, 2001). In the domain of sport, Prapavessis and Carron (1997) undertook an investigation to examine what types of norms typically develop in sport teams. Athletes from elite cricket teams reported norms involving punctuality at practices and competitions, providing support for teammates, staying focused on the field, giving maximum effort during training, and adhering to dress code (Prapavessis & Carron, 1997). Building upon this work, Munroe and colleagues (1999) examined the group norms of 140 athletes (ages 14–25) from 18 different sports. Munroe and colleagues identified norms in four different sport situations: (a) during competitions, (b) at practices, (c) in social situations, and (d) during the off-season. Frequently reported team norms included giving effort (during competition), punctuality and attendance (practice), productivity (practice), respect (social situations), and training (off-season).

In a youth sport setting, two distinct lines of research in group norms have been undertaken. The first line of research focused on the relationship between group norms and performance. Høigaard, Säfvenbom, and Tønnessen (2006) examined the relationship between team norms (productive norms, role involvement, and social support norms), group cohesion (task cohesion and social cohesion), and perceived social loafing among Norwegian junior soccer players. Results revealed that the players' perceptions of the productive and social support norms, as well as attraction to their team's task (task cohesion), predicted perceptions of social loafing. Subsequent interaction analysis indicated that the combination of high social cohesion, low task cohesion, and low team norms was predictive of perceptions of social loafing (Høigaard et al., 2006). The findings from Høigaard et al. (2006) supported earlier research in Japan with 114 high school athletic teams, which found a significant relationship between group cohesion and performance norms (Kim & Sugiyama, 1992). However, Høigaard et al.'s (2006) research did not support previous research by Patterson, Carron, and Loughead (2005) with adult elite athletes that noted stronger social rather than task dimensions of cohesion and social norms to be better predictors of performance. The mixed findings and limited research investigating the interrelationships among group norms, group cohesion, and performance highlight the complexity of these relationships and the need for further investigations.

A second line of developmental research focused on collective norms and moral behavior in sport. Shields and Bredemeier (1995) proposed a model of moral action in which a sport team's collective norms influence behavior. Furthermore, they examined the influence of leadership and peers (operationalized as coach's leadership style and team cohesion, respectively) on two collective norms—cheating and aggression—in a sample of high school and college baseball and softball players. Results revealed significant relationships between coach leadership style variables and collective team norms, and between team cohesion and collective team norms. Specifically, autocratic coach behaviors were significantly and positively linked with the team norms for cheating and aggression. Shields and Bredemeier (1995) proposed that this finding was not surprising given that autocratic behavior tends to reduce the independent, critical thinking skills of the athletes.

A second noteworthy finding was that task cohesion was positively related to expectations that peers would cheat and aggress, and that the coach would condone cheating. The authors suggested that perhaps higher task cohesion may shift the emphasis from fair play to victory, but caution the acceptance of this conclusion until subsequent research has been conducted. In addition to the noted findings, several potential modifiers (gender, level, starting status, team winning percentage) were examined in relation to the norms. Higher propensities for cheating and aggression were found among males, college athletes, winning team members, and nonstarters (Shields & Bredemeier, 1995). Collectively, the work of Bredemeier and Shields has highlighted the important role of the coach and peers in shaping team norms concerning moral behavior.

Given the consistent, growing evidence that norms exert a very powerful influence on individual behavior in a number of settings, including sport (e.g., Munroe et al., 1999), a number of questions emerge as to (a) how to develop appropriate norms in sport teams, and (b) once established, how to enhance conformity to team norms. It has been suggested that team interaction and reinforcement are two key prerequisites for the development of team norms (Carron et al., 2005; Colman & Carron, 2001; Vroom, 1969). In turn, stable group norms lead to increased group cohesion, group effectiveness, and ultimately performance (Mullen & Copper, 1994, Patterson et al., 2005; Prapavessis & Carron, 1997). In regard to the second question, Carron (1980) identified two classes of conditions that influence conformity to group norms: personal factors and situational factors. Examples of personal factors include higher personal status and the gender of the athletes. The literature has suggested that females are more compliant to norms than males (Eagly & Carli, 1981), and are more likely to embrace collective moral norms against tactics that lead to pain or injury (Duquin, 1984).

Of equal and perhaps greater influence on conformity to norms are the situational factors such as the size of the group, the clarity of the group norm, the cohesion of the group, and the leadership structure in place (Carron, 1980; Erickson, Bruner, & Côté, 2010; Shaw, 1981; Widmeyer, Brawley, & Carron, 1985). In a recent study, Erickson and colleagues (2010) explored the relationship between team norms and coach-athlete interactions using a novel state space observation technique (Lewis, Lamey, & Douglas, 1999). The dynamic systems approach delved into the underlying mechanisms shaping the norms on two competitive youth female synchronized swimming teams. Results revealed that specific coach-athlete behaviors predicted norms in practice and social settings. Specifically, practice attendance norms were predicted by the coach's corrective feedback, social attendance norms were predicted by nonsport-related coach-athlete discussion, and social interaction norms were predicted by sport-related coach-athlete discussion (Erickson et al., 2010). The findings of the study support the complexity of coach-athlete relationships and the need for more research to unlock how situational factors influence the development of team norms.

Social Identity

One important, underdeveloped aspect of research in children and adolescent sport settings that may significantly contribute to participation and development in sport relates to the identities that youth form through their membership on sport teams—their team social identities. The identities youth form around membership in sport teams compose an important component of a youth's self-concept and are critical in the establishment of personal identity and moral values (Harris, 1998; McLellan & Pugh, 1999). Existing social psychological research on social identity is based upon Tajfel and Turner's (1979) Social Identity Theory (SIT). The central premise of SIT is that people define and evaluate themselves in terms of the groups to which they belong (Hogg & Abrams, 2001). Social identity has been defined as "that part of an individual's self concept which derives from his knowledge of his membership of a social group (or groups) together with the value and emotional significance attached to that membership" (Tajfel, 1981, p. 255). As highlighted within this formal definition, social identity is conceptualized as having three key dimensions: (a) cognitive centrality (the importance of being a group member), (b) ingroup affect (the positive feelings associated with group membership), and (c) ingroup ties (perceptions of similarity, bonding, and belongingness with other group members; Cameron, 2004). Until recently, only minimal research has investigated the influence of team social identity in sport, especially with youth populations. The subsequent paragraphs will briefly summarize the extant literature in youth sport (Bruner & Côté, 2010; Hogg & Hains, 1996; Murrell & Gaertner, 1992; Zucchermaglio, 2005).

Murrell and Gaertner (1992) are credited as being among the first to examine social identity in sport. They examined the salience of common group or team identity on the performance within four high school football teams. Ninety-four high school football players (ranging from grades 9–12, median age of 16) completed a survey that measured strength of identification with the team as a whole, as offensive versus defensive units, or as individual players. Results indicated that players on winning teams (as determined by season win-loss record) emphasized team unity significantly more than players on teams with losing records.

Zucchermaglio (2005) undertook a qualitative, ethnographic approach to investigating the rhetorical manipulation of social identities arising in the discourses of a professional soccer team. Three interactions between team members were audio-recorded (e.g., after a victory, after a defeat, and in a pregame situation). Zucchermaglio coded the conversations paying particular attention to the pronouns used within the conversations (e.g., I, you.). Results revealed the way in which the outcome of the match influenced how team members referenced team membership and specific subgroups on the team. For example, after a loss, team members were more likely to distance themselves from the team and identify specific subgroups to account for the loss (e.g., forwards were responsible for the loss for not scoring goals), whereas post victory the group was considered as a whole and fewer differentiations were made regarding team membership (Zucchermaglio, 2005).

More recently, Bruner and Côté (2010) began a line of research to examine how team social identity (the identity that adolescents associate with being on a sport team) shapes social development. Results of an initial investigation involving 37 teams and over 400 high school athletes found team social identity to be a significant predictor of prosocial behavior towards teammates (Bruner & Côté, 2010). This line of research built upon previous group-dynamics research with youth examining social identity and exercise adherence in school-based physical activity clubs (Bruner & Spink, 2008; 2009). Bruner and Spink endeavored to examine if perceptions of group membership among 122 male and female youth (13–17 years of age) participating in 10 rural physical activity clubs influenced exercise adherence. Results revealed that an adolescent's perception of social identity with the physical activity club were significantly associated with the adolescent's participation in the club as well as with his or her intention to return to the activity club in the future (Bruner & Spink, 2008; 2009). Collectively, the body of emerging research by Bruner and colleagues highlights the influential role that social identity can play on a youth's participation in activity and psychosocial development. Further research with youth exploring the relationship between social identity and sport involvement and development in regards to the three dimensions of social identity is strongly encouraged.

Interdependence

Another important group construct that has thus far received minimal attention in the group dynamics sport literature is interdependence. Interdependence is said to occur when the actions of one individual within a group have implications for another member, and ultimately for the group as a whole (Johnson, 2003; Johnson & Johnson, 1998). Based upon this definition, interdependence can be positive, negative, or absent. Positive interdependence is often characterized by individuals engaging in promotive interactions, such as offering another group member assistance or sharing information (Johnson, 2003). In contrast, negative interdependence is characterized by individuals obstructing or discouraging the efforts of others while focusing on being productive themselves.

Research in business and education has identified a number of benefits of positive interdependence, including increased individual accountability/responsibility, interaction, social skills, and reflection on group functioning (Johnson, 2003). In sport, limited research has evaluated the construct of interdependence. As one example, Jowett and colleagues examined interdependence in terms of the interactions of coaches and athletes, and its consequences on athletes' feelings, thoughts, and behaviors (Jowett, 2005; Jowett & Ntoumanis, 2004). However, athletes' interdependence in different sport contexts and potential developmental experiences associated with interdependence in a youth sport setting have only recently been explored (Bruner, Hall, & Côté, 2009; 2011).

A possible explanation for the lack of attention to interdependence in sport psychology research may be a common misconception regarding the complexity of the group construct. Interdependence in sport has often been perceived as a unidimensional, static construct focusing on one element—the structure of interactions among the participants in the setting (Rusbult & Van Lange, 2003). From a substantive perspective this suggestion is appealing, as it has been proposed that different types of sports (e.g., individual sports vs. team sports) involve differing degrees of dependence or reliance on another person to successfully execute one's task (Carron, 1988; Chelladurai & Saleh, 1978). Quite often, the interdependence of the sport has been classified based upon a dependency classification system (e.g., Chelladurai & Saleh, 1978). The system proposes that highly interdependent sports are team sports (e.g., basketball, volleyball, soccer, hockey), while athletes in sports that are primarily independent in nature are classified as individual sport athletes (e.g., swimming, gymnastics, golf, track and field). While the type of sport captures the task dimension of interdependence, similar to other group constructs (e.g., cohesion), interdependence has been conceptualized as being multidimensional and dynamic in nature. Organizational psychologists have proposed that interdependence includes two key dimensions: task interdependence and outcome interdependence.

Van der Vegt, Emans, and Van de Vliert (1998) operationalize task interdependence as the "interconnections between tasks whereby the performance of one individual depends on the performance of another individual" (p. 127). As highlighted earlier, this dimension aligns with predominant research in sport psychology examining the task dimension of interdependence operationalized as sport type and a number of outcomes (e.g., alcohol use, coping strategies for stress, moral character, moral reasoning, concern for others; see Bredemeier & Shields, 1986; Martens, Watson, & Beck, 2006; Vallerand, Deshaies, & Cuerrier, 1997; Yoo, 2001).

A second overlooked dimension is outcome interdependence. It has been suggested that interdependence should not only be viewed in terms of the immediate interactions and behaviors, but also as a consequence or future outcome of the interaction (Kelley, 1984; Kelley et al., 2002; Rusbult & Van Lange, 2003). In the organizational psychology literature, outcome interdependence has been operationalized as the extent to which "people believe that their personal benefits and costs depend on successful goal attainment by other team members" (Van der Vegt et al., 1998, p. 130). In a sport setting, the attainment of success for both individual and team sport athletes may be a function of the interdependence within the training and competition environments.

While the two distinct dimensions of interdependence have been highlighted in the organizational psychology literature for quite some time, only recently has research begun to examine the relationship between task and outcome interdependence and the developmental experiences provided by different sports. Bruner and colleagues (2011) examined the relationships between sport type, interdependence (task and outcome), and the developmental experiences and outcomes (enjoyment and burnout) of select male basketball players ($n = 129$) and middle-distance runners ($n = 83$) aged 14–17 years. First, with respect to development experiences, hierarchical multiple regression determined that basketball players reported higher rates of teamwork and social skills, adult networks and social capital, and negative experiences. Furthermore, outcome interdependence was a predictor of identity exploration, initiative, emotional regulation, positive relationships, teamwork and social skills, and adult networks and social capital experiences independent of sport type (Bruner et al., 2011). Conclusions from the study suggest that although different sports may provide different learning environments, the developmental experiences youth garner may be more strongly influenced by how the people involved interact toward achieving their goal(s) (outcome interdependence) than by the type of sport.

Second, as it pertains to developmental outcomes, Bruner and colleagues (2009) revealed that interdependence could significantly predict a young athlete's enjoyment and burnout after controlling for contextual and individual characteristics and sport type. Specifically, participants who perceived greater outcome interdependence—interdependence among the other athletes to attain their goals—reported more enjoyment and less burnout. The study findings offer initial support for interdependence being a more meaningful predictor than sport type for the developmental outcomes of enjoyment and burnout. The results also reinforce the importance of fostering interdependence, regardless of the type of youth sport context, to promote positive youth development. Given the preliminary nature of this developmental group research in youth, further research is required.

SUMMARY OF PREVIOUS RESEARCH

Experiences with peers shape children's motivation to participate in sport, as well as their personal and athletic development. The conceptual framework introduced in the chapter (see Figure 10.1), based upon Rubin et al.'s (1998, 2006) and Hinde's (1987) previous work in child and social psychology, captures the three distinct levels of social complexity (interactions, relationships, and groups) in which peers can influence youth sport experiences and development. Although the literature on peers and on groups is closely related, the research in sport up until this point has not integrated the two areas of study. This chapter has attempted to address this important gap in the literature.

FUTURE RESEARCH

Upon reviewing the chapter, there are a number of avenues of future research on peer and group influences in youth sport. First, there is a need for more theoretically driven descriptive research, in order to both quantitatively and qualitatively gain a deeper understanding of the relationships between the peer and group constructs and developmental outcomes in sport. For example, how do the three dimensions of social identity (ingroup ties, ingroup affect, and cognitive centrality) relate to sport involvement? In addition, subsequent descriptive research may examine the relationships between peer and group constructs (e.g., cohesion, group norms) previously explored in exercise and/or health settings or with adult sport populations.

A second future direction would involve moving beyond descriptive research questions toward higher generations of research questions (see Carron, 1988; Carron & Brawley, 2008). This would entail examining potential moderators and mediators of the relationships. For example, peer interactions may influence prosocial behaviors in youth sport because team members perceive the norm of supporting teammates as a requirement of being on the team. To aid in addressing this future direction, more experimental research is urgently needed. Given the observed, well established powerful influence of groups to act as a change agent (Cartwright, 1951), children can be targeted on the team by coaches and practitioners to change their behaviors. For example, youth participants can develop expectations for behavior (group norms) and be targeted to change inappropriate behaviors (norms) toward performance and development through group-based interventions such as team building. However, there is a dearth of research systematically testing and evaluating theoretically driven interventions targeting youth in sport. Supplemental research should carefully construct and implement coach-oriented interventions to evaluate recommendations put forward by researchers. In one example, Shields and Bredemeier (1995) advocate a mastery-oriented climate and democratic leadership to foster moral development. Steps are necessary to systematically test these assertions.

A fourth and final recommendation for researchers to consider is the use of novel approaches to capture peer interactions and experiences in sport, such as the State Space Grid analysis (Murphy-Mills et al., 2011). While traditional methodologies (e.g., surveys, interviews) are informative, innovative methodologies are encouraged to advance theories and shed new light on how peers and groups underpin children's investment in sport and their talent development.

CONCLUSION

Sport teams constitute peer groups that theorists have identified as the highest level of social complexity (Rubin et al., 2006) and as an important developmental context shaping and supporting the behavior of its members. The present chapter provided an overview of some of the key constructs and theoretical propositions shaping our understanding of peer and group influences in youth sport. It is our hope that this chapter will spark increased research interest in this important topic.

REFERENCES

Allen, J. B. (2003). Social motivation in youth sport. *Journal of Sport & Exercise Psychology, 25,* 551–567.

Asher, S. R., & Coie, J. D. (Eds.). (1990). *Peer rejection in childhood: Cambridge studies in social and emotional development.* Cambridge, UK: Cambridge University Press.

Azmitia, M., Lippman, D. N., & Ittel, A. (1999). On the relation of personal experience to early adolescents' reasoning about best friendship deterioration. *Social Development, 8*(2), 275–291. doi: 10.1111/1467-9507.00095

Bailey, R. P., & Morley, D. (2006). Towards a model of talent development in physical education. *Sport, Education and Society, 11*(3), 211–230. doi:10.1080/13573320600813366

Beauchamp, M. R., Bray, S. R., Eys, M. A., & Carron, A. V. (2002). Role ambiguity, role efficacy, and role performance: Multidimensional and mediational relationships within interdependent sport teams. *Group Dynamics: Theory, Research, and Practice, 6*(3), 229–242. doi:10.1037//1089-2699.6.3.229

Berghout-Austin, A. M., & Draper, D. C. (1984). The relationship among peer acceptance, social impact, and academic achievement in middle childhood. *American Educational Research Journal, 21*(3), 597–604.

Berndt, T. J., & Keefe, K. (1995). Friends' influence on adolescents' adjustment to school. *Child Development, 66*(5), 1313–1329. doi:10.2307/1131649

Biddle, B. J., & Thomas, E. J. (1966). *Role theory: Concepts and research.* New York, NY: John Wiley and Sons.

Bigelow, B. J., Lewko, J. H., & Salhani, L. (1989). Sport-involved children's friendship expectations. *Journal of Sport & Exercise Psychology, 11*(2), 152–160.

Bloom, B. S. (Ed.). (1985). *Developing talent in young people.* New York, NY: Ballantine.

Bosselut, G., McLaren, C. D., Eys, M. A., & Heuzé, J. (2012). Reciprocity of the relationship between role ambiguity and group cohesion in youth interdependent sport. *Psychology of Sport and Exercise, 13,* 341–348. doi:10.1016/j. psychsport.2011.09.002

Bredemeier, B. J., & Shields, D. L. (1986). Moral growth among athletes and nonathletes: A comparative analysis. *The Journal of Genetic Psychology, 147*(1), 7–18. doi:10.1080/00221325.1986.9914475

Bruner, M. W., & Côté, J. (2010, October). *Exploring youth social identity and development in sport.* Sport Canada Research Initiative Conference, Ottawa, ON.

Bruner, M. W., Eys, M. A., & Côté, J. (2011). Group cohesion and personal and social development in youth team sports. *Journal of Sport & Exercise Psychology, 33* (suppl), S133.

Bruner, M. W., Hall, J., & Côté, J. (2009, August). *Examining sport type, interdependence, and developmental outcomes in youth sport.* American Psychological Association (APA) Convention, Toronto, ON.

Bruner, M. W., Hall, J., & Côté, J. (2011). The influence of sport type and interdependence on the developmental experiences of young athletes. *European Journal of Sport Science, 11*(2), 131–142. doi:10.1080/17461391.2010. 499969

Bruner, M. W., & Spink, K. S. (2008, June). An examination of group identity as a mediator of the relationship between group cohesion and intention to return. *International Society for Behavioral Nutrition and Physical Activity (ISBNPA),* Banff, AB.

Bruner, M. W., & Spink, K. S. (2009, June). Investigating the relationship between social identity and exercise adherence in adolescents. *International Society of Sport Psychology (ISSP) World Congress of Sport Psychology,* Marrakech, Morocco.

Bukowski, W. M., Newcomb, A. F., & Hartup, W. W. (1996). Friendship and its significance in childhood and adolescence: Introduction and comment. In W. M. Bukowski, A. F. Newcomb, & W. W. Hartup (Eds.), *The company they keep: Friendship in childhood and adolescence* (pp. 1–15). New York, NY: Cambridge University Press.

Cameron, J. E. (2004). A three-factor model of social identity. *Self and Identity, 3*(3), 239–262. doi:10.1080/13576500444000047

Carron, A. V. (1980). *Social psychology of sport.* Ithaca, NY: Mouvement.

Carron, A. V. (1988). *Group dynamics in sport.* London, ON: Spodym Publishers.

Carron, A. V., & Brawley, L. R. (2008). Group dynamics in sport and physical activity. In T. Horn (Ed.), *Advances in sport psychology* (pp. 213–237). Champaign, IL: Human Kinetics.

Carron, A. V., Brawley, L. R., & Widmeyer, W. N. (1985). The development of an instrument to assess cohesion in sport teams: The Group Environment Questionnaire. *Journal of Sport Psychology, 7*(3), 244–266.

Carron, A. V, Brawley, L. R., & Widmeyer, W. N. (1998). The measurement of cohesiveness in sport groups. In J. L. Duda (Ed.), *Advancements in sport and exercise psychology measurement* (pp. 213–226). Morgantown, WV: Fitness Information Technology.

Carron, A. V., & Eys, M. A. (2012). *Group dynamics in sport* (4th ed.). Morgantown, WV: Fitness Information Technology.

Carron, A. V., Widmeyer, W. N., & Brawley, L. R. (1988). Group cohesion and individual adherence to physical activity. *Journal of Sport & Exercise Psychology, 10*(2), 119–126.

Cartwright, D. (1951). Achieving change in people: Some applications of group dynamics theory. *Human Relations, 4*(1), 381–393.

Chelladurai, P., & Saleh, S. D. (1978). Preferred leadership in sports. *Canadian Journal of Applied Sport Sciences, 3,* 85–92.

Chen, X., Chen, H., & Kaspar, V. (2001). Group social functioning and individual socio-emotional and school adjustment in Chinese children. *Merrill-Palmer Quarterly, 47*(2), 264–299. doi:10.1353/mpq.2001.0008

Colman, M. M., & Carron, A. V (2001). The nature of norms in individual sport teams. *Small Group Research, 32*(2), 206–222. doi:10.1177/104649640103200204

Criss, M., Pettit, G., Bates, J., Dodge, K., & Lapp, A. (2002). Family adversity, positive peer relationships and children's externalizing behaviour: A longitudinal perspective on risk and resilience. *Child Development, 73*(4), 1220–1237. doi:10.1111/1467-8624.00468

d'Arripe-Longueville, F., Gernigon, C., Huet, M-L., Winnykamen, F., & Cadopi, M. (2002). Peer-assisted learning in the physical activity domain: Dyad type and gender differences. *Journal of Sport & Exercise Psychology, 24*(3), 219–238.

Duquin, M. E. (1984). Power and authority: Moral consensus and conformity in sport. *International Review of Sociology of Sport, 19*(3–4), 295–303.

Eagly, A. H., & Carli, L. L. (1981). Sex of researchers and sex-typed communications as determinants of sex differences in influencability: A meta-analysis of social influence studies. *Psychological Bulletin, 90*(1), 1–20.

Erickson, K., Bruner, M. W., & Côté, J. (2010, October). Exploring the relationship between team norms and coach-athlete interactions. *Societé Canadienne D'Apprentissage Psychomoteur et de Psychologie du Sport (SCAPPS),* Ottawa, ON.

Eys, M. A., Beauchamp, M. R., & Bray, S. R. (2006). A review of team roles in sport. In S. Hanton & S. D. Mellalieu (Eds.), *Literature reviews in sport psychology* (pp. 227–255). New York, NY: Nova Science Publishers.

Eys, M. A., Carron, A. V., Bray, S. R., & Beauchamp, M. R. (2005). The relationship between role ambiguity and intention to return the following season. *Journal of Applied Sport Psychology, 17,* 255–261. doi:10.1080/10413200591010148

Eys, M. A., Loughead, T. M., Bray, S. R., & Carron, A. V. (2009a). Development of a cohesion questionnaire for youth: The Youth Sport Environment Questionnaire. *Journal of Sport & Exercise Psychology, 31*(3), 390–408.

Eys, M. A., Loughead, T. M., Bray, S. R., & Carron, A. V. (2009b). Perceptions of cohesion by youth sport participants. *The Sport Psychologist, 23*(3), 330–345.

Fogel, A. (1993). *Development through relationships: Origins of communication, self, and culture.* Chicago, IL: University of Chicago Press.

Forsyth, D. R. (1983). *An introduction to group dynamics.* Belmont, CA: Wadsworth.

Gifford-Smith, M. E., & Brownell, C. A. (2003). Childhood peer relationships: Social acceptance, friendships, and peer networks. *Journal of School Psychology, 41,* 235–284. doi:10.1016/S0022-4405(03)00048-7

Granic, I. (2005). Timing is everything: Developmental psychopathology from a dynamic systems perspective. *Developmental Review, 25*(3–4), 386–407. doi:10.1016/j.dr.2005.10.005

Gunnar, M. R., Senior, K., & Hartup, W. W. (1984). Peer presence and the exploratory behaviour of eighteen- and thirty-month-old children. *Child Development, 55*(3), 1103–1109. doi:10.2307/1130163

Harris, J. (1998). *The nurture assumption: Why children turn out the way they do.* New York, NY: Touchstone.

Hartup, W. W., & Laursen, B. (1999). Relationships as developmental contexts: Retrospective themes and contemporary issues. In W. A. Collins & B. Laursen (Eds.), *Relationships as developmental contexts.* The Minnesota Symposia on Child Development (Vol. 30) (pp. 13–35). Mahwah, NJ: Lawrence Erlbaum Associates.

Hinde, R. A. (1976a). Interactions, relationships, and social structure. *Man, 11*(1), 1–17.

Hinde, R. A. (1976b). On describing relationships. *Journal of Child Psychology and Psychiatry, 17*(1), 1–19.

Hinde, R. A. (1979). *Towards understanding relationships.* London, UK: Academic Press.

Hinde, R. A. (1987). *Individuals, relationships, and culture.* Cambridge, UK: Cambridge University Press.

Hinde, R. A. (1995). A suggested structure for a science of relationships. *Personal Relationships, 2*(1), 1–15. doi:10.1111/j.1475-6811.1995.tb00074.x

Hogg, M. A., & Abrams, D. B. (2001). *Intergroup relations: Essential readings.* Hove, UK: Psychology Press.

Høigaard, R., Säfvenbom, R., & Tønnessen, F. E. (2006). The relationship between group cohesion, group norms, and perceived social loafing in soccer teams. *Small Group Research, 37*(3), 217–232.

Holt, N. L., Black, D. E., Tamminen, K. A., Fox, K. R., & Mandigo, J. L. (2008). Levels of social complexity and dimensions of peer experiences in youth sport. *Journal of Sport & Exercise Psychology, 30*(4), 411–431.

Jewitt, E. (2011). *Assessing the validity of the Youth Sport Environment Questionnaire* (Unpublished master's thesis). Wilfrid Laurier University, Waterloo, Ontario, Canada.

Jewitt, E., Eys, M. A., Loughead, T. M., & Bruner, M. (2010). Validity of a measure of cohesion for youth sport: The Youth Sport Environment Questionnaire. *Journal of Sport & Exercise Psychology, 32* (suppl), S180.

Johnson, D. W. (2003). Social interdependence: Interrelationships among theory, research and practice. *American Psychologist, 58*(11), 934–945. doi:10.1037/0003-066X.58.11.934

Johnson, D. W., & Johnson, R. T. (1998). Cooperative learning and social interdependence theory. *Social Psychological Applications to Social Issues, 4,* 9–36.

Jowett, S. (2005). On repairing and enhancing the coach-athlete relationship. In S. Jowett & M. Jones (Eds.), *The psychology of coaching* (pp. 14–26). Leicester, UK: British Psychological Society.

Jowett, S., & Ntoumanis, N. (2004). The Coach-Athlete Relationship Questionnaire (CART-Q): Development and initial validation. *Scandinavian Journal of Medicine and Science in Sports, 14*(4), 245–257. doi:10.1111/j.1600-0838.2003.00338.x

Keegan, R., Harwood, C., Spray, C., & Lavallee, D. (2009). A qualitative investigation exploring the motivational climate in early career sports participants: Coach, parent and peer influences on sport motivation. *Psychology of Sport & Exercise, 10*(3), 361–372. doi:10.1016/j.psychsport.2008.12.003

Kelley, H. H. (1984). The theoretical description of interdependence by means of transition lists. *Journal of Personality and Social Psychology, 47*(5), 956–982. doi:10.1037//0022-3514.47.5.956

Kelley, H. H., Holmes, J. G., Kerr, N. L., Reis, H. T., Rusbult, C. E., & Van Lange, P. A. M. (2002). *An atlas of interpersonal situations.* New York, NY: Cambridge University Press.

Kim, M. S., & Sugiyama, Y. (1992). The relation of performance norms and cohesiveness for Japanese school athletic teams. *Perceptual & Motor Skills, 74*(3), 1096–1098. doi:10.2466/pms.1992.74.3c.1096

Kindermann, T. (2003). Children's relationships and development of person-context relations. In J. Valsiner & K. Connolly (Eds.), *Handbook of developmental psychology* (pp. 407–430). London, UK: Sage.

Lewis, M. D., Lamey, A.V., & Douglas, L. (1999). A new dynamic system method for the analysis of early socioemotional development. *Developmental Science, 2*(4), 457–475. doi:10.1111/1467-7687.00090

Light, P. H., & Glachan, M. (1985). Facilitation of individual problem solving through peer interaction. *Educational Psychology, 5*(3&4), 217–255. doi:10.1080/0144341850050305

Martens, M. P., Watson II, J. C., & Beck, N. C. (2006). Sport-type differences in alcohol use among intercollegiate athletes. *Journal of Applied Sport Psychology, 18,* 136–150. doi:10.1080/10413200600653758

Martin, L. J., Carron, A. V., Eys, M. A., & Loughead, T. (2012). Development of a cohesion inventory for children's sport teams. *Group Dynamics: Theory, Research, and Practice, 16,* 68–79. doi: 10.1037/a0024691 .

McLellan, J. A., & Pugh, M. J. (1999). *The role of peer groups in adolescent society identity: Exploring the importance of stability and change.* Stanford, CA: Jossey-Bass.

Moran, M. M., & Weiss, M. R. (2006). Peer leadership in sport: Links with friendship, peer acceptance, psychological characteristics, and athletic ability. *Journal of Applied Sport Psychology, 18,* 97–113. doi:10.1080/10413200600653501

Mullen, B., & Copper, C. (1994). The relation between group cohesion and performance: An integration. *Psychological Bulletin, 115*(2), 210–227. doi:10.1037//0033-2909.115.2.210

Munroe, K., Estabrooks, P., Dennis, P., & Carron, A.V. (1999). A phenomenological analysis of group norms in sport teams. *The Sport Psychologist, 13*(2), 171–182.

Murphy-Mills, J., Bruner, M. W., Erickson, K., & Côté, J. (2011). The utility of the state space grid method for studying peer interactions in youth sport. *Journal of Applied Sport Psychology, 23*(2), 159–174. doi:10.1080/10413200.2010.545101

Murrell, A. J., & Gaertner, S. L. (1992). Cohesion and sport team effectiveness: The benefit of a common group identity. *Journal of Sport & Social Issues, 16*(1), 1–14. doi:10.1177/019372359201600101

Newcomb, A. F., & Bagwell, C. L. (1995). Children's friendship relations: A meta-analytic review. *Psychological Bulletin, 117*(2), 306–347. doi:10.1037//0033-2909.117.2.306

Patrick, H., Ryan, A. M., Alfeld-Liro, C., Fredricks, J. A., Hruda, L. Z., & Eccles, J. S. (1999). Adolescents' commitment to developing talent: The role of peers in continuing motivation for sport and the arts. *Journal of Youth & Adolescence, 28*(6), 741–763. doi:10.1023/A:1021643718575

Patterson, M. M., Carron, A. V., & Loughead, T. M. (2005). The influence of team norms on the cohesion-self-reported performance relationship: A multi-level analysis. *Psychology of Sport and Exercise, 6,* 479–493. doi:10.1016/j.psychsport.2004.04.004

Prapavessis, H., & Carron, A. V. (1997). Cohesion and work output. *Small Group Research, 28*(2), 294–301. doi:10.1177/1046496497282006

Rubin, K. H., Bukowski, W. M., & Parker, J. G. (1998). Peer interactions, relationships, and groups. In W. Damon (Series Ed.) & N. Eisenberg (Vol. Ed.), *Handbook of child psychology: Vol. 3, Social, emotional, and personality development* (5th ed.) (pp. 619–700). New York, NY: Wiley.

Rubin, K. H., Bukowski, W. M., & Parker, J. G. (2006). Peer interactions, relationships, and groups. In W. Damon, R. M. Lerner, & N. Eisenberg (Eds.), *Handbook of child psychology: Vol. 3, Social emotional, and personality development* (6th ed.) (pp. 571–645). New York, NY: Wiley.

Rubin, K. H., Chen, X., Coplan, R., Buskirk, A. A., & Wojslawowicz, J. C. (2005). Peer relationships in childhood. In M. H. Bornstein & M. E. Lamb. (Eds.), *Developmental science: An advanced textbook* (5th ed.) (pp. 469–512). Mahwah, NJ: Lawrence Erlbaum Associates.

Rusbult, C. E., & Van Lange, P. A. M. (2003). Interdependence, interaction, and relationships. *Annual Review of Psychology, 54,* 351–375. doi:10.1146/annurev.psych.54.101601.145059

Scanlan, T. K., Carpenter, P., Schmidt, G., Simons, J., & Keeler, B. (1993). An introduction to the sport commitment model. *Journal of Sport & Exercise Psychology, 15*(1), 1–15.

Shaw, M. E. (1981). *Group dynamics: The psychology of small group behaviour* (3rd ed.). New York, NY: McGraw-Hill.

Shields, D. L. L., & Bredemeier, B. J. L. (1995). *Character development and physical activity.* Champaign, IL: Human Kinetics.

Smith, A. L. (1999). Perceptions of peer relationships and physical activity participation in early adolescence. *Journal of Sport & Exercise Psychology, 21,* 329–350.

Smith, A. L. (2007). Youth peer relationships in sport. In S. Jowett & D. Lavallee (Eds.), *Social psychology in sport* (pp. 41–54). Champaign, IL: Human Kinetics.

Spink, K. S., Wilson, K. S., & Odnokon, P. (2010). Examining the relationship between cohesion and return to team in elite athletes. *Psychology of Sport and Exercise, 11*(1), 6–11. doi:10.1016/j.psychsport.2009.06.002

Steenbeek, H., & van Geert, P. (2006). A theory and dynamic model of dyadic interaction: Concerns, appraisals, and contagiousness in a developmental context. *Developmental Review, 27*(1), 1–40. doi:10.1016/j.dr.2006.06.002

Tajfel, H. (1981). *Human groups and social categories: Studies in social psychology.* Cambridge, UK: Cambridge University Press.

Tajfel, H., & Turner, J. (1979). An integrative theory of intergroup conflict. In W. G. Austin & S. Worchel (Eds.), *The social psychology of intergroup relations* (pp. 33–47). Monterey, CA: Brooks-Cole.

Taylor, I., & Bruner, M. W. (2012). The social environment and developmental experiences in elite youth soccer. *Psychology of Sport and Exercise, 13*(4), 390–396. doi:10.1016/j.psychsport.2012.01.008

Thelen, E., & Smith, L. (1994). *A dynamic systems approach to the development of cognition and action.* Cambridge, MA: MIT Press.

Ullrich-French, S., & Smith, A. L. (2006). Perceptions of relationships with parents and peers in youth sport: Independent and combined prediction of motivational outcomes. *Psychology of Sport & Exercise, 7*(2), 193–214. doi:10.1016/j.psychsport.2005.08.006

Vallerand, R. J., Deshaies, P., & Cuerrier, J. P. (1997). On the effects of the social context on behavioral intentions of sportsmanship. *International Journal of Sport Psychology, 28*(2),126–140.

Van der Vegt, G. S., Emans, B. J., & Van de Vliert E. (1998). Motivating effects of task and outcome interdependence in work teams. *Group & Organization Management, 23*(2), 124–143. doi:10.1177/1059601198232003

Vroom, V. H. (1969). Industrial social psychology. In G. Lindzey & E. Aronson (Eds.), *The handbook of social psychology* (Vol. 5) (pp. 196–268). Reading, MA: Addison-Wesley.

Weiss, M. R., & Petlichkoff, L. M. (1989). Children's motivation for participation in and withdrawal from sport: Identifying the missing links. *Pediatric Exercise Science, 1*(3), 195–211.

Weiss, M. R., & Smith, A. L. (1999). Quality of youth sport friendships: Measurement development and validation. *Journal of Sport & Exercise Psychology, 21*(2), 145–166.

Weiss, M. R., & Smith, A. L. (2002). Friendship quality in youth sport: Relationship to age, gender, and motivational variables. *Journal of Sport & Exercise Psychology, 24*(4), 420-437.

Wentzel, K. R. (1991). Relations between social competence and academic achievement in early adolescence. *Child Development, 62*(5), 1066–1078. doi:10.2307/1131152

Wentzel, K. R., & Caldwell, K. (1997). Friendships, peer acceptance, and group membership: Relations to academic achievement in middle school. *Child Development, 68*(6), 1198–1209. doi:10.2307/1132301

Widmeyer, W. N., Brawley, L. R., & Carron, A. V. (1985). *The measurement of cohesion in sport teams: The Group Environment Questionnaire.* London, ON: Sports Dynamics.

Wold, B., & Anderssen, N. (1992). Health promotion aspects of family and peer influences on sport participation. *International Journal of Sport Psychology, 23*(4), 343–359.

Wylleman, P., & Lavallee, D. (2004). A developmental perspective on transitions faced by athletes. In M. R. Weiss (Ed.), *Developmental sport and exercise psychology: A lifespan perspective* (pp. 507–527). Morgantown, WV: Fitness Information Technology.

Yoo, J. (2001). Coping profile of Korean competitive athletes. *International Journal of Sport Psychology, 32*(3), 290–303.

Zucchermaglio, C. (2005). Who wins and who loses: The rhetorical manipulation of social identities in a soccer team. *Group Dynamics: Theory, Research, and Practice, 9*(4), 219–238. doi:10.1037/1089-2699.9.4.219

CHAPTER 11

FAMILY INFLUENCE ON CHILDREN'S INVOLVEMENT IN SPORT

Jessica Fraser-Thomas, Leisha Strachan,
and Sarah Jeffery-Tosoni

INTRODUCTION

The "child-other relation is the basic feature of the developmental-contextual relations that characterize the social creature we call a human being" (Bronfenbrenner, 2002, p. 203). Given the importance of child-other relations, it is critical that athlete development researchers examine the relationships that are most central in a child-athlete's life. In 1992, Brustad suggested that everyone talks about parents' involvement in sport, but no one researches it. In the past two decades, we have seen a surge in research focused on families' socialization of child-athletes in sport; this research not only has offered a greater understanding of how specific parenting styles and behaviors are associated with diverse outcomes in the development of young athletes, but has also shed additional light on the role of siblings in athletes' development.

In the first section of the chapter we consider the parent-athlete dyad. Two models of family influence and past classifications of parental involvement are presented as a lens by which we can examine literature pertaining to the parent-athlete dyad in more depth. Subsections include (a) expectancy-value model (Fredricks & Eccles, 2004); (b) Developmental Model of Sport Participation (DMSP; Côté, 1999); (c) classifications of parental involvement in youth sport; (d) parents' tangible support; (e) parents' emotional and informational support; (f) parents' beliefs, values, and expectations; (g) parent modelling; and (g) parents' role in facilitating personal and social development. The second section of the chapter examines the sibling-athlete dyad, with literature focused on both positive and negative potential influences within the athlete-sibling relationship. Subsections include (a) sibling support and (b) negative influences and outcomes. The third section offers a revised version of the DMSP that integrates family influence. Sub-sections reflect roles of parents and siblings in children's sport experiences across the developmental stages and trajectories: (a) all stages, (b) sampling years, (c) recreational years, (d) specializing and investment years, and (e) early specialization. The final section of the chapter outlines key directions for future research.

THE PARENT-ATHLETE DYAD

In this section, we outline key models and conceptual frameworks that have been developed to examine and account for the influence of parents on children's sport involvement. In addition, we discuss the current research exploring the complex influence of parents on their children throughout their sport development.

Expectancy-Value Model

A model explaining parental influences on children in general achievement contexts (e.g., academics and music) was developed by Eccles and her colleagues (see Fredricks & Eccles, 2004). Their expectancy-value model states generally that the expectation one holds to do well in an activity, coupled with the value that one places on the activity, predicts both persistence and performance in an achievement context. With specific regard to parents' influence on their children in achievement contexts, the expectancy-value model asserts that parents hold (a) general beliefs, which are formed by cultural influence and demographic factors (i.e., family income, gender, marital status), as well as (b) child-specific beliefs, which are based on parents' general beliefs and the child's characteristics. Collectively, these characteristics and beliefs contribute to the family's socioemotional climate, the parents' general child-rearing styles, the parents' role-modeling behaviors, and the specific behaviors parents demonstrate towards the child that lead to the child outcomes (Fredricks & Eccles, 2004).

The expectancy-value model was adapted by Horn and Horn (2007) to specifically address parental influences in sport and physical activity settings. The adapted model proposes that parents' values and beliefs (e.g., parents' expectancies for their child's performance) impact the parents' behaviors toward and with their child (e.g., parents' involvement, emotional support). This consequently impacts the child's value and belief system (e.g., child's perceived competence) and thus affects the child's performance and behavior (i.e., child's participation, persistence, and effort in sport). The primary strength of this adapted model is that it comprehensively yet succinctly accounts for the impact of parental values, beliefs, and behaviors on children's values, beliefs, and performances, with a specific focus on sport contexts and outcomes. However, the model has not been tested in its entirety, given its extensive number of variables. Further, the adapted model fails to acknowledge the bidirectional relationship between the parent and child.

Developmental Model of Sport Participation

Côté's (1999) study of families of elite adolescent athletes and his Developmental Model of Sport Participation (DMSP) advanced Bloom's (1985) work on talented young people, by providing an increased understanding of key sport training factors and psychosocial influences throughout child-athletes' development. The DMSP highlights three conceptually unique stages of sport development: the sampling (ages 6–12), specializing (ages 13–15), and investment (ages 16+) years. With growing research on talent development in youth sport contexts, the DMSP has been modified several times over the past decade (e.g., Côté & Fraser-Thomas, 2011; Côté & Hay, 2002) and now proposes three possible sport participation trajectories: (a) recreational participation through sampling, (b) elite performance through sampling, and (c) elite performance through early specialization. Côté and colleagues' work emphasizes the parents' important changing roles throughout their children's sport development. However, many questions remain regarding the specific processes of influence, interaction, and optimal behaviors on a day-to-day basis, given that this work has been largely retrospective, focusing primarily on "successful" cases of talent development, with not as much attention being devoted to understanding less than optimal cases of parental involvement.

Classifications of Parental Involvement in Youth Sport

A key challenge in studying parents' involvement in their children's sport development relates to identifying the multiple means by which parents may influence their children's sport involvement. Recent reviews of the youth sport development literature have outlined a variety of typologies, dimensions, and classifications of parental involvement. Côté and Hay (2002) proposed a typology highlighting four dimensions of parental support: (a) emotional support, which includes behaviors that provide comfort and enhance children's self-esteem; (b) informational support, which involves behaviors focused on providing advice, guidance, or instruction; (c) tangible support, which includes the provision of physical and practical resources for children's involvement and success; and (d) companionship or network support, which is reflected in the positive interactions of the parent and child surrounding the child's sport involvement. Further, Fredricks and Eccles' (2004) proposed that parents' involvement in their children's sport can be categorized into three major roles: provider (i.e., making opportunities available through enrolment, transportation, equipment, finances); interpreter (i.e., demonstrating values, beliefs, and encouragement related to physical activity and sport); and role model (i.e., influencing children's participation through a personal involvement in physical activity and sport). Clearly, there is a great deal of overlapping in concepts that have been used to classify parental involvement in youth sport settings. In the section that follows we draw upon these categories and discuss research focused on parents' influence on children's sport development in the areas of (a) parents' tangible support, (b) parents' emotional and informational support, (c) parents' beliefs, values, and expectations, (d) parent modeling, and (e) parents' role in facilitating children's personal and social development. A summary of parental involvement in youth sport is presented in Table 11.1.

Parents' Tangible Support

Bloom (1985) and Côté's (1999) seminal works highlight the instrumental roles that parents play in providing children with the opportunity to engage in sport, through the introduction to unstructured sport and physical activity, enrolment in structured sport programs, and the promotion and integration of sport and physical activity into the family lifestyle and routines. Inherent within the parents' roles of providing children with opportunities for sport participation

Table 11.1. Summary of Parental Involvement in Youth Sport

	Tangible Support	Emotional and Informational Support	Parents' Beliefs, Values, and Expectations	Parent Modelling	Facilitation of Personal and Social Development
General Findings	1. Mother's contribution often includes sacrificing social life to arrange transportation, meals, etc.; father's contribution often financial. 2. Tangible support a pre-requisite for involvement, not a distinguishing factor of optimal sport involvement.	**Parenting Style** 1. Stable, supportive, and consistent homes that promote challenging opportunities ideal. 2. Authoritative and autonomy-supportive parenting ideal. **Parents' Level of Involvement** 1. Moderate level of involvement preferred, but it is also important to examine the degree (i.e., too little, too much, just right). **Parents' Sport-Related Feedback** 1. Instructional feedback not necessarily welcomed by adolescents. Honest feedback related to effort/attitude preferred. 2. One-size-fits-all approach not appropriate; feedback dependent on each parent-child relationship, parents' sport background, etc. **Parent-Child Relationship and Communication** 1. Sport can facilitate meaningful relationships due to extensive time commitments and highs/lows. 2. Optimal communication dependent upon developmental stage (e.g., childhood—discuss sport performance, later adolescence—discuss sport career in broader picture of one's life). **Parents' Positive Push** 1. Research inconclusive on whether negative behaviors (e.g., yelling, criticizing) may positively influence the child-athlete (e.g., help to foster motivation).	1. Child-athlete's perception of positive parental beliefs related to sport associated with higher perceived competence, intrinsic motivation, value of sport, and sport participation. 2. Parent-created task-oriented climates related to higher sport satisfaction and persistence. 3. Parents may demonstrate gender imbalance between sons and daughters (e.g., sport valued more for sons).	1. Relationship between parents' physical activity and children's sport participation not clear. 2. Parents' former elite sport participation may negatively impact their child-athletes.	1. Parents have the potential to positively influence their child-athlete's personal and social development (e.g., teaching sport psychology skills, demonstrating a solid work ethic, teaching sportspersonship). 2. Parents have the potential to negatively influence their child-athlete's personal and social development (e.g., poor parent behaviors at competitions linked to children's poor sportspersonship).

are a multitude of tangible behaviors, which include but are not limited to providing financial support for program fees, equipment, books, videos, magazines, and personal training; offering transportation to and from training sessions and competitions; rearranging family schedules to accommodate the sport; volunteering time for coaching, managing, officiating, fundraising, or sport administration at practices and competitions; and relocating the family or the child-athlete to afford them access to optimal coaching and training facilities (see Bloom, 1985; Côté, 1999; Fraser-Thomas, Côté, & Deakin, 2008b; Fredricks & Eccles, 2005; Gould, Lauer, Rolo, Jannes, & Pennisi, 2008; Keegan, Spray, Harwood, & Lavalee, 2010; Kirk, Carlson, O'Connor, Burke, Davis, & Glover, 1997a; Kirk, O'Connor, Carlson, Burke, Davis, & Glover, 1997b). Mother-father differences may exist in how parents offer tangible support to their children, with mothers often sacrificing their career and/or social life to provide transportation and meals, and to manage competition schedules, and the fathers' contributions often being primarily financial (Kirk et al., 1997b; Wolfenden & Holt, 2005). Researchers have suggested that parents' provision of tangible support appears to be a *prerequisite* for involvement, rather than a factor that distinguishes youths' optimal and less optimal development through sport (Kirk et al., 1997a; Lauer, Gould, Roman, & Pierce, 2010; Wolfenden & Holt, 2005).

Parents' Emotional and Informational Support

Parenting style. A substantial body of earlier research concentrated on how parents' general parenting style influenced children's sport development. Csikszentmihalyi, Rathunde, and Whalen's (1993) seminal study of 58 talented American teenagers in a variety of fields, including athletics, examined the role of the family home environment in influencing talent development. Csikszentmihalyi et al. (1993) determined that talented teenagers had four different types of home environments: (a) *integrated,* defined as stable, supportive, and consistent; (b) *differentiated,* described as those that promote youth to take on challenging new opportunities; (c) *complex,* which include both integrated and differentiated characteristics; and (d) *simple,* which do not include integrated or differentiated characteristics. Their findings suggested that complex families were associated with the most positive outcomes related to talent development (i.e., greater happiness, alertness, excitement towards their activities, sense of fulfilment and accomplishment). In a study that aimed to replicate Csikszentmihalyi et al.'s (1993) study, van Rossum and van der Loo (1997) examined the influence of family in talented and less-talented Dutch athletes; their modified measurement tool resulted in one positive categorization of *functional family* and two negative categorizations of *dysfunctional* and *unbalanced families.* In contrast to Csikszentmihalyi and colleagues' findings, significantly more talented athletes were reported coming from unbalanced or dysfunctional families than less-talented athletes. Collectively, these conflicting findings highlight the complexity of interpreting the general style or approach that parents provide in the home environment.

Recently, sport psychology researchers have moved away from using parenting styles to assess parental influence in sport and physical activity settings (Horn & Horn, 2007); however, a few studies have continued to follow this line of research. For example, Juntumaa, Keskivaara, and Punamaki (2005) used the dimensions of authoritative, authoritarian, and permissive parenting styles to examine positive and negative player outcomes among Finnish youth hockey players. They found that players who came from *authoritative* families (i.e., a balance of control and warmth) expressed higher satisfaction in playing ice hockey and demonstrated lower levels of task-irrelevant and norm-breaking behaviors, while parenting approaches traditionally viewed negatively, including *authoritarian* (i.e., highly controlling and lacking warmth) and *permissive* (i.e., low control and high warmth), were associated with greater acceptance of norm-breaking behavior (e.g., breaking rules). Further, gender differences were noted, with mothers demonstrating more authoritative parenting and fathers demonstrating more authoritarian parenting. Additional recent work has offered some insight into how relationships between parenting style and youth outcomes may develop. Autonomy-supportive parents (i.e., parents who allow the child to feel they can initiate their own actions) have been found to show a greater interest in their child's sport involvement, provide an optimal amount of sport structure, better read their child's mood, and engage in open, bidirectional communication with their child, when compared to nonautonomy-supportive parents (i.e., parents that are more controlling; Holt, Tamminen, Black, Mandigo, & Fox, 2009; Keegan et al., 2010). As such, it is clear that parenting styles have the potential to contribute to athletes' sport-related decision making and subsequent behaviors.

Parents' level of involvement. Another line of research of the past two decades has aimed at tapping into parents' level of involvement in their children's sport participation, with a focus on quantifying the optimal amount of involvement. For example, Averill and Power (1995) highlighted the importance of a moderate level of involvement, as they reported that mothers and fathers demonstrating the highest levels of involvement in their children's sports had children with the lowest level of cooperation with the coach. Stein, Raedeke, and Glenn (1999) advanced these findings by examining not only athletes' perceptions of parents' level of involvement (i.e., "not at all involved" to "very involved"), but also their perceptions of degree of involvement (i.e., "way too little" to "way too much"). Results indicated that most parents were involved at a moderate level, which was considered an optimal degree by youth athletes (i.e., "just right"). However, gender differences were again noted: Children of mothers who were "very involved" had more enjoyable experiences, while children of fathers who were "too involved" experienced higher stress. While this study advanced previous work by looking beyond the extent to which parents were involved and placing more emphasis on how athletes perceived this level of involvement, it offered limited insight into what led to or facilitated these perceptions, given its use of categorical quantitative measures.

Most recently, much literature has begun to tap into the specific behaviors that constitute optimal involvement, with a focus on supportive and pressuring parental behaviors. This has consistently been one of the most challenging areas for researchers and practitioners to comprehend, due in part to the methodological challenges of capturing parents' behaviors and parent-child interactions, which most often occur outside public sport fields. As such, many researchers have used qualitative designs to gain an understanding of the perceptions of coaches, parents, and athletes with regard to parents' involvement in youth sport environments (e.g., Gould et al., 2008; Knight, Boden, & Holt, 2010; Knight, Neely, & Holt, 2011). Researchers have generally found that the majority of youth sport parents demonstrate supportive influences and that greater support is associated with a variety of positive outcomes, such as increased sport enjoyment, commitment, and motivation; however, higher levels of support have also been associated with more negative outcomes, such as burnout (Strachan,

Côté, & Deakin, 2009). This highlights that the term *support* often encompasses many very diverse parental actions (Lauer et al., 2010).

Parents' sport-related feedback. Offering sport-related feedback to child-athletes may be among the most bewildering challenges for parents, as findings highlight that child-athletes have a variety of preferences depending on numerous circumstances (e.g., Knight et al., 2010; Knight et al., 2011). While research suggests that parents' presence at competitions is preferred by child and adolescent athletes and has the potential to contribute to a multitude of positive psychosocial outcomes, such as motivation, competence, and enjoyment (e.g., Babkes & Weiss, 1999; Keegan, Harwood, Spray, & Lavalle, 2009; Keegan et al., 2010), results regarding how parents should behave at child-athletes' competitions may sometimes appear conflicting. Two recent studies by Knight and colleagues (Knight et al., 2010; Knight et al., 2011) with high-level adolescent Canadian tennis players and highly invested adolescent female team sport athletes suggest that child-athletes prefer for parents to refrain from providing technical and tactical advice or performance-related comments during or following competitive events, suggesting that such comments are confusing, conflict with coaches' advice, or are seen as an overload of information. Consistent with other studies (e.g., Keegan et al., 2010; Wolfenden & Holt, 2005), the one exception to this is when athletes' parents have extensive knowledge and background in sport as a result of their own experiences as high-level athletes; in this case, athletes tend to be more receptive to instructional or directive parental feedback, but only as a suggestion, and not as a requirement. Holt, Tamminen, Black, Sehn, and Wall's (2008) longitudinal examination of four families over the course of their children's soccer season sheds some light on why parents so often offer their children unwelcome feedback. Parents' verbal behaviors at games were influenced by their perceived knowledge and experience (i.e., if they had a solid understanding of the game, they felt they should provide feedback to their children); however, parents were quick to comment on the behaviors of other parents (i.e., they felt many parents were ignorant, and therefore should not be providing comments). Clearly, parents' perceptions of their knowledge and expertise may be inconsistent with others' perceptions, and as such, they may often act in a manner that they wrongly believe is facilitating their child's optimal development. Knight and colleagues' (2010) work also highlights that athletes are attuned to parents' nonverbal communication (e.g., tense posture, stressed facial expressions, and disappointed tone of voice) and become particularly frustrated when parents' nonverbal communication messages are inconsistent with verbal messages.

While parents' coaching and instructional feedback at competitions does not appear to be welcomed by adolescent athletes in most cases, Knight and colleagues' (2010) work highlights that adolescent athletes are appreciative of parents' honest nonperformance related feedback related to effort and attitude. Further, adolescents preferred hearing positive feedback immediately after performances, while constructive feedback was appreciated later, in the absence of other teammates or parents. Mother-father differences were again seen in the provision of this form of feedback, with mothers tending to offer a great deal of positive feedback, and fathers providing more constructive and critical feedback. These differences are consistent with past work (Averill & Power, 1995; Wuerth, Lee, & Alfermann, 2004) suggesting that mothers see themselves as greater sources of praise and understanding, while fathers feel they offer higher amounts of directive support (i.e., coaching, instruction). While these findings may initially appear confusing, additional research (e.g., Fraser-Thomas et al., 2008b; Keegan et al., 2009) suggests that a balanced parenting approach (i.e., parents who have considerably different and opposing personalities) may be beneficial to children's motivation and continued involvement.

It is also important to understand parents' provision of sport-related feedback within the context of the children's developmental stage. For example, participants in Averill and Power's (1995) study were 6–8 years of age, leading authors to suggest that a father's attempt to help through directive behaviors, particularly when child ability levels are low, may undermine the children's sport effort and enjoyment. In contrast, participants in Wuerth et al.'s (2004) study were 10–20 years of age, with authors concluding that greater amounts of directive behavior are associated with greater success, and a delicate balance of apparently contrasting behaviors (i.e., pushing and pressuring while also praising, listening, and showing unconditional support) may be necessary for talent development. Other authors also emphasize the importance of parental behaviors changing with child maturity. Generally, informational support, coaching tips, and even incentives and rewards have been associated with positive outcomes such as enjoyment, persistence, and talent development during childhood; however, adolescents tend to be less appreciative of these parental behaviors, with some research linking them with negative outcomes, such as dropout (e.g., Fraser-Thomas et al., 2008b; Kirk et al., 1997b; Lauer et al., 2010; McCarthy & Jones, 2007). Finally, a more applied understanding of how parents' feedback should change as children mature is offered by Harter's Competence Motivation Theory (Harter, 1978). The theory suggests that children are motivated to demonstrate their competence through skill mastery, and because young children's competence beliefs are very high, parents should offer primarily positive feedback, which will in turn lead children to perceive skill mastery and stay motivated. However, as children become more abstract thinkers during adolescence, they begin to judge competence to a greater extent through performance outcomes and peer comparison. As such, parents should help children self-reference their performances and integrate multiple sources of informational feedback, in order to optimally promote the children's competence beliefs and continued motivation in their sport.

Collectively, recent research regarding parents' provision of feedback to their child-athletes advances our understanding of optimal supportive behaviors, yet as Keegan et al. (2010) stress, a one-size-fits-all approach does not always hold in child-athlete development, and each interaction must be considered in relation to preceding events, co-occurring behaviors, consistency in behaviors, parent-child relationships, and other environmental factors.

Parent-child relationships and communication. Another line of research has begun to focus on the quality of parent and child-athlete relationships within the sport context. Kirk and colleagues' (1997b) study of 220 Australian junior athletes and their families found that most families reflected positively on the social consequences of their sport involvement, given their shared common interest and the tremendous time spent together travelling and engaging in conversation. Similarly, Fraser-Thomas and Côté's (2009) qualitative study of adolescent competitive swimmers suggests that high investment sport has the potential to facilitate special and meaningful relationships between parents and children, through its extensive time investment and constant highs and lows. Further, Ullrich-French and Smith (2006) reported that when child-athletes have more positive perceptions of their relationships with parents they experience more positive motivational outcomes (e.g., enjoyment, perceived competence).

Qualitative work among adolescent athletes (Knight et al., 2010; Knight et al., 2011; Wolfenden & Holt, 2005) offers further insight into what optimal parent-child interactions may look like. Adolescents in these studies emphasized that in competitions, they welcomed practical advice and care demonstrated by parents addressing their basic nutrition, hydration, body temperature regulation, injury, and mental preparation needs, while also offering hugs and affection as needed; however, the athletes suggested that these behaviors should change over time as they mature. Collectively, findings suggest that parents should be able to read their child and allow them to develop the appropriate level of autonomy in organizing themselves and preparing for their competitions.

Lauer et al's. (2010) study of parental behaviors affecting elite junior tennis players' development also underscores the key role of effective parent-child communication on healthy relationships, with both parents and child-athletes highlighting the importance of emotionally intelligent conversations. During childhood and early adolescence, these conversations were related to knowing when and how to talk to their child about their sport and performances, while during later adolescence, conversations were often related to important decisions regarding athletes' sport careers within the context of their broader life balance—findings supported by others (e.g., Wolfenden & Holt, 2005). Fraser-Thomas et al.'s (2008b) study of highly invested adolescent competitive swimmers also emphasizes the importance of optimal communication during adolescence; while both dropout and engaged athletes considered withdrawing from the sport at some point throughout their swimming careers, only engaged athletes spoke of having constructive discussions with their parents and being presented with multiple creative options to work through this difficult time (e.g., taking a break from the sport, exploring a new approach to the sport, switching coaches/clubs).

Parents' positive push? One overriding question that remains is how much parents should *push* their children and how this push is optimally demonstrated. At first glance, research appears relatively consistent: Praise and encouragement is important for talent development across all developmental stages, but particularly when athletes are younger (e.g., Bloom, 1985; Côté, 1999; Wuerth et al., 2004). However, numerous negative parental behaviors, such as yelling, criticizing, and punishing for poor performance, have been documented in the literature, and in occasional cases have been found to actually motivate athletes to perform optimally, at least in the short term (Keegan et al., 2010; Lauer et al., 2010). It remains a challenge for researchers to interpret how these negative behaviors ultimately affect child-athletes in the short and long term. Lauer and colleagues propose that despite being well-meaning, parents probably do not recognize how their behaviors affect their child and may become so immersed in their investment in their child's sport that they behave in ways they feel will optimize their children's success rather than benefit their healthy development.

Parents' Beliefs, Values, and Expectations

Numerous researchers have noted that parents' beliefs, values, and expectations regarding sport are very influential in the child-athlete's sport-related beliefs, values, and expectations. For example, Eccles and Harold (1991) reported a positive relationship between the child's perception of the degree to which their parents valued their sport involvement and the child's perceived competence. Similarly, Babkes and Weiss (1999) found that when children perceived positive parental beliefs regarding competencies and received more frequent positive comments, they had higher perceived competence and intrinsic motivation. More recently, Fredricks and Eccles (2005) noted a positive relationship between parents' perceptions of the importance and usefulness of sport participation and the child's perceived competence, value of sport, and actual sport participation levels. Of particular interest was that fathers' beliefs were more strongly associated with children's perceptions of competence, possibly suggesting that children continue to perceive sport as a masculine-based activity (Fredricks & Eccles, 2002). Fredricks and Eccles (2005) also found that parents' beliefs regarding children's perceptions of competence were positively related to the children's own perceptions of competence. Collectively, these findings support the expectancy-value model (Fredricks & Eccles, 2004; Horn & Horn, 2007).

Research also suggests that the parents' motivation orientations may influence a child's own motivation orientations, in addition to other child-athlete outcomes. An extensive body of sport psychology research has focused on individuals' motivation orientations; when individuals are task-oriented, they are motivated by and set goals related to skill development, enjoyment, and task mastery, while individuals who are ego oriented are motivated by and set goals related to performance outcomes and peer comparison (e.g., Ames, 1992). In a large study of Greek youth athletes, mothers were found to make a significant contribution to the formation of mastery goals in their children, and further, task-oriented climates as created by mothers and other social agents were found to positively correspond to child-athletes' sport satisfaction (Papaioannou, Ampatzoglou, Kalogiannis, & Sagovits, 2008). Another study (Le Bars, Gernigon, & Ninot, 2009) found parents of older adolescent athletes who persisted in national training centers were perceived by athletes as inducing a more task-oriented environment than parents of athletes who dropped out. Further, athletes' perceptions of parents' task-orientation decreased during the two years of study, suggesting appropriate parent-created climates may vary according to stage of development.

Finally, research has examined how parents' values, beliefs, and expectations surrounding sport may differ for sons and for daughters. Historically, findings suggest that parents place greater value on sport for their sons than daughters (e.g., provide more encouragement, perceive as more competent, and provide more tangible support; e.g., Fredricks & Eccles, 2005). Diacin and DeSensi's (2011) recent qualitative study among sport parents sheds a slightly more optimistic light on gender equality among sons and daughters, finding that parents generally have similar expectations of their sons and daughters, while also supporting them equally; however, this finding was not expressed by all study participants, suggesting a need for further examination of this lingering potential gender imbalance.

Parent Modeling

While most research has supported positive associations between parents' and children's physical activity patterns (e.g., Sallis, Prochaska, Taylor, Hill, & Geraci, 1999), research relating parents' physical activity levels to their children's sport involvement has been conflicting (e.g., Yang, Telama, & Laakso, 1996). Recent research has begun to examine the potential influence of parents' past and current sport involvement on child-athletes' involvement. For example, in their examination of psychosocial influences in a matched sample of competitive swimmers who withdrew and persisted in sport, Fraser-Thomas, Côté, and Deakin (2008a) found that significantly more dropouts had parents who had been athletes in their youth than engaged swimmers, and further, significantly more dropouts had parents who had been high-level athletes (i.e., provincial level or higher) in their youth, than engaged athletes. In a followup qualitative study (Fraser-Thomas et al., 2008b), many dropout athletes spoke directly to this finding, highlighting that they always felt pressure to be high performing athletes like their parents, but suggested that their parents did not overtly demonstrate any specific behaviors that led them to feel this way; rather, it was something that they constantly lived with as young highly invested athletes. In a more exploratory study focused on understanding adolescents' personal and social development through sport, athletes emphasized another important dimension of parental modelling in sport—parents' work ethic (Fraser-Thomas & Côté, 2009). Collectively, these findings suggest that the relationship between parent and child sport participation patterns may be more complex than initially believed.

Parents' Role in Facilitating Personal and Social Development

An emergent body of literature is also beginning to highlight the critical role that parents can play in facilitating children's healthy psychological and social development through sport. Some of these studies (e.g., Gould et al., 2008; Lauer et al., 2010) suggest that parents can play an important role in influencing children and young adolescents' development as well-rounded individuals, not simply athletes in a particular sport, by instilling core values, teaching sport psychology skills, emphasizing a positive attitude, demonstrating a solid work ethic, modelling respectful in-game behavior, teaching appropriate sportspersonship, and facilitating the learning of life skills. While this process occurs through a variety of means, it has been suggested that competitive sport serves as a venue for children to hold their parents accountable to model appropriate life skills, such as resolving conflicts, overcoming challenges, meeting new people, showing respect, maintaining emotional control under stress, and developing resilience (see Fraser-Thomas & Côté, 2009; Knight et al., 2010, 2011).

Also of interest is recent work that has highlighted the potential negative role parents can play in influencing their child-athlete's development through sport. For example, Shields, LaVoi, Bredemeier, and Power (2005) found that spectators' (i.e., primarily parents') poor sport behavior and parents' acceptance of poor sport behavior were significant predictors of poor sportspersonship behavior among young athletes in grades five to eight. LaVoi and Babkes Stellino's (2008) study tapped further into this relationship and found that young athletes who perceived parents as having promoted a task-involved climate (e.g., encouraged mastery of skills, defined success multidimensionally, emphasized mistakes as part of the leaning process) while minimizing their promotion of an ego-oriented climate (e.g., did not pressure to win), were more likely to display good sportsperson behaviors such as concern for opponents and graciousness, and were less likely to display poor sportsperson behaviors such as trash talking, playing outside the spirit of the game, and whining and complaining. Collectively, these findings begin to detail specific ways by which parents can facilitate positive development and minimize negative outcomes in the areas of personal skills, social skills, core values, and life skills, consistent with frameworks of positive youth development (e.g., Benson, 1997; Fraser-Thomas, Côté, & Deakin, 2005).

THE SIBLING-ATHLETE DYAD

As an important part of the family structure, siblings have a potentially strong influence on children and youth sport development. In fact, previous research has discussed that children who have siblings involved in sport are more likely to participate in sport themselves (Wold & Anderssen, 1992). Sibling influence may be direct (e.g., child-sibling) or indirect (e.g., sibling-parent-child), impacting the experiences and perceptions of youth-athletes regarding sport involvement, support, and negative influences.

Sibling Support

Bloom's (1985) seminal work focused primarily on parental influences in talent development, with minimal information regarding siblings and their involvement in child and adolescent sport participation. This work was extended by Côté (1999), who reported that, particularly in the specializing years, older siblings who displayed a strong work ethic acted as role models for youth involved in sport, and these youth emulated those characteristics. Further, cooperation was perceived to be a strong part of the child-sibling relationship, as opposed to competition. Additionally, Fraser-Thomas et al. (2008b) found that siblings generally had a positive influence on sport participation for youth competitive swimmers who remained engaged in their sport. Finally, research has also pointed to the positive supportive influences of siblings in helping youth athletes develop physical skills (e.g., speed), motor skills (e.g., visual-perceptual skill), emotional support (e.g., encouragement), as well as psychological skills (e.g., mental toughness; see Davis & Meyer, 2008; Weissensteiner, Abernethy, & Farrow, 2009; Wolfenden & Holt, 2005).

Negative Influences and Outcomes

Although many positive outcomes have been cited through the research regarding the influences of siblings on sport participation, it has been found that tensions also arise among siblings related to sport participation. Bloom (1985) shares several instances related to talent development, where the siblings of high-level performers felt isolated. In relation to sport development, Côté's (1999) research has also suggested that athletes in the investment years often have younger or twin siblings who felt bitterness and/or jealousy due to the increased amounts of time and resources placed on the developing athlete. Further, research has pointed to sibling rivalry as a concern in sustaining youth sport participation (Fraser-Thomas et al., 2008b), as direct competition between siblings at an elite level has been found to be uniquely different from direct competition with a nonsibling (Davis & Meyer, 2008), often leading to negative implications including affective responses to sibling competition (i.e., anger, frustration).

In exploring the indirect relationship (e.g., sibling-parent-child), parents involved with elite-level youth athletes have expressed concerns for the other children in their families, suggesting that despite their best efforts, they are unable to treat all their children equally in terms of attention and time (Kirk et al., 1997b), resulting in sibling jealousy and resentment (Harwood & Knight, 2009). Parents also feel tension themselves in their feelings that other children often do not enjoy the same amount of time, attention, and resources as the elite athlete. Further, parents experience stress relating to splitting the family, choosing one child over the other, and worry about the quality of the relationships with their other children. This indirect relationship offers a unique perspective into sibling influences, while also emphasizing the need for future research relating to sibling involvement.

INTEGRATING FAMILY INFLUENCE INTO THE DMSP

Since its inception by Côté in 1999, the DMSP has become a significant framework for understanding children's development in sport, with substantial advances over the years in our understanding of training and coaching influences across development (e.g., Côté, Young, Duffy, & North, 2007); however, contextual influences need to be considered further, particularly pertaining to the roles of parents and siblings. In this section, we present a revised DMSP (Figure 11.1), which integrates the roles of parents and siblings in youth sport development, while highlighting practical suggestions for furthering the relational and contextual aspects of the trajectories. While this section does not contain references, its contents and practical suggestions are based upon all of the literature reviewed throughout the chapter.

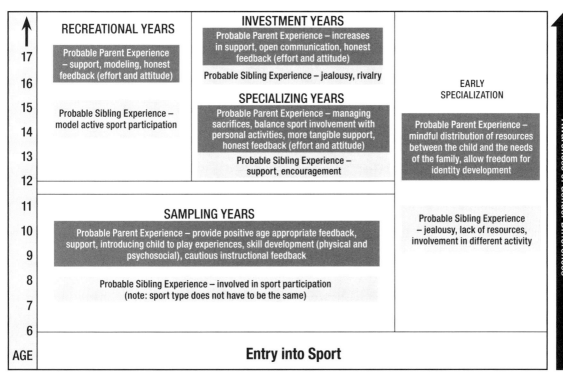

Figure 11.1. Probable parent and sibling experiences within the trajectories of the DMSP

All Stages

Across all stages, parents should create task-oriented climates that are autonomy supportive (i.e., involve children in decision making) and focus on effectively communicating with their child-athletes. Parents should be particularly cautious of pushing their children (e.g., yelling, criticizing); while pushing may motivate some children in some situations, it is also linked with many negative outcomes (i.e., decreased motivation, dropout). Teaching and modeling life skills and positive sport participation is also a key factor to consider across stages, although more research is needed to determine how parents can best facilitate this at each stage. Finally, parents should always consider how their involvement with the child-athlete influences other siblings and be mindful of gender differences in their interactions with son and daughter child-athletes.

Sampling Years

In the sampling years, parents should provide positive, age-appropriate feedback that will encourage and facilitate a supportive environment for their young children as they begin their sport experiences. Parents, especially fathers, should be cautious about providing too much instructional feedback, particularly when the child-athlete's ability levels are low, as this may be detrimental to children's motivation. In these early years, parents should also create more play opportunities for their children (i.e., playing in the park) to help encourage physical and psychosocial skill development. Research suggests that the sampling years also provide an opportunity for positive sibling influences, where child-athletes' older siblings may model positive participation habits and attitudes and where child-athletes may have a similar influence on their younger siblings.

Recreational Years

As samplers move into the recreational years (trajectory 1), parents have an opportunity to continue to positively influence their child-athlete's development by providing support (particularly emotional and tangible), offering honest feedback regarding their children's effort and attitude, and modeling active physical activity and/or sport participation for life. At this stage, siblings may continue to model positive sport participation for each other, and engage in each others' respective sports; however, further research is necessary to better understand how age differences may or may not affect sibling influence within this stage.

Specializing and Investment Years

After age 12 or 13, many children specialize in two or three sports (trajectory 2); child-athletes' increased investment is accompanied by a similar increase in parents' provision of tangible support. Research highlights the importance of parents carefully managing their various involvements (i.e., time, money), as finding time to pursue personal interests may be beneficial for both parent and child-athletes. Generally, adolescent athletes do not welcome parents' performance-related feedback during adolescence, but such feedback may be appropriate if parents have an extensive background as high-level athletes in the sport. Further, adolescents tend to appreciate honest feedback regarding attitude and effort, assuming parents know when and how to communicate this feedback. Parents should also be mindful of maintaining open communication and providing an opportunity to discuss big decisions with their child-athletes, so that transitions into higher levels of investment are smooth. The specializing and investment years may be challenging for siblings of child-athletes. Child-athletes may receive greater attention during these stages, leading siblings to experience feelings of jealousy and rivalry. Optimally, parents should be mindful of meeting all their children's needs, and siblings should provide emotional and sometimes informational support while being encouraging and helpful within the family context.

Early Specialization

When a young athlete shows talent in sports, participation in the early specialization stream may be an option for families (trajectory 3). Parents need to be mindful of the distribution of resources throughout the development of the child and inclusive of the needs of the family. Further, parents also should be aware of changes relating to identity development in their child. If a child's identity is only in sport, outcomes such as burnout, dropout, or difficulty in transitions are possible. Similar to the investment years, this trajectory may breed feelings of jealously among siblings. Siblings may also experience a lack of resources devoted to them, and this may lead to resentment. If there is a talented child involved in early specialization, siblings may be best served by becoming involved in another activity that will give them their own niche, and developing a talent, athletic or otherwise, away from the shadow of the early specializer.

FUTURE DIRECTIONS

While Brustad's (1992) suggestion that everyone talks about parents' involvement in sport, but no one researches it, no longer holds true, contradictory findings and unanswered questions suggest that this field remains in its infancy. Research using longitudinal innovative methodologies is critical for gaining a deeper understanding of ongoing interactions between young athletes and their families over time, and as a way to tap into specific mechanisms by which interactions are perceived by child-athletes, their parents, and their siblings; such research will offer a clearer understanding of optimal support and positive pressure in youth sport contexts (Fraser-Thomas & Côté, 2009). In particular, investigation of similarities, differences, and the matching of parents' and child-athletes' perceptions of optimal behaviors is necessary, coupled with the examination of how optimal behaviors may differ according to parent gender or parents with extensive backgrounds in high-level sport (Fraser-Thomas et al., 2008a; Knight et al., 2011).

Future work should also focus on differences in parental involvement across sport, gender, developmental stage, performance level, and socioeconomic status. While we have seen a significant increase in the depth of understanding in recent years, the breadth of understanding remains less advanced. For example, recent research suggests that parental support and expectations continue to differ according to parent and child gender, and that the distinct cultures of different sports should not be undermined (e.g., Bois, Lalanne & Delforge, 2009; Diacin & DeSensi, 2011). Further, future work should acknowledge and prioritize the dynamic and changing roles of parental involvement throughout the child-athletes' development, as the enormity of changes from children's sport initiation through adolescent levels of expertise or recreational involvement cannot be underestimated. Additionally, future research exploring and comparing family influences across different ability levels and over time would be fruitful (Wolfenden & Holt, 2005). While much research has focused on elite adolescent athletes, little research has focused on nonelite but highly invested youth athletes, and research has not followed youth elite and nonelite athletes' performance results into young adulthood. Also noteworthy, researchers have suggested that because tangible support appears to be a prerequisite for sport involvement (Lauer et al., 2010; Wolfenden & Holt, 2005), the study of talent development has focused on children of middle to high socioeconomic status; yet, further research is necessary to determine if and how families of lower socioeconomic status can optimally facilitate children's sport development (Fraser-Thomas et al., 2005).

With the emerging depth of studies pertaining to parents and their influence regarding child or youth sport participation, research examining the influence of a child's sport participation on parents' experiences is sorely lacking in the literature. Due to the bidirectionality present in relationships, it is crucial to examine both sides of the relationship. The limited amount of research that does exist in this area has found that parents are indeed being socialized by their children's involvement in sport; they are experiencing changes in their thoughts, emotions, and behaviors as a result of their child's sport participation (e.g., Dorsch, Smith, & McDonough, 2009; Harwood & Knight, 2009), with several individual level factors (i.e., age, temperament) and contextual factors (i.e., community involvement, individual versus team sport) influencing the socialization processes. Further exploration will enable greater insight into these complex interactions. In addition, the whole-family dynamic is an important consideration for future research. The inclusion of siblings to this topic of research has many possibilities, including examination of gender difference between siblings, birth order, sibling divergence (Sulloway, 1996), sibling age separation, sibling activity diversification, and sibling participation and interaction throughout the trajectories of the DMSP. Each of these topics contributes to a unique gap in knowledge and may lead to exciting avenues of research.

Finally, given the applied nature of this research, it is critical that the research wheel turn full circle, with researchers assuring that effective knowledge translation occurs, which in turn can lead to effective sport policy and applications. In particular, we are seeing a surge in parental workshops and training sessions affiliated with youth sport programs, which are often a requirement for youth sport involvement; however, these programs are not always evidence-based. While the parents, programmers, and policy makers' willingness to do the right thing is an important first step, we must ensure that the information and education being communicated is indeed consistent with the current research linking family involvement with optimal child development in sport.

REFERENCES

Ames, C. (1992). Classrooms: Goals, structures, and student motivation. *Journal of Educational Psychology, 84*(3), 261–271.

Averill, P. M., & Power, T. G. (1995). Parental attitudes and children's experiences in soccer: Correlates of effort and enjoyment. *International Journal of Behavioural Development, 18*(2), 263–276.

Babkes, M. L., & Weiss, M. R. (1999). Parental influence on children's cognitive and affective responses to competitive soccer participation. *Pediatric Exercise Science, 11*(1), 44–62.

Benson, P. L. (1997). *All kids are our kids: What communities must do to raise caring and responsible children and adolescents.* San Francisco, CA: Jossey-Bass.

Bloom, B. S. (Ed.). (1985). *Developing talent in young people.* New York, NY: Ballantine Books.

Bois, J. E., Lalanne, J., & Delforge, C. (2009). The influence of parenting practices and parental presence on children's and adolescents' pre-competitive anxiety. *Journal of Sports Sciences, 27*(10), 995–1005.

Bronfenbrenner, U. (2002). Developmental systems theory. In R. M. Lerner (Ed.), *Concepts and theories of human development* (pp. 200–242). Mahwah, NJ: Lawrence Erlbaum Associates.

Brustad, R. J. (1992). Integrating socialization influences into the study of children's motivation in sport. *Journal of Sport and Exercise Psychology, 14*(1), 59–77.

Côté, J. (1999). The influence of family in the development of talent in sport. *The Sport Psychologist, 13,* 395–417.

Côté, J., & Fraser-Thomas, J. (2011). Youth involvement and positive development in sport. In P. R. E. Crocker (Ed.). *Sport psychology: A Canadian perspective* (2nd ed.) (pp. 226–255). Toronto, Canada: Pearson Prentice Hall.

Côté, J., & Hay, J. (2002). Children's involvement in sport: A developmental perspective. In J. M. Silva & D. E. Stevens (Eds.), *Psychological foundations of sport* (pp. 484–502). Boston, MA: Allyn & Bacon.

Côté, J., Young, B. W., Duffy, P., & North, J. (2007) Towards a definition of excellence in sport coaching. *International Journal of Coaching Science, 1,* 3–16.

Csikszentmihalyi, M., Rathunde, K., & Whalen, S. (1993). *Talented teenagers: The roots of success and failure.* Cambridge, UK: Cambridge University Press.

Davis, N. W., & Meyer, B. B. (2008). When sibling becomes competitor: A qualitative investigation of same-sex sibling competitive in elite sport. *Journal of Applied Sport Psychology, 20,* 220–235.

Diacin, M .J., & DeSensi, J. T. (2011). Parents' gender role expectations and support for children's sport activities. *Research Quarterly for Exercise and Sport, 82,* A–24.

Dorsch, T. E., Smith, A. L., & McDonough, M. H. (2009). Parents' perceptions of child-to-parent socialization in organized youth sport. *Journal of Sport and Exercise Psychology, 31,* 444–468.

Eccles, J. S., & Harold, R. D. (1991). Gender differences in sport involvement: Applying the Eccles' expectancy-value model. *Journal of Applied Sport Psychology, 3,* 7–35.

Fraser-Thomas, J. L., & Coté, J. (2009). Understanding adolescents' positive and negative developmental experiences in sport. *The Sport Psychologist, 23*(1), 3–23.

Fraser-Thomas, J. L., Côté, J., & Deakin, J. (2005). Youth sport programs: An avenue to foster positive youth development. *Physical Education and Sport Pedagogy, 10*(1), 19–40.

Fraser-Thomas, J., Côté, J., & Deakin, J. (2008a). Examining adolescent sport dropout and prolonged engagement from a developmental perspective. *Journal of Applied Sport Psychology, 20,* 318–333.

Fraser-Thomas, J., Côté, J., & Deakin, J. (2008b). Understanding dropout and prolonged engagement in adolescent competitive sport. *Psychology of Sport and Exercise, 9*(5), 645–662.

Fredricks, J. A., & Eccles, J. S. (2002). Children's competence and value beliefs from childhood through adolescence: Growth trajectories in two male-sex-typed domains. *Developmental Psychology, 38*(4), 519–533.

Fredricks, J. A., & Eccles, J. S. (2004). Parental influences on youth involvement in sports. In M. R. Weiss (Ed.), *Developmental sport and exercise psychology: A lifespan perspective* (pp. 145–164). Morgantown, WV: Fitness Information Technology.

Fredricks, J. A., & Eccles, J. S. (2005). Family socialization, gender, and sport motivation and involvement. *Journal of Sport and Exercise Psychology, 27*(1), 3–31.

Gould, D., Lauer, L., Rolo, C., Jannes, C., & Pennisi, N. (2008). The role of parents in tennis success: Focus group interviews with junior coaches. *The Sport Psychologist, 22*(1), 18–37.

Harter, S. (1978). Effectance motivation reconsidered: Toward a developmental model. *Human Development, 21*(1), 34–64.

Harwood, C., & Knight, C. (2009). Understanding parental stressors: An investigation of British tennis parents. *Journal of Sport Sciences, 27*(4), 339–351.

Holt, N. L., Tamminen, K. A., Black, D. E., Mandigo, J. L., & Fox, K. R. (2009). Youth sport parenting styles and practices. *Journal of Sport and Exercise Psychology, 31*(1), 37–59.

Holt, N. L., Tamminen, K. A., Black, D. E., Sehn, Z. L., & Wall, M. P. (2008). Parental involvement in competitive youth sport settings. *Psychology of Sport and Exercise, 9*(5), 663–685.

Horn, T. S., & Horn, J. L. (2007). Family influences on children's sport and physical activity participation, behaviour, and psychosocial responses. In G. Tenenbaum & R. C. Eklund (Eds.), *Handbook of sport psychology* (3rd ed.) (pp. 685–711). New York, NY: Wiley.

Juntumaa, B., Keskivaara, P., & Punamaki, R. (2005). Parenting, achievement strategies and satisfaction in ice hockey. *Scandinavian Journal of Psychology, 46*(5), 411–420.

Keegan, R. J., Harwood, C. G., Spray, C. M., & Lavallee, D. E. (2009). A qualitative investigation exploring the motivational climate in early career sports participants: Coach, parent and peer influences on sport motivation. *Psychology of Sport and Exercise, 10*(3), 361–372.

Keegan, R., Spray, C., Harwood, C., & Lavallee, D. (2010). The motivational atmosphere in youth sport: Coach, parent and peer influences on motivation in specializing sport participants. *Journal of Applied Sport Psychology, 22,* 87–105.

Kirk, D., Carlson, T., O'Connor, A., Burke, P., Davis, K., & Glover, S. (1997a). The economic impact on families of children's participation in junior sport. *Australian Journal of Science and Medicine in Sport, 29*(2), 27–33.

Kirk, D., O'Connor, A., Carlson, T., Burke, P., Davis, K., & Glover, S. (1997b). Time commitments in junior sport: Social consequences for participants and their families. *European Journal of Physical Education, 2,* 51–73.

Knight, C. J., Boden, C. M., & Holt, N. L. (2010). Junior tennis players' preferences for parental behaviours. *Journal of Applied Sport Psychology, 22,* 377–391.

Knight, C. J., Neely, K. C., & Holt, N. L. (2011). Parental behaviours in team sports: How do female athletes want parents to behave? *Journal of Applied Sport Psychology, 23,* 76–92.

Lauer, L., Gould, D., Roman, N., & Pierce, M. (2010). Parental behaviors that affect junior tennis player development. *Psychology of Sport and Exercise, 11*(6), 487–496.

LaVoi, N. M., & Babkes Stellino, M. (2008). The relation between perceived parent-created sport climate and competitive male youth hockey players' good and poor sport behaviours. *The Journal of Psychology, 142*(5), 471–495.

Le Bars, H., Gernigon, C., & Ninot, G. (2009). Personal and contextual determinants of elite young athletes' persistence or dropping out over time. *Scandinavian Journal of Medicine and Science in Sports, 19*(2), 274–285.

McCarthy, P. J., & Jones, M. V. (2007). A qualitative study of sport enjoyment in the sampling years. *The Sport Psychologist, 21*(4), 400–416.

Papaioannou, A. G., Ampatzoglou, G., Kalogiannis, P., & Sagovits, A. (2008). Social agents, achievement goals, satisfaction and academic achievement in youth sport. *Psychology of Sport and Exercise, 9*(2), 122–141.

Sallis, J., Prochaska, J., Taylor, W., Hill, J., & Geraci, J. (1999). Correlates of physical activity in a national sample of girls and boys in grades 4 through 12. *Health Psychology, 18*(4), 410–415.

Shields, D. L., LaVoi, N. M., Bredemeier, B. L., & Power, C. F. (2007). Predictors of poor sportspersonship in youth sports: An examination of personal attitudes and social influences. *Journal of Sport & Exercise Psychology, 29*(6), 747–762.

Stein, G. L., Raedeke, T. D., & Glenn, S. D. (1999). Children's perceptions of parent sport involvement: It's not how much but to what degree that's important. *Journal of Sport Behavior, 22,* 591–602.

Strachan, L., Côté, J., & Deakin, J. (2009). An evaluation of personal and contextual factors in competitive youth sport. *Journal of Applied Sport Psychology, 21,* 340–355.

Sulloway, F. (1996). *Born to rebel.* New York, NY: Pantheon Books.

Ullrich-French, S., & Smith, A. L. (2006). Perceptions of relationships with parents and peers in youth sport: Independent and combined predictions of motivational outcomes. *Psychology of Sport and Exercise, 7*(2), 193–214.

van Rossum, J. H. A., & van der Loo, H. (1997). Gifted athletes and complexity of family structure: A condition for talent development? *High Ability Studies, 8,* 9–30.

Weissensteiner, J., Abernethy, B., & Farrow, D. (2009). Towards the development of a conceptual model of expertise in cricket batting: A grounded theory approach. *Journal of Applied Sport Psychology, 21,* 276–292.

Wuerth, S., Lee, M. J., & Alfermann, D. (2004). Parental involvement and athletes' career in youth sport. *Psychology of Sport and Exercise, 5*(1), 21–33.

Wold, B., & Anderssen, N. (1992). Health promotion aspects of family and peer influences on sport participation. *International Journal of Sport Psychology, 23*(4), 343–359.

Wolfenden, L. E., & Holt, N. L. (2005). Talent development in elite junior tennis: Perceptions of players, parents, and coaches. *Journal of Applied Sport Psychology, 17,* 108–126.

Yang, X. L., Telama, R., & Laakso, L. (1996). Parents physical activity, socioeconomic status and education as predictors of physical activity and sport among children and youths: A 12-year follow-up study. *International Review for Sociology of Sport, 31*(3), 272–289.

CHAPTER 12

CIRCUMSTANTIAL DEVELOPMENT: BIRTHDATE AND BIRTHPLACE EFFECTS ON ATHLETE DEVELOPMENT

Dany J. MacDonald and Joseph Baker

INTRODUCTION

The identification and development of sport talent has become an important concern for sport governing bodies worldwide. Largely, this is due to countries trying to match or exceed the success of countries such as Australia, China, the United States, and the United Kingdom, who have invested considerable time, money, and effort into developing programs to identify and nurture athletes with the highest potential for international success. However, despite this outlay of resources, the evidence collected to date suggests that talent identification and development programs have generally been unsuccessful at meeting their aim (Vaeyens, Güllich, Warr, & Philippaerts, 2009).

The difficulty in identifying talented young athletes arguably reflects the same difficulty in predicting any future occurrence. In all areas of human behavior, the greater the time between assessment and the date of future performance, the greater the number of variables affecting this future. Consider, for example, the recent study by Koz, Fraser-Thomas, and Baker (2012). They examined the ability of teams in the National Basketball Association, National Hockey League, National Football League, and Major League Baseball to predict career potential in players drafted to their teams. Even when predicting potential in athletes who are in late adolescence or early adulthood (i.e., immediately before they embark on their professional careers), top scouts working with some of the richest sports teams in the world have a wide range of accuracy (between 2% and 16%). When trying to predict success earlier in development the task becomes even more daunting.

Why is it so difficult to predict who will succeed in sport at the adult level? There are several factors, but generally these can be grouped together into three main reasons. First, adult elite performance is usually the end result of at least a decade of acquired experiences, and it is difficult to determine at the start of the journey (or during early phases of this journey) who has the necessary "raw material" (e.g., intrinsic motivation, resiliency) to make it to the end. Second, understanding athlete development is a complex undertaking that is affected by a magnitude of factors at the individual and environmental levels. As previously outlined in the text, taking an ecological perspective (see Bronfenbrenner & Morris, 2006, for a discussion of the ecological perspective) to understanding athlete development is critical, as it paints a more realistic picture of the factors affecting the developing athlete. Third, and the focus of much of this chapter, is that sport programs are inherently flawed in ways that reduce their predictive potential. In this chapter we discuss two phenomena inherent to sport that reflect the difficulties associated with identifying and developing talented athletes. The first, the relative age effect (RAE), relates to selection biases associated with the month of one's birth, while the other, the birthplace effect, describes the disproportionate distribution of athletes who come from geographic regions of a specific size.

THE RELATIVE AGE EFFECT

In order to ensure equal competition among participants who vary in age, most sports will group athletes into one-year (and sometimes two-year) age groups. Although this is done with good intentions (i.e., to limit the developmental differences between athletes playing in the same leagues/divisions), it can have significant negative consequences for many participants. The RAE reflects the asymmetrical distribution of athletes (or students) based on their birth date relative to an arbitrary cut-off date, such as when athletes born closer to (i.e., soon after) a sports cut-off date have a higher representation in elite sport leagues compared to athletes born later. The first studies of the RAE were published in 1984 (Grondin, Deschaies, & Nault) and 1985 (Barnsley, Thompson, & Barnsley) and focused on Canadian ice hockey players. Since these initial studies, researchers have found strong support for the RAE in most sports. One study documented RAE going back at least 30 years in elite Canadian ice hockey (Wattie, Baker, Cobley, & Montelpare, 2007) and another over 40 years in elite German soccer (Cobley, Schorer, & Baker, 2008).

Table 12.1 presents a brief review of studies on RAE. Generally, and with few exceptions (e.g., football, wrestling), there is a robust RAE in competitive sport. There are several hypotheses as to how this effect occurs. The first is that relatively older players experience greater success (because they are older and more capable), and therefore have higher intrinsic and competence motivation than relatively younger players who hypothetically should feel frustration and negative feedback due to comparisons to relatively older peers. Although this hypothesis seems reasonable, it has not been adequately tested (for an exception see Schorer, Baker, Lotz, & Büsch, 2010). Alternatively, a more strongly supported hypothesis suggests that athletes who are relatively older and more physically and cognitively mature are more likely to be identified by coaches looking for the most "talented" athletes, because they appear stronger and faster, and make better decisions when compared with their relatively younger and usually less mature sport peers. Once selected, relatively older athletes gain access to superior coaches and better instruction, in addition to competing against more skilled opponents, which creates a self-fulfilling cycle where these relatively older athletes ultimately reach higher levels of attainment.

There are several assumptions underpinning this second hypothesis. First, coaches and talent scouts must select athletes (either consciously or subconsciously) using a variable confounded by relative age. In sport, there has been some evidence that this variable is size. Baker, Cobley, Montelpare, Wattie, and Faught (2010) noted no differences in height and weight among participants in a representative (i.e., highly competitive) level of junior ice hockey (9–10 years of age), despite the fact that there was up to 12 months' difference between the oldest and youngest players in the sample. Furthermore, the average height and weight would place the participants at around the 75th percentile when compared to national averages. The lack of difference in these anthropometric variables, particularly in populations where normally significant variation exists, is quite telling about what coaches perceive when they think they are seeing talent. More likely, coaches are confusing size and other maturational-related variables (e.g., power,

Table 12.1. Review of Investigations of Relative Age Effects in Sport
(adapted from Cobley et al., 2009)

Sport	No. of Studies	Notes
MEN'S		
Soccer	13	+
Ice hockey	10	+
Baseball	8	+
Basketball	5	+/-
Football	3	-
Cricket	3	+
Rugby	2	+
Tennis	2	+
Volleyball	1	+
Gymnastics	1	-
Swimming	1	+
Aussie rules football	1	+
Golf	1	-
WOMEN'S		
Tennis	2	+
Gymnastics	2	+/-
Soccer	2	+
Ice hockey	1	+/-
Netball	1	+/-
Swimming	1	+
Volleyball	1	+
Basketball	1	+/-

NOTE: + = Evidence of an effect, - = No evidence of an effect, +/- = Mixed evidence of an effect.

speed) for talent. Interestingly, these findings also suggest that relatively younger youth may overcome this effect if they mature more quickly than their peers.

Another assumption relates to how the RAE changes throughout development. At each level of sport, coaches and trainers are required to select the most talented players from an increasingly homogenous group of athletes. If there is a general advantage for participants who are relatively older, there should be an increase in the RAE as the level of competition increases and athletes move through subsequent steps in the talent development system, due to the accumulated effect of the advantage. Data generally support this assumption, at least up to a certain point. Cobley, Wattie, Baker, and McKenna's (2009) meta-analysis found that the strength of RAEs increased until the level immediately preceding the professional level and then decreased. Schorer, Cobley, Büsch, Bräutigam, and Baker (2009) noted a similar effect in team handball. We will return to the reason for the decrease at the highest level of skill later in the chapter, but generally research supports the assumption that there is an increasing advantage for relatively older participants—at least as it relates to being selected for subsequent stages of talent development. Unfortunately, what this suggests is that as athletes move through these stages, it becomes increasingly difficult for relatively younger athletes to stay in the system, and as a result a younger relative age is also associated with dropout from sport (Delorme, Chalabaev, & Raspaud, 2010; Helsen, Starkes, & Van Winckel, 1998).

The Scope of the Problem

The strength of the RAE has been so strong that interventions to remove or decrease the effect have been difficult to implement. Simply moving the selection date is not enough, since the relative age distribution simply shifts to the new selection date (Helsen, Starkes, & Van Winckel, 2000). As a result of this difficulty, researchers in this area have begun to focus on sports where an effect should be expected but has not been found. For instance, gridiron football in the United States has all of the basic requirements to promote a RAE. It emphasizes the physical characteristics of height and weight (among other qualities) and has a highly structured system of competition, particularly in the southern US. However, research (e.g., MacDonald, Cheung, Côté, & Abernethy, 2009) has found no effect in this sport. What makes this sport different is that players' participation is often organized into weight classes during early stages of competition, which seems to reduce emphasis on maturational differences at a time when the difference between the relatively oldest and relatively youngest is greatest. Presumably, this is also why RAEs have not emerged in other weight-organized sports, such as boxing and wrestling.

There is also increasing evidence suggesting that reducing the extent of competition for spots on a team may reduce or eliminate the RAE. For instance, Lidor, Côté, Arnon, Zeev, and Cohen-Maoz (2010) proposed that the smaller number of participants might explain the lack of RAEs in elite sports in Israel. The lower rate of participants has also been proposed to explain the difference in RAEs between men's and women's sports. Examinations of women's ice hockey (Weir, Smith, Paterson, & Horton, 2010), gymnastics (Baker, Janning, Wong, Cobley, & Schorer, in press), and basketball (Delorme, Boiché, & Raspaud, 2009) have noted that the RAE in females reflects an overrepresentation of athletes in the second birth quartile compared to the other three quartiles (i.e., instead of the first quartile as found in males). Some researchers (e.g., Baker et al., in press; Weir et al., 2010) believe that this effect may be due to the lower level of competition in women's sports. Interestingly, a recent study by Baker, Schorer, Cobley, Bräutigam, and Büsch (2010) noted that RAEs remained smaller in female sports even when participation numbers were similar to those in men's sports, suggesting that this factor alone may not be enough to explain the consistent differences between men's and women's sports.

Are There Advantages for the Relatively Younger Athletes?

Recent examinations have suggested that the social structures that perpetuate the RAE might not be disadvantageous to the relatively younger athletes as much as previously suggested. As we noted earlier in the chapter, the size of the RAE decreases at the professional/senior-open level of competition. Although this effect has not been adequately investigated, there is some evidence to suggest that it may be due to relatively younger players being more sought after at the professional level (Baker & Logan, 2007) and having longer playing careers than their relatively older counterparts (Schorer et al., 2009). Baker and Logan (2007) suggested that the highly competitive sporting environment that initially penalized relatively younger players may actually end up making them better players in the long run, because they have to develop superior skills to compete with their relatively older teammates and opponents. Ashworth and Heyndels' (2007) study indicating that relatively younger soccer players obtain higher salaries at the professional level adds some support to this notion.

In another interesting aspect of the RAE, Wattie et al. (2007) found that relatively younger ice hockey players were up to three-and-a-half times less likely to get injured than relatively older players. Although the precise reason for this is unclear, it does add depth to the discussion regarding whether RAEs are actually disadvantageous for relatively younger participants. The subtleties of the RAE are still being revealed; however, what seems clear is that the effect highlights a critical limitation of current athlete development systems, suggesting that coaches and talent scouts are neglecting a significant pool of potential.

THE BIRTHPLACE EFFECT

A second factor linked with the development of expertise in sport is location of birth; commonly referred to as the *birthplace effect*. In Canada, for example, where ice hockey is ingrained within the sport culture, it is common to hear that rural children raised in small towns make it in the National Hockey League at higher rates than their large-city counterparts. A strong work ethic and the development of physical strength associated with small town environments are often provided as reasons why so many of these individuals enter professional leagues. These anecdotal accounts have fuelled interest in the birthplace effect, which aims at understanding if (and why) disproportionate numbers of professional athletes are born in cities of certain sizes.

Early research on birthplace can be traced back to the work of Rooney (1969). His research assessed the development of American football players in order to understand "hotbeds" of talent development. Rooney demonstrated that certain geographical areas produced higher rates of college and professional football players. Broadly speaking, his data suggested that athletes from the southwestern and northeastern regions of the United States produced higher than expected per capita rates of athletes, implying that certain areas are more conducive to the development of American football players than others.

Almost two decades after Rooney's (1969) study, Curtis and Birch (1987) and Carlson (1988) performed two studies essential to our understanding of birthplace effects. Curtis and Birch investigated the distribution of Canadian ice hockey players' birth community size of those who played in the National Hockey League, American Hockey League, and Central Hockey League. Further, they collected information on Olympic ice hockey players from Canada and the United States to determine whether community size and attainment of elite levels were related. Their analysis of the Canadian players showed that when compared to census values, the largest (i.e., cities with more than 500,000 inhabitants) and smallest (i.e., rural areas with less than 1,000 inhabitants) centers yielded lower than expected proportions of elite athletes. On the other hand, cities that ranged between 1,000 and 500,000 residents produced rates that were higher than expected. Although they did not report which areas were statistically under- or overrepresented, their conclusions showed trends towards a birthplace effect for Olympic and National Hockey League players in the North American ice hockey system.

In his study of Swedish tennis players, Carlson (1988) interviewed elite athletes to understand their socialization process into sports. Athletes from smaller cities reported greater access to playing fields, which they felt provided them with better opportunities to develop relevant abilities. Athletes from smaller cities also reported having free (and unlimited) access to tennis courts throughout their development, which allowed them to play and practice as much as they wanted at their own convenience.

The studies by Curtis and Birch (1987) and Carlson (1988) set the stage for more recent work examining the birthplace effect. Côté, MacDonald, Baker, and Abernethy (2006) investigated the birthplace effect in over 2,200 Canadian and American professional athletes. Athletes from the United States were sampled from the National Hockey League, the National Basketball Association, Major League Baseball, and the Professional Golf Association. By determining if discrepancies existed between the expected and observed proportions of individuals born across different city sizes, they determined whether certain areas produced higher numbers of professional athletes than expected. Across all sports, results showed a pattern where athletes were consistently overrepresented in cities of less than 500,000 and consistently underrepresented in city sizes of more than 500,000. When looking at the results more closely, Côté and colleagues observed that city sizes between 50,000 and 100,000 produced the highest overrepresentation of elite athletes. One limitation of the findings was that the US Census categorized all cities with less than 50,000 inhabitants into one bracket, thereby limiting the ability to determine whether small(er) cities would reflect the same effect.

Côté and colleagues (2006) turned their attention to National Hockey League Canadian ice hockey players in order to address this issue. With the Canadian Census using city size classifications down to less than 1,000 inhabitants, it was possible to determine if an effect was present in cities of less than 50,000. Results of this analysis expanded the US data by suggesting that cities as small as 1,000 inhabitants produced greater than expected numbers of professional athletes. Additionally, cities of less than 1,000 were significantly underrepresented in the sample of Canadian ice hockey players. In large cities they found a similar trend to that of the US data, with cities larger than 500,000 producing a lower than expected rate of professional athletes. Together, these results demonstrate an upper (500,000) and lower (1,000) boundary of city sizes in developing elite athletes. These boundaries provide target values for future research to investigate how communities of different sizes produce more elite level athletes.

It is important to be clear that although the effect noted in Côté et al. (2006) was quickly dubbed the birthplace effect, the authors (and those who conducted subsequent studies) clearly intended that the effect was driven by differences in the qualities of the early developmental environments of athletes in regions of different size. For instance, they speculated that cities between 1,000 and 500,000 are more effective at producing elite level athletes because they provide optimal resources (e.g., number of arenas) for youth to participate, and offer a safer environment to play.

Subsequent Research

Although the research by Côté and colleagues (2006) provided evidence of a birthplace effect, it was unclear how generalizable the findings were. This has led to additional studies of birthplace effects investigating how differences in location of birth relate to other variables, such as sport participated in, sex, and country of origin. To date, a number of different researchers have investigated birthplace across a range of sports. For a summary of studies conducted on birthplace effects, refer to Table 12.2.

MacDonald, King, Côté, and Abernethy (2009) examined women's professional sports in the United States to understand if female athletes were affected by birthplace in a manner akin to their male counterparts. Their study consisted of athletes from the Ladies Professional Golf Association (LPGA) and the Women's United Soccer Association (WUSA). Using methods similar to Côté and colleagues (2006), MacDonald et al.'s findings supported the trend of smaller cities producing higher than expected proportions of elite level athletes. However, results of the soccer players deviated from previous work by demonstrating that cities between 500,000 and 1 million also exhibited higher proportions of elite athletes. It is not clear why inconsistencies were observed for female soccer players in the United States, but it is possible that different sport socialization processes exist for males and females and/or across different sports (see Coakley & White, 1992). While it is clear that future research should investigate the relationship between sex, city size, and sport socialization to gain a better understanding of

Table 12.2. Summary of Research Conducted on Birthplace Effects by Sport, Sex, and Country

Authors (year)	Sport(s)	Sex	Country
Abernethy & Farrow (2005)	Rugby, cricket	Male	Australia
Baker & Logan (2007)	Ice hockey	Male	Canada, USA
Baker et al. (2009)	Olympians, soccer, handball, basketball, volleyball	Male	Canada, USA, UK, Germany
Bruner et al. (2011)	Ice hockey	Male	Canada, USA, Sweden, Finland
Carlson (1988)	Tennis	Male	Sweden
Côté et al. (2006)	Ice hockey, baseball, basketball, golf	Male	Canada, USA
Curtis & Birch (1987)	Ice hockey	Male	Canada, USA
Fraser-Thomas et al. (2010)	Swimming	Male/Female	Canada
Lidor et al. (2010)	Basketball, handball, soccer, volleyball	Male	Israel
MacDonald et al. (2009)	American football	Male	USA
MacDonald et al. (2009)	Golf, soccer	Female	USA
Schorer et al. (2010)	Handball	Male/Female	Germany

how these factors affect athlete development, one of the challenges of studying female athletes in the United States (and elsewhere) is the lack of professional leagues available from which to draw. Even the WUSA league studied by MacDonald et al. (2009) had to cease its operations due to lack of financial resources. Such difficulties restrict the pool of athletes from which to sample. In other women's professional sports, such as tennis, there are not enough US athletes at the elite level to allow for proper analysis of a birthplace effect. An alternative would be to investigate the effect in samples of Olympic or National Collegiate Athletic Association (NCAA) athletes, however this may impact (i.e., "water down") definitions of elite or expert.

Other researchers have examined the cultural impact of birthplace by investigating how prevalent these effects are across countries. Studies by Abernethy and Farrow (2005), Baker et al. (2009), Bruner, MacDonald, Pickett, and Côté (2011), Lidor et al. (2010), and Schorer et al. (2010) have researched birthplace across Australia, Europe, and the Middle East. Depending on the country studied, results show slight variations in the optimal city size for producing elite athletes. For example, in their analysis of handball players from Germany, Baker et al. (2009) and Schorer et al. (2010) determined that large cities were just as effective in producing elite athletes as smaller cities. Both of these studies showed that cities of more than 2.5 million inhabitants produced higher than expected rates of elite athletes, although, similar to Côté and colleagues (2006), they noted that cities between 30,000 and 250,000 inhabitants also produced more athletes. Of particular interest in these studies was that in addition to investigating birthplace, Baker et al. and Schorer et al. also considered where athletes were first introduced to the sport (i.e., the location of their first club). They found some disagreement between these two variables, emphasizing the need to adequately measure the variable of interest (i.e., the location associated with an athlete's introduction to sport) to understand the generality of birthplace effects across different geographical environments (e.g., between Canada and Germany).

Lidor et al. (2010) studied basketball, handball, soccer, and volleyball players in Israel, reporting a somewhat different pattern than previous studies. First, they found that basketball was not affected by birthplace, namely that all cities produced athletes at an expected rate. Second, they found that soccer and handball players were overrepresented in cities between 50,000 and 200,000, which concurs with previous results discussed above. Third, they found that cities between 2,000 and 50,000, which were identified as optimal in previous studies (i.e., Côté et al., 2006), did not show overrepresentations of athletes in any sport. In fact, for soccer and volleyball, these cities produced significantly fewer athletes than expected. Finally, they found that cities of less than 2,000 residents produced significantly higher rates of volleyball players, but significantly fewer athletes for soccer.

Although these results do not align perfectly with previous findings, they exemplify, along with the results of Baker et al. (2009) and Schorer et al. (2010) that cultural aspects need to be considered when understanding birthplace effect. More specifically, Baker and colleagues (2009) expanded this idea by discussing how Germany went through significant political changes while the athletes in their sample were developing. Until 1990, Germany was divided into two separate political systems, namely the Federal Republic of Germany and the German Democratic Republic. Each had their own sport system, which uniquely impacted the development of athletes in each segment of the country. Geopolitical changes such as these may partially explain how an athletes' environment affects the development of talent. Alternatively, Lidor et al. (2010) noted the cultural norms underpinning the development of volleyball in Israel. They noted that volleyball has historically been played in very small places (i.e., farm settlements known as Kibbutzes), which may explain why these athletes were overrepresented in cities of less than 2,000 people. Based on these explanations, it is clear that the environmental and cultural makeup of a country can affect the development of elite athletes and should not be neglected in future studies of birthplace.

Birthplace and Other Domains

The evidence discussed above indicates that an athlete's early developmental environment is an important factor for understanding the overall development of elite athletes. However, considering that only a small proportion of athletes will attain elite level status (Danish, 2002), it is important to understand if this factor is associated with other developmental characteristics encountered during sport participation. A recent study by Fraser-Thomas, Côté, and MacDonald (2010) investigated whether city size of birth was associated with indicators of positive youth development in young athletes (e.g., internal indicators such as commitment to learning and positive identity, as well as external indicators such as empowerment and support). Elite level swimmers from large (greater than 500,000) and smaller (less than 500,000) cities completed the Developmental Assets Profile (DAP; Search Institute, 2004) to determine whether athletes from different city sizes developed different types (and amounts) of assets. Results of Fraser-Thomas et al.'s (2010) study demonstrated that athletes from small cities reported significantly more developmental assets than athletes from large cities in three of the eight asset categories (support, boundaries and expectations, and commitment to learning). Although not statistically significant, athletes in small cities reported higher mean values in four of the five remaining asset categories (empowerment, positive values, social competencies, and positive identity), while athletes in large cities reported higher (although nonsignificant) rates of constructive use of time compared to athletes from small cities. Although this study was limited by a small sample, these preliminary results suggest that birthplace effects play a role in domains other than the development of sport expertise.

INTERACTIONS BETWEEN RELATIVE AGE AND BIRTHPLACE

The previous sections show consistent and independent effects for relative age and birthplace, suggesting that both are important in determining an athlete's ability to reach professional levels across a range of sports. However, given the strength of these factors, a reasonable question is whether combining the two variables (i.e., being born early in the calendar year and being from a certain city size) creates a synergistic effect and further increases one's likelihood of becoming an elite athlete. Although the evidence on the interaction between relative age and birthplace is scarce, the findings thus far fail to show a synergistic effect of the two factors.

Côté et al. (2006) investigated the relationship between the two factors by examining the correlations between relative age and birthplace; coefficients ranged between -.02 and .04, suggesting that each factor acts independently from the other. Similarly, Bruner et al. (2011) investigated the interaction between birthplace and relative age using Poisson regression. They included interaction terms in the hope of understanding if the combined effect was useful in predicting athlete success in sport, but these researchers also failed to find a significant interaction between birthplace and relative age. Although interesting, the idea of interactions between relative age and birthplace has not been supported by previous research, and additional work is necessary to validate this conclusion.

CONCLUSION AND FUTURE DIRECTIONS

This chapter has outlined the impact of relative age and birthplace on the development of elite-level athletes. The strength and consistency of the findings across a range of different sports demonstrates that birth date and birth location are factors that should not be neglected when trying to understand talent development in youth. Although these factors do not appear to interact in their influence, further understanding of the mechanisms driving these effects is necessary. Ultimately, minimizing these effects and creating optimal developmental opportunities for all sport participants should provide more youth with the opportunity to develop talent in their sport of interest.

Although the consistency of the patterns in these two effects seems clear, additional research is still required. For example, as illustrated in Table 12.1, much of the work on RAEs has been restricted to team sports (primarily soccer, ice hockey, baseball, and basketball), primarily with male samples (only 2% of relative age data come from female samples), and therefore conclusions drawn from outside this limited sample range should be made with caution. Moreover, although descriptive studies are still needed in areas where samples are limited, researchers should move away from simply describing the effect towards understanding the mechanisms and long-term consequences of this persistent phenomenon.

Furthermore, recent findings suggest RAEs may have greater implications than simply affecting talent development. The RAE has been observed in other domains, such as math and science (Cobley, Baker, Wattie, & McKenna, 2009) and physical education classes (Cobley, Abraham, & Baker, 2008), which highlights that comparisons with peers can take place in multiple domains and could have significant implications on the overall development of children. It is possible that RAEs operate implicitly (similar to the Pygmalion effect described by Rosenthal & Jacobson, 1968), where relatively older athletes are treated in a more favorable manner due to biased comparisons with relatively younger peers. Although difficult to measure, this mechanism highlights the difficulties associated with reducing or eliminating this effect in sport and education.

Similarly, birthplace effects may denote more serious inequalities within the general developmental environments of athletes in particular, and of young people in general. The big-fish-little-pond-effect (BFLPE; Marsh & Parker, 1984; Marsh et al., 2008), for example, suggests that a child's self-concept will not only vary as a function of his or her performance in school, but also as a function of how other individuals within their environment perform. More specifically, a child who performs well in an environment where few perform well (i.e., being the big fish in a small pond) will have a higher self-concept than a child who performs well but is surrounded by many children who also perform well. This effect has not been assessed within models of talent development and the birthplace effect, but it has obvious implications. Within sports, an athlete who performs better than others may develop enhanced self-competency, which will provide her or him with increased levels of confidence. This, in turn, provides the child with more opportunities, as he or she may be identified as more talented by coaches and given more playing opportunities. Children from smaller cities may have less competition and could therefore be identified more easily, given that fewer individuals are competing for the attention of coaches/selection to teams. Although reasonable, this hypothesis requires further research.

Another important aspect to understanding the birthplace effect revolves around why the effect occurs. As noted in the research outlined above, birthplace effects are related to the development of sport expertise; however, direct evidence on the processes that drive this effect is limited. Future research would benefit from qualitative or mixed methodologies for investigating the elements of interest within cities of a certain size, in order to gain knowledge on how certain communities produce higher than expected proportions of elite athletes.

In conclusion, this chapter accentuates birth date and birthplace as factors that relate to athlete development in a complex process that incorporates individual and environmental variables (see also Bronfenbrenner & Morris, 2006). Moreover, these factors highlight how circumstantial athlete development can be, by stressing the need to be in the right place at the right time. To fully understand how sport expertise develops, we need to build on current knowledge by tying in other factors known to affect development. By continuing to investigate the issues raised in this chapter, concurrent with the range of other factors that affect athlete development and performance (many of which are outlined in this book), developmental opportunities for future athletes should improve considerably.

REFERENCES

Abernethy, B., & Farrow, D. (2005). Contextual factors influencing the development of expertise in Australian athletes. *Proceedings of the 11th ISSP World Congress of Sport Psychology.* Sydney, NSW: International Society of Sport Psychology.

Ashworth, J., & Heyndels, B. (2007). Selection bias and peer effects in team sports: The effect of age grouping on earnings of German soccer players. *Journal of Sports Economics, 8*(4), 355–377.

Baker, J., Cobley, S., Montelpare, W. J., Wattie, N., & Faught, B. (2010). Exploring mechanisms of the relative age effect in Canadian Minor Hockey. *International Journal of Sport Psychology, 41,* 148–159.

Baker, J., Janning, C., Wong, H., Cobley, S., & Schorer, J. (in press). Variations in relative age effects in individual sports: Skiing, figure skating and gymnastics. *European Journal of Sports Sciences.*

Baker, J., & Logan, A. J. (2007). Developmental contexts and sporting success: Birthdate and birthplace effects in NHL draftees 2000–2005. *British Journal of Sports Medicine, 41*(8), 515–517.

Baker, J., Schorer, J., Cobley, S., Bräutigam, H., & Büsch, D. (2010). Gender, depth of competition and relative age effects in team sports. *Asian Journal of Exercise and Sport Science, 6*(1), 7–13.

Baker, J., Schorer, J., Cobley, S., Schimmer, G., & Wattie, N. (2009). Circumstantial development and athletic excellence: The role of birth date and birth place. *European Journal of Sport Science, 9*(6), 329–339.

Barnsley, R. H., Thompson, A. H., & Barnsley, P. E. (1985). Hockey success and birthdate: The relative age effect. *Canadian Association for Health, Physical Education, and Recreation, 51,* 23–28.

Bronfenbrenner, U., & Morris, P. A. (2006). The bioecological model of human development. In W. Damon & R. M. Lerner (Eds.), *Handbook of child psychology* (6th ed.) (pp. 793–828). Hoboken, NJ: John Wiley & Sons.

Bruner, M. W., MacDonald, D. J., Pickett, W., & Côté, J. (2011). Cross-cultural examination of birthplace and birthdate in World Junior ice hockey players. *Journal of Sports Sciences, 29,* 1337–1344.

Carlson, R. C. (1988). The socialization of elite tennis players in Sweden: An analysis of player's backgrounds and development. *Sociology of Sport Journal, 5*(3), 241–256.

Coakley, J., & White, A. (1992). Making decisions: Gender and sport participation among British adolescents. *Sociology of Sport Journal, 9*(1), 20–35.

Cobley, S., Abraham, C., & Baker, J. (2008). Relative age effects on physical education attainment and school sport representation. *Physical Education and Sport Pedagogy, 13*(3), 267–276.

Cobley, S., Schorer, J., & Baker, J. (2008). Relative age effects in elite German soccer: A historical analysis. *Journal of Sports Sciences, 26,* 1531–1538.

Cobley, S., Baker, J., Wattie, N., & McKenna, J. (2009). How pervasive are relative age effects in secondary school education? *Journal of Educational Psychology, 101*(2), 520–528.

Cobley, S., Wattie, N., Baker, J., & McKenna, J. (2009). A meta-analytical review of relative age effects in sport: The emerging picture. *Sports Medicine, 39*(3), 235–256.

Côté, J., MacDonald, D. J., Baker, J., & Abernethy, B. (2006). When size matters: Birthplace effects on the development of expertise. *Journal of Sport Science, 24,* 1065–1073.

Curtis, J. E., & Birch, J. S. (1987). Size of community of origin and recruitment to professional and Olympic hockey in North America. *Sociology of Sport Journal, 4*(3), 229–244.

Danish, S. J. (2002). Teaching life skills through sport. In M. Gatz, M. Gessner, & M. Ball-Rokeach (Eds.), *Paradoxes of youth and youth sport* (pp. 49–60). Albany, NY: State University of New York Press.

Delorme, N., Boiché, J., & Raspaud, M. (2009). Relative age effect in female sport: A diachronic examination of soccer players. *Scandinavian Journal of Medicine & Science in Sports, 20,* 509–515.

Delorme, N., Chalabaev, A., & Raspaud, M. (2010). Relative age is associated with sport dropout: Evidence from youth categories of French basketball. *Scandinavian Journal of Medicine & Science in Sports, 21*(1), 120–128.

Fraser-Thomas, J. L., Côté, J., & MacDonald, D. J. (2010). Community size in youth sport settings: Examining developmental assets and sport withdrawal. *Physical and Health Education Academic Journal, 2*(2), 1–9. Retrieved from http://ojs.acadiau.ca/index.php/phenex/article/view/8

Grondin, S., Deschaies, P., & Nault, L. P. (1984). Trimestres de naissance et rendement scolaire [Trimester of birth and scholastic achievement]. *Apprentissage et Socialisation, 16,* 169–174.

Helsen, W. F., Starkes, J. L., & Van Winckel, J. (1998). The influence of relative age on success and dropout in male soccer players. *American Journal of Human Biology, 10*(6), 791–798.

Helsen, W. F., Starkes, J. L., & Van Winckel, J. (2000). Effect of a change in selection year on success in male soccer players. *American Journal of Human Biology, 12*(6), 729–735.

Koz, D., Fraser-Thomas, J., & Baker, J. (2012). Accuracy of professional sports drafts in predicting career potential. *Scandinavian Journal of Science and Medicine in Sports, 22,* e64-e69.

Lidor, R., Côté, J., Arnon, M., Zeev, A., & Cohen-Maoz, S. (2010). Relative age and birthplace effects in Division 1 players: Do they exist in a small country? *Talent Development and Excellence, 2,* 181–192.

MacDonald, D. J., Cheung, M., Côté, J., & Abernethy, B. (2009). Place but not date of birth influences the development and emergence of athletic talent in American Football. *Journal of Applied Sport Psychology, 21,* 80–90.

MacDonald, D. J., King, J., Côté, J., & Abernethy, B. (2009). Birthplace effects on the development of female athletic talent. *Journal of Science and Medicine in Sport, 12*(1), 234–237.

Marsh, H. W., & Parker, J. W. (1984). Determinants of student self-concept: Is it better to be a relatively large fish in a small pond even if you don't learn to swim as well? *Journal of Personality and Social Psychology, 47*(1), 213–231.

Marsh, H. W., Seaton, M., Trautwein, U., Lüdtke, O., Hau, K. T., O'Mara, A. J., & Craven, R. G. (2008). The big-fish-little-pond-effect stands up to the critical scrutiny: Implications for theory, methodology, and future research. *Educational Psychology Review, 20*(3), 319–350.

Rooney, J. F. Jr. (1969). Up from the mines and out from the prairies: Some geographical implications of football. *Geographical Review, 59*(4), 471–492.

Rosenthal, R., & Jacobson, L. (1968). *Pygmalion in the classroom: Teacher expectation and pupils' intellectual development.* New York, NY: Rinehart and Winston.

Schorer, J., Baker, J., Lotz, S., & Büsch, D. (2010). Influence of early environmental constraints on achievement motivation in talented young handball players. *International Journal of Sport Psychology, 41*(1), 42–57.

Schorer, J., Cobley, S., Büsch, D., Bräutigam, H., & Baker, J. (2009). Influences of competition level, gender, player nationality, career stage and playing position on relative age effects. *Scandinavian Journal of Sport Science and Medicine, 19,* 720–730.

Search Institute. (2004). *Developmental assets profile: Preliminary user manual.* Minneapolis, MN: Search Institute.

Vaeyens, R., Güllich, A., Warr, C. R., & Philippaerts, R. (2009). Talent identification and promotion programmes of Olympic athletes. *Journal of Sports Sciences, 27*(13), 1367–1380.

Wattie, N., Baker, J., Cobley, S., & Montelpare, W. J. (2007). A historical examination of relative age effects in Canadian hockey players. *International Journal of Sport Psychology, 38*(2), 178–186.

Wattie, N., Cobley, S., Macpherson, A., Howard, A., Montelpare, W. J., & Baker, J. (2007). Injuries in Canadian youth ice hockey: The influence of relative age. *Pediatrics, 120*(1), 142–148.

Weir, P. L., Smith, K. L., Paterson, C., & Horton, S. (2010). Canadian women's ice hockey: Evidence of a relative age effect. *Talent Development and Excellence, 2*(2), 209–217.

CHAPTER 13

SOCIOLOGICAL ASPECTS OF TALENT DEVELOPMENT

Stephen Harvey, Hyunwoo Jung, and David Kirk

INTRODUCTION

How do talented children develop their ability to become professional athletes? Achieving excellence in sport seems to be not only the result of individual effort involving mental determination and physical power or prowess. The development of any talent implicates a range of factors, including individual characteristics, aspects of the environment, as well as access and opportunity. As such, talent is a multidimensional concept and talent development is a very complex and dynamic process. However, we think the full implications of this view of talent, which we plan to illustrate further in this chapter through consideration of sociological aspects, are rarely recognized. To confirm this point, we need only consider the extent to which the talent development process in sport tends to be limited to physiological and psychological determinants, such as motor and physical ability, evaluation of game intelligence, motivation, and coaches' or parents' perceptions. Accordingly, we propose a closer examination of the possible sociological influences on talent development, which could allow us to gain insight into how social forces such as social class, wealth, and the family impact on talent development. Consider for a moment why there are so many world-leading East African distance runners. How can two soccer players with such different social backgrounds and educational careers such as Frank Lampard and Roy Keane become leading professional footballers in England? Why are there currently so many South Korean female golfers on the Ladies Professional Golfers Association (LPGA) tour? How can one country such as Brazil produce soccer players, gymnasts, and swimmers who are from distinctly different socioeconomic backgrounds?

Of course, much has been made of the statement that "talent is born, not made." The thinking behind this statement has been widely refuted by psychological research, which has demonstrated that a large proportion of talent is derived from both deliberate play and deliberate practice (Côté & Hay, 2002). While many developmental profiles of elite athletes are probably due to their accumulating more deliberate play and/or practice, the access and opportunity to this play/practice is also of central importance to their profiles.

Thus, some of the factors that have already been outlined in other chapters in this text, such as peers (see Chapter 10) and family (see Chapter 11), as well as additional factors such as social class, wealth, gender, race, disability, etc., also interact with individual and psychological determinants to shape talent. Along with Schoon (2000), a number of authors have agreed that there is a need for a multidimensional view of talent (e.g., Bailey & Morley, 2006; Burgess & Naughton, 2010). Such a multidimensional view considers that talent is the expression of many forces that are interdependent, played out in a wider sociocultural context than simply at the individual level. Building on the work of Schoon (2000) and Burgess and Naughton (2010), among others, we will argue in this chapter that talent development is strongly influenced by a number of interrelated factors over the course of the life span. We are aware that there are studies in the literature (e.g., Reilly, Williams, Nevill, & Franks, 2000; Vaeyens et al., 2006) where authors claim their research is multidimensional, but in these only anthropometric, physical, psychological, and sport-specific skills are measured and assessed, typically using solely cross-sectional research designs. Arguably, such studies are not comprehensively multidimensional, since they omit many sociological aspects of talent involving the individual (such as gender, birthplace, race, ethnicity, disability) and their environment or personal circumstances (e.g., family makeup, economic situation, peer influence, access to coaching and education, etc.). Certainly, we feel that there may be a case for some of these sociological aspects to be mediators in any model or framework of talent development.

In this chapter we review the research on sociological aspects of talent development in sport in order to, first, provide an account of the types of research designs most often used, and to, second, examine the substantive sociological aspect of talent that are the focus of these studies. Reflecting on the studies we have reviewed, we then raise and discuss a number of issues for this field of research on talent. We identify some strengths and shortcomings of research design to date and argue for future developments that might better match the complexity of the concept of talent. We also seek to show that more studies are required involving relational analyses of the interactions and interdependency of factors and forces that act within the process of talent development in sport. We begin with a brief note on the method we adopted to review the research studies on which this chapter is based.

A NOTE ON METHOD

Reviewing the literature, we followed the procedures highlighted by Cale and Harris (2009). In accordance with their recommendations we carried out a database search using EBSCOhost (a multidatabase research tool that includes journals from North America, the United Kingdom, Australia, and Europe). Searches used the following terms/combinations of key terms: talent, sport, talent development, talent identification, youth sport, children, young people, sociological, socialization, social, and disability. Using these terms, we conducted multiple searches and crossreferenced until a saturation point was reached (e.g., Cale & Harris, 2009, p. 91). Next, we performed a qualitative analysis of the literature we had identified and retained studies that matched the following criteria:

- It was a study either with and/or about youth sport participants or their participation rates.
- It was a study that reflected on historical aspects of youth sport participation.
- The study included at least one sociological aspect (e.g., gender, race, culture, social class, family, peer relations).

We also included studies that we found referenced in the included studies and that also met the selection criteria. In addition, we included unpublished reports of projects that had been commissioned by relevant bodies in different countries (such as the Kirk, Penney, Carlson & Braiuka, 1998, study in Queensland, Australia—see Table 13.1).

In terms of categorizing the studies, we considered both the type of research design and the focus of the studies in terms of the sociological aspects they included. In the next section we will overview the design types before going on to examine the sociological aspects that formed their focus.

Table 13.1. An Overview of Empirical Studies of Sociological Aspects of Talent Development and Youth Sport Participation (N = 40)

Study/ Country	Cross-Sectional or Longitudinal	Type of Study	Focus	Method	Findings
Fitzgerald (2005) UK (Eng)	Cross-Sectional	Single context multivariate	Embodied conceptions of ability/ disability	Qualitative (Focus group interviews)	A paradigm of normativity prevailed in physical education manifest through conceptions of ability that recognize and value a mesomorphic ideal, masculinity and high levels of motoric competence.
Côté (1999) Canada	Cross-Sectional	Multiple context univariate	Family	Qualitative (interviews)	The role of the family in children's sport involvement is a complex phenomenon because of the diversity of the family context. Concluded that family environment needs to be studied at each stage of a child's development.
Fitzgerald & Kirk (2009) UK (Eng)	Cross-Sectional	Single context multivariate	Family (habitus)/ disability	Qualitative (Focus group interviews)	Three main themes: (a) concerned with the construction and disruption of sporting tastes and other interests, (b) with the generation and conversion of capital through sport, and (c) with the active engagement of these young disabled people in the processes of constructing the *habitus*.

Lauer et al. (2010) USA	Cross-Sectional	Single context univariate	Family (parental relationship & support)	Qualitative (interview)	Revealed three nonfiction stories of three tennis development pathways: smooth, difficult, and turbulent.
Moraes et al. (2000) Brasil	Cross-Sectional	Single context multivariate	Family (parental support)/ Income	Qualitative (interviews)	Young Brazilian pre-elite soccer players reported that they received little familial support when growing up regarding their soccer playing. Most of the players were from poor rural backgrounds where 80% of the total monthly earnings was $150–375.
Rabelo, Moraes, & Salmela (2001) Brasil	Cross-Sectional	Single context univariate	Family (parents)	Qualitative (interviews)	Only 17% of the low class, rural soccer players parents said they made an adjustment in their routines for their soccer playing children.
Wolfenden & Holt (2005) UK (Eng)	Cross-Sectional	Single context univariate	Family (parents)	Qualitative (interviews)	Parents appeared to fulfil the most significant roles in terms of providing emotional and tangible support (with the mother being more involved than the father). Parents were perceived as a source of pressure when they became over-involved in competitive settings. Parents and players were required to make sacrifices.
Gould et al. (2006) USA	Cross-Sectional	Single context univariate	Family (parents)	Quantitative (survey)	Most parents (59%) were seen as having a positive influence on their player's development. However, 36% of parents negatively influenced their child's development.
Fraser-Thomas et al. (2008) Canada	Cross-Sectional	Single context multivariate	Family (parents)	Quantitative (retrospective interview)	Dropouts were more likely to have had parents who were high-level athletes in their youth.
Robinson & Lieberman (2007) USA	Cross-Sectional	Single context multivariate	Family (parents)/ disability	Mixed (questionnaire, activity log, resource manual)	One month after they provided the families of the campers with a parent resource manual, the male participants significantly increased the time that they spent participating in physical activity.
Vianna et al. (2001) Brasil	Cross-Sectional	Single context univariate	Family Income	Qualitative (interviews)	84% of the parents stated that they were forced to re-schedule family routines to accommodate their daughter's participation. 40% of the gymnasts parents had upper-middle class status and earned between $1,500–3,000 per month with 40% of that group earning $3,000 plus and possessing secondary and university education.

Kirk, Carlson, et al. (1997) Australia	Cross-Sectional	Multiple context univariate	Family Income	Mixed (questionnaire followed by interviews)	Family income is a key factor in determining the likelihood of a child's participation in junior sport that challenges the assumption that sport in Australia is open to everybody.
Kay (2000) UK (Eng)	Cross-Sectional	Multiple context multivariate	Family Income/ Lifestyle	Mixed (interviewer-administered questionnaire and interview)	Results revealed the enormous significance of the financial cost of supporting a child's progression to excellence and the impact on family lifestyle.
Durand-Bush (2000) Canada	Cross-Sectional	Multiple context multivariate	Family Income/ Physical and Coaching Resources	Qualitative (interviews)	Parents provided their children with the finances to attain the necessary physical and coaching resources so that they could become the best in their field, even sometimes relocating to better coaching environments.
Kirk, Carlson, et al. (1997) Australia	Cross-Sectional	Multiple context univariate	Family Support	Mixed (questionnaire followed by interviews)	Parents made a substantial contribution to their child's participation in junior sport in terms of time and emotional support.
Rowley (1992) UK (Eng)	Longitudinal	Multiple context multivariate	Family Social class	Mixed	Children from two-parent families were much more likely to progress to levels of sports achievement whereas children from one-parent families were underrepresented. There were fewer children in the four sports studied from the lower socioeconomic groups (measured by parents' work) than from higher socioeconomic groups than was representative of the British population. There were three reasons for the inequality: finance, occupational flexibility, and car ownership of parents.
English Sports Council (1998) UK (Eng)	Cross-Sectional	Multiple context multiivariate	Family Social class	Quantitative (survey)	Of the 924 pre-elite and elite performers across the 12 sports studied, only in rugby league did the social class distribution of players match that of the general population, with the other 11 sports skewed towards children from wealthier backgrounds. Family size and ethnicity also influenced the development of talent.
Laakso et al. (2008) Finland	Longitudinal	Single context univariate	Gender	Quantitative (questionnaire)	There is an upward trend in Finnish adolescents' leisure time physical activity and in organized sport in particular, and that the increase in activity has been greater in girls than boys.

Holt & Morley (2004) UK (Eng)	Cross-Sectional	Multiple context univariate	Gender	Qualitative (interviews)	Girls reported professional/ international ambitions less than boys did. More boys than girls were socialized into sport by their fathers and brothers. More boys attributed their success in sport to physical factors than girls did.
Anderson et al. (2005) USA	Cross-Sectional	Single context multivariate	Gender Disability	Qualitative (interviews)	The responses illustrated the inequities in active recreation opportunities that still exist for girls with disabilities within their communities.
Kantomaa et al. (2007) Finland	Cross-Sectional	Single context multivariate	Gender Family (parent education and income)	Quantitative (questionnaire)	Boys were more often active members of sports clubs than girls. High parental education was associated with adolescents being physically active. High family income was associated with being an active sports club member in boys and girls. Different types of physical activity varied according to family income.
Martin & Smith (2002) USA, AUS, NZ, SA	Cross-Sectional	Multiple context multivariate	Peer Relationships Gender Disability	Quantitative (sport friendship quality scale)	Disability sport is an important vehicle for promoting positive peer relations with females, in particular, seeing their sport friendship as providing more positive benefits than males.
Wright et al. (2003) Australia	Cross-Sectional	Single context univariate	Physical Environment	Qualitative (interviews)	Different spaces and places proved important in the nature of the physical activity available.
Haycock and Smith (2010) UK (Eng)	Cross-Sectional	Single context multivariate	Policy (PE) Disability	Qualitative (focus group interviews)	Using the NCPE as a means to pursue the government's educational inclusion policy goals has unplanned outcomes that undermine the extent to which teachers are able to use inclusion to make a greater contribution to the promotion of young people's experiences of PE. These outcomes may be seen as undesirable consequences emanating from teachers' attempts to manage the contradictory pressures brought about by pursuing the priorities of government.
Curtis & Birch (1987) Canada	Cross-Sectional	Single context multivariate	Relative Age Birth Place	Quantitative	The largest cities are underrepresented as birthplaces of players at each elite level, whereas small towns are overrepresented. Community size does not appear related to the general population of male youths' rate of participation in hockey.

MacDonald et al. (2009) USA	Cross-Sectional	Single context multivariate	Relative Age Birth Place	Quantitative (Monte Carlo simulations)	Players born in cities with populations of less than 500,000 were significantly overrepresented in the NFL. No relative age effects were found for the NFL, possibly due to the elimination/minimization of relative age effects, presumably through the use of sub-classification systems.
Côté et al. (2006) Canada/ USA	Cross-Sectional	Multiple context multivariate	Relative Age Birth Place	Quantitative (Monte Carlo simulations)	A birthplace bias towards smaller cities, with professional athletes being overrepresented in cities of less than 500,000 and underrepresented in cities of 500,000 and over. A birth month/relative age effect (in the form of a distinct bias towards elite athletes being relatively older than their peers) was found for hockey and baseball but not for basketball and golf. Comparative analyses suggested that contextual factors associated with place of birth contribute more influentially to the achievement of an elite level of sport performance than does relative age and these factors are essentially independent in their influences on expertise development.
Ashworth & Heydels (2007) Germany	Cross-Sectional	Single context multivariate	Relative Age/ Income	Quantitative (various statistical measures)	Clear evidence of a month-of-birth-related wage bias with players born late after the cut-off date earning systematically higher wages. This effect was not discernible in all positions; it is strongest for goalkeepers and defenders but not evident for forwards.
Collins & Buller (2003) UK (Eng)	Cross-Sectional	Multiple context univariate	Social Class	Mixed (telephone interviews, social need analysis, documentary analysis)	Majority of participants were from middle class and relatively affluent households. Disproportionately few from lower classes and deprived groups and areas.
Engström (2008) Sweden	Longitudinal	Single context multivariate	Social Class Academic Achievement	Quantitative (questionnaire)	Fifteen year olds with the highest cultural capital (consisting of social class and grades in academic school subjects) in 1968 were five times more likely to be exercising regularly as 53 year olds than their contemporaries with low cultural capital.
Wright & Burrows (2006) Australia	Cross-Sectional	Single context multivariate	Various	Qualitative (phenomenological analysis)	Physical ability is far from a neutral concept and that how it is understood has important consequences for young people in relation to gender, race, and social class.

Humbert et al. (2008) Canada	Cross-Sectional	Single context multivariate	Various	Qualitative (interviews)	Participants identified eight factors that they felt should be addressed in programs and interventions designed to increase the physical activity behaviors of youth.
Carlson (1988) Sweden	Cross-Sectional	Single context multivariate	Various	Qualitative (interviews)	It is not possible to predict who will develop into a world-class tennis player based on individual talent alone. Personal qualifications and early life experiences in combination with social structures, tradition of sport, and tennis culture all worked together in an optimal way, particularly the local club environment and the players' relationships to coaches.
Johnson et al. (2008) USA	Cross-Sectional	Single context multivariate	Various	Qualitative (interviews)	A young swimmers athlete's desires and inherent traits, the efficaciousness of his or her interpersonal relationships, the physical workload experienced, and the level of distractions, interact in a coordinated manner within the context of the athlete's social, structural, and cultural milieu.
MacPhail et al. (2003) UK	Longitudinal	Single context multivariate	Various	Mixed (ethnography – field notes, interviews and a psychometric questionnaire)	The athletics club created a climate for the samplers, intentionally or not, conducive to the development of Siedentop's educative goal, and to a lesser extent the public health and elite development goals.
MacPhail & Kirk (2006) UK (Eng)	Longitudinal	Single context multivariate	Various	Qualitative (ethnography – field notes and interviews)	Four key characteristics of the specialising phase that were evident, one of which was the influence of family, the school, and their clubs.
Scheerder et al. (2005) Belgium	Longitudinal	Single context multivariate	Various	Quantitative (principal component and binary stepwise forward logistic regression analyses)	Structural and positioning variables such as age, sex, and education remain significant determinants for young people's active participation in leisure time sports styles over the observed period of time.
Kirk et al. (1998) Australia	Cross-Sectional	Multiple context multivariate	Various	Mixed (questionnaires and case studies)	Sport participation policy needs to be informed by the interdependency of the factors that impact on young people's participation in sport.

| Elling & Claringbould (2005) Holland | Cross-Sectional (Multiple studies) | Multiple context multivariate | Various | Mixed | Differences in wishes, opportunities, and possibilities to participate in sport and, especially, to participate in specific organizations or types of sports, are still related to unequal access to different economic, social, and cultural resources and the influence of normative images. |
| Smith et al. (2007) UK (Eng) | Cross-Sectional | Single context multivariate | Various (Extracurricular PE) | Quantitative (questionnaire) | Young people's reported levels of extracurricular PE varied significantly and differentially according to gender and, to some extent, social class. The kind of sports and physical activities a school provides appears to be a critical factor in understanding school-level differences in participation particularly among 15–16-year-old girls in lower working class areas. |

TYPES OF RESEARCH DESIGN OF SOCIOLOGICAL STUDIES OF TALENT

We identified two main types of research design—univariate and multivariate. A univariate study focuses on one sociological aspect of talent (e.g., gender; see Holt & Morley, 2004), whereas a multivariate study includes a focus on two or more sociological aspects of talent in the same study (e.g., family and disability; Fitzgerald, 2005). Within these two broad categories, we next asked whether the studies were single- or multiple-context studies. A single context study included only one population group from one sport/activity (e.g., tennis; see Lauer, Gould, Roman, & Pierce, 2010), or case studies such as MacPhail and Kirk's (2006) ethnographic study of a single athletics club in the UK. A multiple context study involved multiple populations from different sports/activities (e.g., Kirk, Carlson, et al. 1997 studied participants in tennis, gymnastics, netball, hockey, cricket, and Australian rules football). These categories (i.e., univariate/multivariate and single/multiple context) were combined to identify four types of studies: (a) single context univariate, (b) single context multivariate, (c) multiple context univariate, and (d) multiple context multivariate. In a final step we asked whether the study was cross-sectional or longitudinal (as defined by the authors where possible), noted whether quantitative or qualitative methodologies (or both, i.e., mixed methods) were employed, and completed a brief synopsis of each study. In total we reviewed 40 studies. More specific details on these studies are outlined in Table 13.1, and the total numbers of each type of study are summarized in Table 13.2.

In reviewing the various studies seen in Table 13.1, we can conclude that a single context multivariate type was the most frequently used research design in studies of the sociological aspects of talent in youth sport. We found all but one of the longitudinal designs (Rowley, 1992) in the single context category, with the majority in the single context multivariate category. The main research design in all categories is therefore cross-sectional, which clearly limits the

Table 13.2. Summary of the Different Types of Research Designs Employed in the Sociological Aspects of Talent Identification Literature

Type of research design	Multiple-context studies	Single context studies	Total
Multivariate studies	8	20	28
Univariate studies	5	7	12
Total	13	27	40

extent to which researchers can comment on the strength of the relationships between sociological aspects of talent. Moreover, an obvious criticism is that most of the quantitative studies employed correlation/predictive statistical methods, and in some cases were unable to show causality for the variables they observed (e.g., Curtis & Birch, 1987; MacDonald, Cheung, Côté, & Abernethy, 2009). Thus, quantitative research may continue to take advantage of developments of more sophisticated statistical techniques, such as multilevel modeling, which may not only add to our understanding of the multidimensional nature of talent, but also help us to consider the variables that influence talent development at *both* the micro and macro levels. We believe it is not possible to explain what may be happening at one level without an understanding of what is going on at the other (Donnelly, 2008). Actions at the micro level include personal (i.e., psychological) and social (i.e., social class, family, etc.) spheres, which are strongly interdependent, while actions at the macro level include, for example, the development of guidelines, policies, and in some cases legislation, with national governing bodies of sport playing an important role at this level. We discuss the implications of this review of research design more fully below, in light of the focus of the 40 studies reviewed.

SOCIOLOGICAL ASPECTS: THE SUBSTANTIVE FOCUS OF STUDIES OF TALENT

For the 40 studies included in this review, we identified five sociological aspects of talent in sport that formed the primary focus of the studies adopting the four research designs. These are family, social class and economic factors, gender, birthplace, and relative age. We also include three studies of other aspects that do not belong to these more frequently researched topics at the end of the birthplace and relative age section. This included one study on the effects of relative age on the wages of professional soccer players in Germany (Ashworth & Heydels, 2007), the physical environment (Wright, MacDonald, & Groom, 2003), and finally, physical education and sport policy for disabled youth in England and Wales (Haycock & Smith, 2010). Thirteen of the studies focused on one sociological aspect of talent (i.e., were univariate studies, see Table 13.2). This does not mean that other aspects were missing, but rather that the interrelationship of aspects was not of central concern. Therefore, in each of the sections below we also consider the 29 other studies we reviewed (see Table 13.2) that adopted multivariate designs, and thus sought to explore interactions and interdependence between two or more sociological aspects of talent.

Family

We found 16 studies that included analysis of the family, eight of which were univariate and centred solely on the family (see Table 13.1). The family is a complex and diverse phenomenon, which plays an important role in youth sport participation and talent development, arguably both positively and negatively (Gould, Lauer, Rolo, & Jannes, 2006; Wolfenden & Holt, 2005), in terms of time (Kirk, Carlson, et al., 1997), emotional support (Robinson & Lieberman, 2007; Wolfenden & Holt, 2005), family lifestyle (Kay, 2000; Vianna, Morares, Salmela, & Mourthé, 2001), size and ethnicity (English Sports Council, 1998; Rowley, 1992), and family relocation (Côté, 1999; Durand-Bush, 2000). Fitzgerald and Kirk (2009) noted the important influence of family on the participation of youth disabled sport participants, while Robinson and Lieberman (2007) outlined the importance of providing a resource manual to parents to help disabled children increase their level of physical activity.

Previous sports participation by parents would appear to be a factor in talent development, with high-level sports participation by parents leading in some cases to early drop-out of their children from sport (Fraser-Thomas, Côté, & Deakin, 2008). At the same time, higher levels of parental education have also been shown to be positively associated with Finnish adolescents being physically active (Kantomaa, Tammelin, Näyhä, & Taanila, 2007).

This research suggests that the family is a primary socializing agency for sport, perhaps the primary agency. What is missing from studies of the family in youth sport is longitudinal research, with only Rowley's (1992) study in this category. This leads us to propose that researchers need to study the family role much more closely over longer periods of time (possibly using ethnographic methods, e.g., MacPhail & Kirk, 2006) to assess how the complex interrelations of the family affect youth sport involvement and talent development (Côté, 1999).

Social Class and Economic Factors

Some of the studies that focused on social class and economic factors were also inevitably related to the family. For example, Kay (2000) in the UK found that there were potential financial costs to supporting progression to excellence within sport. Also in the UK, Collins and Buller (2003) conducted 70 telephone interviews and social need analyses of 319 youths who had participated in a local council's sports participation initiative. These authors found that middle class and relatively affluent households were overrepresented in the study sample, with a disproportionately small number of young people from lower classes and deprived groups and areas. In Australia, Kirk, O'Connor, et al. (1997) reported that family income is a key determinant of a child's participation in junior sport, which challenged the assumption that sport in Australia is open to everyone. This study also showed the considerable differences between sports in terms of costs of participation, particularly for youngsters striving towards the elite level.

These analyses support earlier work from Rowley's (1992) TOYA study, where she found that there were fewer children in the four sports studied (football, gymnastics, swimming, and tennis) from the lower socioeconomic groups (measured by parents' work) than from higher socioeconomic groups, than was representative of the British population. Rowley concluded there were three reasons for this inequality: finances, occupational flexibility, and car ownership of parents. English Sports Council (1998) research also showed that of the 12 sports studied, only in rugby league did the social class distribution of players match that of the general population, with the other 11 sports skewed towards children from wealthier backgrounds. In Canada, Durand-Bush (2000) studied multiple Olympic and World Champions and confirmed that parents provided their children with the finances to attain the necessary physical and coaching resources so that they could become the best in their field.

Using the information from a cross-section of 16-year-old participants from the Northern Finland Birth Cohort of 1986 and their parents, Kantomaa et al. (2007) also found that family income was associated with being an active sports club member. They also showed that different levels of family income are related to participation in particular sports. For example, participation in downhill skiing was associated with higher levels of family income for both boys and girls, while children from lower income groups were more numerous in swimming, ice hockey, bandy, volleyball, and athletics. There was one longitudinal study of social class and economic aspects—Engström's (2008) 38-year study in Sweden. Engström showed that the 15 year olds with the highest cultural capital (consisting of social class and grades in academic school subjects) in 1968 were five times more likely to be physically active regularly as 53 year olds than their contemporaries with lower cultural capital. While these two Scandinavian studies provide many indications of sports participation and its relationship to income, the complex relationships between sociological aspects of talent could be further understood by undertaking ethnographic case studies within each of these cohorts.

Vianna et al. (2001) noted that although elite club gymnasts' parents in Brazil only had primary school education, their earning power in a major city was considerably higher than the parents of soccer players studied by Morares, Salmela, and Rabelo (2000). Most of the soccer players were from poor rural backgrounds where 80% of parents earned $150–375 monthly. In contrast, 40% of the city-dwelling gymnasts' parents earned between $1,500–3,000 per month, with 40% of that group earning $3,000 plus.

In sum, these studies show that social class and economic factors such as family income are key determinants of a child's participation in junior sport and/or being an active sports club member. Family income is also related to participation in particular sports, and this has been shown in Finland and Brazil, where those possessing the highest cultural capital in Sweden are more likely to be physically active. However, future studies need to continue to examine the relationship between income and sports participation in children from both the micro and macro perspective, using the guidelines we highlighted previously in this chapter.

Gender

A number of studies have reported gender differences in youth sport that relate to talent development. Kantomaa et al. (2007) found that boys were more often active members of sports clubs than girls. In their univariate study, Holt and Morley (2004) noted girls reported professional/international ambitions less than boys did, more boys than girls were socialized into sport by their fathers and brothers, and more boys attributed their success in sport to physical factors than did girls. Linking gender with disability sport, Anderson, Bedini, and Moreland

(2005) outlined how girls with disabilities faced a "double whammy" (p. 78), as they illustrated the inequities in active recreational opportunities that still exist for girls with disabilities within their communities.

In a Finnish longitudinal study on physical activity from 1977–2007, Laakso, Telama, Nupponen, Rimpelä, and Pere (2008) revealed that there was an upward trend in Finnish adolescents' leisure time physical activity, and in organized sport in particular. Showing the benefits of longitudinal analysis, Laakso and colleagues noted a different trend to the cross-sectional study of Kantomaa et al. (2007), in that they discovered there had been a greater increase in physical activity over the past 30 years for girls when compared to boys. In a cross-sectional study of 150 disability sport participants (85 male and 65 female) from four different countries, with 17 disability types, Martin and Smith (2002) found that females in particular saw their sport friendship as providing more positive benefits than did the male study participants.

In sum, gender can restrict sports participation, and can even provide a "double whammy" for some girls when combined with additional determinants such as disability and the psychosocial factors associated with sport participation. More research on the interaction of gender with other factors such as social class and family income is needed, so that we can gain an even deeper understanding of how this may influence children's talent development. What is sure at the moment is that boys continue to be more likely than girls to capitalize on opportunities they receive for developing their talent in sport.

Birthplace and Relative Age

The relative age effect (RAE) was initially used in studies that determined scholastic success (Delorme & Raspaud, 2008). "'Relative age' means the age difference existing between two children, a difference that is due to the cut-off dates chosen to define school year" (Delorme & Raspaud, 2008. p. 235). RAE has come to prominence in the sport literature since its first publication by Grondin, Deshaies, and Nault in 1984 (cited in Delorme & Raspaud, 2008. p. 235). Since then a number of studies on RAE have been published, on a range of sport contexts in the youth sport domain, with football (soccer) (e.g., Gutiérrez, Vicedo, Villora, & Jordán, 2010; Helsen, Van Winckel, & Williams, 2005; Mujika et al., 2009; see also Chapter 12 in this text) being the most studied. Studies have also been published in a wide range of contexts in the youth sport domain including basketball (e.g., Delorme & Raspaud, 2008), baseball (e.g., Thompson, Barnsley, & Stebelsky, 1992), gymnastics (e.g., Baxter-Jones, 1995), ice hockey (e.g., Hurley et al., 2001), swimming (e.g., Baxter-Jones, Helms, Maffull, Baines-Preece, & Preece, 1995), and tennis (e.g., Baxter-Jones et al., 1995; Giacomini, 1999). Cobley, Abraham, and Baker (2008) have also found RAEs within school physical education contexts, where current age grouping, assessment, and selection strategies served to compound RAE. Observations of school sport representation data, for example, showed that a higher frequency of pupils born in the first quartile of the school year represented the school in extracurricular teams across genders and sports (netball, soccer, rounders, and rugby). These numerous research studies demonstrate the potential cognitive, physical, and biological variability between young people within an age-grouped cohort (Musch & Grondin, 2001), which may potentially influence talent identification and development.

While RAEs are of interest in their own right, these have recently been combined in research alongside birthplace in an attempt to study birthplace relative age effects. Curtis and Birch (1987) were the first authors to note that the largest cities were underrepresented as birthplaces of players at the elite level, whereas small towns were overrepresented. In an extension to this line of research, Côté, MacDonald, Baker, and Abernethy (2006) and Mac-Donald, Cheung, Côté, and Abernethy (2009) have linked birthplace to RAEs. These studies have substantiated the findings that there is a birthplace bias towards smaller cities, with professional athletes (Côté et al., 2006; American football—see MacDonald et al., 2009) being overrepresented in cities with a population of less than 500,000 and underrepresented in cities of 500,000 and over (see also Chapter 12 in this text). And while a relative age effect (in the form of a distinct bias towards elite athletes being relatively older than their peers) was found for hockey and baseball but not for basketball and golf (in the 2006 study by Côté and colleagues), comparative analyses suggested that contextual factors associated with place of birth contributed more to the achievement of an elite level of sport performance than did relative age. The authors considered that these factors were essentially independent in their influences on expertise development. Similarly, while no RAEs were found for athletes in the National Football League (American football) in the study by MacDonald et al. (2009), there was, again, an overrepresentation of professional athletes from cities of less than 500,000 population and an underrepresentation in cities of 500,000 and over. These authors argued that the environment in smaller cities seemed to facilitate the development and/or emergence of athletic talent in American football, further concluding that birthplace effects are likely to be mediated by psychosocial factors such as positive relationships, opportunities to belong, positive social norms, etc.

Rather than studying RAE and birthplace, Ashworth and Heyndels (2007) analyzed how age grouping in youth competitions and soccer education programs affected wages at the professional level with (native) German soccer players. The authors provided evidence of a month-of-birth-related wage bias with players born late after the cut-off date earning systematically higher wages, though this effect was not discernible in all positions and was strongest for goalkeepers and defenders.

In addition, Wright, Macdonald, and Groom (2003) studied the physical environment, and concluded that different spaces and places affect the nature of the physical activity available. This notion is supported by research in the UK cited in this chapter, where facility availability and location influenced issues with talent development (Collins & Buller, 2003). Using figurational sociology, Haycock and Smith (2010) revealed the importance of the proper implementation of government policy at the macrosociological level in affording disabled participants avenues to participate in sport and develop their talent at the micro level. Figurational sociology is useful in this regard, as it looks to bridge the gap between macro (i.e., structural development of society) and micro (individual agents' behavior) sociology, further examining not only the present but also researching the past to understand the complex relationships between variables (Hopkins, 2008).

In sum, RAEs have been shown to exist in a number of different sports. However, the contextual factors associated with place of birth contributed more to the achievement of an elite level of sport performance than did relative age itself. Sports governing bodies and associations need, therefore, to understand how they can continue to eliminate/minimize RAEs through subclassification systems (MacDonald et al., 2009), and how an understanding of the physical and psychosocial environment of the athlete may contribute significantly to access and opportunity for young people to be engaged in sport, and that these elements may often be more significant determinants of continued participation in sport and talent development than the biological and physical aspects of talent.

The Interaction and Interdependence of Sociological Aspects of Talent

Nine of the 28 studies adopting multivariate designs explicitly considered the interactions of various sociological aspects, further illustrating the complexity of youth sport participation and talent development (see Tables 13.1 and 13.2). For example, in a classic study on tennis by Carlson (1988), he noted that qualifications and early life experiences in combination with social structures, tradition of sport, and tennis culture all worked together in an optimal way, specifically in the local club environment and in the players' relationships to coaches. This study was one of several that considered a macro sociocultural perspective in their analysis (see also Elling & Claringbould, 2005; Johnson et al., 2008; Kirk et al., 1998; MacPhail, Gorley, & Kirk, 2003; Smith, Thurston, Green, & Lamb, 2007).

Smith et al. (2007) showed that extracurricular physical education participation in North West England and North Wales varied significantly and differentially according to gender and, to some extent, social class. These authors further cited the school as an influence on this participation, particularly among 15- to 16-year-old girls where higher rates of female participation (particularly in lower working class areas) were gained when a particular blend of sports and physical activities were available in extracurricular provision.

In a study of the socioeconomic determinants of junior sport participation in Australia, Kirk et al. (1998) argued that "individual motivation to participate is only one of a range of interdependent socioeconomic determinants of sport participation. Sport participation policy needs to be informed by the interdependency of the factors that impact on young people's participation in sport" (p. 1).

The authors concluded that for young people who wish to play club sport, the capability of the family to provide economic, social, and emotional support may be of central importance. However, they found that the traditional nature of sport provision by community bodies such as clubs may be a key factor in limiting the numbers of young people who play sport, particularly girls. Kirk et al. (1998) contend that alternative forms of provision to community sports clubs, including inexpensive local and informal activities, may hold appeal for a significant number of young people.

The findings of this Australian study were echoed in Kirk and MacPhail's (2001) report commissioned by the Institute of Youth Sport in the UK, noting that "the interests of young people must come before the interests of a sport or other party.... [And] modified forms of sports and informal competition are recommended from a talent development perspective" (p. 23).

Furthermore, a study by the English Sports Council in 1998 on the development of sporting talent across 12 different sports revealed that "the opportunity to realise sporting potential is significantly influenced by an individual's social background ... [and] ... clearly affect the country's ability to compete and win in international competition" (p. 13).

DISCUSSION

There are a number of issues we think arise from this review of research on the sociological aspects of talent in sport in terms of what we have learned, where there appear to be gaps in the research, and consequently on future directions in this field. We begin with some reflections on research design before going on to consider issues relating to the substantive sociological aspects of talent.

Reflecting on Research Design

As we noted, a large proportion of the research we reviewed is cross-sectional in nature. Only six studies from the 40 included in our analysis were longitudinal. Of these, three used the same cohort (Engström, 2008; Laakso et al., 2008; Rowley, 1992) while one study drew on data from four cohorts at longitudinal time points (Scheerder, Taks, Vanreusel, & Renson, 2005). The studies by MacPhail and Kirk (2006) and MacPhail et al. (2003) drew on data from 21-month and 18-month ethnographies, respectively. The strength of longitudinal studies is that they provide insights into the relationships between process and outcomes, which is important in relation to a multidimensional concept such as talent in sport. More longitudinal sociological research on talent is needed (Côté, 1999).

At the same time, only one of the longitudinal studies employed a mixed-method design and within multiple contexts (Rowley, 1992). Of the nine mixed-method studies we identified, again only Rowley's study was longitudinal, albeit many were multiple context (e.g., Kirk et al., 1998; Collins & Buller, 2003). A mixed-method longitudinal design could involve researchers undertaking small-scale case studies, ethnographies, and/or interviews to support the findings from quantitative data gained from larger samples of survey research (Rowley, 1992). These data can then be matched to data taken from different domains, such as physiological and psychological measures (Kirk & MacPhail, 2001; Rowley, 1992). We also think that a wider range of qualitative methods could be employed, certainly with more ethnographic studies in multiple contexts that examine multiple sociological aspects of talent (Kirk et al., 1998). Indeed, one other significant aspect to note from our review was the bias toward single-context studies (N = 27). In terms of quantitative research, many more relationships between significant determinants of talent need to be examined within the sociological domain. Once again, we also need to examine how these interact with measurements taken in other domains, such as psychology and physiology (Kirk & MacPhail, 2001; Rowley, 1992).

Few of the studies offer genuinely relational analyses of the intersections of sociological aspects of talent, in terms of the relationships between policies and practices, as well as from both micro and macro perspectives. An example of one study that is relational in nature is the figurational sociology (or process sociology) study by Haycock and Smith (2010), which investigated the implementation of the National Curriculum Physical Education (NCPE) in relation to inclusion of pupils with disabilities. Most other studies, however, have been completed without consideration of the intersections and interactions of these macro and micro sociological aspects, especially as a long-term process.

Studies have been limited geographically to Western Europe, North America, and Australia, with the exception of Brazil. It might be argued that we need to broaden the geography of sociological studies of talent, since youth sport is increasingly a global phenomenon. Furthermore, it is not appropriate to generalize from studies carried out in developed countries to the identification and development of talent in countries in the developing world. We need to know more about the cultural heritage of sports such as rugby in New Zealand, baseball in the Dominican Republic, Central American boxers, African distance runners, and badminton/table tennis in Asia, and how the different cultures of these countries and regions affect talent development (Salmela & Morares, 2003). We also need to understand more about how local cultures are affected by government policies and their effect on talent development. For example, while the UK's population of Asian/Asian British people is 5.87% (Rogers, 2011), only one Asian player has ever played in the English Premier League (Rai, 2011). Reasons cited for children not participating in football (sport) are sociocultural and historical (e.g., the initial need for Asian families new to the UK to simply work to put food on the table, families' perception of sport not being a viable career path for their children, etc.). While some English Premier League clubs like Chelsea have run initiatives to get more children from Asian backgrounds into the game, more intervention may be needed. The English Football Association, for example, may need to adopt notions of subclassification systems (MacDonald et al., 2009), so that all children will have similar access and opportunity for playing football. Additional efforts can be made to promote an appropriate physical and psychosocial environment to support every (Asian) child's desire to achieve their talent in football.

In a second example, research on South Korean women golfers has shown that the two most notable factors behind the victories of these Korean golfers on the LPGA tour are (a) parents' early discovery and devotion, and (b) Korean social structures and culture. Where the social structures and norms have worked against the Asian/Asian British population with football in the UK, Korean social structures and culture have worked in favor of many women pursuing a career in golf. It is acceptable for daughters in Korea to follow such a career path, because it is deemed that sons would have to support their family financially, and a career in golf may not provide stable and lucrative incomes for them. As women's earnings would only be the second source of family income in Korea, young women can afford to take a risk for a career in professional golf (Shin & Nam, 2004). More longitudinal, multivariate, and ethnographic studies examining these phenomena are needed.

Reflecting on the Substantive Sociological Aspects of Talent

We suggest that there is much to learn about talent in sport from sociological studies. We know that in most cases a supportive family environment is a requirement for the development of talented sportspeople. We have suggested that the family is possibly the primary socialization agency in youth sport, although this point does not seem to be acknowledged by policy-makers and strategists for sport development. We have learned that economic issues are important determinants of talent development, the cost of participation varies among sports, and that youth sport in many countries remains inaccessible to lower income groups. This is particularly the case in Western countries, where the inequality gap is growing (Wilkinson & Pickett, 2009). We know that boys continue to be more likely than girls to capitalize on the opportunities they receive to develop their talent in sport, and in any case elite male performers continue to benefit economically at much higher levels than women. We have learned, too, from the studies of birthplace and relative age that the structure of sports participation and the provision of local facilities and opportunities to play are crucial to the development of sporting careers. For example, the quality and quantity of play and practice opportunities in smaller cities may be more conducive to unstructured play activities which "offer fewer safety concerns, better access to open spaces and less competing sources of leisure time for young people … and, possibly, the less competitive psychosocial environment of cities" (Côté et al., 2006, p. 1072).

We suggest that these studies teach us something too about the concept of talent itself. Talent is unescapably multidimensional (Walker, Nordin-Bates, & Redding, 2010), and develops due to the interdependency and interaction of a number of different factors (Kirk et al., 1998). Indeed, talent may arise in different sports for a multitude of different reasons. Talent and its development in youth sport will be influenced by whether the sport is an individual or team sport, by the culture of the country that the person lives in, by family circumstances, and by access to coaching and facilities. The factors that come together to assist one person to develop talent in one sport may not work to the same effect in another sport or in another country or a location within the same country.

It is this multidimensionality that makes the emergence of talent so difficult to predict. Consequently, the development of a sophisticated understanding of talent to match the complexity of the concept would appear to be necessary and would have implications for the future of research in this field. In short, we need more relational analyses of the factors that shape and develop talent. A good example here is the research on relative age and birth date. The relative age studies tend not to take into consideration the multitude of other factors that may impinge on talent development. Studies of relative age could be developed as multivariate projects, and in so doing provide more contextual information. For example, when describing the participants and their performance levels, they could provide more detail on what leagues the participants are competing in and what minimization effects to relative age there are in the leagues (MacDonald et al., 2009), and further, provide more detail about the links to other micro- and macro-level determinants such as school, class, family, culture, and time of development.

We also note that the limited connections to sports policies in the relevant countries of implementation need to be explored and linked to wider sociocultural contexts. In Western countries, which have been the majority focus of this review, there is little evidence, certainly in the UK, that the academic literature has been consulted when sports policy is being configured, and also there has been little evaluation of sports policy and its impact on developing prospective talented athletes. This has been compounded by the fact that researchers of sports policy from a sociological perspective have rarely engaged with sport pedagogy researchers to develop the field of research in sports policy, not only at the macro or structural level, but to further consider the nature of the individual in this relational analysis. Sport pedagogy researchers would be able to support sociologists in researching the impact of a change in policy at the macro level and how these changes are played out at the level of the individual.

CONCLUSION

Our purpose in this chapter was to review the research on the sociological aspects of talent development. We considered both the types of research design employed in the studies and the substantive focus of this research. Reflecting on what we learned from this review, we have argued for more multivariate, multicontext, mixed-method, and longitudinal research designs that can produce data that will permit researchers to better understand the multidimensionality of the concept of talent and the complex, dynamic and hard-to-predict nature of the talent development process. We think that a focus on the sociological aspects of talent concerns simple and simplistic notions of talent, since such research reveals the interacting and interdependent forces at work in talent development. We also argued for research in developing as well as developed countries, since youth sport is increasingly a global phenomenon and sociological research shows that local cultures and circumstances play key roles in talent development.

Notwithstanding the complexity and unpredictability of talent development in sport and the consequent need for relational analyses, we acknowledge the weight of evidence from this field of research that suggests that in developed countries, children from relatively wealthier backgrounds are likely to develop their potential in sport more readily than children from relatively poorer backgrounds. As levels of inequality grow in countries such as the UK and the US (Wilkinson & Pickett, 2009), we think that inequality produced by the intersecting factors of family, economy, gender, disability, ethnicity, and place and date of birth, and how these operate at the macro and micro levels, should be the core concern of social science research into talent development. We need, therefore, to develop and evaluate policies that may or may not be based on this review of the research literature, so that we can understand which elements have the greatest influence on talent development. For example, we know that birthplace is a more important factor than relative age, but this is not to say that it is more important than family income or gender. If we understand these inequalities in more depth and the relational character of them, we can ensure that all children will be given the same access and opportunity to develop their talent, irrespective of some factors that have been predetermined for them (e.g., birthplace, gender, etc.). Knowing which predetermined factors may be advantageous and/or disadvantageous will help in setting the appropriate environments so that all children can achieve their potential, regardless of this access and opportunity. This is not to say that children from within and between different countries and cultures may not be more likely to achieve success in different sports, as we see in Brazil with soccer and East African running, but a greater understanding of the role that local cultures and circumstances play in talent development is required to build an appropriate infrastructure for promoting talent in a globalized world, in order to ensure that sport is for all and not only for a select few (Kirk et al., 1998).

REFERENCES

Anderson, D. A., Bedini, L. A., & Moreland, L. (2005). Getting all girls into the game: Physically active recreation for girls with disabilities. *Journal of Park and Recreation Administration, 23*(4), 78–103.

Ashworth, J., & Heyndels, B. (2007). Selection bias and peer effects in team sports: The effect of age grouping on earnings of German soccer players. *Journal of Sports Economics, 8*(4), 355–377.

Bailey, R., & Morley, D. (2006). Towards a model of talent development in physical education. *Sport, Education and Society, 11*(3), 211–230.

Baxter-Jones, A., Helms, P., Maffull, N., Baines-Preece, J., & Preece, M. (1995). Growth and development of male gymnasts, Swimmers, soccer and tennis players: A longitudinal study. *Annals of Human Biology, 22*(5), 381–394.

Burgess, D. J., & Naughton, G. A. (2010). Talent development in adolescent team sports: A review. *International Journal of Sports Physiology & Performance, 5*(1), 103–116.

Cale, L., & Harris, J. (2009). Fitness testing in physical education—a misdirected effort in promoting healthy lifestyles and physical activity? *Physical Education and Sport Pedagogy, 14*(1), 89–108.

Carlson, R. (1988). The socialisation of elite tennis players in Sweden: An analysis of the players' backgrounds and development. *Sociology of Sport Journal, 5*(3), 241–256.

Cobley, S., Abraham, C., & Baker, J. (2008). Relative age effects on physical education attainment and school sport representation. *Physical Education and Sport Pedagogy, 13*(3), 267–276.

Collins, M. F., & Buller, J. R. (2003). Social exclusion from high-performance sport: Are all talented young sports people being given an equal opportunity of reaching the Olympic podium? *Journal of Sport & Social Issues, 27*(4), 420–442.

Côté, J. (1999). The influence of the family in the development of talent in sport. *The Sport Psychologist, 13*, 395–417.

Côté, J., & Hay, J. (2002). Children's involvement in sport: A developmental perspective. In J. M. Silver & D. Stevens (Eds.), *Psychological foundations of sport* (pp. 484–502). Boston, MA: Allyn & Bacon.

Côté, J., MacDonald, D. J., Baker, J., & Abernethy, B. (2006). When "where" is more important than "when": Birthplace and birthdate effects on the achievement of sporting expertise. *Journal of Sports Sciences, 24*(10), 1065–1073.

Curtis, J. E., & Birch, J. S. (1987). Size of community of origin and recruitment to professional and Olympic hockey in North America. *Sociology of Sport Journal, 4*(3), 229–244.

Delorme, N., & Raspaud, M. (2009). The relative age effect in young French basketball players: A study on the whole population. *Scandinavian Journal of Medicine & Science in Sports, 19*(2), 235–242.

Donnelly, P. (2008). Sport and social theory. In B. Houlihan (Ed.), *Sport and society: A student introduction* (2nd ed.) (pp. 11–32). London, UK: Sage.

Durand-Bush, N. (2000). *The development and maintenance of expert athletic performance: Perceptions of World and Olympic champions, their parents and coaches* (Unpublished doctoral dissertation). Faculty of Education, University of Ottawa, Ottawa, Ontario, Canada. Retrieved from http://www.ruor.uottawa.ca/en/handle/10393/8462

Elling, A., & Claringbould, I. (2005). Mechanisms of inclusion and exclusion in the Dutch sports landscape: Who can and wants to belong? *Sociology of Sport Journal, 22*(4), 498–515.

English Sports Council. (1998). *The development of sporting talent, 1997.* London, UK: English Sports Council.

Engström, L. (2008). Who is physically active? Cultural capital and sports participation from adolescence to middle age—a 38-year follow-up study. *Physical Education and Sport Pedagogy, 13*(4), 319–343.

Fitzgerald, H. (2005). Still feeling like a spare piece of luggage? Embodied experiences of (dis)ability in physical education and school sport. *Physical Education & Sport Pedagogy, 10*(1), 41–59.

Fitzgerald, H., & Kirk, D. (2009). Identity work: Young disabled people, family and sport. *Leisure Studies, 28*(4), 469–488.

Fraser-Thomas, J. L., Côté, J., & Deakin, J. (2008). Examining adolescent sport dropout and prolonged engagement from a developmental perspective. *Journal of Applied Sport Psychology 20*, 318–333.

Giacomini, C. P. (1999). Association of birthdate with success of nationally ranked junior tennis players in the United States. *Perceptual and Motor Skills, 89*(2), 381–386.

Gould, D., Lauer, L., Rolo, C., Jannes, C., & Pennisi (2006). Understanding the role parents play in tennis success: A national survey of junior tennis coaches. *British Journal of Sports Medicine, 40*(7), 632–636.

Grondin, S., Deshaies, P., & Nault, L. P. (1984). Quarter of birth and participation in hockey and volleyball. *La Revue Que 'becoise del' Activite' Physique, 2*, 97–103. (In French: English abstract).

Gutiérrez del Campo, D. G. D., Vicedo, J., Villora, S., & Jordán, O. (2010). The relative age effect in youth soccer players from Spain. *Journal of Sports Science and Medicine, 9*, 190–198.

Haycock, D., & Smith, A. (2010). Inadequate and inappropriate? The assessment of young disabled people and pupils with special educational needs in National Curriculum Physical Education. *European Physical Education Review, 16*(3), 283–300.

Helsen, W. F., Van Winckel, J., & Williams, A. M. (2005). The relative age effect in youth soccer across Europe. *Journal of Sport Sciences, 23*(6), 629–636.

Holt, N., & Morley, D. (2004). Gender differences in psychosocial factors associated with athletic success during childhood. *The Sport Psychologist, 18*(2), 138–53.

Hopkins, G. (2008). *A sociological investigation in to the dynamic power balance between the football league and football association: Using the football league cup as a window for exploration* (Unpublished doctoral thesis). University of Chester. Retrieved from http://chesterrep.openrepository.com/cdr/handle/10034/64013

Humbert, M. L., Chad, K. E., Bruner, M. W., Spink, K. S., Muhajarine, N., Anderson, K. D., Girolami, T. M., Odnokon, P., & Gryba, C. (2008). Using a naturalistic ecological approach to examine the factors influencing youth physical activity across Grades 7 to 12. *Health Education & Behavior, 35*(2), 158–173.

Johnson, M., Castillo, Y., Sacks, D., Cavazos Jr., J., Edmonds, W., & Tenenbaum, G. (2008). "Hard work beats talent until talent decides to work hard": Coaches' perspectives regarding differentiating elite and non-elite swimmers. *International Journal of Sports Science & Coaching, 3*(3), 417–430.

Kantomaa, M., Tammelin, T., Näyhä, S., & Taanila, A. (2007). Adolescents' physical activity in relation to family income and parents' education. *Preventive Medicine, 44*(5), 410–415.

Kay, T. (2000). Sporting excellence: a family affair? *European Physical Education Review, 6*(2), 151–169.

Kirk, D., & MacPhail, A. (2001). *Talent identification, selection and development.* Institute of Youth Sport: Loughborough University.

Kirk, D., Penney, D., Carlson, T., & Braiuka, S. (1998). *Socio-economic determinants of junior sport participation in Queensland.* University of Queensland Foundation.

Kirk, D., Carlson, T., O'Connor, A., Burke, P., Davis, K., & Glover, S. (1997). The economic impact on families of children's participation in junior sport. *The Australian Journal of Science and Medicine in Sport, 29*(2), 27–33.

Kirk, D., O'Connor, A., Carlson, T., Burke, P., Davis, K., & Glover, S. (1997). Time commitments in junior sport: Social consequences for participants and their families. *Journal of Sport Behaviour, 20,* 51–73.

Laakso, L., Telama, R., Nupponen, H., Rimpelä, A., & Pere, L. (2008). Trends in leisure time physical activity among young people in Finland, 1977–2007. *European Physical Education Review, 14*(2), 139–155.

Lauer, L., Gould, D., Roman, N., & Pierce, M. (2010). How parents influence junior tennis players' development: Qualitative narratives. *Journal of Clinical Sport Psychology, 4*(1), 69–92.

MacDonald, D. J., Cheung, M., Côté, J., & Abernethy, B. (2009). Place but not date of birth influences the development and emergence of athletic talent in American football. *Journal of Applied Sport Psychology, 21,* 80–90.

MacPhail, A., & Kirk, D. (2006). Young people's socialisation into sport: Experiencing the specializing phase. *Leisure Studies, 25*(1), 57–74.

MacPhail, A., Gorely, T., & Kirk, D. (2003). Young people's socialisation into sport: A case study of an athletic club. *Sport, Education and Society, 8*(2), 251–268.

Martin, J. J., & Smith, K. (2002). Friendship quality in youth disability sport: Perceptions of a best friend. *Adapted Physical Activity Quarterly, 19*(4), 472–482.

Morares, L. C., Salmela, J. H., & Rabelo, A. (2000). The development of performance of young Mineiro soccer players. *Anais do primeiro congress cíentifico Latíno-Americano.* Fundep: São Paulo.

Mujika, I., Vaeyens, R., Matthys, S., Santisteban, J., Goiriena, J., & Philippaerts, R. M. (2009). The relative age effect in a professional football club setting. *Journal of Sports Sciences, 27*(11), 1153–1158.

Musch, J., & Grondin, S. (2001). Unequal competition as an impediment to personal development: A review of the relative age effect in sport. *Developmental Review, 21,* 147–167.

Rabelo, A., Morares, L. C., & Salmela, J. H. (2001). The role of parents in the development of young Brazilian athletes in soccer. *Proceedings of the Association for the Advancement of Applied Sport Psychology Conference,* Orlando (Florida), 52–53.

Rai, R. (2011). Why are there so few British Asians playing professional football? Sportsmail investigates...*The Daily Mail online.* Retrieved from http://www.dailymail.co.uk/sport/football/article-1371544/Why-British-Asians-playing-professional-football-Sportsmail-investigates-.html#ixzz1fCt9DmjI

Reilly, T., Williams, M., Nevill, A., & Franks, A. (2000). A multidisciplinary approach to talent identification in soccer. *Journal of Sports Sciences, 18*(9), 695–702.

Robinson, B. L., & Lieberman, L. J. (2007). Influence of a parent resource manual on physical activity levels of children with visual impairments. *RE: View, 39*(3), 129–139.

Rogers, S. (2011). The ethnic population of England and Wales broken down by local authority. *The Guardian.* Retreived from http://www.guardian.co.uk/news/datablog/2011/may/18/ethnic-population-england-wales

Rowley, S. R. W. (1992). *Training of young athletes (TOYA) and the identification of talent.* London, UK: Sports Council.

Salmela, J. H., & Morares, L. C. (2003). Development of expertise: The role of coaching, families and cultural contexts. In J. L. Starkes & K. A. Ericsson (Eds.), *Expert performance in sport: advances in research on sport expertise* (pp. 275–293). Champaign, IL: Human Kinetics.

Scheerder, J., Taks, M., Vanreusel, B., & Renson, R. (2005). Social changes in youth sports participation styles 1969–1999. The case of Flanders (Belgium). *Sport, Education & Society, 10*(3), 321–241.

Schoon, I. (2000). A life span approach to talent development. In K. A. Heller, F. J. Mönks, R. J. Sternberg, & R. F. Subotnik (Eds.), *International handbook of giftedness and talent* (pp. 213–226). Oxford, UK: Elsevier.

Shin, E., & Nam, E. (2004). Culture, gender roles, and sport. *Journal of Sport & Social Issues, 28*(3), 223–244.

Smith, A., Thurston, M., Green, K., & Lamb, K. (2007). Young people's participation in extracurricular physical education: A study of 15–16 year olds in North-West England and North-East Wales. *European Physical Education Review, 13*(3), 339–368.

Thompson, A., Barnsley, R., & Stebelsky, G. (1992). Baseball performance and the relative age effect: Does Little League neutralize birthdate selection bias? *Perceptual and Motor Skills, 81,* 952–954.

Vaeyens, R. R., Malina, R. M., Janssens, M. M., Van Renterghem, B. B., Bourgois, J. J., Vrijens, J. J., & Philippaerts, R. M. (2006). A multidisciplinary selection model for youth soccer: The Ghent Youth Soccer Project. *British Journal of Sports Medicine, 40*(11), 928–934.

Vianna, J., Moraes, L., Salmela, J., & Mourthé, K. (2001). The role of parents in the development of young Brazilian athletes in rhythmic gymnastics. *Proceedings of the 16th Annual Conference of the Association for Advancement of Applied Psychology, Orlando, Florida, 61.*

Walker, I. J., Nordin-Bates, S. M., & Redding, E. (2010). Talent identification and development in dance: A review of the literature. *Research in Dance Education, 11*(3), 167–191.

Wilkinson, R., & Pickett, K. (2009). *The spirit level: Why more equal societies almost always do better.* London, UK: Allen Lane.

Wolfenden, L., & Holt, N. (2005). Talent development in elite junior tennis: Perceptions of players, parents, and coaches. *Journal of Applied Sport Psychology, 17,* 108–126.

Wright, J., & Burrows, L. (2006). Re-conceiving ability in physical education: A social analysis. *Sport, Education & Society, 11*(3), 275–291.

Wright, J., MacDonald, D., & Groom, L. (2003). Physical activity and young people: Beyond participation. *Sport Education and Society, 8*(1), 17–34.

Index

About the Editors

Dr. Jean Côté is a professor in and director of the School of Kinesiology and Health Studies at Queen's University at Kingston in Canada. His research interests are in the areas of sport expertise, children in sport, coaching, and positive youth development. Dr. Côté holds a cross appointment as a visiting professor in the School of Human Movement Studies at the University of Queensland in Australia. He has published several influential papers on a variety of sport expertise, youth sport, and coaching topics. Dr. Côté is regularly invited to present his work to both sport governing organizations and at academic conferences throughout the world. Dr. Côté was a co-editor of the *International Journal of Sport and Exercise Psychology* from 2008–2011. He is presently, or has been, on the editorial boards of the *Journal of Applied Sport Psychology, The Sport Psychologist,* the *International Review of Sport and Exercise Psychology,* the *Asian Journal in Exercise and Sport Science, Revue International des Sciences du Sport et de l'Education Physique,* and *Physical Education and Sport Pedagogy.* In 2009, Dr. Côté was the recipient of the 4th EW Barker Professorship from the Physical Education and Sport Science Department at the National Institute of Education in Sinpapore. He enjoys spending time with his wife and three children, and likes to play ice hockey, tennis, golf, and racquetball.

Dr. Ronnie Lidor is a professor of motor behavior and is the director of the Zinman College of Physical Education and Sport Sciences at the Wingate Institute in Israel. His main areas of research are cognitive and learning strategies, talent detection and early development in sport, and sport development. Dr. Lidor has published extensively in peer-reviewed scientific journals such as *The Sport Psychologist, Journal of Sports Sciences, International Journal of Sport and Exercise Psychology, Psychology of Sport and Exercise,* and *Physical Education and Sport Pedagogy.* In addition, Dr. Lidor is co-editor of a number of books, among them *The Psychology of Team Sports* (2003), *Handbook of Research in Applied Sport and Exercise Psychology: International Perspectives* (2005), *Psychology of Sport Training* (2007), and *Psychology of Sport Excellence* (2009). He is the editor of *Movement: Journal of Physical Education and Sport Sciences* (published in Hebrew). He resides in Tel Aviv, Israel, with his wife and three children. In his free time he likes to read, jog, and play basketball.

About the Authors

Bruce Abernethy is currently a professor in skill acquisition in the School of Human Movement Studies, and deputy executive dean and associate dean (research) within the Faculty of Health Sciences at the University of Queensland in Australia. He is also a visiting professor at the Institute of Human Performance at the University of Hong Kong. His research interests include the control and learning of skilled movement, with a particular focus on understanding the processes underpinning the expert perception and production of patterns of human movement.

Paul R. Appleton, PhD, is a teaching and research fellow in the School of Sport and Exercise Sciences at the University of Birmingham, UK. Paul's research interests concern social-environmental and motivational processes in sport and other physical activity settings, including developing a programme of research on perfectionism.

Joseph Baker is an associate professor and head of the Lifespan Health and Performance Laboratory in the School of Kinesiology and Health Science, York University, Canada. His research considers varying influences on optimal human development, ranging from issues affecting athlete development and skill acquisition to barriers and facilitators of successful aging.

Mark W. Bruner, PhD, is an assistant professor in the School of Physical and Health Education at Nipissing University, Canada. His research investigates how group dynamics (e.g., team building, social identity, cohesion) influence physical activity adherence and psychosocial development in youth sport, exercise, and physical education settings.

Chris Button is an associate professor in the School of Physical Education, University of Otago in New Zealand. A common theme of his research is the application of movement science to sport within an ecological framework. Chris also plays and coaches soccer and futsal.

Catherine Capio, PhD, conducts research in the Institute of Human Performance, University of Hong Kong. Her research interests include the overlapping areas of motor learning, biomechanics, and physical activity of children with and without disabilities. Other research involves children with intellectual disabilities and those with mental health issues (psychomotor therapy).

Melissa A. Chase, PhD, is an associate dean in the School of Education, Health, and Society and associate professor in the Department of Kinesiology and Health at Miami University in Oxford, Ohio. Dr. Chase's research interests are in the areas of self-efficacy beliefs, coaching efficacy, and motivation.

Jia Yi Chow is an assistant professor in the Physical Education and Sports Science Department in the National Institute of Education, Nanyang Technological University. His area of specialization is in motor control and learning. Jia Yi's key research work includes nonlinear pedagogy, the investigation of multi-articular coordination changes, analysis of team dynamics from an ecological psychology perspective, and examining visual-perceptual skills in sports expertise.

Keith Davids is a professor in the School of Exercise and Nutrition Science at Queensland University of Technology in Australia. He also currently supervises many doctoral students from Portugal, the UK, Australia, and New Zealand. He investigates the coordination and control of human movement, and skill acquisition. A major focus of his research concerns how ideas from ecological psychology and nonlinear dynamics can be integrated into a nonlinear pedagogy for sport and physical education.

Karl Erickson is a PhD candidate in sport psychology in the School of Kinesiology & Health Studies at Queen's University, under the supervision of Dr. Jean Côté. Karl's research interests focus on coaching and athlete development in youth sport. In particular, Karl's work examines the influence of coach-athlete interactions on athletes' psychosocial and sport skill development.

Mark A. Eys, PhD, is an associate professor in the Departments of Kinesiology/Physical Education and Psychology at Wilfrid Laurier University, Canada, and a Canada research chair in group dynamics and physical activity. His current research interests include role perceptions (i.e., ambiguity, satisfaction, and acceptance) and the measurement and correlates of cohesion within sport and physical activity groups.

Jessica Fraser-Thomas is an assistant professor in the School of Kinesiology and Health Science at York University in Toronto, Canada. Her current research focuses on positive youth development through sport in the areas of life skill development, psychosocial influences (including parents, coaches, and peers), and prolonged engagement in sport.

Wade Gilbert is an associate professor and sport psychology coordinator in the Department of Kinesiology at California State University, Fresno. He has directed research and applied consulting partnerships with coaches and athletes in developmental and elite sport settings across a wide range of sports.

Howard K. Hall, PhD, is a professor of sport and exercise psychology at York St John University in the UK. Howard's research is concerned with the psychological processes underpinning motivation in sport and exercise, and his most recent research is investigating the antecedents and consequences of perfectionism in athletes.

Stephen Harvey is a senior lecturer in physical education and sport at the University of Bedfordshire, England. His research interests include models of instruction, game sense pedagogies and game performance assessment, analyzing coach intervention behavior to effect pedagogical change, competition in physical education, and ethics in youth sport and physical education.

Andrew P. Hill, PhD, is a senior lecturer in youth sport and children's physical activity at York St John University in the UK. Andy's research interests are focused upon the motivational consequences of perfectionism in achievement contexts.

Sarah Jeffery-Tosoni is a doctoral candidate in the School of Kinesiology and Health Science at York University in Toronto, Canada. Her research focuses on facilitating healthy psychosocial development through sport, most recently through the examination of parent involvement and game atmosphere in Canadian minor hockey.

Hyunwoo Jung is currently working toward a PhD in physical education and sport pedagogy at the University of Bedfordshire, England. His research interests include sport policy and sport development in England and Wales, physical cultural discourse embedded in physical education and school sport policy in terms of the social construction of pedagogic discourse, and the indirect teaching behaviors used by physical education teachers.

David Kirk is the Alexander Chair in Physical Education and Sport at the University of Bedfordshire, England. His interests lie in the social construction of physical education and sustainable curriculum renewal in physical education through model-based practice.

Dany J. MacDonald is an assistant professor in the Department of Applied Human Sciences at the University of Prince Edward Island, Canada. His main research interests are in positive youth development through sport. More specifically, he is interested in identifying characteristics of youth sport participation that are most effective for fostering positive personal development through sport. He is presently conducting research on athlete development and coaching to further understand the mechanisms that contribute to elite athlete development and expertise.

Robert M. Malina, FACSM, is a professor emeritus in the Department of Kinesiology and Health Education of the University of Texas at Austin, and a research professor at Tarleton State University, Stephenville, Texas. A primary area of interest is the biological growth and maturation of children and adolescents with a major focus on young athletes and the influence of training for sport.

Rich Masters is a professor and the assistant director (research) in the Institute of Human Performance at the University of Hong Kong. Rich uses experimental psychology to study motor learning and performance. His work in implicit motor learning has received considerable attention across a broad range of disciplines, including sports science, rehabilitation, movement disorders, psychology, speech sciences, and surgery.

Scott W. Pierce, MS, is a doctoral student at Michigan State University where he works in the Institute for the Study of Youth Sports. His research interests include athletic talent development, life skill development, and coaching sciences.

Ian Renshaw is a senior lecturer in the School of Exercise and Nutrition Science at Queensland University of Technology, Australia. His research interests include an ecological dynamics approach to understanding perception and action in sport, with an emphasis on developing effective learning environments. Current research projects include psychology and metastability in nonlinear pedagogy, the implementation of nonlinear pedagogy in schools, emergent decision making in football referees, and representative learning design in sporting run-ups.

Leisha Strachan is an assistant professor in the Faculty of Kinesiology and Recreation Management at the University of Manitoba in Winnipeg, Canada. As a coach and judge in the sport of baton twirling, she has a keen interest in the growth of children and youth in highly competitive sport contexts. Dr. Strachan also continues to examine the experiences of children, youth, and instructors involved in Mini-University at the University of Manitoba, one of North America's largest summer sport camps.

Jennifer Turnnidge is a PhD student in the School of Kinesiology and Health Studies at Queen's University, Canada. Her research interests are in coaching, peer relationships, and positive youth development in sport. More specifically, she is interested in how social interaction can promote positive development in youth, both in able-bodied and disability sport environments.

John van der Kamp, PhD, is a lecturer in the Faculty of Human Movement Sciences at the VU University in Amsterdam. In recent years, John's work has focused on the differential use of optical information in movement control and perception. This work involves various populations, including infants, students, people with movement impairments such as CP and stroke, and sport performers.

Gal Ziv, MPE, is a doctoral student at the University of Haifa–Faculty of Education (Israel). His doctoral research involves attentional focusing, gaze behavior, and the learning of closed, self-paced motor skills. Gal's research interests involve the effects of cognition, attention, and gaze on sport performance, physical and physiological demands of beginner and skilled athletes, and the use of tests in early phases of talent development.